PERISHABLE MATERIAL CULTURE
IN PREHISTORY

Perishable Material Culture in Prehistory provides new approaches and integrates a broad range of data to address a neglected topic: organic material in the prehistoric record. By offering new ideas and connections and suggesting revisionist ways of thinking about broad themes in the past, this book demonstrates the efficacy of an holistic approach by using examples and cases studies.

No other book covers such a broad range of organic materials from a social and object biography perspective, or concentrates so fully on approaches to the missing components of prehistoric material culture. This book will be an essential addition for those people wishing to understand better the nature and importance of organic materials as the 'missing majority' of prehistoric material culture.

Linda M. Hurcombe is Senior Lecturer in Archaeology at the University of Exeter, UK.

PERISHABLE MATERIAL CULTURE IN PREHISTORY

Investigating the Missing Majority

Linda M. Hurcombe

Routledge
Taylor & Francis Group

LONDON AND NEW YORK

First published 2014
by Routledge
2 Park Square, Milton Park, Abingdon, Oxon OX14 4RN

and published by Routledge
711 Third Avenue, New York, NY 10017

Routledge is an imprint of the Taylor & Francis Group, an informa business

© 2014 Linda M. Hurcombe

British Library Cataloguing in Publication Data
A catalogue record for this book is available from the British Library.

Library of Congress Cataloging in Publication Data
Hurcombe, Linda.
Perishable material culture in prehistory : investigating the missing majority / Linda Hurcombe.
p. cm.
Includes bibliographical references and index.
1. Anthropology, Prehistoric. 2. Material culture. 3. Antiquities, Prehistoric.
I. Title.
GN740.H87 2014
930.1--dc23
2013033781

ISBN: 978-0-415-53792-6 (hbk)
ISBN: 978-0-415-53793-3 (pbk)
ISBN: 978-1-315-81772-9 (ebk)

Typeset in Bembo
by Taylor & Francis Books

For Betty, Mandy, Malcolm, Richard, and Robin

CONTENTS

LIST OF TABLES, FIGURES AND PLATES

Tables

Figures

Plates

PREFACE

Serendipity plays a larger role in the direction of academic research than is generally allowed. In my case an initial interest thirty years ago (Hurcombe 1992) in Neolithic long-distance exchange networks in the Mediterranean led me to investigate obsidian, a volcanically formed glass. The relationship between form and function grew alongside an abiding interest in making and using stone tools as a way of understanding the social and practical role of those artefacts. This is easier said than done: as a way of comparison, the edge tools of our society are now made mostly of metal, but imagine having only the metal blades surviving to understand what the tools looked like as a whole, how they performed and what they were used for. In our society, as in the past, the role of tools is mostly connected with one of two major activities: getting food and making things. Both are personal actions and social ones. Prehistoric tools most often dealt with raw materials from plants and animals. Thus, my experiments with stone tools inevitably led me to investigate plants and animals for food and as the raw materials for crafts. As I formed ideas for experiments, I was drawn into researching ethnographic sources to understand better the range of tasks that should be considered and the specific details of how societies might use plants and animals. The extraordinary diversity of materials and crafts made them a continuing source of research interests and led me mentally and physically all over the world. Plants and animals are key resources for humans and though there is much variation, common themes emerge. The most persistent theme was the insights provided by experimenting to understand better the exploitation of plants and animals. The most fundamental insight was how much we have lost from the archaeological past because most of the time it does not survive. More significantly, it is lost from our mindset.

This book builds on *Archaeological Artefacts as Material Culture* (Hurcombe 2007a). The organics chapter of that book is the largest of the four 'materials and artefacts' chapters because plant- and animal-based material culture is so amazingly rich and diverse: it is these media that express so much of the identities of groups and individuals. The need for a much more detailed volume dedicated to this part of the material culture repertoire was obvious. The emphasis here is still very much on ethnographic and experimental data as a key feature of the approach, alongside more emphasis on the opening phases of the object biographies. This latter is a distinctive feature of my current research because plants and animals come from places and landscapes. Both these aspects reflect my personal position on material culture and artefact studies. The tacit knowledge of craft practitioners combined with my own experience and experiments inform the research and its presentation. The illustrations have been used to convey a great deal of technological information succinctly, but also reflect my personal approach to communicating ideas about past sensory worlds.

Many of the perishable material culture items appear after excavation as small dark fragments with textural details visible only on close inspection. They have been muted in size, colour, texture and shape. When I look at these fragments in a museum case, I 'see' a living plant or animal in a landscape transformed by people in moving 3D colours, shapes, textures, smells and sounds. This appreciation and understanding has come from these practical crafts, from experiments and ethnographic studies, which I have tried to pass on to the reader. These features make the book a distinctive personal view of the topic.

The seeds of this book arose decades ago when I looked at small pieces of obsidian whose wear traces suggested plants as contact material, but whose size and specific character suggested working those plants in a manner far more likely to be part of activities associated with basket-making than food gathering (Hurcombe 1992). These ideas have gestated slowly along with a growing recognition that there is far more to plant and animal exploitation than is currently allowed for. This book is thus about expanding horizons and addressing an imbalance. It is about the crafting of an archaeological approach to understanding fundamental craft issues across the full range of human evolution. I sincerely hope that the many craftspeople with whom I have interacted as well as the academic community, will find this book of interest.

ACKNOWLEDGEMENTS

In a book that covers plants, animals, ethnography, archaeology and craft traditions there are inevitably a lot of people to thank.

Thanks to all the crafts people, academics and curators who have discussed ideas and objects with me. Patty Anderson, CNRS, for discussions on plant working, residues and usewear traces over many years. Eva Anderssen Strand, for invitations to conferences in Ostersund and Kalmar, Sweden and for hosting a visit to the CTR. Mary Barlow, for textile discussion and hosting a visit in Copenhagen. Anne Batser, weaver, spinner and dyer, Lejre, Denmark for discussions on nettles and weaving and spinning all kinds of fibres. Marta Bazzanella, Museo San Michele, for hosting a visit and discussions on cordage, basketry and textiles. Mark Beabey, historical shoe and bootmaker, for discussions on traditional tanning and shoemaking. Anders Björnskär, lecturer in leather handcrafts, Nyköpings Folkhogsköla. Anne Beck, formerly Lejre, Denmark, for help with practical experiments and discussion of house structures. Marcus Bingalli and Marcus Bingalli, two identically-named bronze metalworkers for discussion on the hide bellows and style of tongs. Toomai Boocherat, discussions and demonstration of some cordage preparation techniques. Bruce Bradley, loan of objects, discussions on American traditional practices. Eddie and Jill Buckler, for sharing bark cloth information. Dave Budd, knife maker, sheath maker and woodsman. Neil Burridge, for discussions on metal tools and hafting arrangements. Katrin Kania, independent scholar, for sharing knowledge of weaving, spinning and dyeing. John Coles for loan of the experimental hide shield for photography. Bryony Coles for many discussions on wet site organic finds and sharing images and information on beavers and house construction. Lara Comis, for help with Italian translations and discussions on experimental archaeology. Dale Croes for discussions on basketry and organic finds of the Northwest coast. Brian Cumby, shipwright, for discussions on woodworking techniques, moss caulking and organic substances, yew withies. Ide Demant, weaver, spinner and dyer, Lejre,

Denmark, for discussions on all kinds of fibres, spinning and weaving. Susi Densmore and colleagues, John Densmore Trust, for discussions on spinning and weaving the Nepalese nettle. Irene Dorra, traditional Sámi, Funesdalen, Sweden for discussions on tanning and sinew production. Ann O'Dowd and Clodagh Doyle, for discussions and facilitating a visit to the stores, Irish National Museums, Country life division, Turlaugh, Tony Eccles and Tom Cadbury, Royal Albert Memorial Museum, Exeter, UK for visits to the collections and stores. Theresa Emmerich Kamper for sharing photographs and discussions on North American tanning technologies and sourcing some photographs. Lauren Ferrero, spinner and weaver. Richard Fullagar for dicussions on plant, bone and shell technologies in Australia. Sean Goddard, for discussions on wood and wood working. Cozette Griffin-Kremer for help with translation and discussions and information on furze use. Christina Grünefeld, tablet weaving. Smriti Haracharan, discussions on plant practices in India. Ruth Hatcher, felt maker, for discussions on felting and Soay wool. Heather Hopkins for discussion on dyeing and spinning. Padraig Irish National Museums, Dublin, for facilitating a visit to the stores. Isse Isrealsson, for discussions on fishskins. Åne Jepson, Lejre, Denmark, for help with practical experiments. Helle Juel Jensen for discussions on plantworking and usewear traces and Aarhus University for hosting a visit to Moesgaard Museum and showing me some of the Tybrind Vig material. Gill Juleff, for discussions on use of palm and organic materials in making up clay mix for furnaces. Maikki Karisto, tablet weaving. Katrin Koch-Maaasing, ancient shoes. Marisa Lazzari, loan of objects and discussion on South American weaving traditions. Leena Lehtinen, Kierikki Stone Age Centre, Finland, for hosting a visit at Kierikki, Oulu Museum and Turkansaari Tar Pit Museum. Linda Lemieux, rush cutter and basketmaker. Robyn Levitan for discussion on experimental archaeology and sharing photographs and knowledge of North American technologies. Anne Lisbeth Schmidt, for showing me the skin capes from the Danish bog bodies in the Danish National Museum store at Breda and discussing shrinkage temperatures. Ulla Mannering, Danish National Museum, for hosting a visit to the CTR, and stores of the National Museum and especially discussions on nettle textiles. Mary, from Dorset Guild of Weavers Spinners and Dyers for teaching me how to use a drop spindle at one of their open days. Val Maxfield, for many discussions on dry site organic finds and information on the felt yurt. Tom Monrad Hansen for sharing photographs and discussions of north European technologies, working with yew withies. Linda Mortensson, craftsperson, for discussion on weaving and spinning. Museum of Simon Fraser University, Vancouver, and Museum of British Columbia. Johanna Neiderkofler, Director Arceoparc, Val Senales, for hosting a visit to Archeoparc museum and discussing the Ötzi finds and the museum's replicas of these. Marie Louise Nosch for discussions on textiles and welcoming me to the CTR. Clive Ó Gibne, Irish coracle and curragh builder for discussions and allowing me to photograph his coracle. Janine Österman, for help with Swedish translation and discussions on hideworking. Alan Outram, for loan of bones, teeth and shells and discussions on animals as materials. Roeland Paardekooper, for discussions on experimental archaeology. Shanti Pappu, for discussions on basketry and plant management practices in India. Annaluisa Pedrotti, Museo Tridentino delle Scienze Naturali, for hosting a visit and discussions on cordage, basketry and textiles. Aja Petersson, Bäkedal Folkhøgskola, detailed knowledge of tannages and individual skin idiosyncracies plus 'hide glueing'. Harma Piening, nalbinden. Devi Kumari Rai for Nepalese nettle spinning and discussions. Lotte Rahme, fish skins and detailed understanding of tannages and temperatures. Marianne Rasmussen, formerly Lejre, for discussions on experimental archaeology. Anne Reichert, for discussions and information on bast fibre production and sharing her detailed collection of replicas and techniques from the circum-Alpine region. Sabine Ringenberg, dyes and mordants and textiles. Pernilla Salmonson, Funesdalen, antlerworker and tanner. Ann Salomonsson, Umea, tanning sealskins and ostrich skins. Romana Scandolari, Museo delle Palafitte del Lago, for discussions on cordage, basketry and textiles. Bill Schindler, for discussions and sending some of the American fibre plant samples. Linda Scott-Cummings, Paleoresearch Institute, for discussions on phytoliths, residues and plantworking. Alison Sheridan, for hosting a visit to National Museums Scotland collections and organic objects and impressions. South Tyrol Museum of Archaeology, Bolzano, for allowing me to use their library. Southwest Basket makers association visit to Museum of Rural Life, Reading. Sharada Srinivasan, National Institute of Advanced Studies, Bangalore, for discussions on traditional wax casting of religious bronzes in India. Ellinor Sydberg, Bäkedal Folkhøgskola, weaver and for information on traditional shoe hay production. Susanne Swedjemark, Bäkedal Folkhøgskola, for discussions on tanning and sewing hides. Annelou van Gijn for discussions on plantworking and usewear traces. Kate Verkooijen, for discussions on strings and flax productions. Gillian Vogelsang Eastwood, textile research centre, Leiden, Netherlands for allowing me to photograph the felt kepenek. Penelope Walton Rogers, textile consultant, for discussions on fibres and textiles. Åsa Wilhelmsson, Bäkedal Folkhøgskola for discussions on tanning and basketry reproduction. Jackie Wood, independent experimental archaeologist, for discussions of the Orkney Hood and her replica of it.

Images

Copyright permissions were obtained and acknowledged in the captions for animal images provided by Theresa Emmerich Kamper, Tom Monrad Hansen and Chris Madson who gave permission to use Luray Parker's images on behalf of Wyoming Game and Fish; for the Wallace Ruin awls by Bruce Bradley, and for the stunning painted armband by John Whittaker, Grinnell College, USA.

Access to museum stores and libraries have been crucial and I would like to thank the following for allowing me to visit their stores and photograph objects in their collections: in the UK, Anne Tyack, Royal Cornwall Museum, Truro; John Allen, Royal Albert Memorial Museum, Exeter; Somerset County Museum, Taunton; Lynda Aiano, Tom Muir, and others, Orkney Museum, Kirkwall; Gill Varndell, Caroline Cartwright and Pippa Cruikshank, British Museum; in the Netherlands,

Inge Riemersma and Frits Kleinhuis, Alphen aan den Rijn, South Holland Archaeological store; Gert-Jan van Rijn, Museon, The Hague, Netherlands; in the Czech Republic, Ludmila Kanakova Hladikova, Masaryk University, Brno who arranged for me to see and photograph the Palaeolithic clay impressions and art with kind permission of Martin Oliva, Moravian Museum, Institute of Anthropos.

I am also very grateful to many of the people who helped with the images by kindly letting me photograph objects they had made or that they had in their collections and by sending me samples. For sharing information and objects, including personal items and replicas made by them: Bruce Bradley, Jill Buckler, Bryony Coles, John Coles, Peter Rowley-Conwy, Theresa Emmerich Kamper, Tom Monrad Hansen, Marisa Lazzari, Eddie Leggett, Linda Lemieux, Robyn Levitan, Val Maxfield, Alan Outram, Anne Reichert, Bill Schindler. Thanks also to colleagues at Tashkent University, Uzbekistan for hosting a visit to Samarkand province where the ground loom, spinning, and cotton drying images were taken.

The production of the images into the format for this book has been a major part of the preparation and Penny Cunningham, Adam Wainwright, Mike Rouillard, and especially Sean Goddard have helped produced the images with Sean taking many of the photographs and working with me to create the collage used on the front cover.

Pru Manning and Jess Collins have helped with the production of the text. Particular thanks go to Robin Dennell who has been a sounding board for the ideas discussed here and has lived with the research and production of this book, supporting the work in myriad ways.

Grants

The following grants have enabled museums visits and research data collection which have aided the ideas presented here: AHRC-EPSRC Touching the untouchable, AHRC-EPSRC Touching the Past, AHRC Cornwall and the Sea in the Bronze Age in Collaboration with National Maritime Museum, Cornwall; Leverhulme, Alternative methods for studying cordage and basketry in prehistory; REACT HEIF please touch; European Union Openarch project; Lejre Archaeological Research Centre (now known as Sagnlandet Lejre) Research Grants 2006, 2007, 2008, 2009.

1

THE HOLISTIC APPROACH TO MATERIAL CULTURE

Introduction

This book challenges existing conceptions of plant and animal usage and significance within archaeology in order to include their role in material culture. It is time to augment the way that archaeological data is analysed and integrated. That is why this chapter introduces a concept termed 'the holistic approach to material culture' and a problem termed 'the missing majority'.

Archaeologists are used to dealing with fragmentary data and problematic evidence. The history of the subject and the nature of the evidence have allowed the durable materials of stone, pottery and metal to dominate archaeological reports and the resulting discussions, just as much if not more than they dominate archaeological ways of thinking. To re-think not the value of individual studies of pottery, stone and metal, but rather the way in which the agendas arising from these artefacts have dominated material culture discourse is not to negate what has been achieved, but rather to augment and integrate perishable material culture as a fundamental act of enrichment.

Clearly, this is an ambitious agenda and one that many archaeologists may not think worthwhile given that the material culture from plants and animals survives so rarely and is missing from significant periods of the archaeological record. Why then does it matter so much? The clearest demonstration of why it matters is to take a look around you. If you are inside a building, whatever room you are in, living room, library, study, or craft studio, the chances are that you have a range of possessions and furnishings around you which will be dominated by organic materials. Consider clothes, bags, furnishings, furniture and utensils, and then add tools with organic handles. The room you are in will perhaps also have organic structural elements such as door frames. The building may also be made partly or wholly from organic materials. These are far more substantial and durable elements than the organic products that may be present as food and drink. The things around you and what you wear identify your social persona in a moment and signal the relationships you have between other members of your society and your relative status. The perishable organic material forms the majority of the material culture and is missing from most prehistoric sites worldwide. More problematically, it is missing from our archaeological worldview.

Although we live in a world where material culture ownership is significantly higher than most periods of archaeological study, these fundamental truths are just as relevant, if not more so, to the societies of the archaeological past. To think about and discuss organic material culture only on the rare occasions when we find it is simply to miss important facets of the cultural repertoire, and the relationships between the individuals of a society and between people and their environment. It is for these reasons that this book is relevant to more than the set of people who already study plant and animal remains as elements of the archaeological record. Furthermore, the agenda set by the need to produce material culture can be argued to be far more significant than is currently appreciated as a tenet of archaeology. It is recognized that the absence of evidence is not the same as the evidence of absence. In just the same way, the absence of large amounts of good data is not at all the same as a lack of significance of the missing data. Nor can it be argued that its effect on the small amount that does survive can be dismissed as negligible.

The central tenets of this book are therefore that the majority of material culture is made up of organic raw materials, that most of these are highly perishable materials, and that their absence has severely affected our interpretation of their significance. This is the problem that I have termed 'the missing majority'. Just because these crafts are invisible does not and should not preclude them from being an essential aspect of archaeological thinking. The sophisticated techniques that allow archaeologists to routinely extract the maximum amount of information from few and fragmentary remains could equally well be used to address the concept of a holistic approach to material culture and mitigate against the problem of the missing majority. If scientists can now extract the Neanderthal genome from scraps of bone or identify the type of liquids stored in pots, it should be possible to recover far more evidence about perishable technologies than has so far been done. These are scientific breakthroughs and can be literally described as archaeology working on molecules of evidence but although the 'missing majority' could and should use these opportunities, much more could be made of the artefactual, environmental, palaeoeconomic data that we already have. New techniques will undoubtedly draw out more of the 'missing majority' and help develop the agenda but a more fundamental shift needs to ripple through the discipline from fieldwork through analysis to interpretation and presentation.

A key part of this introduction is to set out the approach and its context explaining the ways in which this book can be used. There is no single intended reader of this volume; rather people will come to it and leave with a variety of resonances. For anthropologists and archaeologists interested in material culture studies there is the consideration of complex relationships between individuals and communities, and an argument that the choice of material and its location and place within the landscape is as much a part of the creation of identity as any other aspect of material culture production and consumption.

For archaeologists in the broadest sense there is the consideration of organic eras and agendas in the conception and day-to-day production of material culture. For archaeologists specializing in the analysis of plants and animals and environmental evidence there is a way of approaching the interpretations of different kinds of familiar evidence. Last but by no means least, for the craft practitioners in the contemporary world whose raw materials come from plants and animals, there is an historical depth to their craft traditions. They will know what I mean when I say that they can understand this book with their hands as well as their minds.

Subsistence, scene setting and study strategies

The way in which this discussion is pursued argues that it is not just archaeology that misses some of the significance of plant and animal relationships with the material culture of human beings. Other subjects also preference food sources over material culture sources, and animals, as animal beings, over plants, as fixed resources. It is as though the movement and personality witnessed in animals heightens the ability to perceive the human–animal relationships in a way that cannot be repeated over the human–plant relationships. I believe this difference is false. Plants and sets of plants have 'personalities' by their reactions to other living things and circumstances; it is just that they work and can be witnessed on a completely different timescale. When the wildlife programmes feature animals, the camera works in real time but the BBC's landmark study of the life of plants featured memorable time-lapse footage where the plant grew, reacted and interacted with other plants. The accelerated time footage made them more engaging because their movement and exchange worked on our own 'animal' scale. Animals and people are on permanent 'fast-forward' hectic activity in comparison to plants. If humans touch an animal, it reacts instantly, and familiarity and conditions are built up. A good example would be hand-milking, rearing and feeding. By proximity, interaction and an animal–human relationship is built up. The same is true for plants but the time-scale is different. A coppiced tree reacts to human intervention perhaps on a yearly scale for willow basketry, or a seven-year timescale for hazel rods, or a 20-year timescale for bark production. The plant has 'personality', or characteristics that are valued and exploited by humans who cause the plant to react to some intervention on their part. Those interactions are built up over time into a relationship: it just works on a slower timescale than for animals.

The social role of plants and animals and the intimate relationships individuals and societies can form with them is just starting to become a topic for discussion (Russell 2012). Animals as metaphors and totems are well-known phenomena in the anthropological literature. For example, the role of animals such as the jaguar in some South American societies is linked with divinities and totem spirits (Viveiros de Castro 1992; Urton 1985). Similarly, although perhaps to a lesser extent, the social role of plants is tackled in the anthropological literature. Archaeologists are, however, some way behind anthropologists in the recognition of these topics, and, as importantly, in both cases there is more discussion of the conceptual significance of animals than plants.

Animism and the way in which human–animal relationships are perceived offers a more intimate exploration of societies' relationships to the animal kingdom with which they interact than the plants kingdom. Geographers often discuss the role of trees, but in relation to those in urban landscapes, with individual trees in settings as promenades in parks (Jones and Cloke 2002), or as sources of timber, fuel or paper, rather than the close relationships with tree species or as religious beings or ritual places (Shutova 2006; Stewart 1984). The modern academic world preferences food requirements over material culture needs, and animals over plants. Is this the same for different global traditions of archaeology? Archaeology is behind in some subjects but is moving ahead of others. This book aims to shift archaeology to the fore in this respect.

Where there are still indigenous communities practising traditional ways of life, there is far more awareness of the role of crafts in the exploitation of resources from the environment. In postcolonial discourse and postmodernist paradigms, archaeologists now pay far more attention to indigenous beliefs and practices. This rectifies to some extent the biases of the modern world. The research discussed in this volume has certainly drawn on a wide range of indigenous community practices in developing the central tenet that the missing majority of perishable material culture is a significant part of people's relationships with their world. If archaeologists neglect to consider this they overlook fundamental parameters of social interaction and belief. Later chapters explore the significance of the missing majority and indeed show that there is a global aspect to this.

Three aspects of the current discourse of plant and animal evidence need to be addressed. First and foremost, archaeologists think of food far more than crafts when considering interpretations. Second, there are subtle but key differences in the way in which wild versus domesticated species are explored and third, there are differences in the way in which wild plants versus wild animals are interpreted. In reality these divisions are not binary opposites but more like an axis for a line of thought which needs to be documented and argued thoroughly. Moreover the hermeneutic nature of the task involves perceptions held by the modern analyst and those held by the ancient society.

When the plant and animal remains for a site are identified it is straightforward to focus on domesticated species as key subsistence information because these are so obviously farmed resources. For the most part these farmed resources, whether plants or animals, are seen only as sources of food and fulfilling the subsistence sustenance agenda. (The key exception for animals are sheep because of their wool.) The only domestic plants that are readily assigned to both the food and crafts agendas are flax and hemp. They have bast fibres in their stems and oil and nutrient rich seeds, and *Cannabis sativa* also produces hallucinogenic effects. In contrast, cotton is usually seen as a fibre crop although it too has edible seeds.

This short listing of domesticated fibre plants is more limited than the wild resources that have become used for fine fibres around the world. In North America, these include dogbane, milkweed, nettle and tree basts; in temperate Europe, nettle and tree basts; in New Zealand *Phormium tenax* (known as New Zealand flax but nothing like the Eurasian species of *Linum*). This short list for some areas of the world is by no means exhaustive but is used to demonstrate a point. There are many wild resources that can be used for fine fibre artefacts but the identification of a wild resource in most excavation reports is interpreted as background information whether this is related to the climate at the broadest scale, the regional environment or local site conditions. The interpretations rest on whether the wild resources are seen as 'weeds', 'natural background' or 'brought to the site for a reason'. Archaeological palaeobotanists know that 'weed' species are commensal with the crop species and can characterize different types of husbandry practices. They are thus useful proxies, but are still dismissed as 'weeds', with no intrinsic value. This distinction on many sites is impossible to make precisely. The plant evidence may be in the form of pollen, attributable to a general level of these plants in the vicinity (although different plants produce pollen in greater or lesser amounts and some pollen is much more robust than others), macroscopic plant remains (preserved by charring, waterlogging or desiccation) or microscopic fragments such as phytoliths or starch grains (which are robust but may not be distinctive to species level). Whatever the kind of plant remains, unless there is specific locational evidence to suggest something unusual such as abnormal arrangement or abundance, the information will be attributed to the local environmental conditions. It will be used to set the scene for activities on site, but will rarely feature more strongly as evidence of an activity.

One plant above all others has led me to question this scene-setting fallback position, and that is the stinging nettle, *Urtica dioica*. Nettles grow well in disturbed soil and are usually found in and around settlements in temperate Europe and North America. They are historically known to have been used as a source of fibres for textiles but in the twenty-first century we mostly encounter them, painfully, as weeds. If there is evidence of nettles on an archaeological site, their presence is seen as indicating local environmental conditions, even though they are edible and a potential fibre source. Archaeological caution predicates the minimalist interpretation. However, imagination could at the least consider what might arise from the presence of nettles.

Part of the purpose in writing this book is to raise awareness of the kinds of natural resources that could be used as the raw materials for crafts and to consider the processes by which parts of plants and animals can be transformed into material culture. Cautious interpretations need to be tempered with an awareness of the possibilities. The old adage that you only see what you are looking for is true. In the interpretation of plant and animal remains all too often there is no consideration of the material culture dimension of plants and animals.

Augmenting the archaeological record

The situation is exacerbated by concepts of affordance – the concept of knowing what it is possible to do with a resource. There are innumerable but little-known uses for plants and animals and, worse, uses and processes that no longer exist. The perishable material culture of the past could have used unknown materials and processes to serve needs that may have no modern counterpart. Perception is a fundamental part of the identification and recognition of perishable material culture.

This research cannot claim to present a complete answer, but raising an awareness of the problem and then outlining some of the little-known aspects of organic material culture will provide a platform for more to be recognized. My interest arose from investigating stone tool functions where experimental work assisted the interpretation of the archaeological tools. 'What is the function of this tool?' is a straightforward question to which there was often not a straightforward answer. It was evident that many stone tools were involved not in food production and preparation but in the making of other tools and items of material culture. The same intellectual route has been followed by other wear analysts who have become interested in particular aspects of invisible crafts by trying to interpret and research wear traces on stone and bone tools. For example, Anderson (1980), Beugnier (Beugnier and Crombé 2007), van Gijn (1998a, 1998b, 2005), and Juel Jensen (1994) have been especially interested in plant-working processes, and Beyries (e.g. Beyries et al 2001) and Plisson (1993) have especially pursued hide-processing activities, as well as leading to a more generic interest in the invisible crafts which are so often also a gender issue (see Owen 1998, 1999, 2000; Donald and Hurcombe 2000a, 2000b, 2000c).

Theoretical approaches underpin the research and are interwoven: *actualistic studies* incorporating both experimental and ethnographic data; *affordance* as the knowledge and skill to know what materials and processes could be used to afford a solution to the issue; *chaîne opératoire*, the sequence of operations of processes and their physical and social settings; *extended object biographies*, the conception, procurement, manufacture, use, maintenance, recycling, and preservation/discard of ancient objects, and their recovery and role in our own society. The transmission of materials and technologies as both knowledge and skills takes place within communities of practice and the whole social setting of material choices and practices leads to *agency* and *sensory worldviews*.[1] These theoretical issues do not exist in isolation but interweave in complex ways. They are, however, all united by a common thread, practical understanding. The individual approach encapsulated within this volume is that a physical and practical understanding of perishable materials, gained by years of personal experience and discussions with other craft practitioners, provides insights and understanding that inform and structure the interpretations. This practical knowledge and experience is still situated within academic theoretical frameworks, which are further explained.

Actualistic studies

The term actualistic is an ugly word but a useful concept because it encompasses both ethnographic data and experimental approaches (Outram 2008). For both, a key part of their value is in their realism. In practice, experimental methods can also include laboratory-based experiments with highly controlled variables. These serve a purpose and can isolate cause and effect from individual factors and demonstrate potential issues (Hurcombe 1992). However, these often need to be supported by a demonstration, if not a more extensive experimental programme, which corroborates the highly controlled results when they are applied to a more realistic environmental setting. Experimental work also relies heavily on ethnographic evidence as a source of ideas and inspiration (Hurcombe 2007a: 60–69). Ethnography can incorporate historical accounts from the late nineteenth century or earlier but has been pursued specifically by archaeologists who want to use present-day societies and their practices to understand archaeological issues. This is termed ethnoarchaeology. The data collected specifically for archaeological purposes have proved very effective in the understanding of the processes of production and the patterning of the archaeological remains from them (for a full discussion see Frink and Weedman 2009; David and Kramer 2001). The close interaction of archaeologists and craft practitioners from traditional societies has been a fruitful relationship. Furthermore, the experiential aspects of ethnography and experimentation have a key role in this book in the investigation of in life processes (see Outram 2008). The present study uses both broad and detailed ethnographic examples alongside modern craft practices to inform all of Chapters 2 and 3.

Affordance

The concept of affordance rests on a physical understanding of a material as an appreciation of what it can be used to do. The need and suitability of something to address it are interlinked. When Merleau-Ponty (1962) explained phenomenology as a way of understanding the central role played by perception in understanding the world, and the interaction of all of the senses in making sense of the world around us, he started a train of thought that has since developed into a much more general appreciation of intersensorality and synaesthesia where the holistic appreciation of the totality of sensory experiences is emphasized (Ingold 2000a: 268; Howes 2006). In phenomenology it is recognized that if a quality or a property cannot be perceived then its existence is immaterial. Gibson (1979) and Knappett (2005b) have stressed that it is the performance of objects and materials that lies at the heart of these perceptions, because how objects behave is part of the learned experiences. In this way our worldview is shaped by the practical experiences over a lifetime. Materiality, the way in which materials are understood and perceived, is thus part of the way in which people have experienced those materials and the phenomena generated by their interactions with them. The concept of affordance takes this understanding of materials from learned experiences and links them very firmly to a perceived need. It is this that makes the concept of affordance distinctive. At its simplest, affordance is what somebody knows a material or shape will be able to do in a given situation. If there is no need for a particular property, then that property will not necessarily be registered. That is why affordance is linked so strongly with need. It is also why there are some things for which the modern world has no understanding. In our society, that 'affordance', or need, is not there.

This does not rest simply on the material properties alone, but is also related to shape. For example, if something needs to be propped up, a stone will do, but several tabular stones could be stacked on top of each other to get the right height, in a way that several pebbles, being rounded could not, because they would overbalance. To use an organic example, most people today would understand that wood can be sawn into a shape suitable for the purpose they have in mind. However, that same person might have no experience to draw on to take a nettle growing in the garden and fashion a piece of string from it to serve a different need. Using string made from nettle, and the ability to do it, is thus outside that person's learned experiences. In practice people use the concept of affordance all the time. It is using a screwdriver to open a paint can, using duct tape to stick a key under a dustbin lid, and using a kitchen knife to trim wire. If a nail needs to be hammered in, a hammer or a portable stone will do the job. If the stone is large it will not fit in the hand and will not suit the purpose: it will not suit the concept of affordance.

These complexities are worth exploring because they have allowed archaeologists to think about sensory perception and ways of understanding materiality in different, more practically orientated ways. I have argued elsewhere (Hurcombe 2007a: 105) that the concept of affordance depends upon a perception, but also an ability. Thus the skill of the person concerned needs to be factored in, as well as their knowledge. The easiest way of explaining this is that if a watertight basket is needed, the range of materials may be present and to hand, the knowledge of which materials will serve that purpose may also be known, but if the skill is not there to make the basket so finely that it holds water, then the material cannot be used to meet the intended purpose. So in my understanding of the concept of affordance, incorporating personal knowledge and skill is an important extra layer of appreciating the affordance of materials and objects. It is also, on the one hand, an explanation of why some prehistoric objects are not understood by us and, on the other hand, why there are materials of which many people are uneducated in terms of their affordance. The concept of affordance thus highlights the way in which the sensory experiences, and thus the sensory worldview, of a modern person will be different from those of the people being studied in a prehistoric society. This also explains why Bourdieu (1977) is a philosopher much quoted by archaeologists: he focused on practice. What people do affects how they think about objects, and that intervention also affects their subsequent interactions with objects. This ripple effect, of perceptions of interacting with materials, is in practice an activity-related concept of the way people and objects affect one another.

Chaîne opératoire

This French term for the operational sequence or operational chain is now well established in the archaeological literature, and what started as investigations of lithic reduction sequences has now become more endemic and an approach adopted for all kinds of material culture production sequences (Leroi-Gourhan 1964; Lemonnier 1986, 1993; Pelegrin 1990; Schlanger 2004, 2005). This breakdown of the stages of production takes account of the locations of each step and the cultural settings, as well as understanding the patterning and style of remains that would likely be left to form the archaeological record of these actions. Hence, it is not just a breakdown of technology but a detailed examination of the stages and settings of culturally situated practices that explores locations and settings as much as phases and stages. In some ways this work is allied to the sequential schema of Schiffer (1987). It also leads into Ingold's (2000a) 'taskscapes', which emphasize the characteristic locations of tasks in the landscape as part of the social setting.

Extended object biographies

Object biographies are a more expansive way of thinking through the life histories of objects, and stress the meaning of these objects and their role to individuals and societies (Gosden and Marshall 1999). It is now part of the archaeological framework and incorporates ideas about the shifts in role and value that one object can undergo over time. In the same way that human biography would present sequences of information, clearly signposted key changes, and the place of that individual in society, so too do object biographies stress the negotiated social role with shifts and nuances of their social interaction included as key biographical features. 'Extended object biographies' is a term used to extend this biographical approach into the role objects play in contemporary societies and the way in which archaeologists and museums offer new phases in the artefact's biographical relationship with people (Hurcombe 2007a: 39–41 and Fig. 3.1).

Agency

The concept of agency interweaves with this philosophical position, but different authors use the term in different ways. At its heart agency is focused on the meanings and changes that the actions of individuals and groups have on material culture, and vice versa (Dobres 2000; Dobres and Hoffman 1999; Dobres and Robb 2000; Gell 1998; Hoskins 2006; Johnson 1989; Gosden 2005; Owoc 2005a). For a more fluid concept of how objects and things affect people and vice versa see Knappett (2005a).

It is acknowledged that objects can have agency, the ability to act as a stimulus and intervention for people. The position taken here is predicated upon an under-standing that objects are habitually a part of human material culture and provoke reactions. This is why Gosden's (2005) question 'what do objects want?' teases out the way in which objects often change slowly and do so by means of 'variations around a theme'. There is variation in small details that shift into trends over a longer timescale, but in any one instance the object is easily understood as a known type. Often the category of object serves a purpose, and its affordance as well as its social role needs to be obvious.

These unstated rules allow meanings and uses to be readily understood, while showing individual expression and on occasion, pushing boundaries slightly or shifting sharply into novel territory. This is what is meant by negotiated meanings. Some authors would go further and argue that objects have animacy, i.e. agency and the ablilty to instigate their own reactions. The position taken here is that objects are made by people and the reactions they provoke are reflections of the animacy of people in the same way that waves meet a harbour wall and are reflected back from it. The inanimate wall has caused a particular reaction but that reaction is a material one with the energy coming from a different dynamic entity and, furthermore, the wall has been made and placed by people. Even though they can cause physical and emotional reactions, ultimately these, too, come from people. Objects are more usefully considered as mediators of agency or as interventions rather than direct providers of agency. However, animals and plants are animate and do have agency. They are also the raw materials for objects. Thus objects from them may have powerful emotional attachments and a legacy of agency from the living beings they once were. This can be complicated because the associations could be to a generic animal or plant of the same species, or to a more localized or intensely personal memory of a living creature or plant in a particular place.

Sensory worldviews

Materiality, the concept of how we understand materials, is not an objective way of pursuing an understanding of material culture. It is predicated upon experiences and worldview. That worldview can be described as a sensory perception of the world, learned through experience from birth onwards. There has been a main focus on visual material culture and visual sensory experiences. This focus on the visual is seen as part of a modern worldview and it is recognized that there are other sensory perceptions that need to have more attention paid to them, such as tactile or haptic qualities, or olfactory senses (Classen 2005; Classen and Howes 2006; Classen et al 1994; Hetherington 2003; Ingold 2000a: 155; Patterson 2007).

These issues of sensory perception are also now affecting museum studies (Edwards et al 2006). Archaeologists have argued that material culture is a complex of ways in which humans interact and engage with materials (Knappett 2005a; Malafouris 2010; Renfrew 2004). I have argued that knowledge, skill and aptitude allow people to both perceive their material culture and also to make it (Hurcombe 2000b). Aptitude is emphasized because not everybody in a society will be equally adept at absolute mastery of a particular craft or production technique. It is this way that extra value and individuality can be accrued by individuals, with a consequent rise in their social standing.

Archaeological studies of materiality are thus intricately bound up with trying to understand the ways in which the sensory worldviews of materials and material culture could have been constructed in the past. As an outsider to that culture, it is never going to be an easy or straightforward relationship to match the sensory worldview of the archaeologist with the sensory worldview of the society being studied. Yet if the focus is on what is experienced, recreating some of those materials and technological processes offers new ways of thinking through not just sites, but also sounds, smells and tastes. In this way, sawing an antler releases some of the smells of the blood contained within the spongy cavity. Working bone can be a very greasy experience, where the grease extraction by removal of the marrow still leaves the bone itself with a great deal of the smell of the animal. Or in a fur, the smell of the animal clings, and where the tanned fur is near to the body, being slept on or worn, that smell will become part of the human smell. Thus it may be important to look at the range of sensory experiences and the way in which they can interact with one another, to gain an attention from those working and using these materials. I have argued elsewhere, that to my mind the way forward is to think of the environment as made up of natural and artefactual objects, and to see what is unusual about that as part of an archaeology of attention (Hurcombe 2007a: Ch. 6; 2007b: 538–41).

Strong colours, translucency, shine and flecking may all be aspects of materiality that we take for granted, but are rare in the societies being studied, and could have been aspects of materiality that would have drawn a great deal of attention (Cooney 2002; Cummings 2002; Keates 2002; Saunders 1999), whereas the focus on colour has become more established in archaeological circles (Boivin and Owoc 2004; Jones and MacGregor 2002). The earth tones are the most obvious colours available to traditional societies and there are some colours that draw our eye, to which the societies being studied archaeologically would have had almost no access other than as flowers in the natural world. An archaeology of attention, therefore, draws our attention to what is rare and what is commonplace. The former may mark people out, and the latter may signify powerful, cultural norms and familiarity. The *chaîne opératoires* outlined in the chapters on plants and animals give some indication of the range of these sensory worldviews and allow archaeologists to think through the possibilities for the familiar sensory experiences and the rare sensory experiences. Classen (1997) has argued for an anthropology of the senses: this book argues for an archaeology of the senses. This is a first step to trying to perceive the sensory worldviews of the past.

Integrating the whole

The key structuring principle in this volume is the plant or animal as raw material and the ensuing *chaîne opératoire*. Thus the starting point of a plant or animal in the landscape is emphasized here, rather than using the end-product description as a classifying principle. The materiality of plants comes first, before the chapter dealing with animals because it is very likely that plant materials were used first within our evolutionary pathway. The structure in this chapter has divided categories of plant raw materials according to extraction and exploitation patterns. The discussions cover the growth patterns and the pragmatic constraints and the technological choices made as part of the *chaîne opératoire*, and the roles of these materials and technologies are considered. There are issues of seasonality and location for many of the stages within the *chaîne opératoire*. In some cases the archaeological evidence can be supplemented by scientific techniques that greatly augment particular kinds of identifications of technologies or species or processes; in other cases there are gaps. These different aspects are brought together as a set of issues in the end section. Furthermore, the ways in which people, plants and animals relate to each other and interweave, are discussed later in Chapter 4 and integrated into a wider craft and subsistence network in Chapter 5. This section forms the basis for this later more holistic discussion.

In the modern Western world there is an increased interest in what has become known as 'slow food'. This is a movement that has promoted the idea that knowledge of where food comes from and what has been done to produce that food and bring it to market is an important part of peoples' relationship with food and their understanding of the ethical and sustainable issues connected with it. In some ways the approach in this book also argues for a slow craft movement. Extracting resources from the environment is not something that most people think about when they buy a bag to shop with, or an item of clothing. The modern Western world is divorced from almost all stages of the *chaîne opératoire* for the things that people use and have as their material culture items. Beeswax in candles and polishing products may be scarcely noticeable. The leather car seat, jacket or shoes are more anonymous and are not 'cow crafts'. Furs attract far more emotional connections with animals, but few people own one. There is no sense of how long it took to grow the cotton crop for the T-shirt, nor is there a real sense of where the pine that we buy from the DIY stores comes from, and under what conditions it was grown. In most cases people would not even be able to tell the difference between tree species in a forest, let alone tell the difference between the characteristics of wood when it has been trimmed and processed. This is in direct contrast to the situation that would have prevailed in much of prehistory. People would have been intensely aware of the extraction of the things they needed from their environment. Conversely, items from far away, where this was not known, would have been exotic and may have been marked as special items because of a lack of personal involvement in the *chaîne opératoire*. However, most materials would have had a general familiarity.

It is easy to think of 'wood' as a category that is generally understood by people across the world. If an exotic wood entered a society as part of long-distance contacts and exchanges, people may have recognized that they did not know this particular species or that it held different characteristics from the species they were familiar with, but it would still nonetheless be generally recognizable as wood and they would have had a general level of understanding of its properties and how it might have been processed. Thinking about these kinds of categorizations and the sets of materials that are generally understood is one way in which the structuring principals for the next two chapters, outlined below, have been arrived at. These are by no means perfect, but are an attempt to adopt a system that best fits and facilitates the ensuing discussions, and sits alongside generally perceived qualities of kinds of plants.

There are many places where examples can be used to make the point. In some cases, the full *chaîne opératoire* for a kind of material culture item has been set down, and in other places a generic *chaîne opératoire* approach is used. These two ways of keeping the material broadly relevant, while allowing the exploration of principles in case studies, have been adopted as the best way of showing the approach. There is no way that this book can cover all kinds of materials from all over the world. However, there is enough here in detail and in breadth to allow others, no matter where in the world they are working as archaeologists or as craftspeople, to appreciate the kinds of issues that are raised by this more holistic approach that follows materials from their natural environment to processed item, and integrates these within the whole social system.

Conclusions: perceiving perishable material culture

This opening chapter has shown the scope of the research presented here and outlined the theoretical approaches behind an intensely practical understanding of craft technologies (practices) and material culture. Overall it introduces new approaches and advocates the integration of a broad range of data. It addresses a neglected topic, provides new ideas and connections, suggests revisionist ways of thinking about broad themes in the past, and demonstrates the efficacy of a holistic approach using examples and cases studies. The wide ranging discussions above can be distilled into more succinct aims.

1. Raise awareness of 'the missing majority', the perishable material culture of past societies and make the case for a more holistic approach to material culture.

Since the 1960s archaeology has become increasingly sophisticated in understanding the biases inherent in the archaeological record and as a discipline it has sought to understand the nuances of interpretive possibilities. As a humanistic science with fragmentary and biased remains it has, in the postmodern era, set about addressing the less tangible social questions using a range of arguments and evidence.

Archaeologists have long-recognized the value of rare organic finds and appreciated that they offer a small window on a substantial portion of material culture. Yet nobody has focused a volume specifically on what is missing and drawn together approaches that could augment the evidence available from the rare extant remains. Better recording techniques, improved awareness of excavation and conservation strategies for fragile remains, and the increase in modern building programmes have all contributed to more finds of perishable material culture. The time is now ripe to raise awareness and perceptions of 'the missing majority' – the perishable material culture of the past – by using the extant remains together with ethnographic and experimental data and adopting an integrated approach that deploys other forms of evidence.

No single material category exists in isolation and in life all aspects of material culture are integrated with one another. A more holistic approach allows the evidence from stone tools and ceramics to contribute to a better understanding of perishable material culture. Furthermore, environmental and palaeoeconomic data can contribute in a similar way. To take an understanding of perishable material culture all the way back to the beginning of the object biography profile, to the selection and exploitation of plants and animals perhaps many years before they are harvested, will open up new ways of seeing landscape–people interactions and relationships and offer new interpretive possibilities.

2. Adopt an intensely practical understanding of the possible roles of plants and animals in the formation of a material culture repertoire while emphasizing the social constructs of materiality and technological choices, combining tacit and explicit knowledge in new approaches.

Research interests in a practical understanding have progressed over the years by investigating a range of perishable material culture possibilities drawn from ethnographic accounts and traditional craft practices, and then trying to understand these in practical ways, often involving experimentation (Hurcombe 1992, 1998, 2000a, 2000b, 2004a, 2007a, 2007c, 2008a, 2008b, 2010). A richly varied and detailed practical knowledge offers insights into the ways in which landscapes, and the plants and animals within them, might be exploited for material culture purposes.

The key here is to look at possibilities and rationales in their social contexts, because the plants and animals offer possibilities, but knowledge and practical know-how are socially situated aspects of cultural traditions that contribute to identities. This is why the arguments advanced here are not supporting 'environmental determinism' in any way. The environment offers opportunities and limits what is possible but there is no inevitable pathway of perishable material culture. The approach does not make reductionist or essentialist arguments but will instead inform archaeologists of other ways of thinking about plants and animals than are apparent in the modern world, and will thus result in the consideration of a broader range of interpretive possibilities. In particular, the lesser-known materials and less developed technologies are brought out because more examples would be recorded if the recognition of such artefacts and technologies become better-known.

3. To demonstrate via examples and case studies how to extract information about the missing majority from the inorganic artefacts and environmental data.

The examples and case studies will demonstrate how the ideas and knowledge covered in the opening chapters could be applied in practice. The case studies will follow particular lines of evidence and investigate the issues across one site as a whole.

Impressions of perishable materials in fired clay occur in a number of ways; by accident, deliberate decorative impressions or incidental production-related activities. Each of these offers insights into the missing perishable materials. In addition some artefacts copy the features of the same item produced in a different material. These lookalike skeuomorphs can arise from a variety of causes; interpreting this act of emulation offers a new way of understanding perishable material culture and at the same time bridges traditional artefact study boundaries, contributing to a more holistic interpretation.

Stone tool functional analyses provide information on the processing of organic materials from plants and animals. Many plant foods require only a few tools for harvesting and processing whereas using plants for crafts often requires far more processing time; some of the processes require tools. Likewise, animals may need minimal butchery tools, but working bones and hides takes time and tools. Moreover, plants and animals are often collected for both food and raw materials. This suggests a complex web of interconnections and potential conflicts in scheduling food-collecting *versus* materials-related tasks in different landscapes across the year. Wild, managed and completely domesticated species can be interwoven in complex ways. However, it is usually easier to factor into interpretations the domesticated species that are unequivocally managed for exploitation, whereas the presence of undomesticated species on the site may be perceived as local and regional environmental indicators rather than significant material culture species.

Overall, the ensuing chapters set out an agenda for investigating the perishable material culture of prehistory and emphasizing the role of plants and animals as the raw materials for crafts. If the body is sustained by plants and animals as food, so the social persona and bodily comfort is supported by them too. You are what you eat; and you are what you make, wear, use and inhabit.

Note

1 Material culture has many conceptual issues ranging from gender associations to metaphorical links (see Beaudry 2006; Boivin 2008; Brauner 2000; Conneller 2011; Gage 1993; Gosden 2006; Madden 2010; Meskell 2005; Miller 2007; Outram 2008; Povinelli 2000; Sillar 2000, Tilley 2002a, 2002b; Vandkilde 2007; De Waal 1982; Wincott Heckett 2007). Phenomenology and even the major epochs of prehsitory all rely on materials (Hamilton and Whitehouse 2006; Rowley-Conwy 2006). The use of experimental archaeology, ethnography, craft traditions, historical accounts and the role of perishable materials in the production of pots, goldwork, bow drills and archery equipment have all been used to add to understanding of hafting, musical instruments, textiles, exotic products such as silk and the skill to make then. These are very diverse and show the range of work considered useful to understanding perishable material culture in an holistic way (see Aiano 2006; Anderson 2005; Apel and Knutsson 2006; Dunsmore 1993; Heron et al 2010; Egg and Spindler 2009; Gaddum 1968; Kihlberg 2003; Kovačič et al 2000; Lammers-Keijsers 2008; MacKenzie McCuin 2009; Meiggs 1982; Needham 2000; Oakley 1965a, 1965b; Orchard 1975; Roux 1989; Sillitoe and Hardy 2003; Stocks 1993; Woodward et al 2006).

2

THE MATERIALITY OF PLANTS

Making sense of the plant kingdom as the raw materials for material culture

Divisions of raw material can be seen in relation to the environment in which people live, and to the human body and the ways in which materials are extracted and then processed by people. In different periods and environments plant materials have been exploited in many diverse ways. The social strategies within which materials are exploited affect possibilities, and much of the *chaîne opératoire*. Several concepts and frameworks can be brought into this understanding. The most useful are concepts such as taskscapes (Ingold 2000a, 2000b) and ways of placing actions within locations, and with links to sets of people.

Experiential evidence strongly affected the groupings in this chapter. A combination of size of plant and part used was used to group materials together. The other organizing principle was the kind of technologies associated with different plants. Rushes, reeds and sedges are plants, gathered whole by the armful or handful. The other major grouping of nettle, flax, hemp and cotton is associated with fibre production. Cotton is a seed-head fibre, but the others are all bast fibres. In all of these cases, bundles of material can be extracted from the environment as whole plants, or as gathered seed heads. Likewise, willow and flexible shoots as a category can be taken from the environment as bundles and gathered in the arms. Major differences from the same plant would be when more mature saplings and regrowth or mature trees are exploited. One example makes the point clear. Willow produces young flexible shoots that can be harvested and used after one year. Willow trees with regrowth of five to ten years are still flexible, and can be used in more structural ways. The trunk of a mature willow tree is in a different category. The tree would need to be cut down, and while the work could be done by one person, the material cannot be carried away easily, and in practice it becomes more likely that its exploitation is on an entirely different scale than that of the smaller-scale exploitations of the same plant. Other categories are substances – such as saps, gums and resins – and tannins and dyes.

In this way it is possible to try and conceive of a vast array of the kingdom of plants as they relate to the human scale of exploitation, and the strategies for obtaining the material. The categories of raw material adopted here are broadly based around the following divisions: first wood as the main raw material, and then the bark and roots of trees. The exploitation of bark and roots lead then to discussions of plants as cordage, basketry and plant-based textiles, as well as gums and resins.

Trees as wood

Everybody in the modern world understands wood, because of the way in which it is still used so prolifically as a building material, as handles for tools and for making furniture. Thus, the common sensory perception of wood is as a tough, resilient, warm and comfortable material (Plate 1). Fewer people will have experienced the reality of working with wood in general or with different kinds of species. The reason that this section on plants starts with wood is because the stick so beloved of children on walks has been one of the most influential adjuncts to the human hand. Even an unmodified stick picked up casually can serve as a probe, a weapon and a way of trying out things without risk to the individual concerned. It can also be used to knock down fruit from a tree that is otherwise out of reach, or as an aid to moving around. At its most basic level brushwood and brash can be quickly assembled to make wind breaks and provide the basis for shelters and structures for sleeping. (Brash is the term used by woodsman for the very small twigs at the tips of larger branches.) In many woodland practices, this material is the waste that it is left on the ground, put into piles or even burned. However, around the world this kind of material is used to make quickly assembled hedging and structures. Its springy qualities can also make it very useful for weaving into roof structures and it can make comfortable bedding. The branching habits, springy qualities and the way in which trees grow as individuals and in stands, together with the material that is easily accessible from the ground as either dead, partly rotted or fresh material would have been important ways in which people could have exploited the resources from trees. Figure 1 shows an example of the ways in which different parts of a tree were exploited in a Bronze Age salt mine (Grabner 2009). The mine was on a steep mountainside with limited tree resources nearby. Thus the trees were exploited to make best use of the different parts. Figure 2 shows how one structure could include different species and technologies being used in construction. Wood is not just timber, it is also round wood (poles) and withies.

Bark fibres would have been available from material that had naturally fallen or rotted from material on the ground. Thus, it is even possible to think of trees as providing 'string' in early prehistory. In these ways wood is a diverse and wonderful material. Use is likely to have been early and extensive as an aspect of

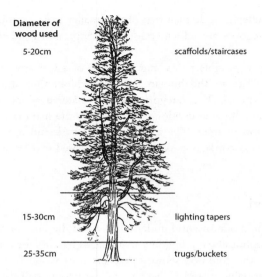

Diameter of wood used

5-20cm   scaffolds/staircases

15-30cm   lighting tapers

25-35cm   trugs/buckets

FIGURE 1 The exploitation of trees used in the Bronze Age salt mines, Hallstatt, Austria. Source: Hurcombe adapted from Grabner 2009: 225.

developing material culture in human evolution. What follows is an explanation of some of the kinds of differences between species of trees and ways in which those qualities could have been used by people.

Tree tissues and structures

Trees lay down new wood each year. This is the basis of the dating technique known as dendrochronology. The process works by an active layer of cells between the bark and the wood known as the *cambium* (Plate 2). In the growing season the cambium cells are active and are laying down both new wood and bark. Thus, in both there is an accumulation of cells and an expansion of the existing structure of the tree. As the tree grows, the wood in the centre of the tree is eventually so far removed from these nutrient-bearing active areas that it becomes heartwood. Heartwood is inert, whereas the area of wood near the cambium is known as the sapwood. This means that even structural timber has two different features, heartwood and sapwood. Sapwood has the highest water content and also still contains nutrients. It has a tendency to shrink more and could split as it dries, and it is also more attractive to attack by insects and fungi. Sapwood is sometimes trimmed off timbers that are used in major structures so that these areas that are more prone to decay will not compromise the desired structural integrity. Differences exist also across species. The bast fibres that make up the layers closest to the cambium layer also gradually expand as new bark fibres are laid down. This gives two areas of bark. The outermost layer is inert and forms a protective skin around

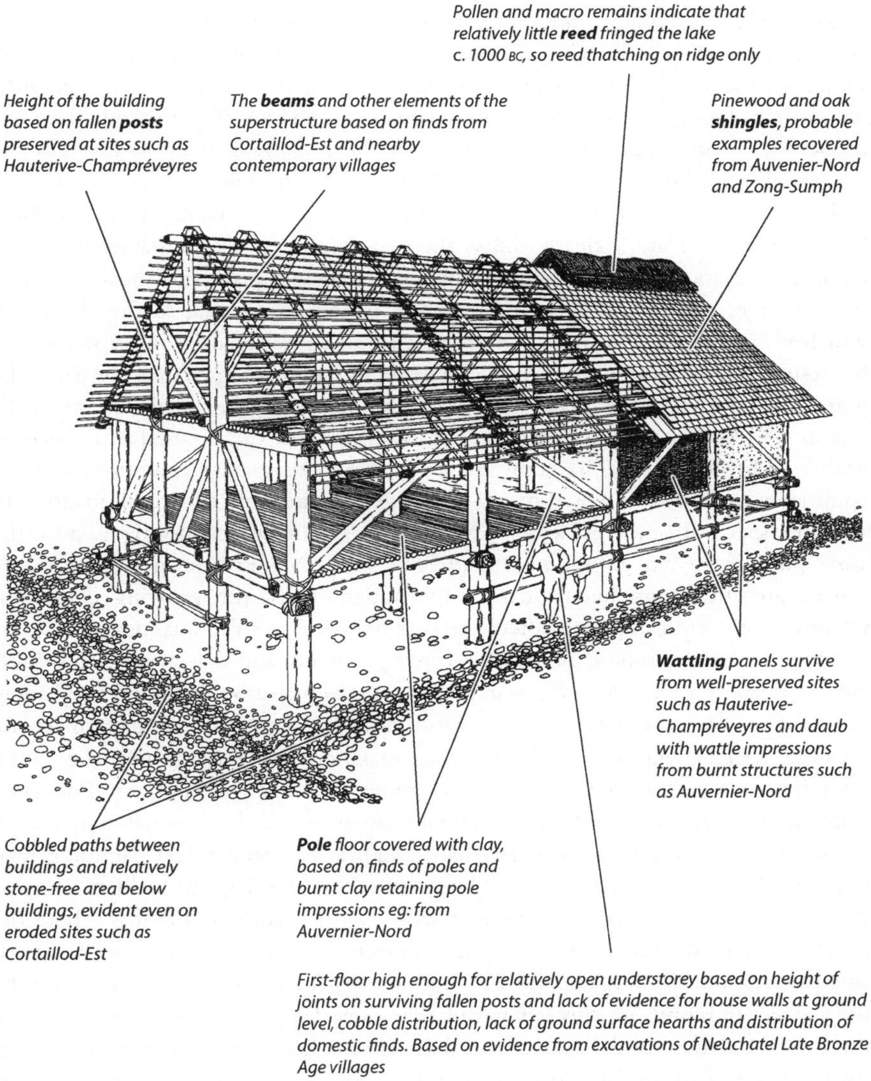

Pollen and macro remains indicate that
relatively little **reed** fringed the lake
c. 1000 BC, so reed thatching on ridge only

Height of the building
based on fallen **posts**
preserved at sites such as
Hauterive-Champréveyres

The **beams** and other elements of the
superstructure based on finds from
Cortaillod-Est and nearby
contemporary villages

Pinewood and oak
shingles, probable
examples recovered
from Auvenier-Nord
and Zong-Sumph

Wattling panels survive
from well-preserved sites
such as Hauterive-
Champréveyres and daub
with wattle impressions
from burnt structures such
as Auvernier-Nord

Cobbled paths between
buildings and relatively
stone-free area below
buildings, evident even on
eroded sites such as
Cortaillod-Est

Pole floor covered with clay,
based on finds of poles and
burnt clay retaining pole
impressions eg: from
Auvernier-Nord

First-floor high enough for relatively open understorey based on height of
joints on surviving fallen posts and lack of evidence for house walls at ground
level, cobble distribution, lack of ground surface hearths and distribution of
domestic finds. Based on evidence from excavations of Neûchatel Late Bronze
Age villages

FIGURE 2 The archaeological evidence for wood used in a house from Cortalloid-Est,
c. 1000 BC.
Source: Adapted from Coles 1992: Fig. 16.1.

the tree. The inner bark is an active area of growth and the fibres are known as
bast. As the tree grows, these fibres expand and strengthen and eventually will
become the inert bark layer. Thus, both heartwood and sapwood and bast fibres
and outer layer of bark give other variations for use by humans.

The other important difference is of that between species.[1] The precise arrangements of cells forming the wood are diagnostic of particular genera and sometime species. There is a broad division of woods into hardwoods and soft-woods. Confusingly, not all hardwoods are hard and not all softwoods have the properties of softwood. Much depends on the precise arrangement of the cells and the growing qualities of the tree. Box (*Buxus* sp.) is renowned as a dense wood. It is the wood selected by flint knappers as their wooden soft hammer for detaching knapping flakes. Plate 2 clearly shows the density of the box annual growth rings compared to another species, pine. However, the same plate also shows that one species, pine, can vary greatly in its growth patterns according to the climate in which it is growing. This is something that is not appreciated by most people and has resulted in the past in mistakes being made in the planting of trees for particular purposes. Two examples make the point; the piece of pine grown in the Baltic region seen on Plate 3 is a solid and dense structure that can be used as a structural timber in boatbuilding. The same species grown in temperate conditions as a fast commercial wood crop would by no means deliver the same structural qualities. In addition, species that are growing in Mediterranean climates cannot be used for the same purposes when grown in Britain. The harsh Mediterranean climate causes slower growth giving better structural qualities. Thus, the growing conditions relating to climate can greatly affect the uses of wood and the qualities.[2]

There is also the issue that wood is a living material and that every tree is indi-vidual. In some cases, there are scar patterns or uneven growth caused by shading out of one side of the tree by competition with neighbours, which can create asymmetries that will cause problems when making material items from the wood. Sometimes the growing in of shapes is going to be very important. For some shipbuilding pieces or handles or structural timbers, wood that it is naturally grown to the desired shape is far stronger than taking a live timber and trimming it as required. Even a short glance at the linear nature of the diagram in Plate 2 shows that the fibres mostly run in alignment with the tree trunk and that is where the greatest structural strength lies. So, when objects are made, the density of growth ring patterns and the way they lie are important aspects of how that material can be used. Trees in temperate climates have large vessels for carrying nutrients as part of the burst of activity in the spring, and these are markedly different from the much smaller vessels that are laid down later in the year. This distinctive banding is part of the way in which the dendrochronological rings can be so distinctive. The term 'ring porous' indicates this marked difference between spring wood and late wood. In general, late wood has more fibres and is the strongest part of the wood struc-ture. Some trees do not grow with such marked differences and are also known as diffuse porous. The other key structures of woods are the medullary rays, which are the transverse connections across the body of the tree. It is this combination of the fibre structures that allows individual species to be recognized from transverse longitudinal and radial cross-sections.

The features and characteristics of four common and useful temperate European species can be described (see Plate 3). Oak (*Quercus* spp.) has distinctive medullary rays clearly visible with large obvious ring porous features. The transverse phase shows very long rays and in between this there are small pores formed by late wood. Its radial phase shows sheaves of rays exposed in a pattern. These are the features that allow the characteristic radial splitting of oak and which mean that, although it will dry into a very dense wood, it can be split and worked green in very flexible ways and with relatively straightforward technologies. The branching habits and growing conditions of each individual species and its localized growing conditions will also be important factors. Oak often grows with high-arched branches, which can be very useful for creating structures. However, log boats will need the trunk to be tall and straight for the desired length of the intended boat. To obtain these kinds of features, trees that are growing in close competition with each other would be needed alongside those that are growing to the required height and breadth desired for the object. In the case of log boats, this could be mature but straight and unbranching trees, growing therefore in a mature, densely-wooded forest.

The characteristic grain patterns of *Ulmus* in transverse radial and tangential views marks it out from the other species depicted. Elm (*Ulmus* spp.) is also ring-porous and has medullary rays but these are smaller and have a wavy appearance as late season wood. These can be seen in both the tangential and transverse places and also as flecks in the radial phase. Elm is good where the objects need to withstand damp and *Taxus* also has this property as well as stunning colour qualities when newly cut and it has differences within the internal wood. Yew (*Taxus baccata*) has annual rings but a very gradual transition from the early to late season wood. The distinctive visual quality of *Taxus* with its dark-red toned wood and distinctive heartwood and sapwood can be clearly seen. *Taxus* is also very resistant to pests and insects and fungal attack with many parts of the leaves, seeds and the wood being toxic (Bevan-Jones 2004; Hageneder 2001, 2005). The same flexibility that makes yew and elm useful for bows also gives yew excellent qualities for use as pins and awls. Taken together these four species in three views demonstrate something of the variation of the characteristics of wood. In each case the wood available in the local area would have been carefully selected and chosen to fulfil its purpose according to the techniques used to work the wood and also the structural qualities wanted for its intended purpose. Other common species can be added to this range.

In general, trees growing near water often have high waer-resistant properties. Alder (*Alnus*) is a good wood for water resistance. Willow, in particular, is a species known for its ability to grow flexible shoots. These shoots have been used traditionally in many areas of the world for making wicker style frameworks and basketry. Ash (*Fraxinus* spp.) is also ring-porous but does not have obvious medullary rays. Ash is a wood known to be preferentially selected for handles because of its qualities of flex, resilience and shock absorption. It is also a species that, as its name suggests, is excellent for firewood.

The use of species for particular kinds of fires and situations is of considerable importance where the interior of a dwelling may need to be kept relatively smoke-free by the choice of wood species and the effect of seasoning in combination. Elsewhere, and for particular purposes, the exact opposite will be important where a smoky fire will be needed to smoke hides or to keep away midges as smudge fires. Different woods burn at different temperatures and in the Northern Hemisphere oak wood is good for fires and hardwood species are chosen for certain kinds of charcoal production. Although Plate 3 shows how four key species from temperate climates differ, exactly the same kinds of issues are there for any other region of the world. Archaeologists can investigate the local uses of wood and the abilities of commonly available local species to fulfil purposes ranging from firewood, charcoal production, wood used in objects that need to withstand wet conditions, wood for handles with good shock-absorbing qualities, flexible bow-making wood, wood that can be used for structures and resists rotting and insect attack, and wood that can be used for the likes of basketry and vessels. Thus, the short discussion here considering common European species could be adapted and considered for other climates and regions. If wood used in planked boat and log boat construction, and bast fibre usage is considered, more species are added to the list. In Northern Europe obvious examples are birch bark canoes, lime log boats as well as those of oak, and in more recent periods such as the Bronze Age, oak in areas such as Britain for boatbuilding versus pine in the Baltic region. In all cases the key species for the region are likely to be those that had been used historically and ethnographically for particular purposes.

This knowledge must be tempered with consideration of the ability of the material to be worked according to the technologies available to the archaeological periods considered. The ability to split wood radially and tangentially will be a key feature in stone tool using communities where iron and steel are not available. To a certain extent bronze and copper allow wood to be worked in different ways than if only polished stone axes or flake stone axes and adzes are available. Thus, the technologies of woodworking have to match the technologies of blades and wedges available to the prehistoric community. In these ways, an idea of how wood might be being used and in some cases managed can be appreciated.

Hazel (*Corylus* spp.) is noted for its ability to grow fine and quite flexible material from its shoots, and is a traditional hurdle-making wood. Wood from both willow and hazel is traditionally made by managing the trees and growth habits of the new shoots in ways described as pollarding and coppicing. The key difference between these two management strategies is the height at which the stump or the original parent tree is cut. Thus, a pollard has many shoots regenerating from an area at usually shoulder or head height of trunk, whereas coppices are cut and regrown from ground level. To this should also be added epicormic shoots from buds that lie dormant in roots close to the trunk and can regenerate and intensify the amount of new growth (see Figure 3). In many respects, archaeologists are familiar with coppicing and pollarding practices because of traditional continuations of these hurdle- and basketry-making based woodland management systems. However, many more species will regenerate and put forward new shoots when cut down in the same way. Willow and hazel are simply trees whose uses have selected them as coppice and pollard products. For example, other species that will coppice include yew. The regenerative properties of this tree follow exactly the same principle, but its slow growth means it is not an economically viable way of

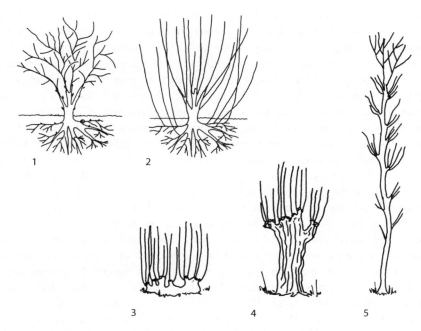

FIGURE 3 The management of bushes, shrubs, and trees to provide straight, flexible, young
shoots: 1. natural bush; 2. bush regrowth after trimming; 3. coppice; 4. pollard; 5.
shredded regrowth.
Source: Hurcombe, 1 and 2 adapted from Anderson 2005: 215, Fig. 27; 3–5 adapted from
Rackham 1990: 66.

managing yew trees to obtain a commercially viable product in the modern world
(Oaks and Mills 2010). Many trees are extraordinarily difficult to kill because they
regenerate as dense growth. In this way, if a tree is deliberately cut down, this can
be for purposes of this regenerative growth rather than to kill the tree. Woods
in other climate zones also have this characteristic. For example, flexible withies
can also be obtained from cedar in northwest America (Stewart 1984: 161–69).
Thus as part of the strategy using the approach adopted here in other climatic
zones of the world, a key feature to investigate would be the regenerative qualities
and properties of the trees species of the area. In many cases these sorts of characteristics can be explored using standard reference works relevant to a particular
area of the world (e.g. Russell 1982; Tebbs 1984).

   The key difference between the way the modern world uses wood and the
traditional use of wood is that with the latter, it is worked green, i.e. fresh rather
than seasoned (Abbott 1989, 2004; Langsner 1995; McGrail 1982; Stewart 1984).
Green wood is softer and therefore easier to use using traditional technologies such
as soft bronze tools or stone tools. In addition, by working it green and hollowing
out or reducing the bulk of the full size of the tree trunk or pole, it is possible to

allow the drying process to act directly on the object made.[3] In contrast, if large pieces of timber are worked after seasoning the craftsperson may have to work around cracks that have developed due to uneven drying. If a large object is required then the first act may be either to use a tree recently brought down from natural causes, or to fell a deliberately chosen tree. In areas where such trees are large, there are always choices to be made according to the size of the desired object, for example the width and length needed in a log boat will require a large size of tree with a long clear trunk before the first branch. Plate 5 shows a large sewn plank boat. The tree for the keel was the most difficult to source. Other desirable qualities in wood are a straight and even grain. For some purposes, this is more crucial than for others but in general wood splits more easily and more predictably where the grain is fine and even. There are three well known ways of working wood; first, by the removal of the material blow by blow, chip by chip. The keel in Plate 5.2. is made by removing material from half trunks with the details axed, adzed and chiselled to shape with bronze tools to make the complex cleats seen along the top of the shaped timber. Second, by using wedges and the grain of the wood to gradually pry it apart and split off material by propagating a crack along the lengths of the grain. The third way is to use the selective and controlled charring of material. The last can be used in addition to other ways of working wood but it is likely to be underrepresented in the way archaeologists think of using tools and manipulating wood into items of material culture. There is ethnographic evidence from places such as the northwest coast of America (Stewart 1984) for other ways of working wood. Stewart shows a series of instances where the tree had a plank extracted leaving the tree standing in the forest (Figure 4). Here, a flitch (a term used to describe a substantial piece of wood the size of a billet or plank, but resembling a large splinter or sliver) is removed from a tree suitable for this purpose. Careful cuts are made in the trunk at either end of the intended flitch or blank. Wedges are used to start the crack and ropes then pull off the wood. In some cases, this material is literally grown off the tree as a crack slowly separates out the desired piece of wood from the parent tree. The use of fire to char wood is also mentioned.

Other ethnographic accounts suggest an even more extensive use of fire. Throughout his descriptions of Ingalik material culture Osgood (1940) refers frequently to the way in which the shaping of wood was augmented considerably by the use of fire to char objects into rough shapes. This is true for a range of different wood types and object categories, for example, a birch wood axe handle is roughly charred to shape, and so are the spruce wood elements that make up the wooden frame within a canoe of birch bark. Even the description of chopping down a tree using a stone axe details the use of fire to char and then remove the pulpy fibres arising from the axe blows (Osgood 1940: 97), see Plate 4.1. Lyford (1945: 61) explains that fire was started at the base of a tree that needed to be felled and when a portion had been charred, a stone chisel was used to scrape this away. The tree would take several repeated versions of this process before it was felled. If a dugout canoe was to be made the same process was used to char and scrape out the hollow

FIGURE 4 Taking tree resources from living trees: 1. removing bark, 2. splitting off a flitch or plank of wood with wedges, then ropes, 3. the same but allowing the tree to propagate the split.
Source: Hurcombe: adapted from Stewart 1980: 115.4 and 42.

cavity to form it. Plate 4.7 shows a canoe log boat being made by the careful use of fire to char the wood, which can then be scraped with simpler tools such as shells. The fire used in these sorts of methods has to be carefully controlled and parts of the tree or felled timber have to be protected from the fire by means of wet clay or a mixture of wet plants and river mud applied to the areas that need to be protected. Wood can be charred to harden a point, although it will also make it more brittle, and the ends of posts are charred to retard the decay process. In these ways a fire can be a tool and an adjunct. There is some doubt as to whether this truly saves time. Partly, this may reflect cultural practices but much depends upon the quality of the tools being used and whether they can be easily replaced. Antler and bone adzes and axes were made by the Iroquois when working with charred wood (Lyford 1943). The tools themselves may be far more important for finer wood-working than we give them credit for. Once a plank or billet of wood is obtained it can be finely shaped to an artefact; see Plates 4.1–4.3 for examples. Holes can be drilled by hand or by bow drill (Plate 4.4). Some objects could be made with minimal shaping, for example the whisk in Plate 4.6, and Lyford (1945: 58) mentions an emergency baby carrier used by the Iroquois made of fine, compactly woven twigs, but considerable effort and embellishment are obvious in others. The replica of the Mesolithic Tybrind Vig paddle (Plate 4.5) accurately reflects the charred pattern created on the original.

Other ways of trimming a large piece of wood to shape include the use of wedges. The cracks can be started by antler, bone or hardwood wedges prepared in advance. Among the Ingalik, the preferred material for wedges was caribou antler. Other kinds of material could be used but were not considered to be as tough because bone will dry and become brittle and break easily, whereas a good antler wedge was regarded as lasting a long time, was more flexible and was thus a tough tool for larger scale tasks. However, for detailed wedge splitting work, the more rigid bone, which could be very finely shaped, achieved fine splitting more accurately. The wedges were used with wooden mauls of spruce wood for medium sized mauls and heavier green birch for larger mauls (Osgood 1940: 102). Once a crack line was propagated, further splitting had to be carefully controlled as this method may result in too much material being removed. It also relied on the grain being relatively straight and even for the crack to propagate in predictable and manageable ways. Where trees are split by using wedges the fibre structures are riven rather than broken, sawed or mechanically disrupted. This allows riven structures to have far greater strength than sawn structures and have more resistance to warping. The lie of the grain is also important: radial planks will warp less than tangential planks.

Where large scale carpentry is part of the project, the careful selection of the initial tree in the forest would probably involve checking the evenness of the grain beneath the bark prior to committing to felling. Even where the bark is even and the tree has been felled, problems may be shown once the tree is down. The commitment of felling large trees should not be underestimated. Felling a tree is inherently dangerous and bringing a large mature tree down using simple technologies still requires space in the forest floor for the tree to fall and careful control of felling to bring the tree down in the desired direction. Then there is the problem of removing the tree from the forest. It is likely that preliminary trimming could have been conducted near or at the place of felling to remove some of the bulk before the material had to be pulled out of the forest and brought to where it was going to be used. The technologies involved would have made themselves part of the working of wood in a community of practice. Thus, large scale carpentry for boats or substantial wooden buildings would inevitably have also involved technologies using other wooden objects such as levers, rollers or runners to manoeuvre those materials into position and to drag them or roll them out of the areas up and perhaps over rough ground and finally bring them to where they were intended to be used. It is likely that trees near rivers would have been preferred.

There would then have been problems of erecting large timbers. The impressive engineering works of prehistory that manifested themselves in stone have their precursors in the manipulation and erection of other large scale heavy objects such as trees and sections of timber. Stones moved across the landscape such as those which make up Stonehenge relied on technologies that were developed to move and work with wood. Large stones or logs were likely to have been moved with the aid of poles as levers and logs as rollers. The use of trees as a transport mechanism, utilizing levers and rollers, is underappreciated.

Plates 6.1, 6.2 and 6.4 show a range of small structures built using only thin wood and various coverings. In these kinds of structures moving individual elements would not be such a problem. Plate 6.2 shows a bent wood frame structure covered with hides as its protection with some mats and matting underneath. The use of twined woven matting as structural elements in houses and roofing is something that archaeologist in general need to consider more often.

The substantial plank built houses from the traditions of the Northwest Coast societies of America (Plate 6.3) offer an insight into what it is possible to do with wood that is high quality and straight grown of substantial size where large scale dwellings and floor plans are required and where storage of food and material products rest alongside people within the house structures. The Northwest Coast building traditions are one of the most stunning examples of the use of wood as a material to build substantial houses (Plate 6.3), but they are by no means the only ones. Plates 6.5–6.7 show ways of using a variety of materials. First, woven wickerwork structures from willow or hazel rods can be seen in the apex of the roof while the roofing material itself is of reed. There is storage under the eaves and the walls are formed by small wood frameworks holding in place reeds and other smaller materials. The whole rests on round wood structures which form the weight-bearing component with a door of solid wood planks. This image was chosen because of the variety of different materials and technologies used in its construction. Plate 6.6 shows that it is not necessarily finely worked and split planks that make substantial structures, but rather the judicious use of smaller tree elements in ways where the greatest load is placed on larger thicker posts, but where much of the structure is instead made of smaller poles. These are in this case plastered over to form floors and walls. Plate 6.7 in contrast is of a house reconstructed at Kierikki, a Finnish site with Neolithic and Chalcolithic style dwellings that were thought to have been of 'corduroy' style house floors and walls with low roof structures again supported by logs. The forested environment would provide plenty of trees but the amount of timber needed for a house of this kind would require a substantial period of felling. The roof is covered by birch bark sheets followed by moss and sod, although reed has also been used in some of the reconstructions.

Ways of working with wood would inevitably have made people aware of the annual growth ring patterns and the best ways to use those, and the ability of different species to split as important aspects of which trees were selected for which purposes. The ability to split radial planks or to halve and quarter trees could have been the first step in making planks. Planks that grow tangential to the growth ring patterns placed in areas where they are subject to wet and dry will warp whereas radial cracks and half splits will be more stable. Wood can be adzed as well as axed to shape and riven surfaces could be left as they were to allow grip. Recent work carried out at the British Mesolithic site of Star Carr (Conneller et al 2012) has shown that planks were possibly used as walkways over swampy areas and that Mesolithic technology was well aware of this kind of larger scale working of wood at 9000 cal BC. There is also wood material from much earlier in prehistory such as a 700–800 ka-old piece at Gesher Benot Ya'aqov (Belitzky et al 1991). There are also Palaeolithic spear shafts that show fine shaping of wood for spears over 2m long from Schöningen in Germany (Thieme 1997) and these are probably similar to the tip of a spear that was discovered much earlier at the British Palaeolithic site of Clacton. These Palaeolithic finds show that wooden spears were finely made about 400,000 years ago.

Later developments of wood would have included the use of bow drills to make holes (see Plate 4.4 for an example) and the development of chisels enabled jointed woodworking. There are polished stone chisels known from Europe as well as metal ones from later periods. Hollowing out wooden vessels by means of fire could have been a very early technique but larger wooden vessels would have been heavy and bulky to carry for mobile societies. Larger ones could have been left as caches and as site furniture for which no trace would remain. Smaller scale pieces could have made simple, personal wooden vessels and although such vessels have been known from the Neolithic they are likely to have been in use much earlier. Other ways of working wood involve the use of heat in the form of steam and direct application of heat to make the material more malleable and flexible. The use of this kind of technology could have been very early indeed as spear shafts and then arrow shafts would all have needed to be straight.

Simple technologies for cooking in an earth oven using hot stones or ashes placed in a pit (with food protected by moss or leaves buried inside) and then covered over with material, could also have been used for steam-heating wood so that it could be bent or straightened, but this would only have been likely for thinner pieces as for thicker ones the steam would not penetrate sufficiently. For smaller items a vessel with boiling water could have been used. Steaming and bending wood into shape is covered by modern technological greenwood specialists and is shown from ethnographic societies (Abbott 1989: 115–23; Stewart 1984: 84–92).

In the Iron Age, a simple pole lathe was used for wood turning. The pole lathe works by a large pole of springy wood being placed firmly in the ground at an angle and the free springier end has a cord passed around it, which is then attached to a pedal operated by foot on the ground. Between the springy end and the pedal, the cord is wrapped around a rod of wood. Thus, as the foot presses down, the springy end of wood is drawn towards the ground as the foot comes up the pole flexes and pulls back up. In this way, the cord can be made to transfer energy between the moving foot and pole, through the cord. This movement allows the cord to be passed around the rod and to roll the rod backwards and forwards as the user depresses the pedal at the base. With the right rhythms and sharp metal tools, pieces of wood placed in the centre of the rod can be gradually shaped into true turned wood. Although on a much larger scale, the pole lathe is similar to the way in which a bow drill works.

Where wooden objects require fine finishing then the use of smaller sharp tools to refine the surface and to smooth it down can be the last phase of working the wood. A finer surface still can be obtained by rubbing it on gritty rocks or sand, or by using sand with wet leather.

Tree exploitation

The material properties and characteristics of the different elements of a tree thus show an extensive range and need to be understood according to the technologies available to ancient societies. For tree materials, these range from massive structural work to very fine lashings from roots, and cordage from material removed from the tree and processed further. In some cases, the exploitation would leave very little archaeological signature and would not even kill the tree. However, in the living system the scars and manner of regrowth may all signify cultural management and in some cases personal ownership rights of those resources or at the least be a visible mark of exploitation or testing lasting tens if not hundreds of years (Garrick 1998; Rhoads 1992; Pole et al 2004). There is a mismatch between the ways in which the living trees can be exploited and the ways in which archaeologists collect their evidence. The most obvious finds from trees tend to be the larger materials because they survive better, with the materials deliberately deposited in the ground either as the basis of structures and posts, or as grave goods, or those where the manner of use made it likely that they would be preserved under exceptional conditions, such as log boats preserved in waterlogged deposits. Much of the primary exploitation of tree species exists in the landscape with only small elements brought back to site. There are sites with woodchips and evidence of woodworking, for example, Etton Causewayed Enclosure from Neolithic Britain (Pryor 1998), but these are few and far between. The exploitation of trees is about more than the exploitation of whole tree trunks. This aspect will be addressed later, and further information on the technologies involved is covered in the next section.

Bark

Bark is arguably one of the most important organic materials available to prehistoric communities from at least the Mesolithic onwards. The significance of bast fibres as part of the European Neolithic and Bronze Age traditions of cordage, basketry and textile production means that people in these periods were well aware of the properties of bark, but this is likely to be part of a much older tradition. Plate 6.1 shows a Mesolithic style reconstruction of a possible dwelling from Europe, with bark as roofing. In many traditional North American structures bark forms the walls and roofing of large dwellings (e.g. Nabokov and Easton 1989: 89). Bark can be used in very diverse ways from clothing to roofing.

The uses of bark as a material are explored by outlining the production methods for bark cloth traditions, before moving to European traditions, which differ slightly, and then finally onto birch bark use which is very particular to the qualities of that tree species. The discussion of bark starts with bark cloth. These traditions can be seen in Africa and also over much of the Pacific.[4] In the latter region the paper mulberry tree (*Broussonetia papyrifera*), is widely used and also *Ficus* species. Where the bark cloth is very fine, the surface can also be painted and decorated in intricate ways, such as with the bark cloth brought back from Cook's expeditions to the Pacific. At its simplest, incisions are made around the circumference of a straight even-growing trunk and then the material is slit down the length before being carefully prised-off in sections or as one piece. The bark is removed whole and beaten to make bark cloth. Water can be used to soak the bark before and during the process. As Plate 7 shows, trees with no branches and relatively straight and even trunks are selected and the bark is peeled off. Even in the tropics, this is more easily done in the rainy season. It is then pounded either by using smooth stones or wooden beaters. These gradually loosen the fibres and expand the network so that individual fibres become clearly visible as they cross one another and open up as seen in the African barkcloth shown in Plate 7. The material expands greatly and becomes more flexible. It would not be unusual for a piece of bark removed from the tree to grow to double the size or more once this pounding and softening has taken place. The beating also softens the material and makes it more flexible. This pounding technology is also used extensively in the Northwest Coast of America where it transforms the bark of red cedar (*Thuja plicata*) and yellow cedar (*Chamaecyparis nootkatensis*) (Stewart 1984) into softer material. Thus in the Northwest Coast, the Pacific, South Asia and some areas of Africa, bast fibres offer an important means of making cordage, containers, clothing and matting.

Other species from temperate Europe have been investigated to explore their potential for use in a similar manner.[5] Other bast fibres are also important, for example the work of Reichert and Hurcombe has shown that hazel, elm and willow along with other species such as poplar and spruces all have potential uses.

Plate 8 shows a different operational chain for other forms of bark. For temperate trees, the bark can still be processed by pounding, but other ways of exploiting it have become part of the traditions. In some cases the outer bark is first removed in a layer before the inner bast fibres are beaten and exploited. In other cases this material sheds naturally as the bark is beaten. Beating softens and separates the fibres but many do not need this. Other common practices for exploiting bast fibres are retting, i.e. partial rotting, of the material in water prior to working. In particular, lime bark (*Tilia cordata*) has become synonymous with a whole range of clothing and cordage textiles and matting from prehistoric sites in the Circum-Alpine region. In Plate 8 the top two images show the ways in which one bark material can have very fine longitudinal fibres and much coarser ones depending upon its proximity to the wood or the outer bark respectively. Lime bast when soaked readily laminates into radial layers which can then be further split apart longitudinally in the manner shown. This means that this material is very adaptable. Both coarse and fine materials are possible, and by finely separating the longitudinal material, the precise quantities for cordage and matting and looping technologies can be refined and controlled. The American basswood *Tilia americana* is similarly an important source of fibre (Plate 8.6).

In addition, if lime bast is not retted in water, it has a particular problem in that pectin from the material oozes out in a gelatinous mass. Bast fibres have particular prevalence for key species. One such is undoubtedly the use of lime bast in prehistoric Europe as witnessed by the finding of the Iceman's knife sheath and cordage used in his shoes (Egg and Spindler 2009; Egg et al 1993) and also the many clothing fines of lime bast and matting finds from the Circum-Alpine region of Europe. Even when treated by retting, lime bast still sheds water very well and has a pleasant smell that lingers despite many months of use. Bark is also a material that, much like wood, is a good insulator. Modern descriptions of the properties of plant fibres are based on individual fibres of very finely processed cotton and linen. Bast fibres in contrast still have more bulk and when linked together and put into layers act as traps for air and are quite warm clothing materials.[6] The hat and rain cloak shown in Plate 11 on bast fibres show how these kinds of clothing systems resemble loosely constructed thatch and shed water away from the body. They would become heavier with rain and water may penetrate but they would keep the wearer relatively dry and a lot warmer than if they were not worn. The Portuguese shepherd cloaks described from the recent past by Kuoni (1981) are another example of the same kind of clothing system, although in their case they are using *Juncus* species. In North America cedar wood and juniper wood can also be used in these sorts of ways as can many other kinds of wood. The bast fibres produced by different trees in North America and in Europe does offer many different ways of using this material as cordage or as whole material (Plates 8, 10 and 11).[7]

Plates 8.3, 8.5 and 8.7 show experiments with a range of temperate European tree bast fibres. When the sap is rising small (15–35mm) straight branches can be easily peeled or material can be peeled off much larger trees (Figure 4). The bast fibres can be used with the outer bark on, and can also be prepared by carefully peeling the bark off the fibres, or by scraping it off prior to stripping the branch. Boiling in water, or wood ash and water, or pounding, are other ethnographic practices. The bast fibres of hazel are very strong, and willow can be prepared to form very fine fibres. Oak gives a soft bast that is good for insulation. Traditional retting suits lime and also enables elm bast to split more easily. Some basts are stronger than others, and most can be twisted, with the exception of oak.[8] The simpler production methods offer opportunities for very early exploitation using minimal technologies for this particular kind of material. However, bark can be used as a solid mass from a large tree, stripped while the sap is rising from a smaller tree and bent into shape as containers, or be used as bast fibres alone with or without further work. The preparation of the material, artefact type and manner of entering the archaeological record will all affect the survival of bast fibre products. Even in areas with generally good preservation conditions some organic finds are still very rare. One example is the painted bast fibre armband shown in Plate 10.3 (Whittaker and Kamp 1992). The armband was found in a prehistoric Sinagua burial at Lizard man village (North America) in the grave of a 17–18-year-old woman who had the band on her arm just below the elbow and also had another shell bracelet and grave goods. The find dates from AD 1200–50 and is made from bast fibres (probably juniper) painted with azurite, a copper salt that helped preserve it. Plate 10.1 shows a replica of a Neolithic find of a willow bast knotted net from Finland and Plate 10.2 shows a contemporary cedar bark pouch worked in a variety of thicknesses. As outlined above, bast fibres offer particular qualities for making cordage and fine string in some species such as lime and willow and hazel. The example below shows the range of uses of bark for one society.

Bark use amongst the Iroquois, North America

North American ethnography has some outstanding examples of the ingenuity that native communities used for working bark, and for cordage and basketry. Lyford (1945: 58) mentions the Iroquois made bark baby carriers. Lyford also describes the use made of a variety of plant materials and bast fibres from trees for cordage and ropes. They used the inner bark of Basswood, (*Tilia americana*), loose wood (*Dirca palustris*), slippery elm (*Ulmus fulva*), Indian Hemp or Dogbane (*Apocynum* sp.), nettle and milkweed fibres (*Asclepias syriaca*). The basswood fibre was specially valued for heavier duty ropes. Canoes were made by the Iroquois from oak and red elm bark. This was lashed to a frame and could be of considerable length, with many 40-feet long and able to carry 30 people. The bark of red elm or black ash were used to make bark vessels. In general, the Iroquois used bark for a variety of purposes. Elm bark was particularly favoured. Containers of all kinds including quivers and bowls, trays and troughs as well as canoes, traps and sledges were made of bark. Bark vessels were made by using large sections of the material and folding them slightly to pinch together the two distal ends of the tubular section of bark before adding a handle and stiffening material at the opening. Springs were lined with sections of bark and caches were lined and covered with these same bark materials and used to store fruit and vegetables. It was noted that the bark would come off the tree readily when the leaves were the size of a squirrel's ears. Incision was made near the base of the tree and another some 7-foot up the tree and a vertical cut made between the two. A wedge was used to gradually open up the cut and work the bark free or around from both directions. This came off in one large sheet when it was undertaken successfully but this thick sheet could be thinned by separating the laminating layers. Provided the sap layer was not harmed, the tree would recover and eventually grow new bark. Lyford (1945: 53) states that bark for thread was also gathered in the spring but peeled off in narrow strips about 6 or 8 feet in length. These were loosely braided to keep them tidy and stored until they could be further processed. In order to make the cordage, the bark strips were boiled and pounded up to three times. This softened the fibres, which were then washed and dried in the sun, then separated into very fine threads and braided for storage. This material formed the raw material for netting and a wide variety of cordage tasks. Elm, basswood and cedar, as well as Indian hemp were favoured for their strength when making tumplines (strong braided straps that could be used to carry loads on the back with the strap passing across the forehead). The finest and strongest were the slippery elm fibres although basswood was very good for heavy straps. Again, boiling, stripping, rubbing and twisting are mentioned as processing before making these kinds of cordage products. Tumplines could also have a variety of animal hairs such as moose, buffalo and elk as well as porcupine quills used to weave complex designs with some threads and quills being dyed to add to the pattern variations.

Bark was also used for roofing material and long house construction as the final covering. The bark was gathered in the spring or early summer in long sheets from the elm, hemlock, basswood, ash or cedar trees, but elm was considered the best. The sheets were flattened and then attached to the poles and frames of the long houses with bast fibre, withies or strips. A bone punch was used to make holes so that the bark sheets could be tied down, the sheets being placed like shingles so that water shed from them. A set of poles parallel to the house framework was constructed and placed on the outside of the house so that the bark layers were sandwiched between the two sets of pole structures. Gaps were left in the roof to enable the smoke to escape but these could be closed in exceptional weather.

This short review of the uses of bark by one society shows its potential importance: the bark harvesting season would have been an important fixed point in the annual cycle of tasks.

Birch bark in northern Eurasia

The bark of birch (*Betula* spp.) was particularly important in northern Eurasia (Gramsch 1992). This is because birch bark is a very flexible material which in these colder zones grows more thickly, and as a tree, birch is a first colonizer and grows well under cold conditions. Thus, it is the combination of availability and exceptional properties that make it such an important species in those areas of the world. Birch bark tends to be used as the inner bark with the outer bark removed. The bark is springy and from larger mature trees provides material in sheets suitable even for building canoes (McGrail 1987) and it can also be used for a variety of containers and as roofing material as well as for rain cloaks, shoe manufacture and backpacks (see Plate 9). Birch bark also floats as do many other barks. Rolled up birch bark is interpreted as floats from Mesolithic sites such as Tågerup, Sweden (Karsten and Knarrström 2003: 186) and at Star Carr, Clark's (1954) interpretation was as material for floats or simply a stored set of material placed in water to soak prior to being used. The key tools for working with birch bark are awls and more spatulate but slightly dull blades with a variety of different light curves at the end for prising apart the bark layers during the harvest (Yarish et al 2009).

Birch bark harvest chaîne opératoire

As with many other craft raw material selection processes, birch bark is dependent upon selecting the right kind of material and cues in the environment need to be recognized. Yarish et al (2009) suggest that the bark of birch is better in regions of mixed forest rather than wetter lower lying areas or in stands where the birch is next to fir and pine trees. Better conditions are where the birch is near aspen and alder trees. In this type of deciduous stand the birch grows towards the light and a good area of trunk clear of branches make suitable material for harvesting. If growing in birch groves alone, it is not as tall and the branches occur closer to the ground and closer to each other, affecting the ability to harvest the bark successfully. Where a good length of smooth bark is available, spiral cuts are initiated high up and then the strips carefully controlled and wound off, using tension and angle to maintain an even width that can result in a 10m-long strip, which is carefully rolled into a bundle to be stored in a dry place. Bark is generally taken from trees 15–25cm in diameter. When the strips were being prepared for weaving, they can be re-immersed in water and heated slightly to improve their flexibility and material such as oils and fats can keep the strips oiled so that they glide over each other easily. Birch bark sheets are used for tar production or for making products from the whole sheets. When testing birch to see if the bark is good quality, colour can be important with the best bark being a yellow or yellow-brown tone. The reddish or darker shades tend to dry out more rapidly and are weaker and more brittle, making working them difficult. Again, the ability of the test strip to separate into thin layers is another way of finding out the quality of the bark. If the bark is very wet it might need to be dried slightly before being stored. Thus, harvesting bark is not a good idea in a period of rainy weather. Sheets that show good qualities of evenness and flex can be set aside for the highest quality of work, which is generally airtight containers from whole sheets. A higher level still is the ability to harvest a whole cylinder entire from a section of the birch. These are known as *skolotni* in Russia and are priced as high quality vessels. These have a very limited number produced by master craftsmen each year and have a key season of a few days in early June when the bark is at its best for removing in cylinders. Suitable trees are not easy to find. It is said that you can walk through the forest for more than an hour before finding a tree that is suitable.

This short account shows how vital it is to select the right kind of tree, taking account of growth conditions, and then to test it. As with so many crafts, the finest quality material is very rare, even where there are many trees of the right species.

Once the material has been harvested and dried it can be placed in storage, the key features of the chain of operations for the next phases can wait until the crafts-person is ready to begin their weaving or round work project. Prior to this, warm moisture – perhaps provided by immersing the strips in boiling water and greasing them – may be necessary and, if not done shortly after harvest, the thinning and evening up of the material can be undertaken at this stage. The outermost layer of bark that is discoloured and peeling can also be trimmed off at this stage. Many of the processes for the woven styles of birch bark use imitate those known for weaving rushes. Round containers can be woven at the sides, or made from solid sheet at the side, with a base of wood other pieces of birch bark. The material is usually stitched using either lime bast or root material.

Birch bark artefacts

Woven birch bark shoes are slightly different in parts of Russia for men and women, and different regions also have slight variations. The products of birch bark can range from all kinds of storage containers such as baskets, packages and back packs to muzzles for calves, mats and straps as well as items of clothing such as shoes (Plates 9.1, 9.2, 9.4 and 9.5). It is also used in dwellings as both waterproofing and insulating material for roofs or around and between logs and stones, acting as a kind of damp-proof course (Plate 9.3). It also has nutritional, medicinal and ritual uses. One significant aspect is that airtight containers in a prehistoric context would have been highly sought-after because of their preservative effects on foodstuffs and also to contain embers for fire and control the amount of oxygen reaching the embers. One such example is the Iceman's fire-carrying equipment (Egg and Spindler 2009).

Birch bark finds or vessels are well-known across the Northern Hemisphere although their survival depends largely upon waterlogged conditions or preservation through ice, such as with the Ötzi, the Iceman. There are some from Britain, such as a set of Neolithic birch bark vessels that were found in a ditch context at Horton in Berkshire (Cartwright 2003). One bowl had a diameter of 475mm and another had a maximum surviving depth of 203mm. Such vessels have also been found in Northern Europe and in Switzerland and are outlined as domestic items in Earwood (1993). The birch for such vessels may have been local although, in general, birch bark of this nature is more likely to be found in mature birch stands in colder climates than the present-day climate of the UK allows. It is difficult to obtain good quality birch bark from mature trees growing in present-day conditions in Britain.

Roots

Roots of trees are a neglected form of exploitation of tree species in the minds of archaeologists. Roots are known to be used as lashings for fences in Norway (Monrad Hansen, pers. comm.) and as sewing materials for stitching birch bark as seen in Plate 9.1. The young roots of even mature trees can be dug out and carefully removed, usually in the spring when the sap is rising (Yarish et al 2009). The thin parchment-like or tougher outer layer can be carefully pulled off or stripped using two branches held closed together and the roots can be either split and then stored or vice versa. When used in basketry and cordage, these materials will need to be soaked and where these items are finely made they will be worked further by making sure that they are even along the entire length. Stewart (1984: 171–77) explained this process for cedar where roots of approximately 2.5cm thickness are used, but spruce and birch roots can also be similarly treated. In all cases, loose even soil, in particular sandy soil, gives roots that are straighter with fewer kinks. Roots from trees growing in sandy soils are also easier to extract. In contrast, stony soils have gnarled and angled roots as they grow around the stones and are not suitable for this kind of use. Elsewhere is it described how even the roots of species such as bulrush (e.g. *Cyperus, Scirpus* spp.) can be carefully cultivated and used in a similar manner and likewise they require finer and even soils in order for them to be kept long and straight and these are the most sought-after and useful for basketry (Anderson 2005). Nettle (*Urtica dioica*) roots can also give long tough binding materials.[9]

The roots of birch and other coniferous trees such as spruce are traditionally used as stitching materials and basketry materials. Birch bark containers have such stitching. Roots can be harvested throughout the summer and autumn when the ground is not frozen and when the soil can be loosened most easily. Again, the local indicators of good roots are sandy soils and mossy ground where the roots are even and long. Coniferous trees have roots near the ground and so harvesting the runners is not difficult. The roots of fir trees are much tougher than those of other trees with which they maybe intermingled such as aspen (*Populus* sp.), or alder (*Alnus* sp.) or rowan (*Sorbus aucuparia*) (Yarish et al 2009: 36–39). They also have a different aroma. Gathering roots carefully can result in pieces 2m long. Those gathered are cleaned of the external layer within the first day or so of harvesting and the small shoot roots can be cut off with a sharp knife before the bark is removed. This is so that the bark peels off in the same way as one peels off bark on a branch. Bark processed in this way is then rolled into loose rolls and stored to dry out slowly. Prior to working, the root must then be soaked to make it flexible again, preferably in warm water. It can be split into finer units with a knife or a thin wedge and the crack can be propagated carefully by hand, not unlike splitting willow, and can then be used for fine basketry work and fine lashings.

Plants as stems, leaves and fibres

Plants provide flexible stems, leaves and fibres for a wide range of materials. These raw materials are explained further below, but the technologies for this group open up a wide range of processes related to the materials culture items they produce.

Cordage, basketry, mats and textiles are a wonderfully diverse category, but problematic because the technologies borrow and crosscut each other so much. At one end there is simple twisted cord and at the other end are complex weaves with textural and dyed alterations. The fibres in the high-end textiles are very well processed and managed to produce fine and even products. Although cordage today is mostly of materials such as hemp and in finer terms cotton, the cordage of the past involved a great deal of tree bast materials and also animal skins. A range of scholars, such as Adovasio, Barber, Hurcombe, Jolie and McBrinn and Soffer have been promoting more awareness of the perishable technologies of prehistory. The earliest examples of perishable textile technologies that are known to us are plant fibres.

The great advantage of plant materials over animal ones for making cordage is that they do not shrink in the same way. Nor conversely do they loosen when they become wetter. Even seemingly simple cords can have multiple different structures with just one element untwisted or a twisted element, which is usually recorded according to the direction of the twist as S or Z (see Figure 6). These twisted cords can be combined in different numbers and in different ways to produce complex ropes, even if they still remain one linear element. The development of these into cordage technologies where simple cordage is used in woven and looped structures gives the possibilities for making lashings, flexible objects and even clothing of these kinds of materials. The other key aspect is containers, some

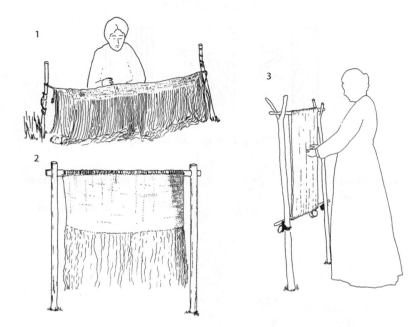

FIGURE 5 Simple two-post structures as aids to weaving.
Source: Hurcombe, adapted from: 1. Del Mar 1924: 32; 2. Stewart 1984, Fig. p 141; 3. Dockstader 1993, Fig. 87.

of which are flexible bags, others of which are more rigid baskets but these are questions of semantics, which is why this category is a closely connected and interwoven one.[10]

Textiles themselves are normally understood as products produced on a loom with finely processed fibres. Towards the end of prehistory that is certainly the case but there were many simpler methods of production before this stage was reached. There are a whole series of devices that would have aided the production of these kinds of products and some technologies used simple frameworks (Figure 5). Even in the modern world, textiles themselves have two dominant raw materials: animal fibres notably wool, and plant fibres, notably cotton and linen, although others such as hemp and jute are also possible. In this book, the more complicated textiles are covered under the animal fibres section in Chapter 3 whereas the more cordage-based and simpler technologies are covered in this chapter as part of plant products. Textiles are the category of plants and animals where the technologies crosscut most closely with one another. However, the object biography approach adopted here means that it is the origin rather than the technology that drives the structuring principles. To take the cordage, basketry and textile traditions from plants is to take a good look at the landscape and the plants available within it and their relative quantities and properties. In the past these kinds of products would

Direction of fibres

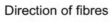

Spinning, plying and cabling

single **strand**
(single Z twist)

two strands plyed into
string
(double S Twist)

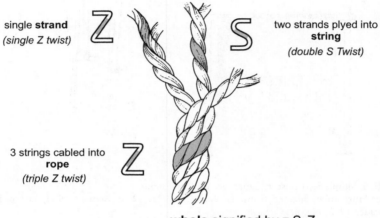

3 strings cabled into
rope
(triple Z twist)

whole signified by $z\,S_2Z_3$

Linear plaiting

3 strands   4 strands   5 strands

FIGURE 6 Twisted fibres, cordage and plaits.
Source: Hurcombe.

have been those that were mostly locally available. Everybody in a community would have needed cordage, containers and textiles even if some had more finely produced ones. Thus the tree bast and the plants used in making cordage, containers and potentially clothes would have been necessities for all and required sufficient raw materials in the environment.

Understanding of cordage technologies and textiles show the amount of time, effort, and status put into and accrued by the production of such goods. The skill of the weaver and basket-maker ranks alongside the skills of woodworker and metalworker (Hurcombe 2000b), it is just that the time constraints are different and the elaboration techniques are also, to our eyes, less obvious. However, the clever use of colour and dyes to create patterns and the extra effort involved in fine fibre production and textural patterning were all employed by prehistoric societies to establish difference, status, and complexity in their craft sphere.[11] Traditional cordage and basketry accounts show some of the possibilities.[12] Many more accounts give specific information about the operational chains that allow individual plants to be used as they are or processed into the raw materials for other cordage and basketry products.[13] In many of the societies mentioned the spinning activities start when girls are young, between the ages of five and seven, and are part of the social life of these children as well as important aspects of their adult life where they spin while walking and doing other tasks (Dunsmore 1985; Franquemont 2009). In each society, there are both a variety of techniques to serve different needs and also particular techniques that seem to be norms within the society. Thus, in the Bronze Age there were both loom-woven textiles and also *sprang*, which uses a different system. While looms are relatively well understood, sprang is a technique where the string elements are held under tension on a frame and the warp threads are crossed to interlace them in ways which give a flexible fabric with a lot of expansion, whereas the loom-woven textiles of the same period are tabbies and twill weaves that give more rigid cloth, especially the latter technique. The sprang is used in items such as the cap from one of the bog bodies (Hald 1980). Carey (2003) shows how, if only a fragment survives archaeologically, the structure can be described but the method of producing it remains unknown (see also Plate 7.17 in Hurcombe 2007a). Looping and looping-around-the-core are fairly well-known technologies explained below but ply-split braiding is a technique that was documented relatively recently (Collingwood 1998; Harvey 1976; Hedges 2006).

Function

Cordage, basketry and textiles serve transport, storage, cooking, clothing, food catching and preserving technologies as well as universal ties and warm and comfortable matting and bedding. They are the most diverse of all of the technologies, except for hides, and between them, the cordage and the hides offer such a great range of flexibility in their uses as to be the prime reason why stone tools and later metal ones might have come into existence. This is controversial because the earliest evidence for material culture is the stone tools starting with Gona in Ethiopia

2.6 million years ago (Semaw 2000); however, many of these early pieces would themselves have been carried around. They could of course have been carried in the hand but at some point a flexible bag made carrying such items a hands-free activity. In addition, children carried with the support of some form of device can be held in better positions, enabling the mother to use both hands, at least for short periods. There are a wide variety of studies of early baskets and cordage[14] and there is also substantial evidence that nets must have existed in order to catch particular kinds of prey (Pringle 1997; Lupo and Schmitt 2002) and of course hafting material (Bocquet 1994) where the lashings are often made from plant materials. For textiles, there are significant recent developments from the Centre for Textile Research in Denmark and others.[15] Within these collections of assemblages, there are also stylistic characteristics and social identity issues, for example, in basketry and clothing.[16] Taken collectively, far more attention is now paid to the social identity that lies behind these fragmentary remains. In most cases, the first act is description but the second is to see beyond this to the people of the society and the significance of textiles, basketry and cordage to their lifestyles and needs and their expressions of self and status and belonging.[17] Thus, ethnographic and archaeological evidence are being meshed together into complex discussions of the sophistication and significance of basketry and textiles as weave structures and as symbolism. It is also worth pointing out that cordage and weave structures rely on understanding mathematical concepts such as pairs of numbers and general numeracy skills in the divisions of sets of elements in order to create particular shapes (Gerdes 2010). The differences that could exist symbolically between looping versus knotting (Küchler 2002a; MacKenzie 1991) and the way in which colour and design are used (Balfour-Paul 1997; Hall et al 1984; Wickens 1983) could also be added to this range of significance. The cordage, basketry and textile sphere of material culture is as rich and significant in the creation of status and identity as any of the other craft spheres. In particular, the numbers and the weave structures have entered our own subconscious as symbolic and powerful metaphors, thus, 'to weave a spell' and 'tie a knot' can mean much more than the words themselves.

Basketry and clothing

Basketry and clothing might at first sight seem strange items to put together. That is because they are different systems in our modern world. This was not the case in the past where the twining and production of softer bags and basketry style technologies were also used to provide fabrics, sheaths, bags and shoes, which merged into true items of clothing.[18]

The twining technologies, and the looping and looping-around-the-core technologies, merge basketry and textiles. That is because these systems have flex within them. Because the material is twisted and can be quite bulky compared to a fine flax cloth, it becomes much warmer. Wearing a rush cloak is to wear plants that already have a layer of air trapped inside them. They also serve as effective windbreaks and can help shed water. To take an example of this, Plate 11 shows some of the bast fibre clothing and sheaths from the circum-Alpine region in prehistory, made up as modern replicas by Anne Reichert. The image shows a reconstructed version of the possible twined cape found with Otzi. The example shown is worked in lime-bast, whereas Otzi's was worked in a grass, most likely *Molinia careulia*. The other items illustrated are the shoe from Otzi, where the inner construction of lime-bast cordage held in place the shoe hay, which provided the insulation material, on top of a bear skin base, with a leather upper. This would have been an effective shoe system, made of a combination of different materials, but featuring plants as part of a clothing system. Woven sandals such as the example shown (Plate 11.4), also from lime bast, are also known from St-Blaise Neuenburgher. The page is dominated by cordage and twining systems. The picture of the knife sheaths shows Otzi's on the left, with the sheath reconstructed from lime-bast loosely twined to make the sheath, and the sheath on the right is made from elm bast.

The archaeological fragment shows how fine some twined work could be. Not all of the materials used have been identified in these finds, many of which were excavated in the late 1800s, but the fineness can be clearly appreciated, with the scale showing that the longer passive elements are mostly 2–3mm in thickness, and that the spacing for the weft twining, which holds the system in place, is less than 1cm apart. Taken altogether this is a complicated system that shows considerable potential to be seen as either a fabric for a bag or mat, in which case it is very fine, or as a clothing system. By knowing the kinds of materials available and the way in which lime bast can be worked very finely, people could have made this kind of weft twined fabric that would have been comfortable to wear, flexible and very effective.

Thus our notions of what might constitute textiles for clothing have to stretch to encompass these kinds of systems.[19] There are also ways in which whole sheets of bark or material from bark, such as bast as a sheet, could have been used as cloaks in much the same way as bark cloth from the African and Pacific traditions is today used to provide material for skirts and such kinds of clothing. There are going to be more discoveries of these kinds of items and it is up to us whether we think of them as part of the clothing systems, or see them simply as mats of some kind or sheaths or bags. My experience suggests that we would do better to consider them as potential clothing items.

If bags become clothes, then what happens to our other definitions of basketry? This is really best seen in terms of a range of plants used in their entirety or with further work, by humans, to serve various container and processing needs. Some of the materials for basketry are woody, and these woody stems have not been used for soft textiles or clothing. However, many of the softer plant materials have. Plate 12 shows some of the useful plant raw materials. These range from traditional textile plants such as flax (*Linum*), dock or *Rumex*, which is used as a basketry material in parts of Ireland, reed (*Phragmites*), which can be used when dry as traditional thatch but can also be cut green when it is far more flexible.

Other plants illustrated are the traditional willow, and soft rush (*Juncus*) as well as bulrush (*Scirpus lacustris*), sedge species known to be used for making shoe hay

(*Carex*) and sets of lime and willow bast and hair moss (*Polytrichum commune*) and birch root. This image was put together to show this kind of range, and how the materials can differ in colour, tone and rigidity, with different kinds of processing techniques. For example, *Phragmites* can be put into very different thatch systems for roofing, with the leaves as well as the stalks forming the cover. This plant has also been worked green to soften and flex the stems, which can then be used in different kinds of ways than our notions of the plant stalks envisage.[20] Plants as roofing, floors and wall materials would have been important in many societies. This variation from mats to walls to clothing, will be expanded on later. Also, every system for clothing and basketry makes use of local available materials, and in some environments there are particular plants that lend themselves to one or several of these needs.

Shoe hay from sedges chaîne opératoire

The case study outlines the use of a 'soft' plant for use as insulating material for shoes as an example of a little-known but very important plant use.[21] People went out to collect shoe hay each year in order to obtain enough to see them through the cold winter period. The shoe hay needs to be soft, but acts as an insulating material within leather shoes. It can be taken out and dried, in much the same way that one can dry off socks. Eventually it will wear out, even with this reuse. It has to be collected when the plants are in the right season. Sources used show that both men and women possessed this knowledge. A person would need ten bundles for a year's supply of shoe hay. Adults doing the processing would be preparing material for the whole family. The remnants from the combing can be used as summer shoe hay material or as toilet paper. Sometimes scrapings from willow bark are also used in combination with shoe hay in the summer. This is said to be good for the feet, with antiseptic properties, and good for the shoe because of the tannins.

The species used are primarily, bottle sedge (*Carex rostrata*) and bladder sedge (*C. vesicaria*). Mostly the shoe hay collection and processing is women's work, but it is something that children learn and help with as they grow up, so everybody knows how to do it. The shoe hay is used by the Sámi and farmers alike in northern Scandinavia. Some processing is done in the field and one account states that all of the pieces with seed heads are removed and discarded. Strength is important and those with seed heads may have different characteristics because of the energy used in seed production. The sedges are grown in marsh conditions but insights from informants show that it is important to gather them from grounds where there are also willow bushes growing. Testing this out is hard, but it might be that the willow signifies a slightly drier set of conditions than those immediately beside a lake, and there is a suggestion that although the wet lakeside conditions allow the sedges to grow longer, their stems are slightly weaker. These subtle aspects are discussed further for other plants in Chapter 4.

The length and conditions of the material harvested result in the collection of a knee- or thigh-height bundle. The collection season is early summer, perhaps from the end of July or August, in the latitudes where these accounts were documented. Bundles are picked and kept bunched and even. Primary processing begins in the field. The roots are rinsed and then, grasping the bundle towards the top, the whole can be beaten against a rock or other convenient surface to get rid of the short pieces. The tops have less breadth than the bases, so usually two bundles are tied together at the top, but remain as two separate bundles near the base. Other sources suggest using a tree for the beating, and loosely knotting the tips to make the bundle. Small twists of cordage can easily be made in the field from nearby willow, to loop around the bundles, which are then carried on the back, to the home. The bundles can be lightly dried to enable them to be stored, and the knot at the top of the bundle can be used to allow the bases to dry and then this situation can be reversed.

Other processing can be done at leisure and involves combing the material. There are metal pronged and wooden handled tools used as shoe hay combs. As shown by Ellinor Sydberg, one such tool (Plate 14) has been used within one family and is now over 100 years old. Combing the sedges cannot be done all at once, nor for a whole bundle as collected in the field at once. Instead, the bundles are made slightly smaller and separated, then the material is grasped about halfway and the tops are combed out first and the tangles and crossing material are gradually aligned and separated. As work progresses, the grasping hand, or the knot, whichever is in use, moves down the stem until finally the direction can be switched; the roots are combed out last. The material can then be hung outside to dry further. One account uses the reverse and starts with the bases and gradually works up to the tips. Some combs have two rows of teeth and look a little different, but the process is essentially the same.

Once the material has been combed it needs to be softened. This involves grasping a small section of the stems in one hand and keeping this stable while twisting the area immediately above the stationary hand and whirling the material around gently in an action not unlike cranking in basketry. This action is repeated all the way down the stem and the fibres are kept in alignment but merely bruised and the whole softened by this process.

Shoes that have hay stuffing within them would need to be two to three sizes bigger than the foot size and the most famous example is the shoe construction from the ice mummy Ötzi found in north Italy (Egg and Spindler 2009). The moss (*Neckera crispa*) serving much the same function has been found in shoes (Leuzinger 2004). Experimental evidence shows it is comfortable and quickly conforms to the shape of the footstrap under the instep.[22]

The breadth of plant species and processes

Plate 13 illustrates a range of useful plants from across the world. Canes and bamboos (13.1, 13.3) are important for structures and basketry, but they can also be used for simple hafts and tubular containers, and split bamboo can make sharp knives. Plates 13.2 and 13.4 show New Zealand Flax (*Phormium tenax*) as the plant and as fibres, whereas Plate 57.4 shows that the leaves can also be split and plaited or woven.

The significance of the shell illustrated with the piece of twined work (Plate 13.4) is that the shell is one of the tools used to scrape the fleshy part off the leaves and release the fibres. Other issues arising from the illustration is the way in which dyeing the fibres black in this case using combinations of natural dyes and muds to achieve a range of mostly earth tones and green colours, allows patterns and variations to be achieved, and strikingly here, the naturally white fibres have been used as the twined element against the dark dyed passive elements, to good effect. Plate 13.5 shows hairmoss (*Polytrichum commune*). The main stem is tough, and as the leaves shrivel, the stem can be used as a fibre in its own right. This can be dried and used or be stripped carefully and prepared very finely. There are special tools for this in the historical period in Scotland, where the material is made into a basket or a hat of this material. Here the illustration (Plate 13.6) is of a plied cord made of the moss imitating one found in the seam of a Bronze Age boat. Plate 13.7 shows *Giardinia diversifolia*. It is a member of the nettle family, but its size and vigour and geographical location in Nepal, mean that in this volume I will refer to it by its local name 'allo', to make sure it is not confused with the kinds of nettles found in temperate climates in the north of America and Eurasia. These will instead be what is meant by 'nettle', which in Europe is *Urtica dioica*. The Nepalese allo is the basis for textiles tumplines and bags and cordage, and is an important part of the local traditions and economy. The women walk for many hours to get to the part of the mountain where this nettle grows well above head height, and its sting is so vicious it can cause severe pain for several days. They use gloves and protective clothing to harvest the nettle, and strip the fibres and epidermis from the stem together. The stripped elements are then bundled up, and when they have a full load they walk for many hours back to their community, taking the material with them. It is processed using strong lye solutions with wood ash and water, and boiled for hours and allowed to stay overnight on the fire. It then needs further pounding and separating, but eventually it is washed and hung up to dry (Dunsmore 1985; Hwang 2010). One of the interesting aspects of this *chaîne opèratoire* is the use of clay as a final coating for these long cellulose fibres, in order to help the fibres come free and slide across one another easily in the drop spindle spinning process.[23]

As an introduction to the range of plants the illustrations in Plate 13 show the spread, but it is also useful to focus on one kind of environment and look at the possibilities created within this. That is the subject of Plate 14, which has a range of wetland associated plants, which are widely available across the northern hemisphere of Eurasia and North America. Plate 14.1 shows a wetland flora comprising of *Iris pseudacorus* and *Typha latifolia*, which are the plants otherwise known as cat tails, with the cigar-shaped brown heads. Plate 14.4 shows the professional basket-maker Linda Lemieux harvesting rush (*scirpus lacustris*) on a Somerset river in the UK, from her coracle. Rush such as this grows in slow flowing rivers and streams and is harvested in July. Iris and *Typha* can also be used as their leaves are tough.

Plate 14.2 shows the preparation of *Carex* sedge species into softened shredded material for stuffing inside hide shoes. As explained above, this kind of prepared material is part of the northern European Sámi traditions of preparing for winter, as the material forms the insulation inside their hide boots. Moss can also be used in this way, and as a packaging material. Leuzinger (2004) states that there are small wads of moss found in various wetland sites in Europe, but that he had found one such wad as the lining of a leather shoe. He believes that the wads of moss found on some other European sites are the remnants of this practice of shoe-stuffing. It is certainly the case that such finds and knowledge of the relevant *chaîne opèratoire* open up interpretive possibilities. In the same way Plate 14.5 shows the gathering of soft rush *Juncus effusus*. At first sight this plant looks like a smaller version of *Scirpus lacustris*, which is the bulrush, but it has a slightly different internal structure, as seen in Plate 14.6. A detail from the iris is also shown in 14.3. These show that the size and uniformity of relevant plants can be an important factor if they are to be used whole, rather than shredded. Dried iris leaves can be twisted and made into cordage to be used in basketry and twining systems, but it is also possible to process the plant so that the stiffened midrib is dealt with separately from the smaller fibres in the blade of the leaf. Thus one plant can be processed in a number of different ways, either whole or broken down into fibres and these fibres and elements sorted in relative hardness. Much depends upon what the desired end product is and how crucial it is to make it as finely as possible. This is where there are complex inter-actions of utilitarian need with display and status, factoring in cultural choices in the processing of materials in the environment.

Following on from this, Plate 15 shows different ways of processing *Juncus*. It is possible to take *Juncus* stalks, and starting with a small slit in the base, use a blunt tool to strip out the internal pith. The different, more cellular structure of *Scirpus lacustris* as shown in comparison in Plate 14.6, shows that this plant does not behave in the same way. The *Juncus* allows the pith to come out in one whole round, and the natural curl of the outer material then curls back in on itself. This *chaîne opèratoire* processing stage is part of the manufacture of field rush cloaks traditionally worn by pastoral shepherds in northern Portugal (Kuoni 1981). That is why *Juncus* has been processed in this way and used to explore ways in which the material can be more finely worked and the technological systems that can be used to turn it into mats and potentially garments such as cloaks. The material can also be placed in water to soften it, and a hollowed-out log boat that has reached the end of its life makes a useful container for soaking all manner of basketry materials and bast fibres for retting, in a controlled way so that they cannot be lost, as shown in Plate 15.4. The same *Juncus* material can also be shredded as shown in Plate 15.2. A comparison between the top two images in this plate shows exactly the same material, pro-cessed initially in the same way, but then one is worked more finely into shredded material, but the pith is left in. This allows the twining process to slightly cross over each set of fibres making for a dense weave. In Plate 15.1 the larger elements have been used with just the pith removed and no finer working, but the twining has taken place in alternating layers across the two sides of the work. Thus the finger is opening up the material to show the twining that is running across the back face of this material. This was in response to observations of some of the Must Farm material, which looked like there were crossovers of the weft elements. Thinking through these kinds of issues, the solution proposed in Plate 15.1 certainly means that there is no gap for the wind and rain to get through. In the Portuguese shepherds' cloaks, the reason given for removing the pith is to reduce the amount of water that is soaked up when it is raining. The shepherds reported that they switched to more modern materials, not because their cloaks were not keeping the rain off, but because they became very heavy under prolonged rain. This is because the water would gradually seep into the cracks and crevices of the *Juncus*, and while much of it would be shed, some of it would be taken up by the forces of adhesion, and the cloak became very heavy. This suggests that the processing of the raw material visible in Plate 15.2 would, although warm and flexible, not be as effective in the rain as the pith remains with the fibres and would soak up a lot of water. It is in these exploratory experiments that the parameters of some aspects of operational sequences and processing techniques can be understood, or at least their potential revealed.

Plate 16 has more useful plant materials. The first is the centre of a St Bridget's cross made from straw. This was traditionally made from the last sheaf of material brought in from the harvest, but it has also been made of field rush, *Juncus effusus*, and also *Scirpus lacustris* (Hogan 2001: 204). Plate 16.2 shows a plaited straw coil. Coiled up like this, materials could be kept safely and tidily away, without becoming tangled, and the stems would support each other, as shown also in the sweetgrass coil (Plate 16.5). However, plaited material like this can become ropes. In parts of Orkney and Ireland the making of straw ropes is important for many tasks around the farmstead, but can also be used for major items like a roof, thatched with straw rope. Hogan reports on the formation of straw rope granaries using this material (Hogan 2001: 190). Also, Park (2004) has explained the use of straw to make ropes, roofs, baskets and chair backs in the Orkney traditions. Here, black oats are said to be the best types for use in these sorts of craft industries, although their use now is specifically for this, as there are other crops that give higher yields for their food content. The stalks are good because they are flexible, and if they are to be used for craft, they have to be worked by hand and left to dry in the fields in sheaves. Again, the threshing system had to be adapted if the straw was to be used at its best. In this way it was hit against a stone so that the seed heads fell off, rather than the whole being heaped on the barn floor and then flailed in the usual way. A double-plied rope made of such straw could be wound up into a huge ball, waist high, which could be stored and used in roofing. Such ropes could be used to tie down and thatch granary stores, and they were also used to weight down other kinds of thatch. The thatch works by laying down layers of rope and then straw, and then another layer of rope, until the roof is sufficiently thickly formed. Straw was also used as a way of keeping feet and lower legs warm by being placed under the instep, and over shoes on cold days and could be wound around the leg up to knee height in a similar way. The straw thatch would need to be replaced about every two years, which if it were conceived today, would involve a lot of work every two years. Thus plaited material found on archaeological sites, such as the Neolithic village at Skara Brae Orkney, can be seen in two ways. It could be part of a larger rope system or it could be a way of storing material neatly, ready for smaller projects.

The care taken with the straw to be used for craft purposes shows that in the past many crops would have had two uses, one for their food value and the other for the stalk, which could have been used for many other domestic purposes. Likewise the rush has many different ways of being used. There are bundle rafts and raft boats, which have a wood framework based on bundled up rushes. There are also ways of using rush for seating chairs and as caulking material (Hogan 2001: 191). The process for preparing the material would depend slightly on the intended use, but the key phases would have been, first, to harvest the rush in July, usually when the river was low and ideally in a period of good weather so that the rush could be spread out to dry. If the weather was good the drying could take place and then the rush bundles could be sorted and tied into similar length and quality categories, ready for projects later on. If the weather was poor then the rush would have had to be brought inside so that it would not spoil and lose both appearance and overall strength. Thus the timing of the harvest was crucial. Once the material had dried and was been brought inside, it would keep well for several years if it was kept in a shady place with good humidity. The management cycle for harvesting such rush works on harvesting only every two or three years. Where rush cutting is practised, the rush beds are maintained at a high quality, and the river flows freely, because material is not left to die in place and clog up the river bed. It is possible to cut rush by standing in a slow flowing river, or by leaning down from a coracle or other similar simple boat.

In other areas of the world plants have been used in ways that rely very much on their local qualities. To take two contrasting ideas, first of all, the papyrus plant (*Cyperus papyrus*, or a variant of it), which grows in wet conditions in Egypt, is famous for being raw material for a system of paper-like sheets, on which could be recorded scenes and written material. The earliest is from the third millennium BC. Papyrus was produced by cutting the plant stems (the lower part is best), then reducing them to manageable lengths. The rind is stripped off and the pith cut into strips, which are laid down in one layer, edge to edge, with a second layer at right-angles to the first. The layers are beaten or pressed together (Leach and Tait 2000). It is possible that favourite strains of plant were managed or cultivated, but this is difficult to prove (see Chapter 4). In contrast, gourds require little processing, as the raw material lends itself to be being used as storage for liquids, as in Plate 16. 4, which shows a natural gourd, and one that has been turned into a flask, alongside a gourd base, turned into a small dish with a wax setting into which beads have been placed.

Image, 16.5 is of a sweetgrass, *Muhlenbergia sericea*, which is plaited and coiled in much the same way as the straw in Plate 16.2. This plant is used for fine coiled basketry in the southeast of the United States, and has important connections with black American basketry traditions from the former plantations in this area, which is the subject of plant management problems today, as discussed in Chapter 4.

Tough cordage in northern climates can instead be met by using plant bast fibres, tree bast fibres and roots. Birch roots shown in Plate 16.6 show that it is possible to harvest very fine roots that are flexible and can be wound into ropes, if such are needed, although in such climates birch bark can be used for the same purpose. Birch roots have instead provided fine sewing materials for making much finer basketry, and also for lashings to attach the rim systems to birch bark vessels. Tougher birch twigs and other evergreen materials such as spruce can be used as shoots in their own right as tough lashings and for tying poles to fences.

Plate 17 shows a range of finer materials from around the world that are used in fine basketry and cordage production. These include: nettle fibres (*Urtica dioica*, 17.1); sage brush (a North American plant *Artemisia tridentata*, 17.2); and yucca fibres (17.3), which form a very important raw material for basketry and cloth in the American Southwest and further south. Other important plants are Indian hemp (known as dogbane, *Apocynum cannabiun*, 17.4) and milkweed (*Asclepias syriaca*, 17.5). Both dogbane and milkweed provide finer fibres. Plate 17.6 shows coir from the coconut plant and palm. This raw material is used for tough cordage all over the areas where the palm grows.

All of the materials on Plate 17 have the ability to provide finer materials for fine cordage and bags and basketry style materials. The yucca leaf must be processed by allowing the fleshy yucca outer layer to rot slightly, then scraping off the outer material to reveal the fine fibres. This process is time-consuming and can be aided by periods of retting and also by lye solutions. Many of the others can also be processed in this way, but in practice much depends upon the use. If only a short fine string is required, then hand processing by stripping off the outer bast fibre layer from the woody stems and then rubbing the dried material through the fingers and rolling it in both directions, so that the twist breaks up the outer layers, can release the inner fibres adequately for making fine string. This is visible in several of the images in Plate 17.

The manufacture of such string can easily lead to flexible carrying devices which are of universal utility. Plate 18 shows looping and netting using examples from two different regions. The thicker looping system has been used to make a carrying bag in the aboriginal Australian tradition, where the addition of coloured ochre has coloured the plied string that forms the looping with one layer around the bag worked onto the next layer, whereas the bag below has much finer cordage, produced from Allo, and knotted into a fine even mesh gauge, and is part of Nepalese traditions. Both show the range of styles, but the basic need fulfilled by a flexible light container.

Basketry

These looping techniques lead into basketry. The aboriginal looping technique is also known as Fuegian basketry, because the native communities in Tierra del Fuego at the tip of South America were using this same technique to make their bags and baskets. The same looping system can also be used with rabbit skin cordage, to make rabbit skin blankets. Figure 7 also shows the looping systems with addition of a core around which the loops are made. If those cores are removed,

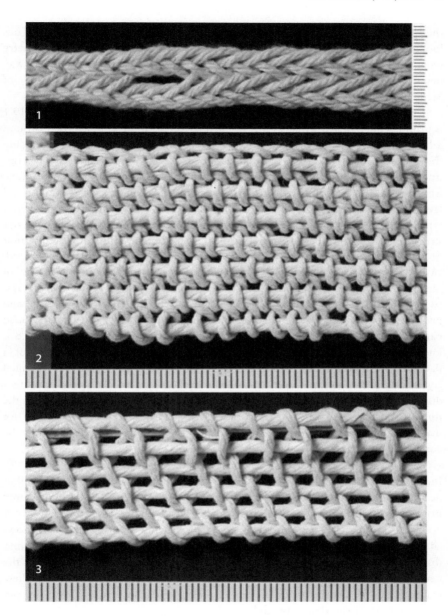

FIGURE 7 Looping technologies: 1. braid with slit made by loop manipulation; 2. looping around the core Tybrind Vig system; 3. looping around the core, Schipluiden Neolithic system.

Source: Hurcombe.

then the system can be seen to be exactly the same as in the aboriginal bag. Thus looping merges into looping around the core, which merges into coil basketry techniques, some of which pick up the stitching from the layer below in the way described by Figure 7.3 and Plate 2.3, as in the basket made at the Neolithic site of Schipluiden (Netherlands).

Plate 19 shows different styles of basketry technologies in closer detail. Plate 19.1 is plain chequer weave while 19.2 is a coiled basket with the core exposed, around a bundle start. The coil material is exposed and the string is the element binding the coils together. Plate 19.3 shows a detail of a twisted willow handle with long-itudinal splits, known as cranking, clearly visible. Plate 19.4 shows a twill weave from a Near Eastern basket, and 19.5 shows a coil basket with a star start of several layers of material on its side being banged in to form the centre. Plate 19.6 is a typical stick basket, but this is a very finely executed one, with an openwork structure at base and sides, because this is a herring cran, which was used as a unit of measure for herring. Plate 19.7 shows an example of rush basketry, using paired, twined weave, with different coloured weavers at 'a' and 'b', and a change of direction at 'c', creating patterns and textural interest. Just visible at the top is a band of darker material, which is a hoop of wood, to add rigidity at the top, and just below this is an extra thickening line of weaving, again adding textural interest. Such baskets, when closely woven, can be rigid, long lasting and watertight. Figure 19.8 is known as a straw three-strand plait technique weave. However, this is not a flat plait, but instead includes small fletches of straw added in to each of the plaited layers, so that the previous layer can be bound in and the whole worked in three-dimensions, into shapes such as cylinders, containers, mats and even doors. Thus the three-strand plait is worked in three dimensions and is a very flexible system for making substantial items out of much smaller material than would normally be considered for large items.

This is explained very well as part of the Irish traditions by Hogan (2001: Ch. 7). In areas of Ireland where wood was rare, straw, rush, grass and dock, as well as heather, were used for many items that elsewhere would have been manufactured from tree materials, such as bast fibres, or from wicker. There are even straw work doors and heather crab-pots worked in a very challenging material. Plate 19.9 shows an open woven paired system around a variety of different stakes, of (a) a wood splint, (b) stripped willow stakes, and (c) a hazel rod stake, halved. Again, this is from the herring cran basket and is a good example of the different ways in which these materials can be incorporated. The basket itself is open, so that when fish are put in, the sea water can drain out easily.

Plate 20 shows at the top a variety of coil woven baskets, and at the bottom a set of interwoven baskets. Coils can be very closely wrapped and form dense materials, with very rigid forms, or can be much more loosely wrapped, to create flexible basketry. Some have been made into sieves and some have lids, some are trays and serving baskets, others are for storage. It can also be seen that the variety of stitching can vary from interlinking with the next layer, such as in the basket top left, or where the stitching material is hardly visible and it is the core which is exposed, for example top right and mid left. There are within the image many different ways of creating textural and patterned interest, from selecting materials which are slightly darker to create the large star shape in the basketry tray from Sardinia, made of *Asphodelus ramosus*. Brightly patterned dyed material used sparingly in the image bottom left from Africa. The coil materials for the inside need only be small enough to keep adding in more material, which is tucked inside the coil, and the stitching is carried on round. Where the material is uneven, the coil will be more difficult to control for evenness, size and ability to bend. The stitching material can be fine cordage or pieces of flexible material, such as paired, split and thinned bramble (*Rubus fruticosus*), palm, raffia or any other material that has sufficient length and flexibility, or can be prepared to have such, to form the close coil material.

In the lower image all the items are interwoven. Some have the weaving structure clearly visible and shapes include squared twill woven items with lids. Others have stick and strand style basketwork, and have been made using a central set of sticks and weaving sets of material around these, with the corner being carefully worked to start the sides, then expanded upwards and out. There is a hat woven with twill weave that also has a band in hexagonal weave on the inside, which shows a slightly different twill weave as it is a double woven structure (for interior see Plate 21).

The pine needle woven basketry is also a double weave structure, see image mid-right. The openwork cane basketry in the centre contrasts in flexibility with the broad tray top left, woven out of carefully thinned and regular elements of bast. Some of the twined baskets have used decorations of slight variations in thickness, such as centre, and other use openwork, bottom centre, and crossed warps, mid-centre, to achieve textural and colour interest.

To these kinds of baskets should also be added frame woven baskets, which are better illustrated in Plate 21. Here, similar items have been made from different kinds of materials. All the items in the top image are made from willow, showing that it can be very finely worked, that it can be stripped and light, or have the bark left on, but that the bark can be coloured, particularly in modern basketry willow varieties, and that the material can also be split into skeins (often a third or a quarter of the stem) and pared down further for finer work, see bottom left.

The top right image in Plate 21 shows a fish trap worked in willow, and below it a frame basket. These baskets do not start with the sticks laying across the base and then weave material around it. Instead these baskets start with a hoop of material such as those bottom centre, and the weaving willow rods are put around this framework, as in the material in the centre, and sometimes a second hoop is attached at right-angles to the first to make the handle. This style of basketry, known as hoop basketry, has great structural strength. Also, many of the items in this image, such as the hamper and the wicker log basket at the back are sturdy and can be used to carry heavy materials. The log basket at the back was used to carry stones to make a cairn as part of an experimental project. It wore a little, but survived a day of very heavy use, where it took two people to carry the basket between them. The interesting points of contrast and similarity in the bottom image are of cane basketry from Mediterranean and East Asian traditions. There are scoops, the inside view of the twill woven hat (seen first in Plate 20), and a robust fruit and vegetable basket for farming work, top centre. More intricate work is possible with pared down split canes as can be seen in the centre, and rattan cane examples are included, such as the fishing basket on the top right. A comparison between the two sets of images shows the flexibility of one kind of material to create a variety of different shapes, with slight differences, according to the underlying structures of the material itself.

The way in which the material is prepared influences heavily the kinds of flex and possible artefacts made from it. Wicker and cane are two of the most well-known and available basketry materials throughout the world. That is why these two have formed the comparison in this image.

As the different kinds of baskets illustrate, the various techniques lend themselves to sieves, scoops, watertight baskets, flexible protective containers and small serving bowls or large substantial trays for heavy duty use, such as in winnowing or collecting agricultural produce. The same techniques and systems can create mats and bedding, be used to construct walls for dwellings or mats used as roofs, or have roofs tied down with ropes of these kinds of materials or materials woven onto a roof shape. The cordage basketry axis of material culture is thus a seamless flow.

Pine needles chaîne opératoire

Pine needles have been used traditionally for both coil and woven basketry. These are narrow leaves and grow in small clusters. This example of an operational chain is drawn from Mallow (2001) and has been selected because pine needles are widely available, and well suited to basketry, with any flexible thin string as stitching. In basketry, it is better to remove the brown caps or sheaths at the base of the needles. The operational chain and gathering period for these is that they can be gathered at any time of the year, but they are in better condition if they are collected from the ground as recent falls before they deteriorate. Thus, early autumn as the weather cools is a good time to collect them. They are gathered in bundles all facing in the same direction and can be laid out to dry indoors or in dry conditions outside for a few weeks with occasional turning to ensure even drying. Green needles plucked from the tree can also be collected, but this should be done in only small amounts from any one tree to avoid compromising its viability. These needles too need to be allowed to dry thoroughly so that they have shrunk before being used in any project. In much the same way as mellowing for reeds and rushes, so pine needles are lightly soaked and then kept moist by wrapping in old cloth so that they are soft enough to work with. The caps should be removed from the end before being incorporated into the coil or woven, and soaking in boiling water can help to soften them immediately prior to working. Pine needles made into coil basketry usually start with the wrapped thread technique and the coils are stitched with good overlap through the previous coil so that not all of the strain is placed on one or two pine needles. New needles will need to be frequently joined in to the short working material and they should always be placed in the centre so that the material on the outside lies flat and even, making sure that it wears well. Pine needles worked in this way make good use of the exposed core style of coil basketry. The stitching material can vary, but is usually a strong thread or plied thread of some flexible material and is considerably finer than that used in many styles of basketry. Joints in this material can also be hidden inside the coils. Where pine needles are intended for decorative effect, they can be dyed, but if so, it is best to collect green pine needles and bring them in to dry slowly in the shade. Sunlight will cause them to darken irretrievably and thus dyes will not show well. It is reported (Mallow 2001) that green needles collected in the first warm months of the season are softer and take dyes more easily than older needles. Even if no dyes are used, these variations in collecting season and treatment of drying will allow subtle variations in tone forming contrasting patterns. The caps can be left on and form decorative features as well.

In general, basketry-style work offers many opportunities for fine work and decorative effects. Plate 22 shows a variety of different patterns and technologies to create different textures and colours and tonal contrasts. Plate 22.1 shows Ramie (*Boehmeria nivea*) with the details of the weave showing a varied warp of loosely twisted fibres, a half stem with the bark on showing as dark, and clean fibres with no twist showing as very light, all of which are woven together with one kind of the processed material in an even strand, creating a tabby weave effect at the top, but a more open tabby weave at the bottom. In this way, one plant can be used to create flex, tonal and textural contrast.

Plate 22.2 shows willow bast finely processed with a flint tool, and woven first in a balanced tabby, then second a more closely packed tabby constituting a weft faced weave towards the base. The scale in millimetres shows how finely this material can be processed and used. Plate 22.3 shows nettle (*Urtica dioica*) processed with a stone tool, and also in a lye solution. In the darker set of material on the left, the only difference is that it has been placed with tannins in the solution and has become dyed and stained by the tannins and ash. In this way tonal contrast can be achieved even with bast fibres, which are generally seen as more difficult to dye. Plate 22.4 shows the same sorts of fibres, naturally lightened by the sun and in this case worked into a looping around the core technique, copying that of the Tybrind Vig style material. Plant dyes for basketry can use woodash, urine and pigeon faeces as mordants (dye assistants); many tannins, plants and muds can be used to give colours (see Chapter 4).

As part of an experimental programme, these materials have also been explored using the patterns from prehistory and the known materials as a starting point, but working the same patterns in different materials and the same materials in different pattern systems.[24] The top image in Plate 23 shows a fine basketry style fragment of willow bast from Schipluiden, Holland. Plate 23.2 is a small sample, woven to understand that technology, which is a looping around the core technique, where the stitching material has been worked into the preceding row's stitch material.

Returning to the archaeological artefact, some things become apparent. The archaeological piece was deliberately made with the interior bast, as the shiniest and finest surface, facing outward. A new version of the replica sample could take this into account, and also adapt to several other small variations that were noted because of the practical experience of working up the sample.

Plate 23.3 is an example of the Tybrind Vig style looping around the core, worked in lime bast, which is the archaeological material. The same system worked in *Juncus* that has had the pith removed, creates a completely different flex and feel to the finished object. Lime bast is a very good soft and flexible material, but *Juncus* would make a good more rigid version of this. In these ways the understanding of the capabilities and capacity of the materials relevant to prehistory can be explored and understood as a first step to understanding cultural choices.

Textiles from plant fibres

The preceding discussions show how difficult it is to draw a line between fabrics of baskets and bags to those intended as clothing. The word textiles has usually been used to denote loom woven cloth made from fine fibres such as flax, cotton, hemp and ramie. To this set of fibres, nettles – both *Urtica dioica* and the giant Nepalese nettle *Girardia diversifolia* – must be added along with other plants. Furthermore, not all clothing is woven on a loom. Therefore textiles could also cover the bast fibre twined clothing used in the pacific Northwest Coast societies of America made from red and yellow cedar bast *Thuja plicata* and *Chamaecyparis nootkatensis*, and the *Phormium tenax* twined clothing from New Zealand. Grass boots and coats are also known from the Arctic (Fienup-Riordan 2005). Confusingly, 'textiles' have also been used as a synonym for clothing to include discussions of hide-based clothing. Thus with no clear boundaries in purpose distinguishing clothing fabrics from those of bags and matting, and no division between loom types or freely made clothing, the materials, technologies and purposes all merge. This is saying something interesting about the fluidity of concepts of materials and technologies. The soft plants and tree bast fibres as well as the lesser-known plant bast fibres have been covered but these blend into the materials which are still important textile crop plants today. Plate 24.1 shows cotton bolls drying on the ground on a tell rising above the fertile plain in Samarkand area, Uzbekistan. Cotton is the fibre from the seed head of the cotton plant (Plate 24.2). This distinctive shape is stylized and featured on many items of material culture in Uzbekistan. Cotton symbolism is also important in other areas where cotton has been a longstanding crop, such as the American Southwest, where the boll is likened to cumulus rainclouds.

The significance of the cotton plant in the prehistoric southwest United States has been fully covered by Kent (1957), who shows the central role of textiles and cotton in the place of Southwestern prehistory. The introduction of cotton plants built on the existing textile traditions using yucca and dogbane (*Apocynum*) as well as animal hair. Likewise, textiles were simply made prior to the introduction of cotton but were adapted and changed with the advent of this material. All this took place before the Spanish traditions were introduced with the addition of wool textiles and yarns. Even in the exceptional preservation conditions of the South-west, the evidence is fragmentary and in some cases the fabric remains can be supplemented by loom weights, spindle whorl weights and by loom parts. Kent concludes that of the known loom types in the Southwest, the back strap loom was the one that came with the cotton plant from the south and that the stationary frames both upright and ground that were part of existing conditions adapted to some extent some of the developments that went with this such as the heddle (a device for making a space between sets of fibres in weaving). Kent's conclusion that there were finger-woven objects before loom-woven ones parallels the opinions of the European traditions (Rast-Eicher 2005). The finger-woven techniques before the loom were given as looping, netting, braiding and twine platting. Kent's analysis of the colours and motifs decorating the textiles link these with basketry motifs in the same region (Kent 1957: 627–30), and the traditions of creating textured fabrics by open work were also well-documented by her. The cultivation of cotton by Hopi in the Southwest of America was an annual crop, planted in May on land that was likely to catch rainfall. Bolls were gathered before they were fully ripe and were dried on rooftops, after which the seeds and fibres were stored. When there was time, usually in the winter, the cleaning or 'ginning' process occurred, when the seeds were picked out (and eaten) and the fibres pulled apart ready for spinning. The fibres could also be beaten lightly with sticks to further separate them (Kent 1983: 26–28). In this society men were the weavers and cotton played an important role in the creation of ritual objects with cotton associated with clouds.

Other major fibre crops are flax (*Linum usitatissimum*) and hemp (*Cannabis sativum*) (see Barber 1991; ramie, sunn hemp, sisal, jute and other fibres are described in Franck 2005). Plate 24.3 shows both dark retted and light unretted flax stems broken to reveal fine fibres and epidermis.[25] Rast-Eicher (2005) has characterized the sequence of fibre crafts in Europe very clearly as 'bast before wool' but she has also drawn attention to the use of tree bast before flax bast. The intensification of flax production in the later phases of the Neolithic (Maier 1999; Maier and Vogt 2001; Maier and Schlichtherle 2011) has evidence of retting as part of the processing sequence but some very clean fibres show no traces of fibre damage suggesting that in earlier phases a manual process of stripping the fibres from the stem was employed.

The other important difference in considering plants such as flax compared to nettle is the ease with which the plant can be grown and managed. This is why in Plate 24.5 the root of the hemp plant has been included, to show that it is a single root and not especially deep. This same root system exists for flax and is in direct contrast to other fibre plants such as nettle. Thus flax and hemp are annual crops that are easy to pull up and harvest, and with thin stems the fibres and pith can be separated in relatively straightforward ways. This contrasts with nettle, where there are nodes at intervals up the stem and where the root system is usually tougher and requires a set of plants to be pulled up, or the stems to be cut.[26]

Plate 25 shows some of the post-harvest processes for plant fibre crops. The most obvious one is spinning the fibres, but any spinner knows that this stage will be far easier, and the finished product finer and more regular, if the fibres themselves have been carefully processed before they get to the stage for spinning. In Plate 25.1 the spinner is clearly making a clean thread from the short cotton fibres, but these have been processed already by removal of the seed heads and careful opening out of the fibres, and preliminary combing and processing into a roving. A roving is a set of uniformly ordered fibres, of even thickness, which allows the fibres to be drawn out easily as the spinner progresses. In Plate 25.1 the prepared material is wound around her wrist, so that she does not have to keep changing fibre bundles: an additional set of prepared fibres can be seen near her knee.

For flax and hemp the seed heads are removed. This could have been done much earlier, or the plants could have been gathered while green and ripened at a settlement so that fewer of the seeds were lost to birds and other species. The seed heads must be removed, and the tough roots will gradually be removed as the plant is processed. One of the advantages of flax is that the whole plant can be processed. The flax stems can be processed in one of two ways. They can either be dried and then spread out on dewy grass for several weeks, or placed in water for a few days or weeks. In both cases, the material has to be carefully watched as what is desired is the partial rotting, known as retting, of the plant stems so that it is easy to separate the woody core from the fibrous outside layer. In both the dew and pond retting systems much depends upon the weather, so that in a shallow warm pond the process will be far quicker than in a cold stream. If the material is left for too long the process will go too far and the fibres will be weakened or lost entirely. Once the material is at the right stage of the process it is taken out of the water, or off the field, and dried thoroughly. Once dried, a device called a flax brake, or a wooden mallet, can be used to lightly flatten and break up the stems and then the fibres can be extracted and most of the woody pith removed. After this stage there are still a lot of small pieces of pith attached, as can be seen in Plate 25.2. These have to be gradually combed out, or hit out using a scutching knife. If the fibres are to be finely processed, once the woody material is out they are drawn through progressively finer combs, which also remove the remains of the epidermis. Finds from the circum-Alpine region show these kinds of combs, known as hackling combs, made from bone or blackthorn spines bound together. Once finely processed, the material can be spun in the traditional manner, but these long threads require slightly different techniques, and the use of a distaff to hold the threads while the user spins from the end of the set of threads.

If the alternative manual processing method already mentioned is carried out, then the retting stage is omitted, but the material will still need to be released from the stems by gently splitting the stems and stripping the fibres, and then rubbed between the hands or processed slightly so that the fibres can be loosened from one another and from most of the epidermal layer. Again a succession of combs can be used to separate these in the same way as the retted fibres. Alternatively still, the fibres can be split longitudinally and then spun in much more of a stop–start motion, where splicing is interspersed with the spinning action.

Variations of these processes have been explored for flax, hemp and nettle. While exploring the possible uses of serrated flint tool edges, which are a common feature of Neolithic European sites, the author has used extensive experimentation with nettles, with the following results. In Plate 26 there is a bundle of stripped stems removed from green nettles at the end of summer by manually stripping the bast fibres and epidermis from the woody inner core of stems harvested both dry and fresh. In the experiments some of the stems were lightly scraped to remove most of the epidermis before being carefully split and left to dry. The bottom image shows all of these processes, with the middle set showing that the woody core can be gradually peeled away with care, leaving just the fibres, which are now devoid of much of the epidermis. The bundle to the right of the scale shows the fibres extracted from one nettle stem using the finely serrated tool beside the coil. Plate 26.3 is a comparison of the fibres which can be spun and produced from, on the left hand side, the tool processed stems, and on the right hand side, the stems with both bast and epidermis remaining, as seen in Plate 26.2. With two or three minutes' active use of the tool, together with more passive storage and drying time, the fibres can be much more finely produced (Hurcombe 2010). Further experimentation involved spinning up some of these fibres as they were manually processed with the tool, and also after further preparation by lightly combing with a variety of devices, including a hedgehog skin, as shown in Plate 27.3. (There was a hedgehog-skin hat in a grave from Sweden, see Burenhult 1997.) The different qualities of yarn produced from drop spindle spinning, thigh rolling and hook spinning, are also illustrated, although much also depends on how much time and care is taken with each of these methods.

Plate 27.6 shows nettle cloth produced on a traditional loom using drop spindle spun yarn from nettle fibres processed manually with a stone tool, rather than by retting. In contrast, Plate 27.5 shows nettle fibres produced by retted material, which was very finely processed using a variety of combs before drop spindle spinning and weaving in a similar manner.[27] Both methods produced acceptable cloth but there are differences in the colour, texture, and drape. These sorts of factors will be the reasons why *chaîne opèratoire* and processing sequences switched. It may also be a reason why the more time-consuming individual stem processing selects the raw material very carefully and then makes the most of all that is picked and processed, whereas the retting process collects large numbers of more varied stems and bulk processes these. However, retting and then processing will shift the balance in activity times, from processing the stems to processing the fibres. Using a flax brake, then scutching, then hackling and combing the material finely, gradually improving the alignment of the fibres, will 'waste' a lot more of the raw material, but give a finely made end product. In practice the waste material could be used as shoe hay or for some other purpose. This fine processing of materials is something that seems to have happened as part of the elaboration of textiles, which are best seen as part of major shifts in societies (Rast-Eicher and Bender-Jørgensen 2013; Michel and Nosch 2010).[28]

Resin, tars and glues

Organic material culture is about more than artefacts. It is also about glues and resins, and other amorphous substances that contribute to composite artefacts and material processing. Resin can be collected after it exudes from the tree, but in many cases the gums and saps need to be extracted. Where these are important, trees will have small incisions to collect the material oozing from a wound in the bark. Examples of this are rubber, turpentine and tree resins, and birch bark sap. For the most part tannins and dyes require further treatment. Usually these kinds of substances will need to be extracted from material taken from the plant itself, whether this is bark, which can then be soaked or boiled to extract tannins, or plants where bruising and heat will extract the dye principle. These kinds of materials can be central aspects of a culture. For the Semalai from Malaysia, resin is central to their way of life (Gianno 1990) and they have sophisticated ways of tapping it from the trees by hollowing out the base of the tree to about halfway and then protecting the new opening by making a small rain shield from plant leaves, allowing the resin to gradually exude and collect down in the base of the new wound in the tree. In this way, they collect the resin they need for a wide variety of different items of material culture. It is known that from the Middle Palaeolithic onwards, pitch and resins were used to fix tips into hafts in composite tools of stone, wood and the resin glue (Koller et al 2001; Mazza et al 2006). There are also examples of birch bark tar being used as chewing gum since this substance has some healing properties and human teeth imprints are left in some of them (Aveling and Heron 1998, 1999). These same kinds of resins and tars cannot only be used as fixing but can also be spread over a surface to help mend or waterproof an item. It can even be used as a sticky substance to help entangle birds (Beck and Borromeo 1990; Brzeziński and Piotrowski 1997; Charters et al. 1993a, 1993b; Connan 1999; Connan and Nissenbaum 2003; Gianno 1990; Langenheim 2003; Nagar and Misra 1994: 178; Newman and Serpico 2000). To this list of botanical substances, one must also add those from animals including insects such as bees, which are important in providing wax. Some of these substances also act in combination with wax, for example, waterproofing properties and fixing qualities. That is why Plate 28 includes examples of wax and resins as well as mineralogical bitumen and runny extracts of tar from pine to show the range of different products that can be used in isolation or combination to achieve particular goals of waterproofing and stickiness. Plants can also provide soap in the form of saponins and poisons for arrows, and of course medicines (Turner 1998, 2001, 2004). Soap root (*Chlorogalum pomeridianum*) was one of the species that the Pomo tribe in California cultivated as part of their management of the land (Anderson 2005: 143). Soap and saponin-bearing plants could thus have been important aspects of the chemicals used from plants. Oils act as lubricants, preservatives and waterproofing agents, and can be aromatic. Hafting processes are one of the markers of sophisticated multicomponent tools (Mazza et al 2006; Rots 2010; Shaham et al 2010; Wadley 2005).

Study strategies

Strategies for studying wood

The problems of wood identification and interpretation from archaeological remains are ably set out by Lev-Yadun (2007). The wood identification is the first step but the desired end result is more specific information on the growing conditions of the tree, the part selected by humans for use and the manner in which those growing conditions have been utilized and exploited. Thus knowledge of the relevant species and their microscopic wood anatomy is a prerequisite, but knowledge of the branching and ecology of the different species and the manner in which they occur in different environmental conditions are important aspects of understanding human exploitation in the past. The movement of timber or finished items between regions may be impossible to determine unless strontium or DNA analysis is used. Lev-Yadun points out that if generic ecological information or climatic information is derived from the wood remains, these may of course reflect instead human choices of what materials were brought on to the site or could be influenced by disease and pests. In particular firewood has been used for hundreds of thousands of years and wood as raw material for perhaps two million years. Generic charred wood samples can be taken in the field but may be preserved minimally and disintegrate on movement or under examination. Where this occurs impregnating the deposits in the field with resin and then identifying the charcoal in the lab is a possible way forward. Ash layers with phytoliths in some cave sites have the potential of indicating the key types of wood used for burning. Because charcoal is such a significant aid to high temperature metalworking, these kinds of studies may show the role of wood in other technologies as well as the technology of cooking (Alperson et al 2007).

There are also prospects for obtaining more information from starch grains present in some woods and barks, but this again relies on reference collection material and is in its infancy. Calcium oxalate and silica phytoliths are both wood cellular structures that can in some cases aid identification of the species. It is often impossible to identify to the species level and a generic identification can be useful but only if its limitations are clearly understood. Wood can also vary according to its age and position in the plant. This is little recognized as a feature of wood analysis in archaeology. Yet from previous discussions in this chapter, it is evident that humans may be preferentially influencing these sorts of factors. Thus the skills of identifying not just the species but also the variations that might occur within one species between young wood, wood from the central trunk and roots differs considerably and adds another layer of knowledge and awareness onto the study of this material.

The phenomenon described by Lev-Yadun as 'traumatic tissues' is also a significant archaeological feature. The structure of the wood will be changed but often the traumatic factor can be a deliberate management or felling policy. This can include the coppicing and pollarding regimes and resin tapping. Whole tree felling and regeneration from the stump can also be affected. In some cases, this traumatic event provides the wood with characteristics that are advantageous to humans.

Thus trees with resin production may lay down extra layers of resin which can lead to a better impregnated and more robust wood for humans to exploit or can exude from the tree and be collected by humans. Elsewhere, I have already mentioned the use of old tree stumps regenerating as a strong wood source for making buckets for use in the Iron Age salt mines in Hallstatt, Austria. Lev–Yadun (2007) also points out that often identification manuals do not state the position of the samples described and so cannot be used where these sorts of studies are required. Thus at the moment, reference sample publications and collections do not adequately cover the problems of juvenile wood, traumatic wood, and branch junctions. Nor is the localized effect of the removal of neighbouring trees or significant changes in local growing conditions adequately referenced and understood.

Where there are substantial wooden structures because of wet site preservation, large numbers of tree rings may be present. These can be dated and the individual results fed into a master chronology for the site that can then be compared to regional chronological sequences. Even where the dendrochronological dates cannot be precisely related back to the present, approximate period indications can be given and AMS dates can provide indications of the date. Often the dating of precious objects has not rested on the rare wooden finds but has been provided by other means. The key development was with the very small amounts of carbon needed for AMS ^{14}C dates where smaller samples measure the exact proportions of radioactive carbon present in the sample rather than the emitting particles from a larger sample.

Isotopic and DNA advances

More recent work has shown that genetic and isotopic information from wood species is likely to advance swiftly in the next decade or so from techniques that provide genetic information on a tree species and the identification of its likely growing area via other isotopes (Deguilloux et al 2006). This gives the intriguing prospect of not just relying on dendrochronological work to identify imports of timber but also on isotopic evidence to do likewise and to analyse much smaller samples, even from those sources that are very precious. In these ways, the growing conditions of the tree can suggest places where a wooden object was made even if it was found in a different area. The key drawback with these kinds of techniques at the moment is the lack of adequate reference collections and comparisons. In some cases, the isotopic evidence suggest a broad range of regional possibilities and extra links will be needed from the material culture evidence on a site to suggest the most likely place from which the original wood was imported. It is then an archaeological question once more as to whether it is the timber that is moving or the object. In these ways, it can be clearly appreciated that the scientific techniques are assisting archaeological interpretations while not denying their centrality.

Hydrogen, carbon, nitrogen and oxygen all have both stable and radioactive isotopes. The ratio of isotopes is dependent on those present in the soil and so the isotopes present in the plants reflect the growing conditions. This is useful to archaeologists who want to understand where a particular plant or tree was growing. The isotope can indicate the relative humidity of the growing conditions but also the mineralogical soil component specific to an area. Using both these kinds of evidence, archaeological implications for imported species can be useful. One such was reported by English et al (2001) when looking at the origin of wood from Anasazi material in Chaco Canyon, New Mexico. DNA studies are developing rapidly but one area in which they have already been of use is in the refinement of understanding the area of origin of so-called founder crops for the Neolithic Revolution (e.g. Morrell and Clegg 2007). The key problem is that most wood on archaeological sites is degraded so that any DNA is poorly preserved or even destroyed if the wood is preserved by charring and carbonization. Lev-Yadun (2007) interestingly prophesized that proteins and other molecules that can now be extracted from archaeological wood could become a developing technique to get around some of the problems of the lack of surviving DNA. In addition, these kinds of studies can clearly be explored as indicators of trade, although it is not expected that early periods where trees were readily available would have seen much timber exchanged or traded. However, evidence is cited for the trade of wood in the early Bronze Age using species which are distinctive of some regions being found in regions where they do not naturally occur, notably *Cedrus libani*, which was found in the early Bronze Age site of Ashkalon, Israel. In regions growing olives and fruit trees, the pruning and related activities to keep these trees at their most productive will produce ready supplies of dense hardwood. This can be useful for fine pieces of woodworking and is known to have been used for furniture-making in Jericho (Cartwright 2005). So far, the origins of woodworking are definitely evidenced by the 780,000-year-old finds from Gesher Benot Ya'aqov where the traces of the polishing and smoothing of a large piece of wooden plank made from willow species was found. However, earlier evidence from microwear analysis of stone tools shows that wood was one of the materials being worked with stone and to this now must be added plant remains on stone tools at very early hominid sites (Keeley and Toth 1981).

Cordage basketry and textile study strategies

Technological systems for cordage basketry and mats can be described as active and passive (Wendrich 1991, 1999) and thread twist direction, angle and breadth measured, along with counts of threads and descriptions of the weave structures. Technologies of manufacture may be identified and some have major documentation on techniques (Collingwood 1974, 1982, 1998). Broad reviews and detailed studies of regions exist (e.g. Bender-Jørgensen 1986, 1992; Gleba and Mannering 2012). These are the first steps but more is being made now of the fineness of the processing and quality as an understanding of fibre preparation and social shifts in textile production (Rast-Eicher and Bender-Jørgensen 2013). However, the microscope or eye is still the first port of call for a description of many of the finds from prehistory. It might be that species identification is not possible except on DNA grounds but similarities with experimental and ethnographic situations can be established and certain elements or treatments ruled out, for example, some kinds of tannage and some kinds of preparation techniques for fibres for cordage. In plant husbandry and DNA analyses of the origin of domestication and variations in genetic traits, the term 'landrace' is now being used as one word. The principle is that the seed for small farms is kept within the farm system and sometimes through many generations, with some genetic material being passed on to neighbours or relatives, but essentially it is a very closed system compared to modern intensive breeding cycles. Recent developments have included DNA evidence that uses the estimated rate of mutation to indicate when genetic populations diverged. These kinds of methods to provide estimates of the dates when domestication or other genetic modifications occurred are new additions to the perishable material culture dating framework.

The biggest revolution in study strategies will come from the sourcing and provenance possibilities provided by isotopic analysis (Benson et al 2006; Frei 2010; Frei et al 2009a, 2009b, 2010). It has long been thought that these organic material culture elements are part of the important trade and exchange in prehistory that is more often witnessed through metal analysis and long-distance exchange of exotic stones. Soft perishable goods could have been part of these trade networks as well as travelling with people as personal items and buried with them as part of their social identity and death as much as in life. As example, the fine nettle cloth from a bronze age cremation burial at Voldtofte, Denmark, has fibres from nettles most likely growing in Austria (Bergfjord et al 2012).

The technology of how objects were made has for a long time been known as a set of possibilities but as more people study these perishable material culture technologies, so there is a great awareness of the sophistication of some of the early techniques that leave little or no trace for machinery or devices in materials that will survive better. Some microscopic treatments of the technologies will be possible but residue analysis may yet prove adventitious in providing new ways of thinking about extra technological processing to provide colours and dyes or sophistication in tanning. The dating prospects had their biggest improvement with the advent of AMS ^{14}C dating. These have become increasingly sophisticated with smaller sample sizes, and have opened up not so much a revolution in the dating technique as a widening of the applicability of known techniques to rare and precious finds that cannot be completely destroyed in order to date them. In these ways, the accumulation of dates throughout regions has allowed more sophistication and new interpretations of the role that perishable material culture played in these regions. An exciting development is that the same analysis which allows residue studies from pots to extract the degraded products of lipids can also be used to provide dates. Thus, some of these techniques may prove useful because the same sample could do two different jobs. In terms of function, some objects are self-evident in the generic functional sense such as a basket as a container. However, specific functions are always going to be problematic but perhaps, in the future, a wicker basket can have samples taken to see what kinds of objects were placed within it and the microscopic remnants of the material carried could, in future decades, provide evidence of very specific functions or generic ranges of functions for these objects. Otherwise, there is the old fall back of shape and form determining the range of possible uses. Taken all together, the techniques of analysis and the study strategies for perishable material culture still rely on, first, the identification early on in the excavation process that something is precious and needs to be carefully handled and lifted for more detailed excavation under laboratory conditions; second, that the structures and information from this may mean that conservation techniques should be selectively applied to preserve some samples for analysis that have not been affected by conservation chemicals and treatments; and third, that there are more identifications and technologies possible to consider than those which are either simply woven cloth, basketry or cord. The way in which these elements are linked are important parts of the development of understanding of functions and possibilities and sophistication from these very early periods. Here, it is sufficient to say that the analyses of DNA, isotopes and residues are the key developing fields in these studies but they still depend upon the skill of the excavator and conservator to recognize the significance of what they have just exposed. It is a salutary lesson that both the material from Schipluiden (Netherlands), which has basketry style and fabric style looping work, and Tybrind Vig (Denmark), where a Mesolithic fabric was found, that if it was not for the quick understanding of the person excavating, those items would have been trowelled away. Thus, all of the sophisticated techniques in the world cannot replace the person on the ground that finds and recovers the objects. In this respect, all sophisticated post-excavation techniques rely on the excavator.

Conclusions

Wood, bark, bast fibres, roots, stems and leaves can be used in an amazing number of ways to produce almost anything from a house to a shoe. Most archaeological attention to plants as a raw material has been on wood, as it is commonly preserved and widely used for radiocarbon dating and, if preserved in sufficient size, for dendrochronological dating. In general, far too little attention has been paid to the potential uses of bark, bast fibres and roots. As the ethnographic examples cited in this chapter indicate, these were probably vitally important materials for many prehistoric societies for making much of their material culture. Likewise, it is insufficiently appreciated that plants such as nettle – today regarded as an irritating weed – could have been one of the main sources of fibres for textiles. Archaeological investigations into prehistoric plant usage need to widen their scope beyond the study of edible plants to the potential ways in which plants can be used as a raw material.

Excavators, environmental specialists and academic archaeologists need to be aware of the kinds of materials that could be excavated and the interpretive possibilities for the evidence recovered in environmental samples. Wherever sites are being excavated there will be traditional knowledge of plants and trees as the raw materials for crafts. This chapter provides a starting point for the kinds of resource exploitation that is possible. It has shown both the breadth and depth of possibilities drawing on examples from different environments. The pattern of evidence and the rare preservation of recognizable material culture could both contribute to a better appreciation of the exploitation of plant materials at a particular site and within a region or period. Plants are not just about food, they offer a rich basis for hard, flexible and soft materials for shelter, clothing, containers and equipment as well as providing fuel for cooking and craft processes. Many aspects of social and personal identity as well as survival depend upon plant-based material culture. Much of the food-getting equipment and facilities requires plant materials. Some plant materials have a distinct period of harvest and the collection and processing of materials would have been important aspects of how people organized their annual cycle of activities and day to day time. The way people exploit their environment for plant resources for food and crafts is an intimate connection with places in the landscape.

The material in this chapter provides a framework for addressing points 2, 3 and 5 below.

For any site, region and period:

1. What trees and plants are there in the environment?
2. What trees and plants are being exploited and how might these be being used for material culture production as well as food?
3. How might plant-based material culture be contributing to the need for transport, structures, bedding, containers, clothing, cordage, food-getting tools, equipment and facilities, material culture producing tools, equipment and facilities?
4. How does this integrate with animal-based material culture and with inorganic material culture?
5. Are there selective or intensive exploitations of trees and plants or evidence of symbolic relationships?

Notes

1 There is a broad range of literature looking at particular tree and plant species or a set of species as part of identification and characteristics (Atzei 2009; Bevan-Jones 2004; Bowes 2010; Cooper 2006; Gale and Cutler 2000; Franck 2005; Hather 1993; Mabey 2001; Milliken and Bridgewater 2004).
2 This aspect of understanding wood arises from discussions with Dave Budd, Sean Goddard and personal experience in a variety of experiments and in building the full scale Bronze Age sewn plank boat with Brian Cumby as shipwright and with academic colleagues Robert van de Noort, Anthony Harding and Lucy Blue.
3 Green woodworking traditions and coppice crafts are a growing field of literature and wood and bark finds sometimes survive in sufficient quantity to merit specific publications (Abbott 2011; Brisbane and Hather 2007; Clark 2004; Coccolini 2006; Coles 2006; Dehn and Hansen 2006; Killen 1994; North House Folk School 2007; Oaks and Mills 2010; Rackham 1996; Van de Noort 2003; Vogt 1949; Wood 2005).
4 The Royal Albert Memorial Museum, Exeter, has a range of pacific bark cloth materials in its ethnographic collections including wooden bark stripping and processing tools as shown to me by the curator Tony Eccles (see also Pole et al 2004), which equate to the metal scudding blades used in bark stripping for the tanning industry. Jill Buckler kindly shared information on African traditions.

5 The discussion of European material is drawn from the experience of Anne Reichert who has replicated many archaeological bast fibre artefacts and and my own experiments funded by Leverhulme, and Lejre, Denmark.

6 Based on my experience of handling and wearing a variety of rush, *Juncus* and bast fibre items.

7 Information from experiments by the author in the UK and Denmark, as part of research grants from Leverhulme and Lejre.

8 The importance of string and cordage is recognised as both an end product and also as a component of bags, mats, fabrics and structures in more complex cordage technologies (Collingwood 1974; Griffiths 1997; Hardy 2007; Hedges 2006; Harvey 1976; Hurcombe 2010; Médard 2000; Médard and Moser 2006; Myking et al 2005; Paama-Pengelly 2010; Ronald Smith 1975; Vaughan 1994).

9 Lemieux and Hurcombe have investigated this and made coil basketry bound with nettle root.

10 There is a long history of basketry and textile analysis in the Americas for a number of reasons: wet site conditions in the Northwest Coast and Florida, dry conditions in the Southwest and in the Andes there are also high altitude burials with excellent preservation. Added to this there is the ethnographic and recent history of native communities who have strong traditions in these fields (Adovasio and Gunn 1977; Adovasio et al. 1999; Andrews and Adovasio 1996; Bennett and Bighorse 1971; Blaine 1979; Carter 1933; Costin 1993; Douglass 1946; Drooker 1992, 2001; Drooker and Webster 2000; Ellis 1976; Follensbee 2008; Hurley 1979; Goldstein and Freeman 1997; Jakes and Ericksen 1997; Green 1997; Hamann 1997; Heckman 2005; Holmes 1896; Keith 1998; Kiviat and Hamilton 2001; Kuttruff and Kuttruff 1996; Lasiter 1946; Lyford 1943; Mason 1997; Overstreet 1997; Peterson 1996; Quimby 1961), and from other areas (Barber 1991; Burnham 1965; Helbaek 1963; Kemp and Vogelsang-Eastwood 2001; McCorriston 1997; Ryder 1965; Scholtz 1975; Tehanetorens 1983; Turner 1973).

11 See Friedl (1989); Hurcombe (2007a, 2007c, 2008b, 2010); Silvester (1994).

12 See Daugherty (1986); Florance (1962); Gabriel and Goymer (1991); Gillooly (1992); Maynard (1989); Peabody Turnbaugh and Turnbaugh (2004); Wright (1983). Many basketry books explain the technique and range of materials or focus on one kind of material or one region. There are many examples drawn from ethnography and living traditions which suit particular environments (Butcher and Hogan 2008; Dalland 1999; Fariello 2009; Fontales Ortiz 2006; Geib and Jolie 2008; Hogan 2001; Kitchell 2010; Mallow 2001; Mason 1890, 2010; Maynard 1977; McGuire 1990; Musée de Préhistoire d'Ile-de-France 2004; Nishida 2008; Okey 1912; Park 2004; Schlick 1994; Wood 2005; Wright 1972). For example, in Ireland and Scotland the use of more unusual materials such as straw, heather, dock and furze is known as well as the relatively recent traditions of cordage, basketry and textiles (Evans 1957; Lucas 1958; O'Brien 2010; McGrail 2002; MacPhilib 2000, 2007; Shaw-Smith 2003).

13 See Andersen (1967); Carey (2002, 2003); Collingwood (1974, 1982, 1998); Densmore (1929, 1974); Dunsmore (1985); Grieve (1931); Gustafson (1980); Hald (1980); Kuoni (1981); Latz (1995); Mowat et al (1992); Stewart (1973; 1977); Zola and Gott (1992).

14 See Adams (1977); Adovasio (1970, 1977); Andersen (1987a, 1987b, 1995b); Barber (1991), Bennike et al (1986); Broholm and Hald (1940, 1948); Burov (1998); Connolly et al (1995); Earwood (1998); Gramsch (1992); Lee (2005); Hurley (1979); McGregor (1992); Pétrequin and Pétrequin (1988); Pétrequin et al (2001); Soffer et al (2001); Wendrich (1991, 1999, 2000).

15 See Bender-Jørgensen (1986, 1992, 1994); Harris (1999); Henshall (1950); Médard (2000, 2005); Vogelsang-Eastwood (2000); Wild (1970, 1988).

16 See Bernick (1998a, 1998b, 1998c); Buijs (2005); Evans (1989); Hays-Gilpin (2000); Heckman (2005); Rodman and Lopez (2005); Stig-Sørenson (1997); Rimantiene (1992); Warnier (2006).

17 See Barber (1991); Boetzkes and Lüth (1991); Harvey (1996); Kent (1957, 1983); Stevenson (1974); West (1989); Paine (1990, 1994).

18 Good (2001) has given a good review and see also work such as Emery (1966).
19 There are finds perhaps similar to Otzi's cloak in other parts of Europe, see for example the Must Farm material from Britain, which has been seen by the author with thanks to Mark Knight and Penelope Walton Rogers and is currently being prepared for full publication.
20 Annelou van Gijn and Patty Anderson have both worked with dry and green plant materials from temperate Europe and also the Mediterranean, showing that the time when these kinds of plants are harvested and processed can lead to them being far more flexible and able to be used in different ways.
21 This account is drawn from two main sources: one, a film about shoe hay making, made in 1970 by the Westerbottens Museum, Umeå, Sweden. The film features Maria, who was born in 1896. The account is supplemented by a presentation by Ellinor Sydberg who has researched shoe hay over many years from her base within Sweden, and whose husband has personal knowledge of shoe hay within his family. In addition, shoe hay materials on display at Funesdalen Museum, Sweden, were noted and used in this generalized account.
22 Information from Anne Reichert who has worn replicas, but these finds are reinterpreting wadges of moss found in the circum-Alpine sites, as hide from shoes does not survive well there. What was once a hide shoe with moss forming a shoe lining is now found only as the shoe-sized compacted layer of moss.
23 John and Susi Dunsmore have established a foundation to promote this traditional craft practice in Nepal and are working with the local community to help the women find new markets for the materials they produce from Allo. Thus as well as the traditional preparation techniques and weaving practices and cordage manufacture, the women are now also knitting goods and producing bags and other items with more tourist appeal as a way of bringing money into their families. The trust established by John and Susi Dunsmore hosted an open-day at which I met and was able to talk to both of them and also to one of the traditional weavers and spinners from the region Dev Kumari Rai. All had useful discussions, and in particular explained the role of the clay in the process.
24 The variations in *Juncus*, different types of tree bast fibres, from hazel, lime, elm and willow, and others, as well as rushes (*Scirpus*), reeds (*Phragmites*) and different ways of processing all of the above, using water, stone tools and boiling, and boiling with wood ash, in different combinations, were all possible with thanks to three grants from Lejre for supporting this research and from Leverhulme.
25 Authors have investigated issues of crop managements and production (Beugnier 2007; Candilo et al 2000; Ibanez Estévez et al 2001; Morsbach 2002, Mrozowski et al 2008; Turner 2001).
26 Based on personal experience from harvesting and hand processing flax, hemp and nettle over many years.
27 The nettle cloth in both cases was produced by Anne Batser, an experienced weaver, spinner and dyer at Lejre. The tool processed cloth was made on an upright loom using flints as weights as part of my research project (Hurcombe 2010) and the water-retted and finely combed yarn cloth was made as part of Ulla Mannering's project on nettles (Mannering 1996).
28 Colour can be argued to be a large part of the shift to greater complexity. Whole books have been written on this topic and there is a great deal of literature. Plants as dyes and plant dyes for animal fibres have been studied from an archaeological, chemical and ethnographic perspective. Much of this discussion comes either from traditional dyeing or from extensive descriptions of dyes as part of the weaving, spinning and dyeing traditions in a region. The discussions include the use of mordants that are chemicals which assist the take-up of the dye substance and also help fix the colour so that it is not as prone to fading or running (Adrosko 1971; Balfour-Paul 1997; Bennett and Bighorse 1997; Bryan and Young 1940; Buchanan 1995; Cannon and Cannon 1994; Cardon 2007; Casselman 1993; Crook 2007; Dean 2010; Delamare and Guineau 2000; Flint

2008; Fraser 1996; Goodwin 2003; Grierson 1986; Hardman and Pinhey 2009; Hilu and Hersey 2004; Mairet 1964; Polakoff 1982; Rudkin 2007; Walsh 2009; Wells 1969; Wickens 1983). The role of colour in archaeology is becoming better-appreciated (see Cooney 2002; Boivin and Owoc 2004; Deutscher 2010; Menz 2004; Clarke et al 1985). Mushroom and lichen dyes can also be used and the lichen ones are a feature of some Scottish and north Eurasian traditions (Bolton 1960; Rice 1980; Waldner Mcgrath 1977). Recent advances have investigated the extraction of dye principle to identify it, and also the separation of this from the animal fibre so that there is greater clarity in the identification of genetic material (Cardon 2007; Hofenck de Graaff 2004; Vanden Berghe et al 2010).

3

THE MATERIALITY OF ANIMALS

Introduction

Animals provide an enormous range of raw materials that can be processed and used in a variety of ways to make items such as a horn comb, bone needle, ivory carving, antler harpoon, feather arrow fletching, fur clothing and a hide container. The most obvious raw materials are those parts of the skeleton that can be fashioned into a wide range of tools. Antler, ivory and horn are the other skeletal products that have often been utilized. Because skeletal elements are durable in many types of deposits, they have attracted considerable attention and generated a substantial literature. The soft products of animals are a different matter, but no less important: the skins and often fibres of animals have immense importance in the ethnographic present and were doubtlessly important in prehistory. The kinds of materials and the ways these can be processed and used are divided here into hard products, soft products and animal substances. Shells have been included with the hard animal products and feathers and felt are added to the softer animal materials. The first examples give a whole animal approach in order to emphasize the way in which animal resources would have occurred in the past, often providing both food and materials.

Hard products: bone, antler, horn and ivory technologies

Bone, antler, horn and ivory are grouped together because between them they offer greater hardness and tensile strength qualities than hides and the other components of animals used in craft products. However, there are significant differences between bone, antler, ivory and horn. Ivory is the hardest of these structures whereas horn is markedly softer. Bone, antler and ivory all contain mineral components that make them heavy and suitable for working into points and projectiles and many other kinds of implements. Horn, depending upon the animal it originates from, can be a dense heavy material but it is made from keratin which is much softer. Thus, of the four, horn is the least likely to survive archaeologically whereas the mineral components of bone, antler and ivory make them amongst the most hard-wearing in life and most long-lasting in deposition of the animal materials (Goss 1983; MacGregor 1976, 1985, 1998; Penniman 1984; Ramseyer 2001). Antler has been the subject of much attention from the medical world because it is a very fast-growing tissue and its regenerative properties outstrip those of other tissues (Goss 1983: 172).

An example of the differences between bone, antler, ivory and horn would be that needles made out of these materials could be used in very different ways even if they all had a similar size and overall shape. A horn needle will flex and will push apart the fibres but not necessarily keep a sharp point if used to penetrate fibres that are tough, such as a hide. Where a sharp point able to penetrate a hide is needed, ivory and bone would make better choices. If antler is used for a needle, it will work well provided that the antler section chosen is the densest available and can be worked smooth. Otherwise antler has too many rougher parts with a looser structure, which will create rough edges. In all cases, the original shapes of the bones, teeth, antlers and horns affect what kinds of objects can be made from them. The four needles made from these different materials would all have different densities, with ivory having the greatest and horn the least, and they would also differ in their appearance and performance, with the translucency of horn showing through and the flexibility of horn, then antler and then bone being more obvious than that of ivory. Finely worked and polished examples of all of these have their own natural flex and in the case of ivory, distinctive patterns as part of the growth marks. Where surfaces have been finely shaped and polished smooth these qualities can sparkle or shine, and their white or strong clean cream colour could have been part of their attraction in the manufacture of fine objects.

All of these materials are anisotropic, meaning that their qualities differ in longitudinal section versus cross-section. Within each of these materials, the species of origin and, in the case of bone, the anatomical part can affect the qualities of the raw material for craft purposes. In addition, a horn, bone or piece of ivory or antler will vary over its entirety according to where pulp cavities, Haversian canal systems, and blood supplies are placed. Young animals tend to have weaker bones than more mature ones and the general health of the individual will also be reflected in its antlers, bones, ivory and horn structures. When thinking about these kinds of materials, it is important to recognize that antlers can be regenerated and are materials that do not necessarily require the death of an animal before humans can exploit them. In all of the other cases, horns, ivory and bone are only available from animals that had died by natural causes and were then scavenged by humans, or ones that have been deliberately killed. As such, it is important to see the whole animal and its exploitation as part of the human predation pattern rather than extracting only the artefactual evidence.

A range of animals across the world that are useful for their fur, fibre, hides, horns and antlers are shown in plates 31–35. Two of the plates show the availability of materials from two contrasting species available in two continents as an example of this whole animal approach. The first of these is beaver (Plate 31) and the second is red deer (the European red deer, *Cervus elaphus*), also known as wapiti or elk (*Cervus canadensis*) in North America (Plates 32, 34 and 35). Beaver is an important source of landscape regeneration and alteration, but is also underrated as an important source of food, weighing when adult the equivalent of a small deer. It also provides secretions from its glands. It is also useful in other ways. Its teeth are exceptionally hard and grow throughout the animal's lifetime because of its habit of felling trees with them. There is also its skin, its distinctive tail and its fine underfur, which is spinnable and can be made into felt. In these ways, taking a beaver for its meat opens up a wealth of other possibilities for craft material exploitation. This is even more the case with the red deer, which has been chosen because it spans two continents but it also is an example of the deer group that is widely available all over the world where, in many cases, deer form a significant part of the wild animal exploitation. Male deer shed their antlers each year. Plate 39 shows that different species have their antlers growing at slightly different stages, and antlers differ in shape and growth patterns as the animal ages and matures. The only species where both males and females have antlers are reindeer (Goss 1983: 33). The diagram for red deer also includes all of the other things that can be obtained from this animal in particular but this group of animals in general. The brains can be used for tanning hides. The fattier parts of the carcass can be rendered down to provide fat and the bones could also be crushed and exploited for this purpose as well. The hides can be used entire or be made into lashings and rawhide babiche. The sinew obtained from the backbone, known as back–strap sinew and also available from each of the lower leg limbs, is an exceptionally strong and important material for lashing and sewing as it is both fine and strong.

Ways of working bone, antler, horn and ivory

All of these materials have in common the fact that they are easier to work when they have been soaked for a while. While this might not matter too much for soft horn it matters a great deal for bone, antler and ivory, especially if these have been worked with stone tools because their sharp but brittle edges need to be protected. Small chisel-like flint implements known as burins (or gravers) are particularly associated with making grooves and working the hard materials, and their other name of 'graver' indicates the manner of their use. Many worked pieces of bone and antler show that natural grooves in the bone such as the mid-line in metapodial bones or the lines of veins in antler are deepened. In these ways, the natural shape of the material is used to help in the splitting and working process. Other ways in which the material can be worked is by gradually making parallel longitudinal grooves into the soft or spongy core and then splitting from there. Antler and bone can also have a groove worked around their surface and eventually a small snap can achieve the break. In antler, charring this area slightly will allow the material to be snapped more easily. Other ways of working with these materials used their qualities of flex, as at the Mesolithic site of Star Carr in England (Clark and Thompson 1953). Parallel grooves are made in the antler and its natural curve is accentuated by pressure and flexing, which will gradually propagate a crack through the material where it has been grooved and eventually a long sliver will be prised out. This is the way in which barbed and tanged antler harpoon points have been made. Other examples of working deer antler at Star Carr were in the manufacture of deer antler frontlets as presumed masks. In this, the setting of the skull is the mask part; it is reversed with new holes assumed to be for attachment or for eye holes (although they are very narrow for this) and the brow time is in effect turned into the main branch of antler with a stump thinned down to make the new brow tine (the projecting spike near the brow). In this way, the antler headdress echoes the animal but is much smaller and in fact reverses the position of the wearer versus the original animal.

Differences also exist between bone, antler and ivory in the amount of fats and blood residues left in the material. If the material is soaked with many of the nutrients still remaining, it will eventually deteriorate and start to rot. The centre of red deer antler smells of the blood contained within it; this can penetrate the antler causing flecking and staining. Fat is more of a problem when working bone although the material can be soaked and some grease removed, but if the material is boiled excessively then the bone itself will denature. Grease can be removed physically and the central spaces of bone and antler can be charred to remove the honeycomb structures or small remnants of bone material if this central cavity needs to be clear and smooth. The smell of burning bone, antler and horn is pungent and not easily forgotten. If material is left unsoaked it can be flaked in the case of bone and ivory and to some extent antler. Where material has been soaked well, antler can also be shaved in much the same way as wood. Antler is known as the 'wood of deer', in French (*bois de cervide*), as these materials are interchangeable and can be swapped where there are few trees to use.

Flaked bone can exhibit conchoidal fracture in the same way as flint although it is much more elastic than stone (Hannus 1985, 1989, 1997). Denser areas of bone are more easily flaked. Some bones have natural holes in them for nerve and blood vessels and these are sometimes used as part of the feature of a worked artefact. An example is a needle from the Greek site Ayia Irini, Keos, which is made from a metapodial but uses the natural hole, the foramen, for the eye (Krzyszkowska 1990). Where items need to have holes drilled these can be bored through by using a small flint tool. All this category of materials can be polished to some extent, although antler is the most problematic. Much depends on the density. If the materials are soaked, they are all softer to work, but for final polishing they need to be worked dry. This is because even ivory visibly swells when put in water, and the surface expands so the final polishing is best achieved when dry.

Early bone tools

The evidence for the earliest use of bone tools is always likely to be problematic but it is like to have been occurring early on in human evolution with some evidence for 1.5 to 2.0 Ma (Backwell and d'Errico 2001). These seemed to be fractured pieces with wear traces that suggest they were used for digging. However, there is little evidence for the routine use of bone for tools before 100 ka. Examples are an antler soft hammer from the Lower Palaeolithic site at Boxgrove, England, c. 500 ka (Pitts and Roberts 1997: 296, Fig. 54), and a flaked bone hand axe from Castel Di Guido, Italy (Gaudzinski et al 2005). Evidence from the Middle Palaeolithic is better – as at the site of Salzgitter Lebenstedt (Gaudzinski 1999) – but it is not until the Upper Palaeolithic that bone, antler, horn and ivory become routine and important aspects of material culture. Importantly, they were not merely flaked at this time, but also sawn, shaped, polished, drilled and carved as required for particular purposes.

Bone and antler natural characteristics

The antler from male reindeer regenerates annually throughout its life and gradually the maturing stag achieves a number of branches on the brow and crown giving a variety of different possibilities for tool manufacture. Larger red deer antler make good raw materials for harpoons and similar hunting point weapons and can also be used for manufacturing weaving combs such as those from Iron Age Britain and antler combs known from the Neolithic. Deer bones tend to be gracile compared to those of bovids and suids, and the long straight length of the limb bones are some of those most often used as the raw materials for tools and craft purposes. The best bones are marked on the diagram in Plate 35 and include the scapula, which can be used as a natural shovel and as a material for making disks and other flat bone objects. In contrast, long bones make good round and D-shaped tubular raw materials and these can incorporate one articular surface as a natural handle making them comfortable to grip. An example of this kind of tool is the bone deflesher in Plate 37. In addition, ribs are often selected as they make good spatulas and polishers. Metapodials (forming the lower leg) are well suited for making awls and again the articular surface can serve as a handle. The metapodials have a groove along the centre line, which lends itself to splitting where a half bone is required. Metapodials are often split along this line to make awls. The examples of awls in Plate 38 are from Wallace Ruins in America and these show different bones and shapes being used including some that have the articular surface missing because the epiphyses was unfused as the animal was juvenile. Juvenile bones such as this can be lighter and less dense although the qualities of the awls generally show that each has been selected appropriately for the purpose intended. Some show clear signs of polish and prolonged use.

In general, long bones have two kinds of bone, a very dense bone on the articular surfaces and down the shafts and then cancellous bone, which is more sponge-like and can form much of the bulk of the bone at either end and in some cases in the middle of the bone as well. Other bones are hollow with clean surfaces. Some of these are natural splits and different bone qualities are reasons why different bones are selected for different purposes and how the tool or object lies within the original bone. The densest bones in the skeleton and densest areas of bones are exactly those where the animal has most skeletal stresses or has the greatest need of protection. Thus, cranial bone can be thick but also the bones of the limbs and the articular surfaces need to take the impact of the animal's weight when running and these can also be very dense areas of bone. The denser areas of bone are good for making tools such as points, oars and needles. In general, this kind of bone can be much denser than antler.

Deer antler is an important raw material but the quality, size and shape vary between species and by age as the antlers are shed each year after the rut (Figure 8). Some animals have very dense antler, e.g. moose or elk (*Alces alces*) and reindeer (*Rangifer tarandus*) antler is a material with good shock absorbing qualities and better tensile qualities than bone (MacGregor and Currey 1983; MacGregor and Main-man 2001; Scheinsohn and Ferretti 1995, 1997). Some antler materials have a natural shape that lends itself to a particular purpose, for example, red deer antler have a brow tine at right angles to the main shaft, which means they make very effective picks if the shaft is cut short and the round tine used as the pick element. The curve of some antlers also lends themselves readily to having flint inserts along the inside to haft blades to make effective sickles. Flatter, palmate shapes are available from some species such as European elk (*Alces alces*) (known as moose in North America), fallow deer, and male reindeer, which offer different possibilities for tool manufacture. Some three-pronged fishing spears are made from these kinds of branching palmate arrangements. When material is found as objects it is not always possible for the exact anatomical part to be identified. For antlers, it may not be possible to say whether the antler is shed or taken from a dead animal unless the pedicle is present. Antlers have been used as shock absorbers for polished stone axes in the Swiss lakes area of Europe in the Neolithic so that the polished stone elements fit into an antler socket, which in turn fits into a wooded haft, making a complex hafting arrangement that preserves both the stone edge and the wooden handle. Elk antler is the densest antler and it has been used in Europe to make antler mattocks in the Mesolithic where the area at the base of the antler with the very dense material is used to weight the whole piece. In a similar way flint knappers use the pedicle base of elk antler in preference as soft hammers (Bruce Bradley, pers. comm.). The cross-section in Plate 40 shows that this area of elk antler is dense and hard-wearing. In species such as red deer, there is also a dense area of antler at the base of the pedicle, but the centre of much of the rest is much more open and honeycomb-like. Thus, antler harpoons use outer areas of the antler and some of these clearly show on the surface where the more open network of material is beginning to appear. Antler and bone are both elements that can be chewed by dogs. These, along with other animals' predation, can be recognized as distinctive archaeologically, but dogs can entirely chew and consume antler leaving no trace whatsoever.

Ivory

Ivory too comes in different shapes depending upon the animal. The pattern of enamel as it is laid down and the overall shape of the piece allow the identification to species of different ivory elements, where the object is both large enough to examine

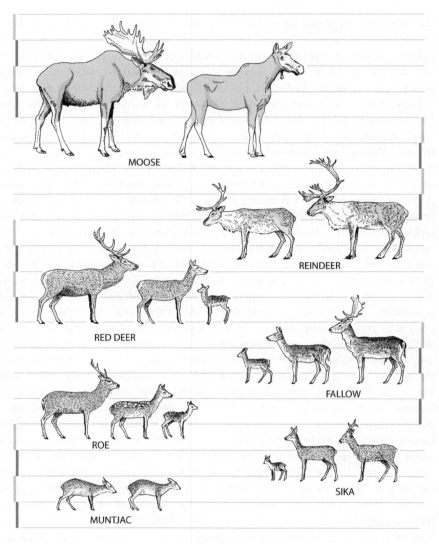

FIGURE 8 Deer and moose showing relative body sizes and antlers for male, female and young animals.
Source: Hurcombe.

and has exposed planes to see the characteristic features (Krzyszkowska 1990; Penniman 1984). Elephant ivory has very distinctive patterns which are also visible in the mammoth ivory polished section area shown in Plate 36. Other animals with tooth enamel of a size useful to humans are walrus and narwhal. Ivory can be flaked or chipped or split along longitudinal planes. In order to work it, it can also be soaked, to slightly soften it. Another form of ivory is hippopotamus tooth. The whole teeth of small animals are often used as beads and as decoration by having holes pierced usually in the root and then being suspended in this way or attached to garments. One such example is included in Plate 36. The Palaeolithic-style point shown in ivory in Plate 36 is a modern replica of a Palaeolithic artefact showing how the polished up material is hard, dense and makes a very effective weapon. In contrast, the carved figure of the head of a woman shows the concentric cracking that ivory tends to exhibit under depositional conditions as it deteriorates. However, these do not detract from the qualities of this exceptional piece of Palaeolithic art, which is one of the few examples of a human face. The flaking qualities of the raw material can be clearly appreciated in Plate 36 and it is also possible to see how the concentric rings of growth can also form natural breaks in the material.

The use of ivory as a carved material is known from the Late Palaeolithic onwards with notable pieces being the 30,000 year-old figure from the Palaeolithic German site of Hohlenstein-Stadel (Conard 2003). The so-called 'lion man' from Stadel cave in Germany is just such one piece. It is a standing figure of a lion's head on what becomes a male person's body. It is a large figure, 30cm in height, which makes use of the shape of the mammoth tusk from which it is carved. This was made from the tip of a tusk using the curve and shape and the shaped and pulp cavity in knowledgeable and skilful ways. The carving itself is a hard material to work with that has been executed to a high level by somebody who was clearly skilled in working with this material and achieving the artistic vision that they wanted. A replica made by Wulf Hein took around 400 hours to produce (Cook 2013: 33).

In more recent times, ivory was an important luxury item that was traded over long distances and was used for high-status items (Gelvin-Reymiller et al 2006; Krzyszkowska and Morkot 2000; LeMoine and Darwent 1998). In ancient Egypt, hippopotamus and elephant teeth were important sources of ivory. They served as inlays and veneers as well as items entirely of ivory. The first step is to recognize the species but while these are clear in prepared sections and from whole examples, it is more difficult to recognize these features in carved and finished items. In some cases, slight decay can enhance the ease of identification as the growth structures become apparent. Krzyszkowska and Morkot (2000) state that though isotopic studies would be useful, they are impossible on small well-worked items. On other grounds, the elephant ivory used in Egypt is thought to primarily originate from Africa but the recognition of the use of hippopotamus ivory may well be under-acknowledged in some of the collections. Some of the items made include solid ivory furniture such as folding stools. In Egyptian Nubia, hippopotamus ivory dates back to pre-dynastic times. Even in a society in which ivory featured and that has both images and written sources, the manufacturing processes and organization of ivory workshops and exploitation in Egypt has many aspects yet to be fully explored.

Horn

Horn also comes in different shapes and densities depending upon the species (Plate 39). It is not mineralized as the other materials described here are but is essentially the same material as fingernails. The material retains flex and translucency even though it is laid down in dense thick layers that grow from the base. In some species such as the North American big horn sheep (*Ovis canadensis*), the horn has clear annual rings of growth but this does not occur in tropical species and the pronghorn antelope (*Antilocapra americana*) is the only species to shed its horns annually, although European bison can shed horn occasionally (Goss 1983: 60–63; and see Plates 32 and 33). The horn is supported by a bony projection known as a horn core. Plate 41 shows longitudinal and transverse sections of cow and buffalo horn showing the lamination patterns along which horn can be opened up. Where an animal has a horn damaged, this will have affected not just the horn that covers the outer surface, but also this bony projection giving a damaged horn core. Sometimes where horn does not survive, this bony horn core can show the marks where the horn has been cut away or removed. It is possible to soften horn considerably by soaking it in water, which makes it easier to work and with moisture and warmth the layers can be split apart. For complex objects, the process of working and carving horn can take several weeks and involve charring and hot oil as well as soaking and carving.

The use of animal horn extends back into the Upper Palaeolithic. There is a figure of a woman engraved on the cave wall at Laussel who is clearly holding a horn (Bahn and Vertut 1988: 99, Fig. 67), which may indicate its use as a drinking vessel, symbol or both. In Egyptian society, the commonest use of horn was as drinking vessels. Plate 41 shows the typical kinds of objects made from horn: containers, combs, and spoons.

Bone, antler, horn and ivory study strategies

In recent years, bone and antler wear studies are regular features of publications (horn less so because of its poorer survival) and the role of bone and antler and ivory as tools is much better understood.[1] Whale bone and mammoth bone can also be used as structural elements, notably with mammoth bones in the hut from Mezherich in the Ukraine (Soffer et al 1997), and also as elements such as sled runners and other large structural elements as in the Thule culture in the Arctic where whale ribs fit the post-hole forms in the ground (Renouf 2009).

For archaeological study strategies, bone antler, ivory and horn from acidic soils are all problematic because they will not survive. Neither will shell. In areas where the acidity is not too much of a problem, the bones of younger animals may be weaker and missing, even if those of adult bones survived. Likewise, the stronger bone elements with denser bone may survive preferentially while the smaller or spongier bone elements deteriorate and are missing. Teeth generally survive the best, so that some graves are known only from the teeth. Most study strategies focus on understanding where skeletal elements have been modified by wear, by splitting, and by manufacturing traces, and where whole artefacts survive by understanding the artefact as a whole and the wear traces from its use. For antler, some care needs to be taken to distinguish wear from use by humans because the deer will use the antler for fighting during the rut and also for browsing and some antlers will have wear because of these natural occurrences in life (Olsen 1989). Decorative objects such as beads offer information from close examination of the surfaces of the drill holes, the manner of suspension can sometimes be indicated and even whether beads were strung together, as they can have rubbed surfaces where they contact other beads on a string. In the Palaeolithic, the arrangement of some of these beads in graves clearly shows the patterns achieved by strings of beads and by rows of ornament around hoods and the edges and fringes of garments (Gilligan 2010; White 1989a, 1989b, 1989c; 1992). Information on fat extraction and exploitation can be provided by careful understanding of the fracture qualities and patterns of assemblages as a whole and anatomical element as a whole (Outram et al 2005). The identification of cutmarks on bones that were not used as raw material is nonetheless an extra way in which bones can be studied for human exploitation patterns (Blumenschine et al 1996). As with stone tools, it is important also to understand the transportation and post-depositional factors that may affect bone that has been in stream environments and has been transported under natural conditions (Andrews 1995; Lyman 1994).

The range of uses for these kinds of materials is broad but they feature particularly as carved items, needles, awls, spatulas and handles. The wear and modification traces are a growing branch of archaeological study strategies (e.g. Antipina 2001; van Gijn 2005, 2006; Jensen 2001; Luik et al 2005; Lyman 1994; Lyman et al 1998). The flat surfaces of bone and antler are also used for making marks and engravings as abstract designs or as notational systems.

Hard products: shell

In general, shells used for material culture and craft purposes are either tools or decorative items. Plate 43 shows a range of different shells and shapes including abalone (*Haliotis midae*), which is used for decoration but also as a container for ochre at Blombos Cave, South Africa, 100,000 years ago (Henshilwood et al 2011). Some form natural scoops, containers and hollows, and larger ones can be used as scrapers and, with a hole through them, can be hafted or turned into shaving and grating implements. The Spanish early Neolithic site of La Draga has the classic pottery impressed with *Cardium* shells and also shell tools (Conte and Solana 2011). Larger shells are available; for example in the Caribbean, Lammers-Keijsers (2008) has shown their use for a variety of purposes and these kinds of shells can even be robust enough to be used as tilling artefacts. In the Aegean, shell items include trumpets, scoops, lamps, beads, pendants, polishers, spatulae, mace heads, buttons, bracelets, figurines, vessels and spools, all of which are found as a mixture of artefacts and imagery from seals and pots (Karali 1999). McCarthy (1976) and other authors also show extensive use of shell materials for chisels and knives as well as water holders and fish hooks in Australia (O'Connor and Veth 2005) and Claassen (1998) adds shells as mesh gauges, handles and spindle whorls. Large shells such as ostrich shells can be used to store water or used to make beads (Phillips 2000). In general, shells made into beads can be used and widely traded showing the links between different areas (Cribb 1986). Shells can be used as metaphors for a wide range of purposes as described by Claassen (1998) and Bayman (2002). In this way it is significant that some shells have their shapes copied in other materials such as in limestone or as the imagery of the Triton's trumpet (Oakley 1965a, 1965b; Skeates 1991). However, by far the most attention has been paid to Palaeolithic bead production using shells. Vanhaeren et al (2006) and Vanhaeren and d'Errico (2006) have explored Palaeolithic ornament production that included several shell beads. The techniques of working shell are straightforward because it is brittle and so grooving and snapping as well as grinding and drilling all lend themselves to this material readily. If large, dense shells are available the material can also be flaked. There is some suggestion that fresh shell is easier to work. Moir (1990) has suggested that immersion in seawater changes the crystalline structure slightly to improve the shell's properties for some purposes. Shells can be dated but usually where the shells form artefacts of significance such as in beads, these sorts of techniques may compromise the artefacts themselves. Likewise, although it is theoretically possible for shells to be sourced to their growing environments, there are complex issues around seawater variation and in practice these avenues have not been explored. They are able to attest some evidence of the seasonality of exploitation of shells and the areas of ocean or coast visited. However, Claassen (1998: 199–203) identifies the key problem in the ad hoc use of shells as one of artefact recognition. If shells are being exploited for food then the numbers resulting from this activity will far outweigh the numbers that are artefacts. It is very difficult to spot these kinds of short-term, quickly made tools with minimal breakage and working features among all of the food debris from shells.

In general, larger shells come from more biologically diverse environments such as deep rivers and the sea where the rich environments can sustain larger body mass. Smaller shells can be used whole, whereas larger ones can be worked further into tools or shaped and turned into many decorative items. Because shell is a calcium-based mineral it is susceptible to acid environments where it will disintegrate and be destroyed. Many shells are also light and laminate easily also aiding their destruction. Shells may also symbolize the environments from which they originate. There is some suggestion that tempering of pottery with shell in the British Neolithic could emphasize a symbolic reference to the sea (Parker Pearson et al 2006).[2]

Study strategies

There are several ways of studying shell. In recent years studies of shell have been involved in discussions about the emergence of modern human behaviour in terms of their symbolic value, and even the linguistic capabilities of Middle Stone Age inhabitants at Blombos Cave, South Africa, 75,000 years ago. There are also discussions on the use of hafting in the formation of compound tools (including ones of shell) with adhesives from the Middle Stone Age of South Africa as an argument for 'human' cognitive abilities (Wadley et al 2009). Stone tool technologies have long been used to investigate the mental capabilities of early human ancestors but the extension of these proxies to include perishable material culture is now also happening and has generated considerable debate with shell beads, hafting and compound adhesives all featuring heavily in these traditional arguments on complexity and the human mind (Ambrose 2001; Wadley 2010; Wadley et al 2009). Vellanoweth (2001) has been able to show using AMS radiocarbon dating that in a limited Mid-Holocene period there is widespread trade along the Western area of North America in shell beads derived from California.

Soft animal products – skins, furs, intestines, sinews

The species, sex, age, season of death and health of the individual animal all affect the qualities of hides. Things that happen to our own skin also happen to animal skins, so that if male animals are killed during the rut then their skins will have bruising and tears from their recent activities. There are also seasons when there would be small holes in the skin from where insects had laid eggs that hatched in their skin, and areas of the skin such as the stomach that are very variable in quality and much more flexible, particularly for female animals because of pregnancy. To this variegated set of individual characteristics of hides must be added the season and environment in which people are exploiting them. The processes for skinning and tanning skins that are useful for a small animal may differ from those for a large animal; also, some environments may lack resources for tanning that are available somewhere else. Tanning techniques that are effective in warm climates might be inappropriate for use in cold climates, and vice versa, for example. In some circumstances, tanning processes that used liquids or required a lot of heat might not work locally if there is insufficient firewood to boil liquids or not enough water to be used for that kind of process. As an example, hot climate nomadic skin tanning processes do not in general, use pots and water. In the far Arctic, animal fat (primarily from seals) is used for lighting and for other purposes – there are no trees, so tree bark cannot be used. Instead, smoking is the ideal tanning technique for a cold dry environment. In Northern Europe where the climate is warmer, methods include both fat tanning and tree bark tanning. On the equator, shade has to be used when working on the skins because the sun will otherwise shrink the skin and dry it in ways that will affect its quality. Here, there are trees and herbs to use. Pastoral societies in Africa use buttermilk and yoghurts as tanning aids. The skinning and tanning equipment available in different societies also takes account of different situations and different tools to use for different animals. Thus, the scrapers that are used for seal hide are not used on reindeer because seals have a lot of fat that needs to be cut free from the hide; this is not the case for reindeer. Studying the treatment of hides has to deal with this variety.[3]

Ethnographic and recent hide-working traditions show that there are many ways of tanning a hide that would not be recognized and identified as true leather production using modern definitions. Fat tanning and brain tanning for example would not be true leathers in the eyes of the more recent leather experts. Likewise, tree bark tanning is believed by some to be a Roman tanning technology but not present earlier. In some respects, these suppositions rest on the definitions. The recent Neolithic find from the Alps (Spangenberg et al 2010) has shown that tree bark tanning is possible although wood smoke can deposit tree products onto skins. Given the use of a wide range of medicinal plants and bark for other purposes, it seems likely that soaking or boiling bark to obtain chemicals is something that may have been known from the production of medicinal teas. In these ways, it seems better to incorporate the possibility of tree bark tannins being a form of ancient tanning technology available to prehistoric people but one that we would not find easy to recognize in surviving hide work. Furthermore, modern bark tan methods are used on very thick hides requiring many months of immersion in progressively stronger bark tan solutions: experience and ethnographic studies suggest thinner skins such as deer skins do not require as long nor even complete penetration for the bark tan process to be of use. Sámi techniques sometimes deliberately leave an untanned core within the skin as an aid to waterproofing qualities. Many authors give very good accounts of different kinds of tanning processes ethnographically and as traditional tanning techniques as well as archaeological studies.[4]

The best part of a hide is the area in the lower neck to just before the tail area of the back extending down the flanks but stopping before the legs and the stomach, where the skin tends to be thin and elastic, particularly for female animals. The leg skin is not so elastic and can make useful cordage material. Much depends upon what the skin is intended to do and what area of the skin is required. There are different ways of skinning an animal depending upon which parts of its skin might best suit the purpose: cutting along the back will allow the softer stomach skin to be kept intact to be used for a stretchy item (but note that the skin would need to be removed immediately so that the guts could be removed to stop the meat from tainting). As with other aspects of organic material culture, the person who harvests the raw material of skin will be well aware of these differences and if they have a particular purpose in mind will already be making selections of how they will adjust the *chaîne opératoire* and select the raw material to give them the best outcome at the end of the process. Skins have points at which the collagen fibres and the skin itself start to shrink in irreversible ways. Generally, the body temperatures of the animals cannot be exceeded. In practice, for animals, temperatures over 20°C are avoided. For fish this is rather lower and it maybe that temperatures over 18°C will cause them to harden and spoil. This heat hardening is known from later periods as *cuir bouilli* and can be used to advantage in setting the shape of an object by shrinking it round a mould. It will harden the skin but higher temperatures will make it brittle so the process has to be carefully managed.

Very thin skins such as those from rabbits have been used by cutting the pelt into a long strip of skin with the fur still on: the furry cord is then woven or looped into a fabric, e.g. in the Arctic (Thompson 1994: 13) and in California and Nevada (Dockstader 1993: Fig. 68).

Tanning technologies and sequences

Tanning is a term to describe a raw skin that has been processed and preserved. Many authors reserve the term 'leather' for fully tanned irreversible processes such as vegetable tanning or bark tanning, whereas other techniques such as alum taw, fat tanning and smoking are regarded as 'pseudo-tanning' (van Driel-Murray 2000). This has led to some issues of nomenclature. Thus van Driel-Murray's assessment of Egyptian practices is that these are pseudo-tannages as the pale 'leather' for which ancient Egypt is noted could have been produced by flour, chalk, egg yolk or brains as fat; minerals could help preserve the raw skins in the hot climate; ochres could have been colouring substances and the alum found is a mordant (dye assistant associated with madder, *Rubia tinctorum*) from the third millennium BC in Mesopotamia, with true bark tan coming much later in Greek and Roman periods. In this book with the focus on prehistory, all of the simple techniques are likely to be part of the early methods of working skins but they are useful in their own right and so the term 'pseudo-tanning' does not suit the ethos of animal materialities. Thus here 'tanning' describes a hide that has been treated and worked no matter the process but it is understood that many of the methods would be regarded as 'pseudo-tanning' by other authors. The methods for turning a fresh skin into something useful and durable would have been an important augmentation of human material culture and a new relationship with animal materials. The tanning methods are diverse but have common themes and largely follow a sequential path.

Once killed, the animal is likely to be skinned very rapidly thereafter. There are different ways of dealing with the skin to stabilize it if it is not going to be worked on straightaway. This can be drying, salting, freezing or smoking. The stabilization process is essential for the qualities of the skin to be retained later. The way in which this initial stabilization process occurs very much depends upon the environment and cultural practices as well as on the size of the dead animal. In cold regions, the skin can be spread out to dry on snow or it can be tacked up on a wall to dry in the cold dry air (see Plate 44.2). If the climate is wet, the skin can be put on a frame so that it can be brought indoors and rested against a wall so that it is not in the way (Plate 44.3). Sámi traditions of storing skins and drying them include inserting small sticks as frameworks for drying the skin.[5] These skins can then be stacked and stored inside ready to be worked on at a later date. Methods of storing and stabilizing skins using salt are likely to be restricted to coastal areas or be relatively late techniques simply because salt would have been an important commodity and expensive when it was first known (even though recent work in Europe has shown the use of Bronze Age salt production sites [Harding 2000; Harding and Kavruk 2010, 2013]). In cold climates, freezing works but more importantly the freezing process will help dry the skin, which is why the skin is exposed to extremely dry cold if possible so that the moisture is drawn out of it by freeze-drying it. Very fatty skins will eventually be changed by freezing conditions and will not store indefinitely in this way. They keep better in more extreme cold but still have a limited storage capacity. The other stabilization method is smoking; this both dries the skin because some mild heat is involved but it also partly cures the skin by allowing it to take up some of the phenols in the smoke. This can work because some of the tanning methods described later are not mutually exclusive. Some work very well in combination, most famously the brain tan method followed by smoking, which is a traditional practice over much of the plains of North America. Also bark tan followed by applications of fat works well or fat tan followed by a bark tan solution painted onto the skin. Alum taw will not work with smoke as this combination will mean that the skin goes hard.

Defleshing is the initial phase of all tanning processes. All the remaining meat, fat and connecting tissues have to be removed from the flesh side (interior) of the skin. Ideally this process happens soon after skinning. Defleshing can use a half log or other smooth round surface, and a stone scraper (Plate 44.4 and see Weedman 2002) or bone deflesher (often with serrated edge as shown in Plate 37) to push the remaining material off the skin. The next key decision is whether to keep the hair or fur on, or off and whether to take off the grain layer (see Plates 46 and 47 and Figure 9).

Hair and fibres can be retained for warmth, appearance, or water shedding qualities but they make the tanning and softening processes more challenging. The hide of the deer is suitable in its size, flex and drape for a wide range of purposes, including for making into clothing. Larger animals can have hides that are so thick that they will never achieve a soft drape, thus making them uncomfortable as

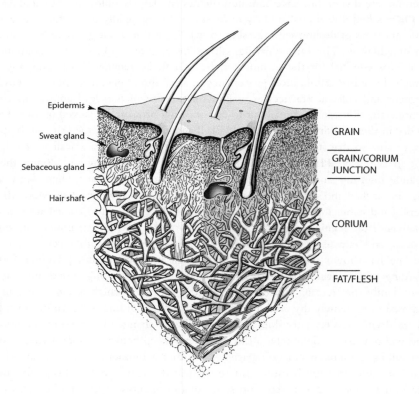

FIGURE 9 Generalized diagram of the layers and structures of skin.
Source: Hurcombe.

materials for clothing. Deer hides are often used without the hair on because the hair has a tendency to break and to come off during the tanning processes (see deer hair on Plate 46). The general exception is that reindeer skins with the hair on have the full value of the insulating hair and are used as materials for bedding and the like and ground covering in cold northern climates. When working with skins and wanting to keep hair on, once cleaned they cannot be left in solutions for too long or the hair will start to slip, which is when the hair starts to pull away in the grain layer. Similarly, when the requisite process using liquid has finished it is a good idea to dry the fur as much as possible, perhaps with the assistance of moss or other natural materials so that it does not stay damp for too long as this will encourage mould and the skin will be ruined. There are several layers to the skin as shown in Figure 9 and Plate 44.1. The main skin layer is mostly made up of collagen fibres in bundles, interwoven in different animals in slightly different patterns. Generally, these fibre bundles lie parallel to the skin near to the surface and gradually become more angled, being at 45° as it nears the internal edge of the dermis. If waterproof qualities are important, it is best to leave the grain on. If the hair or fur is not desired it can be shaved off leaving the grain intact or carefully allowed to soak for some days until the hair comes off: it is difficult to achieve this process across the whole skin as hair grows differently over the body. Lye solutions of woodash and water can also be used to remove the hair. In South Africa pastoralists crush up particular plants and spread these over the hides: the salt in the plants works in a similar way (Webley 2005). Plate 44.5 shows the bone defleshing tool being used to take the grain off an ostrich skin. The other method for removing grain is to dry the hide, usually in a frame, then using a very sharp tool edge scrape off all of the top layer of the skin. The process of removing the grain can substantially reduce the thickness of the skin overall which may be a useful effect (see Plate 47 for a direct comparison of the difference in thickness).

The tanning processes can employ a wide range of different materials and methods as outlined below but many other possibilities exist. Some processes work in combination with others.

Enzymes and biological activity can be useful. *Puering* or *bating* are historical tanning processes that use enzymes from materials such as dog, pigeon or poultry manure but early use is not documented. These are mostly used in solutions and warmed as necessary to allow the enzymes to work. Other processes use the fermentation of bran as a tanning aid, chopped grass may work in a similar way. The fermentation process releases the carbon dioxide that, again, makes the skin very loose and opens up the fibres.[6]

Fat tan

Fats can be reactive with hides in two different ways. First they can penetrate the skin in much the same way as face creams. This can help soften the skin, but it is not a permanent solution because if the skin is wet and then dries, it would become stiff.

Unsaturated fats can be manipulated and mechanically processed to enter into a more permanent relationship with the dermal fibres, and in particular will oxidize, thus coating those dermal fibres and creating a true fat-tanned skin. This fat-tanned skin will stiffen slightly on wetting and then re-drying, but will retain much of its former softness and tanned skin appearance. The unsaturated fats that are best used in this fat tanning process are those contained within brains, known as brain tan and very familiar to a North American audience (buckskin), and also fish eggs, seabird eggs, marrow and a variety of fish oils and plant oils such as rapeseed and olive oil. Most fish skins are simply fat-tanned so that they are cleaned and then dried and softened using the natural oils present in the skin. Materials such as grains and egg yolks have phospholipids that can, in themselves, be excellent for tanning, but also aid in drawing other fats into the skin.

Brain tan

Brains are used by macerating the material (this can be done by cooking the brain for a few minutes in water), or they can be broken down mechanically. A mixture can be spread on the skin, or the hide can be dipped in the solution, wrung out and the process repeated at intervals. As the brain tanned skin dries it is stretched and worked to soften it. The brains of the animal can be used to tan its skin but brains can be kept specifically for this purpose. Lyford (1945: 70) explains that deer brains could be kept if they will not be used straight away by mashing them up with moss and making them into cakes that would be dried thoroughly and kept until needed. These were reported to be viable even for several years. Spinal cord of an eel is also mentioned as a substitute for brains, and also a mixture of eggs and corn mill beaten to a pulp.

Urine tan

Traditionally, the Inuit have used urine to tan their fish skins. Urine contains a mixture of formic and uric acid, and when urine is left to stand, ammonia is formed. This ammonia can break down the fats in this skin and these fatty acids will penetrate the skin and react with the fibres tanning the skin. Rahme (2006: 39) reports that urine from younger people has less smell later on although does not state whether male or female urine differs. She can say that experience suggests that adult urine causes the tanning to make leather a little more brittle with a shorter lifespan. She reports a tanning process used in Alaska where the skins were scraped with a seashell, descaled if necessary and that the urine was preferred to come from a young baby boy before weaning, whereas for the strongest skins, the urine from an older boy is better. Her informant goes on to describe that traditionally soap and aspen shavings in water were also used as part of the process, and that moss was also used to absorb the water. Skins were then left on the wall to dry before being used.

Vegetable or bark tan

Tanning can also be undertaken with vegetable products, such as berries, tree barks and twigs, and various plant substances. This is usually given the name of vegetable or bark tanning. Vegetable tanned leather is a permanent change of the material which means that when it is wet and then re-dries, it will be slightly stiff but retains its suppleness. It can be further waterproofed by the addition of fats and oils, and the amount of softening will determine how supple the material becomes in tandem with the original thickness of the skins. Vegetable tanning probably has a long history in temperate and northern latitudes. In general, most tree barks are good sources of tanning materials, and oak, spruce, willow, birch, ash and alder, acacia and sumac are all used, as well as plants such as heather (*Erica* sp.) and tormentil (*Potentilla* sp.). The amount and quality of the tannins in these vegetable products is variable. Oak bark is excellent whereas some of the other materials would require more to achieve the same level of tanning. Trees should not be too mature as sometimes the tanning content will decrease more with prime condition for oak bark being somewhere between 15 and 30 years of age. The traditional age for stripping oak for tanning in the UK was about 20-year-old pole trees (Bodman 2008). In all cases there is more tannin present as the trees come into leaf and the sap rises. This is also the time when the bark can be most easily removed from the tree. Again, the final stage of bark tan has to include a softening phase if the end result is to be flexible.

As with other chemicals used in skin processing, it is best to start with weak solutions and allow the material to be slowly drawn into the skin. This is particularly the case with bark tan because if stronger solutions are used first, the material in effect tans the outside of the hide and this will then resist the penetration of the tanning liquid into the inner parts. In the debate on the origins of vegetable tan, recent evidence from an ice preserved find in the Alps from Schnidejoch from the Neolithic period have tested positive with the presence of tree tannins (Spangenberg et al 2010). It is impossible to perform the same test on the Iceman's garments because of the conservation treatments already applied to the skin materials.

Smoking

Smoking can be achieved by forming a small wicker tent structure with the hide draped over or by sewing skins to be smoked together as shown in Plate 44.7. Smoking a hide is another form of tanning that was usually used in combination with some other tanning techniques such as fat tan or brain tan. Van Driel–Murray (2000) describes smoking as an aldehyde tannage and makes the important point that smoking hides are known in Europe from the late Neolithic onwards. To quote directly, she also explained why the smoking process can sometimes give a positive reaction for tannins: 'burning wood releases aldehydes and phenols, the latter being responsible for the mild positive reaction to standard test for vegetable tannins (phenols) which are occasionally noted' (2000: 302–3). The scenes from

Egyptian tombs show the de-hairing process of hides as one of dipping skins into jars that are assumed to contain fats or oils and then staking them in order to dry them. This would seem to be the more common technique and may indicate that Egyptian tanning in the first instance was a fat tan method rather than a vegetable-based method for which there is no unambiguous evidence. In a later text, the oil used is listed as sesame oil although other fats could have been used. She cites Mann describing a treatment involving flour, tallow, fat and salt (7:7:2:1), which could be a pseudo tannage that would then be used to oil the skin. There may be something in this tanning technique which particularly affects their survival rate in tombs. Even Tutankhamun's tomb, with its outstanding preservation, has untanned skins that were in a poor condition as their oil decayed into a gelatinous mass after the breakdown of the collagens.

Softening and oiling

The final phase of tanning is the softening process unless the hide is to remain stiff. Softening can be carried out by working the slightly damp hide over a rounded branch or stake. Other toothed wooden pieces can be useful such as the wooden item on the post in the right of Plate 44.6. The brain tan process includes a final phase of wringing and stretching the hide as the solution, which has oils within it, penetrates the skin. Bark tan can be worked damp but the tannins tend to dry out the skin and oils are often applied at the end of the whole *chaîne opératoire* for bark tan and other processes as a way of getting oil into the skin. The softening process works the fibres against one another and frees them up. Oils can help this process and give some protection against wet. Unsaturated and dispersed oils are the best to penetrate the skin and coat the fibres. However, after getting wet, fat tanned hides will still need to be re-softened and bark tan ones may require a little softening. Smoking is often the finishing technique for brain tan and the smoke coats the fibres. Hides treated in this way will remain soft after washing.

The tanning techniques for furs and hides greatly affect the flexibility and colour of the finished pieces. Plate 45 shows that fur and skins can provide a range of colour and textures in material culture. They can be stiff, as some of the rolls show, or very soft. Specific areas of some animals give strong colour tones or piebald markings. The pelts of young animals can give stripes or spots such as the young wild boar piglet with stripes, and furs from animals like fox and lynx can give soft warmth (see Plates 32, 33, 45 and 46). Removing the hair or the grain makes substantial changes to drape and texture. The tanning technique also affects the colour because the tannins dye the skin whereas fat tan and urine tan keep the light tone of the skin. The single skin treated in four different ways shows this and the range of colours along the bottom is not all that can be achieved. The willow gives a nut brown that darkens on the addition of fat to the skin, reddish tones can be created by adding rowan or alder bark to the tanning solution, spruce gives a darker colour as does oak; the golden brown is from a smoked brain tan hide. If iron-rich material is added to the bark tans the tones will darken further. The tonal contrasts, together with decorative effects from textured skins like fish, and the beaver tail, and the addition of tassels, appliqué, lashings, *Dentalium* shell work and beading can all embellish and decorate the finished objects as shown in Plate 50. Hides are a rich aspect of the material culture repertoire.

Uses of hides

Hides can be used in an extraordinary range of ways. At its strongest, a hide can be used for a shield (Plate 49.3). It has qualities which allow it to be waterproofed and to serve as tent coverings and structure coverings, and it also has flexibility and warmth and wind-proofing abilities in clothing. There are also ways of making a hide into a fixed rigid shape and animal products such as the guts can also provide other forms of connective tissue structures. The range of animals used and the range of animal parts used is thus far wider than is generally acknowledged. A clear example of this is the use of fish skins (see p. 86), which in Northern climates are important ways of covering work projects and have also been used to make bags and clothing items (Hurcombe and Williams 2002; Owen 2000; Rahme 2006; Reed 2005). Thus, animals that we do not necessarily think of as hide animals provide skins for human use and larger animals provide a more diverse range of products than might be immediately apparent. Guts of animals are important as thin flexible skins for storing liquids and other materials as ready-made tubular containers (for example, sausage skins). The bottle shown in Plate 49.2 is made from a goat bladder, cleaned and then inflated while fresh and allowed to dry in shape. Raw hide is flexible and heavy when wet but shrinks considerably on drying. This factor has allowed it to be used for bindings where the drying tightens an already tight binding significantly. Water-proofed hides can be used as parkas, or in skin-framed boats (although these become heavy and waterlogged after submersion for several days). A finely-crafted coracle is shown in Plate 49.1. This is similar to a more ad hoc bull boat where a wicker frame is covered with a large skin.

Because hides come in so many different sizes and can be treated in such a variety of ways, they, along with intestines and other types of tissue, serve a very broad range of purposes. One unusual purpose is the use of fleeces to trap gold in streams (Ryder 1991) versus the more obvious uses of hides as clothing, for example the bog bodies of Europe include caps and capes and cords of hide and there are numerous shoes. Also preserved are hide sacks from the salt mines in Hallstatt (Reschreiter and Kowarik 2009; Ryder 1992) and the Iceman's finds (Egg and Spindler 2009). The carrying sack used in the salt mines is particularly interesting because it has a folded over rim, reinforced thong stitching and wooden supports but the design allows a quick release of the material in the sack so that the workflow was smooth, suggesting highly organized labour and artefacts to aid this. The use of ox hide ingots in the European Bronze Age is perhaps an indicator that hides were also likely units of trade that were well understood in much the same way as happened in the fur trade in Canada (Briard 1976). Scoops and containers of hide are other well-known ways of using this material. Hides are the ultimate all-purpose material.

Their use may start with small thin hides that could be relatively easily shaped while fresh to make small containers, which were then rigid when the material dried. In hot climates, this may have been a useful way of making containers. Elsewhere, in order to make useful products of hides, the basis of tanning – even if not fully sophisticated – would have substantially increased the effectiveness of these kinds of products. Even small animals such as rabbit skins can be worked up into larger scale garments where they are reduced to cordage, which is then treated as looping material or woven into larger items. In these ways, hide serves a variety of different purposes as containers and as importantly as lashings and cordage.

In most societies cordage is an important aspect of everyday life, used for a wide range of things. The raw hides give one such raw material to a society in a ready-made form. Yet even in this simple use of cord, complexity and logistical choices can be evident. Binford (2009) describes rope making in the high arctic by Nunamiut societies, explaining that the rawhide for the rope that was used as snares was usually from spring-killed caribou. This is because in this season the caribou pelts are not good for other uses because the hair is beginning to fall out and skins taken at this time of year are full of holes where insects have burrowed under the skin. Thus, although caribou were killed at this time of year, they would be selectively skinned and those skins with the least damage would be carefully stored for use for these rope-making activities. The operational chain consisted of wetting the hide, then rolling it and keeping it indoors usually in the roof area for one to two weeks. After this, the hair would be easy to detach and the rawhide would be cleaned on the inner surface while damp before being cut into thumb-sized strips. The single rawhide strips could be strung over bushes to dry and rolled up for storage.

Fish skins

Fish skins are one of the most neglected aspects of material culture possibilities of the past. Because fish skins are not a normal part of most people's experience, they do not necessarily think of them as being of use to people. However, there was considerable evidence especially in Northern climates for the use of fish skins as an important lightweight and very waterproof material if prepared in the right way. Examples from the Ingalik material culture shows how fish skin blankets could be taken and used to cover projects to protect them from the rain, an important aspect of managing production activities such as canoe-building (Osgood 1940: 170). In many ways, they observe the purpose that today is reserved for tarpaulins. However, fish skins have also traditionally in northern regions been used for items of clothing, bags and in particular for waterproofing materials. Rahme (2006) reports the use of fish skin from around the globe including China and Russia, some of whose communities have traditions of using fish skin for clothing and straps and bags. The fish skin shoes – in this case made of wolf fish skin – described by Rahme are very similar in design to the rawhide shoes known as *pampooties* in Ireland. In many of the recorded uses, the fish skin is simply allowed to dry and softened using its own oil as the lubricant. In effect, this is fat tanning.

A variety of fish skins can be used. For example, the salmon (*Salmo salar*), which can grow up to 1.4m long, offers large skins with distinctive patterns (see Plates 50.2 and 50.3). There is a fin in the middle of the fish's back and this can be simply cut round and the material later sewn up to make a slightly triangular or trapezoidal but effective skin. The kinds of objects known to be made from these skins are items of footwear and examples of hats. Other items of clothing and bags were also used (Hurcombe and Williams 2002: 17; Rahme 2006). Rahme gives an overview of useful species: pike (*Esox lucius*) growing over 1m in length can also be used; burbot (*Lota lota*) is another fish that can be over 1m in length, the position of the dorsal fins mean that small pieces can be obtained from one side, but it is a tough skin that has been used for tanning and for making straps and bindings and for its translucency; cod (*Gadus morhua*) can grow to over 1.5m in length – in Norway, shoes were made of cod skin in the Second World War. Spiny dogfish (*Squalus acanthias*) offer a completely different kind of skin; they are members of the dogfish family and as such their skin has small dermal teeth. These have a distinct direction so that in one direction, the feel of them is smooth and in the other direction it is very rough. The skin is called *shagreen* because of its distinctive qualities. It is sometimes used today in places where the potential for grip is crucial such as the bindings of sword hilts. It has also been used as a sandpaper for wood.

The spiny dogfish is significant because it has a small, but very fine pointed spine. One such was used at the Mesolithic site of Smakkerup Huse in Scandinavia (see Chapter 5). A wide range of other fish can be used for their skins such as grayling, trout, shar and various types of flat fish. Some produce large areas of skin: for example, turbot (*Psetta maxima*) can be over 1m long, brill (*Scophthalmus rhombus*) a little smaller and halibut (*Hippoglossus hippoglossus*) up to 2m long. These all have distinct textures and in some cases, patterns on them that might make them good sources for detailed smaller pieces where pattern can be used for decoration as well as using the whole skins. Eel (*Anguilla anguilla*) are also very important. Mature ones can be between 0.5m and 1.5m in length, and their skin is so exceptionally strong that in historic periods they have been used to drive machinery in water driven mills. The shape of the eel skin means that long thin strips can be obtained that can then be sewn together to make larger items. In recent times, eel skins have been used as the toe and heel bindings of skis, and for making harvesting gloves. The texture of the skin has many different scales at right angles to each other so that the texture almost looks as though it was woven.

As this short review of fish and eel skins shows, a wide range of different species can be used, when sewn together their combination of lightness, strength and waterproofing makes them excellent materials for overshoes or waterproof garments, and they were used as such by many societies in Northern Europe and Alaska.[7]

Properties of fish skins

Most fish have a protective covering of scales that grow through their life. Some fish have small tooth-like scales of dentin and enamel that give the sandpaper effect described above. As with mammals, the key layer of the skin is the dermis, which has larger intersecting collagen fibres. For fish, the epidermis obviously does not have an outer layer of dead cells, but instead have cells that secrete mucous and help the fish move easily through the water by reducing friction. The *stratum compactum* is the key collagen fibre layer, but above this, there is the grain, the *stratum laxum*, and it is in this layer that there are the scales. Fish skin is often much thinner than mammalian skin, and varies in thinness over the body of the fish. In most cases, it stretches longer along its length than in its width. Fish skin is described as more sensitive to acids and high temperatures than animal skins. The collagen fibres of the dermis are highly organized in fish and occur in tightly compacted structural layers. This gives fish skin its greater strength despite its thinness. The collagen fibres are spiralling chains of proteins called amino acids. They are held together strongly but also need to be kept apart so that the structure of the skin can flow freely. It is this process that tanning assists. Tanning can occur in different ways and to different degrees, but it will eventually make the skin more resistant to the effects of temperature on the collagen fibres. Normal collagen fibres untanned in the skin layer of fish and mammals can be turned into gelatine at high temperatures. Fish skin, like mammal skin, needs to be conserved once removed from the living animal. Freezing, salting and drying are three possibilities. All three work better if the material is cleaned first. If freezing is used to preserve a fish skin, it needs to be done quickly. Rahme (2006) clearly states that as the water in the skin freezes, it pushes the fibres apart mechanically and helps to soften the final product. Rahme (2006: 33) also reports that drying is not a good way to preserve fish as they become brittle and difficult to tan. Salt is useful in working with fish and either wet or dry salting can be used. Since many of the fish that might be used are caught near or in the sea, then using saltwater to assist this process is a possibility. A blunt edged knife-like tool traditionally made from slate in the Northern lands can be used to descale the fish. Rahme reports that these have been dated to approximately 5000–4000 BC.

Sinew

Sinew is an invaluable cordage material as it is light and strong and can be split and twisted to make up cordage of different thickness. In particular it is able to be used where both fine and strong material is need. It forms the wrapping material for hafting arrowheads and fletchings, snares, bowstrings and is especially useful as sewing thread. The material can be obtained by making careful incisions in the leg of an animal at either end of the leg bone or by carefully releasing the ligament from a long slit cut. The back strap sinew is pulled away from the backbone. In all cases the material dries hard and in order to be used needs to be lightly broken up until individual fibres are visible as shown in Plate 34. Sets of individual fibres can then be twisted and spliced together to make the desired thickness of thread. Dorra (pers. comm.) shows the rolling process and the direction of the splicing needs to be constant so that the thread will pull through without snagging. The threads can be kept in a loose plait until used.[8] The sinew was also important for decorative work using porcupine quills and sewing and pattern cutting were important skills (Orchard 1971, 1975; Pedersen 2005; Hungry Wolf 1982; King et al 2005; Thompson 1994: 13–18; Wilder 1976). Whale sinew can also be used and in some *chaîne opératoires* the sinew is not allowed to dry out completely (Issenman 1997: 84–85). When it is damp the sinew will expand and retain the waterproof qualities of the footwear by filling the sewing hole. This is also why the needles used are so fine. In a different environment among African pastoralists, goat backstrap sinew is used (cow sinew is too thick; sheep sinew is unsuitable, Webley 2005).

Feathers

While feathers have been known to be used in many societies, archaeologists are not often able to find such material, although there is extensive use from arrowheads of the use of feathers for fletching materials. Plate 42 shows some of the ways in which feathers have become incorporated into archaeological artefacts. As whole objects, they can be part of soft surfaces, and wadding for warmth. They can also be used as parts of the skins, and Plate 50.6 shows an entire bag made from Loon skin, with the feathers still attached. There are also accounts of northern Inuit using bird skins with feathers attached as soft but warm garments for children.

The insulating qualities of feathers are one important aspect of their materiality. Other aspects are the colours and possibilities they give for decoration. In many societies in the Pacific and in North America, feathers of particular birds, either for their colour or their symbolism, are important aspects of decoration for ceremonial equipment and clothing. Plate 42 shows a detail of a Hawaiian headdress, which has been used for the colour, as the feathers were originally red. These have been joined onto fine cords, to construct the headdress, as the image shows. The centre image shows the ways in which feathers can be split, using an example of a turkey feather. In America the domestication of the wild turkey and the use of turkey feathers to make blankets is well-known. The blankets, likewise, are made by incorporating the feathers into cordage and then making cordage technology blankets. To do so each of the feathers is split along its length as shown, then the clean end is inserted into the cord, and bound tightly in as part of it, with the feather wrapped around and the final end tucked in and bound into the cord. In this way feather blankets, as warm insulating garments, were produced.[9]

Plate 42.3 shows a finely fletched detail of an arrow. While archaeologists often think about the need for straightening arrow shafts, they more rarely think about the need for careful selection and preparation of feathers for fletching material. The feathers can be attached by means of pitch or similar materials, and also can be bound with sinew or other very fine thread. Feathers thus have both utility and important metaphorical and symbolic roles in many societies. Where there are bird bones on site, it is worth considering what role these birds may have played. Note also that bird bones can be used to decorate pottery and could have further symbolism in this way. Although feathers rarely survive, their use could be surmised and brought into archaeological arguments to augment the way in which the materials used by prehistoric societies are considered.

Study strategies for skins, furs, sinew and feathers

It is possible to examine skins microscopically and use the pattern of hair follicles and grain structure to determine species of origin (Bonnichsen et al 2001; Körbe-Grohne 1988; Meeks and Cartwright 2005; Procter 1922; Reed 1972; Woodroffe 1949; van Driel-Murray 2002). In all these cases, the light microscope can provide a preliminary assessment but for problematic determinations and greater depth of field the Scanning Electron Microscope (SEM) is useful. However use-wear traces can show that hide working was taking place and have been famously used as indicators of an increase in the finishing of hides in the Upper Palaeolithic (Hayden 1990) and also have made several use-wear specialists take particular interests in hide working technologies, notably Beyries and Audouin-Rouzeau (2002), Mansur-Franchomme (1983) and Plisson (1993). Less successful has been the ability to understand light tanning processes, as these involved natural tannins and fats that have historically proved difficult to distinguish from natural traces and, in any event, lesser tanning usually affects the survival prospects of such material. Thus, there may be whole tanning traditions that have not survived well archaeologically and are missing from our understanding of hide-working traditions and developments. The recent find from the Iceman has shown the complexity of hide-working and hide items on one individual (Groenman-van Waateringe 1967, 1993), where it is obvious that very fine shaping and alignment of the skins was undertaken to make a well-constructed and fitted outfit of coat and leggings designed for that specific person and indicating different animals and different tanning techniques with hair on and hair off according to the purpose of the garment or object. The coming decades are likely to see an increased use of genetics to identify species of origin when this is not clear microscopically, and there is potential for residue analysis to explore the use of fat tanning processes. Tannins from trees could also be explored using chemical analysis techniques. In the longer term, the isotopic analysis is increasingly likely to be able to indicate where a species grew versus where it was found. In these ways, it may be possible in the future to look at the trade in live animals or the trade in the goods produced from animals in ways that are not at present possible. The process of tanning hides deserves further elaboration.

Study strategies of sinew stitching now include x-ray analyses, 2D and 360° surround photography (Schmidt and Pederson 2009).

Hair and wool as fibres for cordage and textiles

Two sets of fibres can be recognized: protein-based animal fibres and cellulose-based plant ones. Animal fibres are more resistant to fire whereas cellulose fibres in the form of charred cloth were often used as tinder. Each has different characteristics, which can be generalized as follows: animal fibres are more susceptible to attacks by moths whereas cellulose fibres are more susceptible to attack by fungi and mildew. Cellulose fibres are more robust and are less likely to be damaged by strong alkalines but are vulnerable to acidic conditions. The reverse is true of protein fibres. This is why animal fibres tend to survive in acidic conditions such as the peat bogs of Northern Europe whereas animal fibres will survive better where conditions are alkaline. Protein fibres shrink in hot water, but cellulose fibres less so. Generally, cellulose fibres are thought to provide less insulation and warmth value than protein-based ones but these vary greatly. Protein fibres resist wear and abrasion more than cellulose ones and also allow moisture to be absorbed and kept away from feeling wet in proximity to the body better than cellulose fibres. Fibre elasticity is less in cellulose fibres, but the strength is greater. What we think of as wool is better described as a type of protein-based animal fibre, as it is formed from a protein called keratin along with other molecules.

Animal-derived fibres generally take three different forms. The first is kemp, which is the coarsest and is the only one to have a central hollow called a medulla. These are sometimes called medullated fibres or med fibres. They can be much more brittle than the other fibres and will not take dye well. Because they are the coarsest fibres, they tend to be the ones that makes a yarn feel prickly or hairy. The term 'hair' in animal fibres usually refers to fibres that are not medullated but are nonetheless straighter, smoother and more inelastic than the very finest fibres. The latter have 'crimp' (a term used to describe the wavy structure of the fibres), and are described as fluffy, furry or fuzzy. In an animal coat each of these fibres has distinct benefits. The under down, i.e. the short woolly fibres, keep an animal warm. The hairy fibres help keep the coat in good order and help shed rain, and the kemp too will help protect the other hair structures and will shed water. All of these fibres have complex structures with microscopic scales on the outside. Domesticated species have been bred especially for some aspect of these fibres if they are fibre animals. Domestication tends to either make the coat much finer in general but still include a lot of different varieties of length and fineness, or it may be polarized into very coarse material and very fine under wool. When it is polarized in this way it is easier to separate the two types of fibre from each other. Kemp has a shorter growth cycle than some of the other fibre types and will break and shed first in the spring. The shepherd who waits a little later in the year will get a fleece with less kemp in it (Robson and Ekarius 2011: 9). However, many animals reported in the same source also shed the down before the hair; combing the animal can provide a way of making sure that the differences in the fibres collected are concentrated into the fine end rather than across the whole range of fibres. Thus the timing of the harvesting of fibres and the manner in which they are combed, plucked (rooed) or shorn will affect what kind of fibres are collected and how much work there might be to sort the fibres into the different grades if that is what is required for particular projects. The hairs of animal fibres are produced by follicles located within the skin. The pattern and structure of this make up distinctive patterns known as 'grain' types on the surface of the animal's skin. There are many different ways of measuring the fineness and quality of animal fibres across the world, but these commercial grade systems are not necessarily harmonized and are problematic in their use. The handling properties of the fibres are also dependent upon something called 'locks', which is the way in which the fibres group together into a lock of hair or a clump of different kinds and qualities of fibres (see Plate 52 and Robson and Ekarius 2011). Locks still have all the fibres aligned and the range of lengths and colour tones can easily be assessed by hand and eye.

Modern-day sheep are all shorn but in the past the natural shedding would have released clumps of material that could have been collected from scratching posts and bushes or could have been combed from tame animals or those that could be captured. The sorts of factors that affect the commercial value of a modern fleece have some parallels in the past. Animal that are in poor health will tend to have a poor coat and excessively dirty and matted fibres will be difficult to work with and will be of less value. Some of the best fibres will be located in specific parts of the animal where they are more sheltered and protected from harsh conditions. Wool can be spun in the grease. Lanolin is a grease that the animals produce naturally to coat their hairs and help protect them. Some animals produce more grease than others and some breeds produce more than others. This is in fact a combination of lanolin grease and a sweat product called *suint*. This can colour the lighter wools but it is usually able to be washed out. Not all the sticky and greasy material is washed away unless higher temperatures and in some cases soaps are used. Guard hairs refer to the coarser fibres that have the important job of overlying and protecting the softer, shorter down. Some kinds of animals have heterotypic hair, which changes its nature according to the season, having more woollen fibres in the winter and becoming more hair-like to shed water in the summer. Fulling is a process described in later historic periods as a process associated with felting. Its use should be confined to filling out the spaces in the weave structure of a fabric. This is achieved by a process akin to felting, but that stops short of the true felting process. Fulling makes the yarn structure becomes less evident and causes the material to have few spaces between the weave structure.

Sheep are the dominant fibre animal today but other fibre-producing animals have been domesticated and there are wild animals whose fibres are important now and in the past.

Russell (2012) has usefully covered and summarized the key domesticated species and the regions and dates at which domestication is currently thought to have occurred. This information is reorganized and augmented in Table 1 to show how different areas have treated domesticated animals and the potential for fibres in amongst these animal species. The size of the hides available is also indicated as well as the possibilities of using birds for their feathers. The hides are given as a relative size order, which generally ties in with their thickness, such that the likes of guinea pig or a turkey have very thin skins whereas the larger animals have much thicker skins. Horses have good skins although they are not commonly used in that way in societies where riding horses is a sport. Animals such as the water buffalo and camel present their own problems. Although they are domesticated species, these large

TABLE 1 The domestication of major animal species with approximate dates and their potential for the provision of skins, fibres and feathers (adapted from Russell 2012: Fig. 6.1)

Taxon	Region	Date BP	Size of skins; fibre, feathers
Dog (*Canis familiaris*)	Central Europe	32,000	Small: potential for fibres
Sheep (*Ovis aries*)	Near East, S Asia	10,500	Medium–small: fibres
Goat (*Capra hircus*)	Near East	10,500	Medium: fibre, sinew?★
Cattle (*Bos taurus*)	Near East, S Asia, N Africa?	10,500	Large: fibre
Pig (*Sus scrofa*)	Near East, E Asia	10,500	Medium: bristles and hair
Water buffalo (*Bubalus bubalus*)	E or S Asia	5000	Very large
Chicken (*Gallus gallus*)	SE Asia/E Asia	8000	Very small (feathers)
Horse (*Equus caballus*)	Central Asia	5500	Large, good: hair
Bactrian camel (*Camelus bactrianus*)	Central Asia	5000	Very large: possibly fibres
Dromedary (*Camelus dromedarius*)	Arabian Peninsula	4500	Very large: fibre possibly
Cat (*Felis catus*)	Near East	4000	Very small
Llama (*Lama lama*)	Andes	5000	Large medium: fibres
Alpaca (*Lama pacos*)	Andes	5000	Large medium: fibres
Guinea pig (*Cavia porcellus*)	Andes	1000	Small
Turkey (*Meleagris gallopavo*)	Middle America/SouthWest	2000	Small: feathers
Muscovy duck (*Cairina moschata*)	Northern S America	1000	Small: feathers

★comment on sinew is based on Webley (2005)

animals have pronounced humps and back ridges that are difficult for traditional hide-working techniques as an area of very tough skin. However, this allows the tougher qualities of the hides to come through so, if drape and homogeneity are not important, these hides can be very useful additions to the material culture repertoire. Reindeer should be added to this list for much more recent times but it is worth noting these are the only species of deer that are truly domesticated even though deer are kept and farmed in many places; for example, red deer in the UK. Overall, the list is dominated by ovicaprids, bovids and camelids. These three groups are also found in different areas though species that, generally speaking, were domesticated in broad phases. One anomaly on the list is the dog. The dog has to be seen as something quite different from the other domestic animals and the reasons for its domestication are absolutely separate from those of the other groups.

In discussions on animal and plant domestication, most attention is understandably given to the dietary aspects of particular plants and animals, and also their social implications in terms of status, ownership and capital (see discussion, for example, in Russell 2012: Ch. 6). Similarly, Upper Palaeolithic discussions focus on the meat from animals, but mammoth hair and muskox fibre could have been very important cordage and insulating materials; fibres, skins, furs and sinew could all have been useful resources as well as antler and bone. Changes in environment and lifestyle would have been affected by the shifts in animal exploitation that mark the Mesolithic, as well as the change to farmed resources in the Neolithic. The bestiary changes would profoundly affect the materiality and both food and material culture are deeply embedded social practices that would have needed a shift in attitude as well as practice. What is omitted from almost all these discussions of subsistence shifts are the consequences for the rest of the material culture repertoire. For example, the Neolithic sheep, goat and cattle also give the farmers or herders the benefit of antlers or horns. All of the larger animals except the water buffalo also offer the possibilities of using the hair whether it is fine underwool fibre or coarser hair material or in the case of the horses, the mane and tail hair as well as the coat brushings. Tail hair and forelock of cattle may have been particularly useful as might the areas of longer hair on goats. These materials could have formed soft unstructured insulating material (or a matted product if some part of the fibres would felt), or be twisted into fine yarns or coarse strong cordage. There is undoubtedly no need to think of these fibre-producing animals as being domesticated for their fibre alone or even at all. Rather the forces that drove domestication could have included the use of fibres. In general, common archaeological perceptions are that fibres are about wool. Woolly under down is certainly useful and is the subject of much study from later periods. However, even though it is a change in coat that comes subsequently as part of what Andrew Sherratt (1983) described as a 'secondary products revolution', it cannot be said that the fibres of these animals would not have been useful. It could be that the skins are kept intact and that the hair coats form part of the resources available on an animal's death. However, many of these species in the wild progenitors have annual moults that shed the fibres at particular times of the year. In the wild, this would shed naturally. Some would catch on bushes or scratching posts, where it could be collected by people. However, once people were in close proximity to these animals, then the closeness of that relationship might have meant that where animals were kept in fenced enclosures, the material was noticeably collecting on the fence; or if animals were being herded more closely still and in close human contact – through, for example, milking, or being kept inside houses – then opportunities would have presented themself to remove the fibres as they were being shed. Plucking or combing off the fibres from such contacts could have been the first form of actively collecting the shed material from animal coats whether on the hairy or the woolly side of fineness. Cordage is something that would have been important to human communities in many different ways and animal husbandry practices could have contributed to the overall amount of cordage material or the ability to collect it ready-sorted by natural shedding sequences.

I have also perhaps controversially added fibres to the table under cattle. Ryder (1969, 1980, 1984, 1987, 1992, 2005) has suggested that the same processes of domestication which gradually increased the quantity and quality of wool in sheep did the reverse in cattle where domestication has gradually turned the coat more hairy. Research in the 1970s by Payne (1973) showed the way in which animals kept for different purposes had different kill patterns. This is a classic piece of work, but in the early phases of domestication it is not thought that this patterning is as clear cut. Furthermore, work by Cribb showed by computer simulations of herd management that managed herd patterns would favour sets of changes: to maximize milk would also increase meat and wool yields (Cribb 1987). For societies early in prehistory, husbandry practices may have been more holistic. Given this, it seems that the arguments for holistic approaches and for the consideration of a variety of fibres to be used including the fine wool and the coat, and for the animals to be used for their skins as well as everything else seems to fit this maximum optimization of the use of domesticated animals. There may also be different scenarios at work for the original domestication of the species and its development in the areas of origin as compared to the thoroughly domesticated animal arriving in new areas and being incorporated into existing peoples, regimes and subsistence practices much later on in time. One such scenario is therefore the early Neolithic pottery, which shows clear traces of milk in Britain (Evershed et al 2008, Copley et al 2005a, 2005b).

Primitive sheep breeds such as those preserved on the Isle of Soay off the northwest coast of Scotland have reverted to more feral qualities and are seen as the present-day sheep breed most similar to the Bronze Age breeds. Primitive fleece breeds vary slightly in colour but tend to have lighter coloured tips to their coats and weathered lighter on the back. Rams are known to have a coarser mane on the neck, shoulders and buttocks. Descriptions (Fournier and Fournier 1995; Robson and Ekarius 2011) state that the Soay fleece yields about 0.3–0.9 kilos of wool with a staple length of 3.8–10cm. There is a wide range of fibres with the broader range as kemp. They have persistent skin flakes at the base of the locks that do not wash out (see Plate 52). It can be spun from carefully teased out locks and the material will also felt.[10]

There is one type of goat, *Capra hircus*, which is used to produce all of the domestic animal fibres from goats. This one is believed to have developed from the bezoar ibex (*Capra aegagrus*). This wild goat still exists and it is likely that the domesticated form was first used about 10,000 years ago in the Zagros Mountains area of western Iran. Modern-day bezoar is a large animal with males weighing 23–26kg and 1.2m tall at the withers. They also have tall backward-curving horns. Thus the animal is a good source of meat, horns and fibre as well as skin. Its behaviour is described as gregarious with herds of 50 or more of females and young and males living in more dispersed groups during the breeding season. The most specific breed of goat, the mohair goat (sometimes also called the Angora goat) is thought to have originated in Turkey in later prehistory perhaps around 1500 BC. They have curly coats and are very distinctive in this respect from other kinds of goats. As with all animals, the young tend to have the softest finest fibre and this might be a reason for treating this kind of fibre separately from that from the mature adults.

There are the sorts of factors that people using the fibres in prehistory would have been well aware of and they would have perhaps reserved the finest materials for special uses. With individual animals, males tend to have coarser hair and the best fibres for spinning come from the sides. In particular, their coats have more lustre than wool because the fibres are coated in scales that are smoother and larger than those of sheep wool. They can be matted together firmly, but it is not easy to make goat hair felt.

The Toggenburg goat produces cashmere and has a fine set of horns. Hand spinners report that the traditional practice of hand-plucking cashmere-producing goats allowed a very easy way of separating the coarser goat hairs from the finer down because only the down would shed at this initial phase. Of course commercially that is no longer the case and this has resulted in changes to the breeding populations to polarize the coarse hairs versus the down in size. However, this would not have been the case in the past and the practice of rooing may well have meant that the fine fibres from goats could have been accessed easily if the animals were tamed and would allow rooing to take place. A short review of present-day knowledge of goat fibres suggests that in the past these fibres would have been silkier than wool, more lustrous and more robust and that they may have required rooing practices that would have greatly aided the separation of the coarser hairs from softer down fibres. This could lead where desired to two qualities of products from goats being available. Some goat hairs are spun and made into cloth, which is then used as tent material in the nomadic tribes of the border area from Turkey to Iran and across into areas of Baluchistan and Afghanistan (Cribb 1991).

Camelids

Camelids exist today in two main groups, in Asia and in South America. These are respectively the camels in Asia and the llama, vicuña and guanaco in South America. In South America, camelids survived to become alpacas, llamas, guanacos and vicuñas. The vicuña and the llama guanaco are ancestral creatures from which the present-day alpaca (*Vicuna pacos*) and the llama (*Lama glama*) are domesticated varieties. Llamas have mixed coats that can be brushed out of does. Of the two domesticated animals, alpacas are smaller than llamas and llamas are used as pack animals as well as having fibres: alpacas are mainly used as fibre animals. Today neither of these animals is used primarily for meat, although older animals may become food. Prior to European contact, however, these were important food sources and at the point of European contact there were herds of both animals over much of the region. However, the fibre qualities and the herd structures changed completely with contact so it is difficult now to know what those original llamas and alpacas might have been like. The modern animals have more kemp and are also more variable in their coats than the consistently fine earlier herds. The wild guanaco and vicuna have some of the softest and finest fibres found in the world.

Bactrian camel (*Camelus bactrianus*) sheds its undercoat in spring and this can be gathered by hand or by combing so that less of the course guard hair is present. Dromedary camels are found extensively across Central and Southwest Asia, with several subtypes. They are used for a combination of milk, meat and yarn (Robson and Ekarius 2011: 387).

Dogs

In many areas of the world, dogs are not just animals that are used in hunting or as family pets, but the combings of their hair are also used for fibres. Some dogs are double-coated and the hair will need to be separated from the down. The Coastal Salish people in North America used the fibres from dogs in part of their weaving traditions for making blankets (Gustafson 1980).

Horse

The brushings from the body hair give short fluffy material whereas the mane and tail hairs are generally stiffer and longer. Because of the lack of elasticity in the tail and mane hairs, felting techniques, knotting and similar adaptations would tend to be used rather than finely spun techniques. Interestingly, soaking horse hair for a couple of days before construction is said to make it easier to work in looping style techniques (Robson and Ekarius 2011: 399). Steppe nomads who milk horses also make ropes and cordage from them (Outram pers. comm.).

Bison

There are two subspecies of bison: *Bison bison athabascae*, which lives in the north of present day Canada, and *Bison bison bison*, which is the traditional plains bison, and is also known as buffalo. These animals traditionally gave indigenous American communities meat, bones, hides and horns, as well as being important conceptually and ideologically. They also produce five different types of fibre that is shed every spring. The outermost coat is shiny coarse hair. There are mid-range hairs to provide bulk and there are several shorter types of guard hair and a very fine soft down. It is impossible to shear a bison. Thus most of the products currently available as bison fibre come from the hides from animals slaughtered for meat. The wool can be collected from bushes and scratching posts but not when the animals are in the vicinity. The quality of the down varies and some experience suggests that it will felt, but others have reported problems.

Yak

These large hairy animals are found on the Tibetan Plateau and are cold-adapted (like the muskox) with thick coats. Domestication seems to have occurred between 10,000 and 4,500 years ago in the region of present day Tibet soon after sheep and goats were domesticated. Today, two species exist, the wild *Bos mutus* and the slightly smaller domestic *Bos grunniens*. People keep them for their meat and milk and ride them as traction animals. Yaks can also be used to pull ploughs or even used for racing. The fibre varies greatly but all yaks produce usable qualities of fibre. Wild and domestic animals can also interbreed. Tail hair is cut every other year and the undercoat can be harvested with some having varying degrees of lustre. The hair fibres generally do not felt well but the down fibres do. Yak herders usually use the mixture of hair and down together to make a range of clothing and other items. If desired the fine fibres can be combed out before the whole of the rest is removed by shearing. Where the animals inhabit cold environments, they produce more of the fine fibres.

Muskox

Muskox (*Ovibos moschatus*) live in northern Alaska, Canada and Greenland, and are adapted for old conditions; this species extended across Eurasia in Pleistocene, and is shown in some Upper Palaeolithic art. Their hair is a major reason for the ability to endure exceptionally low temperatures. This is known as *quviut* and is exceptionally fine. Muskox also house a range of guard and skirt hairs and an intermediate fine hair. It can be combed out of a muskox in a single mass of fibres because all of them shed at the same time. Thus a great deal of time would need to be spent preparing it if it is to be spun.

Fur and felt animals

Beaver, mink, muskrat, chinchilla, New Zealand possum and fox all produce fibres that can be used. Most of these are more likely to have been used as furs. However, where animals shed their fibres naturally, this can be collected. In particular, beaver and muskrat were traditionally the materials for making felt hats, including top hats.

Fibres and textiles

Fibres can be used unstructured but also twisted into yarns and then made up using a variety of techniques to become mats, bags, nets, and textiles. Spindle whorls and loom weights are clear examples of textile productions but their absence cannot be used as evidence of an absence of textile production. However, much has been achieved with the existing evidence of tools and devices. For example accounts of weights and whorls, and the technologies assessed as parts of the research programmes of the Centre for Textile Research are advancing these fields. Likewise the analysis of spindle whorls to look at the momentum of spin and how the weights would have worked, and the way in which small weights might have been preferentially used on fine thread production, have all been assessed experimentally.[11] Plate 52 shows Soay sheep wool. The range of colours and wool fibre lengths in the locks can be seen. The detail shows a layer of skin cells and the short coarse fibres below the better locks of the layer that is being naturally shed. It is possible to spin a range of different thickness yarns but coarse yarns cannot be spun on small spindle whorls and longer fibres sorted well will allow finer yarns to be produced. In the Bronze Age spinning systems, most yarns are hard spun and single rather than plyed. The difference between spinning a lofty woollen yarn versus a worsted yarn is the disordered loft of the former and the parallel fibres of the latter. Thus the manner of sorting and aligning the fibres, perhaps by careful maintenance of the lock structure to keep the fibres aligned or the careful sorting and combing, are the groundwork on which the finished yarn rests.[12] A variety of hooks, spindles and whorls are illustrated showing something of the possible variety in Plate 53. The fibres can be sorted for colour, but if a weighted loom system is used then the warp threads (see below) will need to be strong and tightly constructed.

It is possible to finger-weave narrow sashes entirely by hand. Larger weaving can also progress by hand if there is some means of keeping the threads ordered and in the right position as in Figure 5. These show simple frames to suspend the work but Figure 5.3 is slightly different as it has a lower horizontal bar around which the threads pass so that they are held in place top and bottom. This kind of frame can be described as a loom, specifically, it is a kind of two-bar loom. Many looms are more sophisticated versions of this allowing the bars to be moved up and down slightly to give adjustments to the tension. The framework also allows a tubular warp. The warp threads are held under tension while the weft threads are woven in and out. Another way of describing these elements is to term the warp threads the passive elements and the weft the active one.

The weaving process goes quickly on a loom where the threads are kept in order and heddles are employed. Heddles are the name given to a means of creating the space (known as a shed) for the yarn to pass through. This avoids having to pick out the right threads to raise each time. For plain weave known as tabby only two shed positions are needed. In Plates 54 and 55 a variety of different looms used are shown. The ground loom is useful in warm climates and for making large sections of tough cloth. Plate 54 shows an Uzbek weaver, spinner and dyer using her ground loom on the porch outside her house. The cloth is for a hall runner and is being densely woven with the cloth well beaten down with a heavy wooden weaving sword, which has gloss along the leading edge. There is a heddle system of fine threads tied to a stick supported on a bent wood frame. Pulling the stick up will raise the lower threads creating the second shed. The pattern is achieved by the coloured stripes in the long warp threads and by varying the colour of the weft. The warp weighted loom is illustrated in Plate 55.1. The whole frame leans against the wall and the bar at the bottom is used to partition the warp threads alternately. Here the heddle threads also go around a stick but this has one position in the curve of a forked stick and another position illustrated below where it rests against the frame. The weights keep both sets of threads under tension but when the heddle is in the forked stick position the alternate threads are drawn to the front, thus creating the two sheds for plain weave. More complex patterns can be achieved using more heddle rods and forked sticks. Warp threads are constantly under tension and moving against one another, which is why they have to be strong and not likely to fray. Plate 55 shows other frames. The small bentwood frame (Plate 55.2) is for sprang where one set of threads are wound around the two horizontal sticks. These longitudinal threads are then crossed over each other to create the pattern, with a stick inserted to stop the material springing back to its original position. The structures progress at top and bottom as mirror images. A backstrap loom is shown with the tension provided by the body the other end can be on a hook, branch or peg. The heddle system (Plate 55.3) shown is a rigid set of slots and drilled holes so that one set of threads is free to move up or down according to how the rigid heddle is pulled upwards or pushed downwards to create the sheds. Plate 55.4 is a detail of tablet weaving. Cards with, in this case, four holes are threaded with different yarns. The weft passes between the sheds created by turning the cards. This system is good for dense narrow bands with the weft completely hidden. The patterns are formed by varying the turns across the set of tablets so that different colours are brought to the surface of the weave. Tablet weave is also used to form starting borders and selvedges.

All these different looms offer different possibilities for creating textural, tonal and colourful patterns.[13] Plate 56 shows a range of woollen textiles from an Iranian baby's blanket, with woven figures and patterns to a piece of tablet weave (Plate 56.2). Plate 56.4 shows a hard spun tabby but the detail shows that the spin direction of the two sets of threads is different. This makes the weave close up and when used in a series of stripes gives a spin patterned cloth. Plate 56.5 shows a twill weave where the weft threads pass over more than one warp thread in a shifting pattern. Herringbone zigzags, diamonds and other patterns can be created using this floating thread technique. The example show has a simple twill but also regularly spaced thicker threads forming a second textural pattern; Plate 56.6 shows a detail of a check two tone weave pattern with four shed positions. Not all animal fibres are woven on more complicated looms. Plate 56.7 of nalbinden (needle looping) is created with a needle and looping system. In Plate 56.3, the dense thick cords of camel hair have been split apart and inserted through one another to create a heavy duty strap in the ply-split braiding technique (Collingwood 1998).

Fibre and textile study strategies

Macroscopic features are usually recorded for yarns as breadth, twist direction and angle along with plyed structure details. Textile analysis includes these aspects but usually measures the thread count for both directions of woven textiles. The weave structure is also recorded along with any information about the technology used to produce it. Selvedges, hems, fringes, sewing, repairs and conditions are all studied. Early written records are often accounts and textiles form significant aspects of these accounting systems showing the importance of textiles in the economy of these early complex societies (see Michel and Nosch 2010 for recent reviews). Under the microscope fibres can be measured and their shape and surface detail used to characterize the samples to species.[14] Pigmentation can be noted, natural and dyed.

Recent work by Rast-Eicher and Bender Jørgensen (2013) has used micron counts systematically and developed a method for exploring the changes in fleece in European samples drawn from the Bronze Age and Iron Age. Iron Age wools show that some types have less pigment, whereas these features are not present in Bronze Age skins, although some Bronze Age types had some very fine wools.

They also have evidence of different kinds of sheep in size and wool qualities from different regions, so it would appear that there are different breeds emerging as human interventions. In general, the Bronze Age wools have a fine underwool with coarser kemp and upper fibres, but their methodological paper stresses the need for micron count graphs as a way of truly understanding the range of fibres present. Of course, there is always the possibility of the wools being processed and some of the less desirable fibres being manually removed from the material, which is then spun up. However, their sample also includes skins, so that this effect is mitigated.

From the Iron Age Hallstatt period there is evidence for a few rare fleeces with light wool that has been dyed. These are not typical of the region and could be interesting evidence for trade in textiles at this period. This evidence, taken together with a range of discussions of terms used in written sources from the third and fourth millennia (Michel and Nosch 2010) indicate that there is perhaps a flourishing of the production and controlled production of wool and textiles with a view to trade in these materials. The closer reading of changes in the herd structures – with, for example, the Linear B texts recording more wethers (castrated males) – could indicate that the yield of wool was important since male animals will yield more wool than flocks with more females and young. Rast-Eicher and Bender Jørgensen (2013) summarize several places in Europe where the herd structure seems to change and where sheep are generally increasing in respect to cattle on archaeological sites. They also point out the evidence for shears, which are present in the Near East at the end of the second millennium BC. The micron histograms also pick up where the wool has been processed and aspects of the fleece quality had been changed as part of human processing and selection. Rast-Eicher and Bender Jørgensen (2013: Fig. 21) clearly shows that, while changes occur with a slight delay – starting in southwest Asia and spreading through southern then central Europe then Scandinavia – there is a general move to a variety of sheep, some of which have DNA evidence suggesting that there are sheep sources moving in northern Europe, from Siberia towards Scandinavia as well as the Mediterranean route (Brandt et al 2011; Tapio et al 2006).

Felt

Wool is unique in having fibres, the surfaces of which are covered with scales that point in one direction. These scales under conditions of moisture, pressure and warmth, gradually tangle and interlock turning the loose fibres into felt.[15] Bunn (2010) gives a succinct summary of the place of felt in the sequence of textile history and origins. In particular she explains that the earlier sheep would have had an undercoat that could have been felted, but they would have had much more kemp than modern sheep and this does not felt well. It is well-known from traditional and modern felting practices that fibres can be mixed and those fibres that do not felt can be incorporated with fibres that do felt well to make textured felts. Sometimes this compromises their integrity. In other cases, it makes an effective use of the available material. Just as with goat fibres where early traits would have led to the combing of goats releasing more of the undercoat and the fine material, so to the practice of combing sheep at early periods may have allowed the finer material to be separated out from the much of the coarser hair and kemp. The ability of wool to felt is something that could easily have been discovered by the circumstances in which it is used. Indeed the way in which it can be collected from bushes or scratching posts may have led to the beginning of the felting process, as might have close proximity to animals that cough up fur balls. (Bunn 2010: 15–16). Soft clumps of fur picked from the wild can be used as stuffing for shoes or as bedding and in these circumstances the moisture, warmth, and pressure are exactly those conditions that are most likely to cause felting. Despite the problems arising from the poor survival of woollen material because it is an animal protein, there is nonetheless every reason to suppose that woolly material would have been appreciated and used at very early times. The richest archaeological remains of early felt are those preserved in the deserts of Central Asia and the frozen tombs of Siberia. Some authors are happy to accept that there are Sumerian and Akkadian names for felt, but others are more sceptical and suggest that these terms require argument (Bunn 2010: 16; Breniquet 2010: 56). In addition, Desrosiers (2010) points out that the traditional idea of the origins of felt arising in nomadic Eurasian communities is linked with the material finds of large quantities of felt from 700 BC at Gordion near Ankara in Turkey, which shows urban people in clear contact with the steppes and Steinkeller's (1980) ideas of early Sumerian felt material cannot be substantiated.

Both Bunn (2010) and Breniquet (2010) mention the use of analogies between the styles of paintings at Çatal Höyük and actual felt carpets. Although these are interesting they cannot be regarded as proof of an association with felt. Breniquet (2010) is sceptical that the early Neolithic form of wool would have allowed felting to occur. Certainly, there is no clear evidence of felt from this period. However, as stated above, wool is unlikely to survive and where there is a tangled matt of fibres, these are going to be most problematic to identify during excavation. However, given the evidence of early goat and sheep fleeces and camelids and other wild animals (generalized from Robson and Ekarius 2011), the pattern amongst natural wool collection is that the fine undercoat in many species sheds naturally towards the end of the cold season and that material collected at this time may contain less of the hairy kemp. This seems to be a more generalized situation than is commonly allowed for and it could be a reason why the preparation of woolly fibres would have resulted in the discovery if not the use of fibres matted together.

Felt-making techniques

In the pre-felting stage, the wool is laid out and the design, if used, is created; water is added and the mass of laid out fluffy fibres is rolled. At this stage, the fibres are rolled backwards and forwards in order to gradually tangle the fibres together. As the fibres become more fully felted, the material must be taken out, rolled extensively, laid out, reworked, stretched, and rolled in other directions as the direction of the roll will cause the fibres to shrink more in that direction. In order to produce an even felt, it is necessary to pull and stretch the fibres and change direction occasionally. In the full felting stage, the fibres are integrated with one another in irreversible ways and it is at this stage that the material can also be pulled by pressure and further compacted. Felt-making can be undertaken in nomadic communities or within workshops. The former tend to be female based and the latter male based. The technique of bowing can be used to help fluff up the fibres and a few other tools, such as rods, can be useful for this. Approximate quantities can be given for the amount needed to produce an area of felt. Five or six sheep or goat fleeces can make a piece of felt 4m × 2m, which in turn would make one section of a tent wall. In this, as with other things, there are subtle changes in the *chaîne opératoire* and precisely who is doing which aspect of those phases varies according to ethnic traditions. In some cases, the material is tied up in a roll and pulled using ropes or even animals. In the early phases of the work, grass can be spread out on top to stop the new felt from sticking to itself when it is rolled up. In the later phases, the emphasis is on pulling the fibres as much as on moving them against one another. Pressure is often applied by individuals leaning their forearms on the fleece in rows. This is arduous and can last for hours. Plate 51.1 shows a felt yurt made up of sheets of felt over a wooden frame and a thick shepherds coat known as a *Kepenek*, traditionally with no sleeve opening. This is a fine example with well sorted wool fibres and stitched couch-work. Much rougher felts can be made which make more use of a range of fibres in colour and texture as shown in Plate 51.3 where the disordered structure can be seen. Rugs and yurt walls can have dyed fleece added to create colourful traditional patterns. Felting along with all other lines of material culture production has many ways in which the *chaîne opératoire* can be varied.

Animal substances: beeswax and glue

The role of bees in providing wax and honey has been studied by archaeologists (Brown 1995; Crane 1983: 240–46). Wax can also be burnt to give off light, form part of hafting substances and provide a waterproofing material. Although bees can be taken from the wild, they may increasingly have been managed and tended as hives and valued not just for their food content but also for their wax. In the UK today, beeswax is worth more pound for pound than the honey. Crane (1983) shows some of the images featuring honey-gathering from rock art in Spain and also the gold bee pendant from the Cretan site of Mallia on the Greek island of Crete. The latter is a Bronze Age site and the role of wax in the metal working process known as lost-wax (*cire perdue*) would have meant that Bronze Age societies employing these technique would have had strong reasons to value wax in its own right as a resource to be used carefully when working metal.

Animals can also provide glues by boiling up hooves and scraps of skin and horns. This process makes a strong glue that is soluble in water, so it is only effective in dry conditions. Other useful animal substances should not be forgotten. For Palaeolithic paintings, blood and eggs are useful as binding agents. Eggs can also be used to help emulsify fats and deliver them to hides more evenly in part of the final stages of the tanning process. Brains can also be used in tanning and serve much the same function as a readily dispersed fatty medium. Urine is discussed as a chemical used in tanning. This is usually taken from humans since it is a readily available natural product but it is another way in which animal substances become incorporated into items of material culture. Urine can be used as a fresh tanning agent but it can also be allowed to become stale when it turns into ammoniacal solution that also has bleaching properties. The latter will also act to degrease materials and of course though hides in general have their own place in this volume, the role of finely worked surfaces as a medium for recording important visual information reaches its apogee in the historical periods with the use of parchment as a writing surface. The role of flat fine portable surfaces also includes papyrus in Egypt. The role of hides in prehistory with respect to conveying information or notations is entirely unknown but could well have been taking place. There are suggestions that some of the grooves and patterns of marks on Palaeolithic antler, bone and ivory materials are tally sticks or notation systems or mnemonics of some kind but these may be the ones that we see whereas items of hide could have been filling something of the same purpose. While some of this is supposition, it is also about expanding how we might see the missing element compared to the known element.

Animals are also an important source of oils and fats. The former are liquid at room temperature and the latter are solid. Both act as waterproofing agents and as lubricants (Serpico and White 2000a, 2000b).

Conclusions

The range of ways in which animal materials can be processed into useful and expressive material culture items is nothing less than stunning. In many areas of the world people rely on animals to give them both their food and the majority of their material culture. This broad sweep reviews potential methods and processes across time and space and has inevitably not dwelt on any one instance and yet that is what needs to be done next. Archaeozoologists need to widen their horizons to think about animals not just as a source of meat but about the value of their skins and sinews. The purpose of this chapter was to provide sets of possibilities to assist people as excavators, academics and craft practitioners to think through the animal-based relationships of materiality for sites, regions and periods, and then to integrate these with other parts of the missing majority, the plant materiality. The material in this chapter provides a framework for addressing points 2, 3 and 5 below.

For any site, region and period the agenda is:

1. What animals are there in the environment?
2. What animals are being exploited and how might these be being used for material culture production as well as food in terms of the whole animal, hard animal materials, soft animal materials and substances?

3. How might animal-based material culture be contributing to the need for transport, structures, bedding, containers, clothing, cordage, food-getting tools, equipment and facilities, material culture producing tools, equipment and facilities?
4. How does this integrate with plant-based material culture and with inorganic material culture?
5. Are there selective or intensive exploitations of animals or evidence of symbolic relationships?

Notes

1 The functional analysis of bone and antler uses a variety of a magnifications but is now well established (Choyke 2007; Choyke and Bartosiewicz 2001; Choyke and Schibler 2007; Dart 1957; David 2007; d'Errico and Vanhaeren 2002; d'Errico et al 2001; 2003; Gates St-Pierre 2007; Gilmour 1997; Goss 1983; Gronnow 2009; Henshilwood et al 2001; Legrand and Sidéra 2007; LeMoine 2007; Louwe Koojimans et al 2001a, 2001b; Osipowicz 2007; Sharples 2000; Stanford et al 1981; Van Gijn 2007; von den Driesch and Peters 1995).
2 Research on shell tempered pottery has investigated aspects of provenance, thermal shock and toughness (see Blitz 1993; Bronitsky and Hamer 1986; Cogswell et al 1998; Feathers 1989; Stimmell et al 1982).
3 Hides and leather are described by characteristics, technologies and chemistries of tanning (Baillargeon 2005; Beyries et al 2001; Carrie and Woodroffe 1960; Covington 2009; Delaporte 2004, Edwards 1984; Frink 2005; Gilmore 2005; Grant 1978; Groenman-van Waateringe 1967; Habichte-mauche 2005; Hurcombe and Österman 2010; Issenman 1997; Lockhart-Smith and Elliott 1974; Mason 1889; Mould and Mould 2011; Pante and Blumenschine 2010; Peter 1980; Rahme 2003; Richards 2004; Rizopoulou-Egoumenidou 2009; Ryder 1969, 1970, 1983, 1984, 1987, 1991, 1992, 1999, 2000, 2005; Ryder and Gabra-Sanders 1987; Schlumbaum et al 2010; Schmidt and Pederson 2009; Schwebke and Krohn 1970; Spangenberg et al 2010; Spencer-Wood 2005; Tunón 2010; Weedman 2005; Wilder 1976; Young 1998).
4 See Bahnson (2005); Beattie et al (2000); Brandt and Weedman (1997); Crowell et al (2010); Delaporte (2004); Frank (1998); Harris (2010); Mould and Mould (2011); Procter (1922); Rahme (2003, 2006); Reed (1972); Richards (2004); Thomson (1998); Thompson and Jakes (2002); Tunón (2010).
5 Note this technique can be seen in Funesdalen Museum, Sweden, where stout sticks or staves no longer than an arm are inserted across the two edges of the skin near the head and tail by means of intermittent cut holes see also Delaporte (2004).
6 A sheep skin produced in this way was one of the lightest and fluffiest skins that I have made. Pernilla Salamonson also explained how to tan with oats as she had learned from a traditional Sámi tanner.
7 The information on fish skins was obtained from an excellent book by Lotta Rahme (2006) explaining all of the details of fish species and giving an overview of a wide range of information on how it was used as well as intense practical detail on the recipes and systems that work best for fish skin tanning. Aja Petterson was able to give strong practical information. In addition, practical experience with this material and a range of other fish were reported much earlier but with more experimental learning by Hurcombe and Williams (2002) and further experiments in recent years.
8 The sinew was described by Irene Dorra, a traditional Sámi of over 80 years of age who had learnt the technique as a young girl. She reported that her mother was adamant that only the backleg sinew should be used for making shoes as it was strongest. Other accounts suggest the backstrap sinew is best because it is longer and finer and is prepared by careful extraction from the tenderloin meat, scraping the fibres clean, and then finely

splitting them (Issenman 1997: 84). For use of backstrap sinew see Thompson (1994: 12–13). The demonstration by Irene Dorra and the set of made up threads both showed that the full length of the leg sinew was used but that the thread was kept to this short length – not more than 23cm. Thus the thread for sewing was immensely strong but would frequently require a new thread. In an environment where a damaged shoe can mean losing a foot to frostbite these small distinctions might be critical.

9 Sean Goddard drew my attention to the feathered headdress and Theresa Emmerich Kamper demonstrated the turkey feather process for me.

10 Ferrero (2013); Ruth Hatcher, feltmaker (pers. comm.) and personal experience.

11 Andersson Strand (2003) assessed these for Viking evidence but recent work has worked across other periods and on the general problems and issues (Andersson Strand and Nosch 2013; Hopkins 2013) and a number of experiments using different forms of spindles were also conducted at Lejre by Linda Mortensson and Anne Batser as part of this programme of work. Gromer also experimented at Lejre with banana-shaped loom weights as an aid to twined work among other forms of use. The wear on the weights is an important part of these assessments. See Gleba and Mannering (2012) for many examples.

12 There has been a resurgence of craft interest in recent years in the production of felt. New kinds of techniques and new possibilities have emerged (Belgrave 1995; Burkett 1979; Docherty and Emerson 2004; Vickrey 1987). There also the classic guides to sheep wool (Fournier and Fournier 1995; Robson and Ekarius 2011). These sources between them cover a broad range of fibres and their ability to felt or at least to mat up, as well as the techniques for using them. Key texts on the archaeological significance of felt are Bunn (2010) and Burkett (1979).

13 The treatment of wool and other fibres prior to spinning is part of an extensive literature from modern craft practitioners and more ancient traditions in particular communities and region. The style of spinning feeds into the style of weaving and both are based around the fibres available in terms of their length, elasticity, and fineness (Boeger 2008; Chadwick 1980; Field 2010; Fournier and Fournier 1995; Franquemont 2009; Kania 2010; Teal 1976). The role of fibres in producing the social 'costume' to express identities is also a subject of study (Bergerbrant 2010, Mannering 2008, Nosch 2008).

14 There are many books that cover weaving in specific areas or in the specific technical systems from either an archaeological study perspective, an ethnographic perspective, or as archaeological finds. Many such authors rely on practical knowledge shared with them by their community or by the craft community. Mannering et al (2012) offers a good introduction of a range of European evidence (see also Adovasio et al 1996; Alfaro Giner 1980, 1992; Andersson Strand 2008; Andersson Strand et al 2010; Bazzanella and Mayr 2009; Bazzanella et al 2003; Bender-Jørgensen 2007; Betancourt 2007; Bennett and Bighorse 1997; Burke 2007; Burningham 1998; Callanaupa Alvarez 2007; Coles et al 1999; Croes 1997, 2001; Drooker 1981; Frei 2010; Gabra-Sanders 1994; Gillow 2003; Gillis and Bert-Nosch 2007a, 2007b; Gleba and Mannering 2012; Gleba et al 2008; Hammarlund 2005; Harris 2007, 2010; Hoffman 1991; Hwang 2010; Innes 1977; Killen 2007; Ling Roth 1918; Maik 2004; Martial and Médard 2007; Militello 2007; Möller-Wiering 2007; Nordfors 1974; Rast-Eicher 1992; Rast-Eicher and Schweiz 1994; Rast-Eicher and Windler 2007; Rimkuté 2010; Robson and Ekarius 2011; Rœder Knudsen 2007; Rothe 1934; Sayer 1985; Schutten 1975; Soffer 2004; Soffer et al 2000; Taber and Anderson 1975; Tzachili 2007; Waetzoldt 2007; Warburg 1974; Whittaker and Kamp 1992; Wood 2003).

15 Scientific studies investigating microscopic characteristics or conservation issues have aided many of the interpretations and identifications (see British Leather Manufacturers' Research Association 1957; Chahine 2000; Cohen et al 2000; Evershed 2008; Firth 2007; Kooistra 2008; Larsen 2000; Wilson et al 2010).

4

INTIMATE RELATIONSHIPS BETWEEN PLANTS, ANIMALS AND PEOPLE

Introduction

There are major defining boundaries within archaeological perceptions of the human exploitation of the natural world. One of these is the longstanding biological dichotomy between plants and animals. Others include subsistence and material culture, and wild and farmed resources. These boundaries can be gradations, and people's belief systems, as well as their actions, will affect these conceptual distinctions. This chapter explores some of the conceptual relationships between people and the plants and animals they use, with particular respect to crafts, but also to food. If people want containers then it does not matter from a pragmatic point of view whether that problem is solved by making a basket from plant materials, or a hide vessel from animal skin. Likewise, if people need food, it does not matter whether it is wild or farmed, as the calories are the relevant parameter. However, it will matter that people's attitudes to wild versus farmed resources differ.

Up until this point much of the consideration of the raw materials for crafts has been focused on practical constraints, technological sequences and social and personal choices. The next step is to discuss the holistic plants-animal-people relationships in a freer way and at a larger scale. The examples indicate that people often use what is available and suits their technology, but this often means that in particular environments there are key resources. The relationship with these key species can be very close and intense. One way of thinking about wild versus farmed food systems is to see relationships with wild animals that are increasingly intense. Domesticated species originated in this way but not all intensive exploitations strategies are on an inevitable pathway to domestication (Rowley-Conwy 2001). There is not a goal in mind, nor is there a single trajectory. However, there are logical reasons why intense relationships would be built up with key animal and plant resources. The ensuing discussion explores some of these relationships and crosscuts the boundaries of plant and animal, wild and farmed. In thinking through these issues for the raw materials from plants and animals, food has not been neglected here, but the reverse is not often considered. In general, archaeological discussions of plants and animals as food often lack any consideration of their use as craft materials. It is the craft implications of the intimacy between plants animals and people that will be explored here.[1]

Craft-makers and landscape resources

Traditional exploitation patterns of craft resources often recount ownership of stands of plants, the management of these and some form of emotional connection to the material culture, its production and its raw materials (Hurcombe 2000a). As an example, sweet grass (*Muhlenbergia sericea*) has traditionally been used by the African American communities of South Carolina in the production of coil basketry (Dufault 2013). For these communitiues, this craft plant represents a longstanding and emotional connection with their African American roots. The basket-making families harvested the green sweet grass leaves from coastal dunes and allowed them to dry out for up to ten days. The slender leaves are a rich yellow-green and form the heart of coils sewn with palmetto leaves (*Sabal palmetto*). Other traditional materials such as pine needles and *Juncus roemerianus* have also been used as coil materials.

In recent years, this tradition has been threatened as the stands of wild sweet grass have deteriorated in quality and quantity because of modern urban development. Basket-makers were stopping manufacture as the journeys became too difficult, especially for elderly basket-makers. The stands had traditionally been harvested by particular families but these were now under threat as were the foundations of this important cultural tradition. Very unusually under these circumstances, Dufault (2013) relates his attempts over several decades to investigate ways of providing crop plants for farming or re-establishing more wild growing areas of sweet grass. Modern circumstances show how reliant basket-making traditions are on particular sets of stands of plants and growing conditions. His report shows that the plants growing in particular dishes and bowls in the sand dunes were favoured by the basket-makers and that the richest soil made grass grow luxuriantly but the plant then had too little strength for the basket-makers to use it effectively: the growing conditions were specific to providing the right qualities for the plant to be used for its craft purposes. This is one of the very few examples where a wild plant has in effect been assessed for its production as a crop plant to serve a *craft* purpose. In its natural habitat, the plant lives for many years. In the cultivated plots, it had a far shorter lifespan. Likewise, planting showed that mature plants took two or three years to establish themselves and be suitable for harvesting for basket-making. Harvest time is in the spring and practices such as combing the plants to remove the dead leaves may prolong the productive life of the plant. The suggested regime is to crop the leaves in January; even though they are growing slowly, they are still active and this method will allow light and air to the centre of the plant. Although this case study is a modern issue, it shows the problems of harvesting and relationships of traditions on a local scale and the suitability of plants for basketry purposes as entirely a product of their growing conditions at the local level rather than in the plant growing under any conditions. Management practices that enhance the desired qualities and maintain the plant would be favoured.

Although it is not often covered, the transmission of basketry knowledge in present-day traditional societies has been compromised both in terms of the quality and variety of products and also in the accessibility to raw material sources. Here, Dufault (2013) comments how his attempts to provide more sweet grass stands for the basket-makers in South Carolina run alongside those of Novellino (2009), who recorded Batak basket-weaving knowledge and the problems of cultural transmission faced by the women in this community in the Philippines. Although a paleoethno-botanical collection was being established alongside a record of the traditions, the fieldwork undertaken by him showed that some of these ideals were going to be highly problematic given the current state of basketry and the ability of the people holding the knowledge to convey complex issues to him even though he spent considerable time in the field. Similarly, the problems of maintaining cane brakes for the large cane (*Arundinaria gigantea*) in the Southeast of the United States and the ecological system that supports this important source of basketry material has been found to be complicated as traditional management patterns involving fire have ceased and stands have been compromised because of a lack of traditional management (Platt and Brantley 1997). They report that if fired every year the cane stands will die, but if fired about once every ten years the stands will be maintained because this kind of burning will clear competing woods. This may also have attracted bison since they prefer to graze on recently burnt grasslands. The historical accounts suggest that there was a burning regime of approximate intervals of seven to ten years and that this occurred in the autumn when the weather was dry. Many similar accounts of the harvest and management practices of 'wild' resources exist.

Tending the wild

Research into plant materials in ethnographic accounts and traditional craft practices inevitably led to ideas about how materials would be harvested, and in what ways they might be dealt with to maximize their use in the future. The harvest cycles of plants such as *Juncus* and *Scirpus* have husbandry aspects. These are not crops, but when they are harvested repeatedly by a basket-maker neither are they wild resources left to their own devices.[2] There is a developing sense that management cycles for plants go alongside strategies of exploitation, and that husbandry practices are an important part of human relationships, with plants as much as animals, and with particular stands of plants, or areas in the landscape, as key resources for craft purposes (Hurcombe 1998, 2000a, 2007a). Where the same area of landscape is repeatedly visited to harvest resources, these relationships can quickly lead to observations of cause and effect and an appreciation of how human intervention is affecting the resources. Humans would be able to learn what actions allowed good resources for the future to be maintained, but when the resource is only visited for several weeks a year specifically to harvest material this is clearly not farming nor even by many definitions husbandry.

It was not until 2007 that a phrase leapt out of a bookstand. Kat Anderson's book, *Tending the Wild* (2005) was an extensive documentation of Californian Native American knowledge and management of natural resources. Both the phrase and the data encapsulated my ideas about the integrated relationship of exploiting and caring for particular plants. In many ways this concept already exists within studies of wild animal species, where practices such as burning have long been appreciated as ways of opening up glades in the forest and attracting animals to come to newly burnt material, because of the salts released in the soil, and also because of the new young shoots which are regenerated from the burnt area.[3] Thus a sense of humans intervening in the landscape in order to attract animals, has been a longstanding feature of ideas about human and animal relationships, prior to – and alongside – more domesticated species. It is also seen as one of the ways in which species became domesticated and thus studied as part of the origins of agriculture.

What is well documented by management practices in harvesting plant raw materials is that careless harvesting will irrevocably damage, weaken, or kill the plant harvested. For marram grass, cutting too close the root stock will kill the plant. For *Juncus,* cutting every year will weaken the plant, so that the existing regrowth will get progressively less suitable for its intended purposes. Conversely, harvesting every couple of years benefits the plant by clearing out dead material and encouraging good conditions for strong regrowth. These kinds of issues are repeated throughout the plant kingdom. They culminate in the way in which basketry plants rely on fresh, flexible, disease-free, smooth, straight, young growth. That young growth can be provided by naturally fallen trees, trees damaged by animals or by fire, or trees felled by beavers. Thus the growth and regrowth patterns would have been part of the archaeology of attention and of sensory worldviews in the past, as discussed in Chapter 1. The places where natural fire or tree or branch damage had occurred would have been noticed by people as places where they could go and find resources that suited their purposes. This close attention could over time have led to and been reinforced by deliberate interventions by people to recreate those same conditions. Some trees regenerate by suckers from the roots (for example, cherry) and some trees regenerate by coppice (for example, hazel). In these ways the management of food resources and craft resources would have incorporated in people's mindsets the cause and effect of natural and human interventions in their growth patterns. In animals this would be seen as manipulating animal populations to human advantage. In plants the same is true. The phrase 'tending the wild' encapsulates this idea that the wild resources are being exploited and husbanded for human benefit.

As an example Anderson (2005: 196–99) describes the cultivation of sedge beds. This was to obtain rhizomes used by the Pomo (California) and other tribes for a wide range of burden baskets, cooking baskets and seed beaters. The rhizomes are known as 'white root' and are soft, supple, very strong and were able to be split. Thus *Carex barbarae* roots were one of the chosen sedge types for use in basketry, and were preferentially obtained from soft silty soils where the roots grew straight. In order to obtain this kind of material, the plants were cultivated. Dead branches and debris were removed from around the plant, the soil around was carefully picked over to

PLATE 1 Variety of objects made from tree materials including spear throwers, hafted points, arrows, knives, containers, bowls, spoons, cups, mask, shoes, comb, mallet, flint-knapper's soft hammer and chest press for pressure flaking, Y stick as distaff for spinning, or frame for fingerweaving, shuttle, and bentwood collar for goat bell.
Source: Hurcombe.

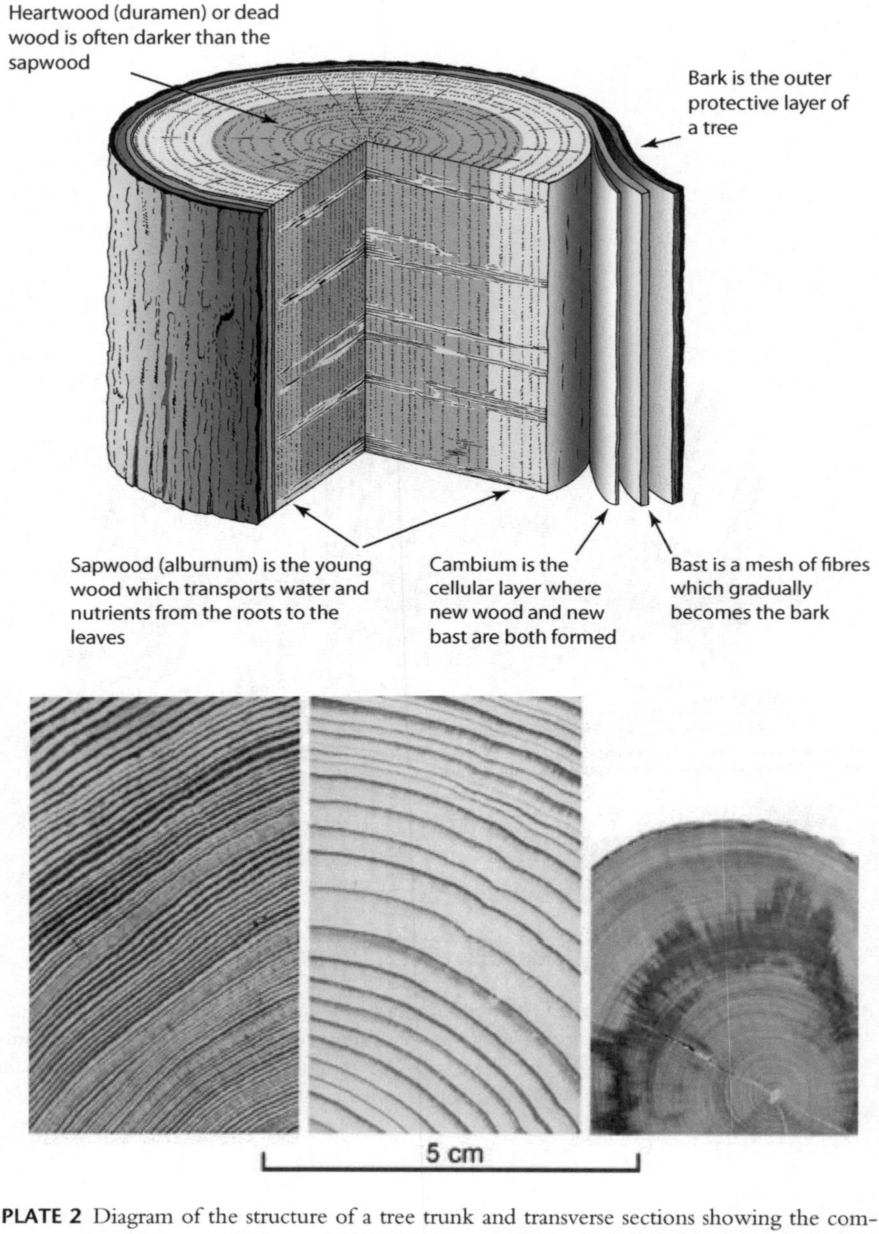

Heartwood (duramen) or dead wood is often darker than the sapwood

Bark is the outer protective layer of a tree

Sapwood (alburnum) is the young wood which transports water and nutrients from the roots to the leaves

Cambium is the cellular layer where new wood and new bast are both formed

Bast is a mesh of fibres which gradually becomes the bark

5 cm

PLATE 2 Diagram of the structure of a tree trunk and transverse sections showing the comparative growth rings of; left, slow grown Baltic pine; middle, commercial pine; right, boxwood (*Buxus*).
Source: Hurcombe.

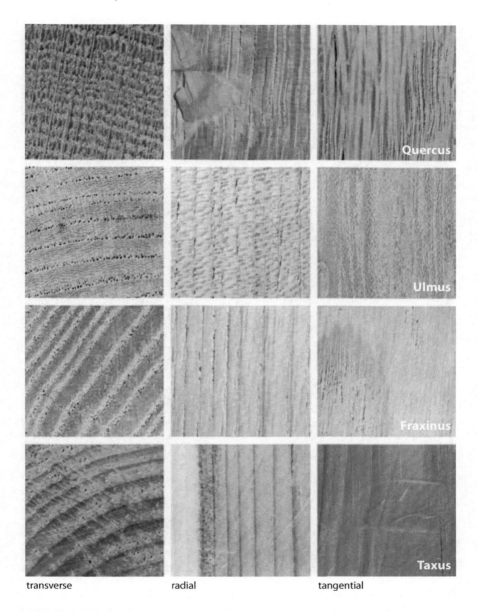

transverse   radial   tangential

PLATE 3 Wood grain macroscopic characteristics.
Source: Hurcombe.

PLATE 4 Working wood: 1. antler wedges splitting off wood; 2. shaving wood surface; 3. Sequence for carving a spoon from a billet; 4. Bow drill; 5. replica Mesolithic Tybrind Vig paddle, charred decoration; 6. replica whisk, Terramare; 7. scraping charred wood away to hollow out a logboat.

Source: Hurcombe.

PLATE 5 Sewn plank Bronze Age boat: 1. the finished boat, 2. the keel made from two half trunks with cleats carved out, 3. a joint showing the moss caulking and lath placement, 4. Yew withy stitch holding hewn planks together.

Source: Hurcombe.

PLATE 6 Structures of wood, bark, reed and hide: 1. bark covering on simple pole frame-work; 2. hide covering on bent pole frame; 3. Cedar plank houses and totem poles; 4. reed mats over bent pole frame; 5. reed thatch over wooden frame with infilled walls of stacked reed, wattle and a plank door; 6. reed thatch and pole framework of a stilt house; 7. a northern row house with walls, floors and roof of poles and birch bark and moss layers on the roof.

Source: Hurcombe.

PLATE 7 Making bark cloth: 1. removing the bark from the trunk; 2. wooden mallets for beating; 3. and 4. the finished bark cloth showing the fibres.
Source: Hurcombe.

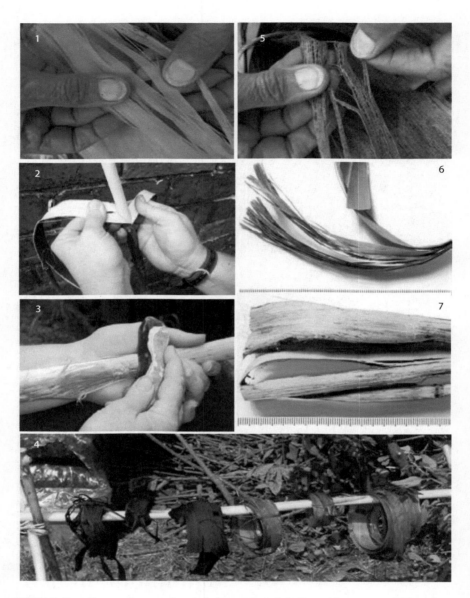

PLATE 8 Bast fibres and processing techniques: 1. and 5. fine and coarse retted lime bast; 2. peeling bast; 3. scraping off outer bark; 4. willow and hazel bast after boiling with and without woodash; 6. basswood bast; 7. cottonwood bast.

Source: Hurcombe.

PLATE 9 Birch bark usage: woven open bowl (detail shows birch root stitching), backpack and shoes, closed containers, roofing and protective material.
Source: Hurcombe.

PLATE 10 Bast fibre usage: as 1. replica Neolithic willow knotted net, Kierikki, Finland; 2. modern cedar bark twined and woven container; 3. bark painted armband.
Source: Hurcombe, except 3. John Whittaker.

PLATE 11 Bast fibre clothing and sheaths from circum-Alpine prehistory: 1. limebast twined cape based on the finds with Ötzi; 2. Ötzi's knife and limebast sheath (left) with elmbast sheath (right); 3. Ötzi's limebast inner shoe structure; 4. limebast sandal from St Blaise Neuenburger, replicas by Anne Reichert, 5. archaeological fragments of fine weft twining, Robenhausen.
Source: Hurcombe.

PLATE 12 Useful plants for raw materials: flax (*Linum*), willow (*Salix*) as withies and bast roll,
dock (*Rumex*), reed (*Phragmites*), bulrush (*Scirpus lacustris*), soft rush (*Juncus*) and sedge
(*Carex*) as well as moss (*Polytricum commune*), birch (*Betula*) roots and lime bast.
Source: Hurcombe.

PLATE 13 A range of plants used around the world: 1. Mediterranean tall reed (*Arundo donax*); 2. New Zealand flax (*Phormium tenax*); 3. bamboo; 4. fibres extracted from *Phormium* with a shell scraper; 5. hair moss (*Polytricum commune*); 6. hair moss rope, 7. Allo, giant nettle, Nepal (*Girardinia diversifolia*).

Source: Hurcombe.

PLATE 14 Wetland plants and processing: 1. *Iris pseudocorus* and *Typha latifolia*; 2. Sedges used as shoe hay; 3. Detail of Iris stems showing midrib; 4. harvesting rush (*Scirpus lacustris*) by coracle; 5. Harvesting soft rush (*Juncus effusus*); 6. Scirpus and Juncus showing size and internal structures.

Source: Hurcombe.

PLATE 15 Different ways of processing one plant, *Juncus effusus*: 1. Alternate twinings of *Juncus* with the pith removed; 2. Simple twining of shredded *Juncus*; 3. Removing the pith from *Juncus* with a wooden tool; 4. Soaking *Juncus*, bast fibres and other plants in an old logboat.
Source: Hurcombe.

PLATE 16 Useful plant materials: 1. straw made into the centre of an Irish St Brigid's cross; 2. plaited straw coil; 3. papyrus; 4. gourds, including a base decorated with wax and beads; 5. sweetgrass plaited and coiled *Muhlenbergia sericea*; 6. birch roots.
Source: Hurcombe.

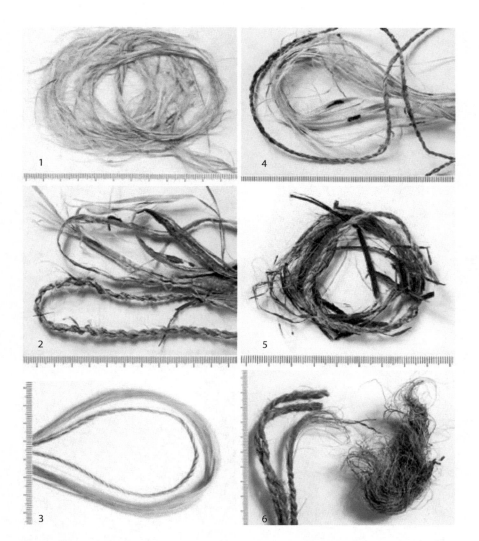

PLATE 17 Useful plant fibres: 1. Nettle fibres (*Uritica dioica*); 2. big sagebrush (*Artemesia tridentata*); 3. yucca fibres and plyed; 4. Indian hemp, dogbane (*Apocynum cannabium*); 5. milkweed (*Asclepias syriaca*); 6. coir.
Source: Hurcombe.

PLATE 18 Looping and netting: top traditional Australian aboriginal bag in looped cord, bottom traditional knotted bag made from 'allo', Nepal.
Source: Hurcombe.

PLATE 19 Basketry technologies: 1. plain/chequer weave; 2. coiled basket, core exposed, bundle start; 3. twisted willow handle; 4. twill weave; 5. coil basket, star start; 6. stick basket; 7. twined (paired) weave with different coloured weavers (a, b) and change in direction (c) creating patterns; 8. straw 'three-strand plait' worked in three dimensions; 9. fitching around (a) wood splint, (b) willow stakes and (c) split hazel.

Source: Hurcombe.

PLATE 20A Coiled and woven basketry techniques: a variety of forms and materials all worked in the coil technique.
Source: Hurcombe.

PLATE 20B Coiled and woven basketry techniques: a variety of forms and materials worked by interweaving the elements.
Source: Hurcombe.

PLATE 21A Willow basketry styles: fishtraps, containers, hat.
Source: Hurcombe.

PLATE 21B Cane basketry styles: fishtraps, containers, hat.
Source: Hurcombe.

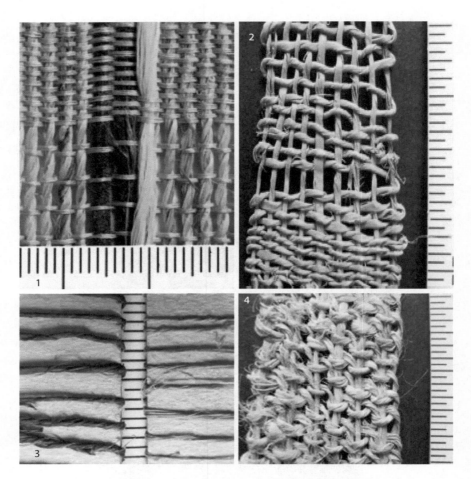

PLATE 22 Patterns from weaves, textures and tonal contrasts: ramie (*Boehmeria nivea*), showing varied warp of loosely twisted fibres, half stem with bark on, clean fibres with
weft tabby-woven; 2. Willow bast finely processed with a flint tool and woven in
balanced and weft faced tabby; 3. nettle (*Urtica dioica*), tannin dyed and undyed;
4. processed with a flint tool and worked in a looping-around-the-core technique.
Source: Hurcombe.

PLATE 23 Looping-around-the-core technology and materials: 1. a fine basketry style fragment of willow bast from Neolithic Schipluiden, Holland; 2. a modern sample made from bast processed with flint tools; 3. a replica sample of retted lime bast in Tybrind Vig style technique; 4. the same technique worked in Juncus with pith removed.

Source: Hurcombe.

PLATE 24 Plant fibre crops of cotton, flax and hemp: 1. cotton bolls drying, Uzbekistan; 2. the cotton seed head; 3. retted and unretted flax stem broken to reveal fine fibres and epidermis; 4. base of hemp plant to show some of the fibres and the root.
Source: Hurcombe.

PLATE 25 Processing plant fibres for textiles: 1. Uzbek weaver, spinning cotton with the fibre supply wrapped around her wrist; 2. flax fibres, with those on the right still containing remnants of pith; 3. removing flax seed heads.
Source: Hurcombe.

PLATE 26 Processing nettle fibres: 1. nettles (*Urtica dioica*); 2. A bundle of stripped nettle fibres and epidermis; 3. nettle fibres and epidermis twisted into cordage (right), and twisted after removing the epidermis (left); 4. scraping the epidermis off the stem, splitting the stem, then peeling the fibres away from the pith to give a bundle of fibres from one nettle plant.
Source: Hurcombe.

PLATE 27 Processing nettles for textiles: 1. spinning manually processed nettle fibre; 2. simple
bentwood weaving frame; 3. hedgehog skin used as comb; 4. manually processed
fibres spun in different techniques; 5. nettle cloth retted and finely processed;
6. nettle cloth, manually processed and spun fibres.

Source: Hurcombe with thanks to Anne Batser.

PLATE 28 Resin, tar and wax: 1. resin from (a) pine, (b) wild plum, (c) pine tar, (d) beeswax and (e) bitumen; 2. flake with fibre and pitch haft; 3. resin oozing from a tree; 4. making pine tar using two pots, one buried to collect the tar and the other with the resinous material around which a fire is burnt.

Source: Hurcombe.

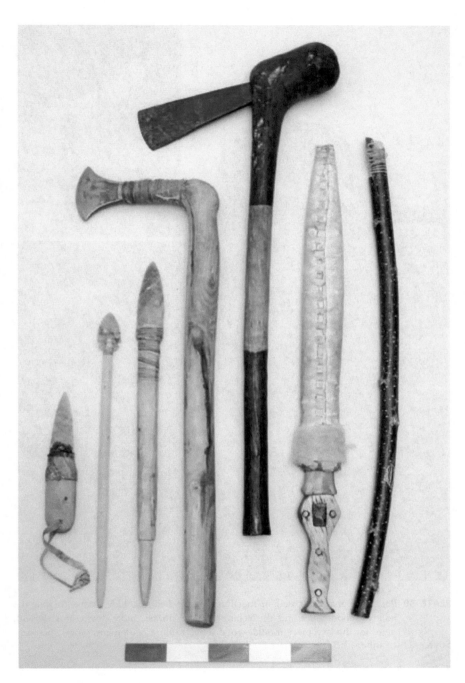

PLATE 29 Hafts and sheaths.
Source: Hurcombe.

PLATE 30 Perishable materials used in metallurgy: hide bellows, hide sleeve to join the
hollow wood tubes and the ceramic tuyere nozzle, hide gloves (not shown),
straps for the two piece mould, wood tongs and fire equipment, wood charcoal.
Source: Hurcombe.

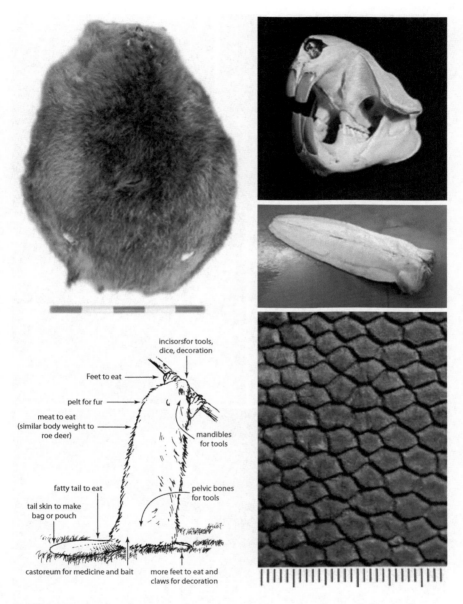

PLATE 31 Food and craft resources from a beaver: skin, teeth, tail and tail skin detail.
Source: Hurcombe incorporating data from Coles and Rouillard.

PLATE 32 Animals for fur, hides, antlers, and horns: 1. Wapiti, American elk, Red deer (*Cervus canadensis*) with antler in velvet; 2. aurochs; 3. llamas; 4. brown bear (*Ursus arctos*); 5. pronghorn antelope; 6. mountain goat.

Source: Hurcombe, except 1. Theresa Emmerich Kamper; 4. Tom Monrad Hansen; 5. and 6. Wyoming Game and Fish Department.

PLATE 33 Animals for fur, hides, antlers, and horns (cont.): 7. wild boar piglet; 8. bison; 9. Soay sheep; 10. bighorn sheep; 11. lynx; 12. musk ox.
Source: Hurcombe, except 8. and 10. Theresa Emmerich Kamper; 11. Tom Monrad Hansen.

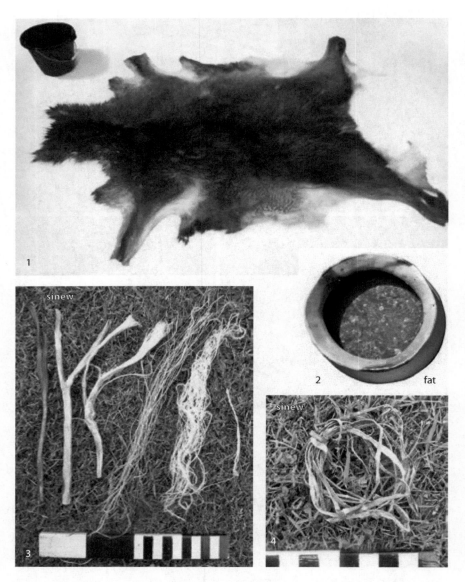

PLATE 34 The raw materials available from one European red deer (*Cervus elaphus*).
Source: Hurcombe.

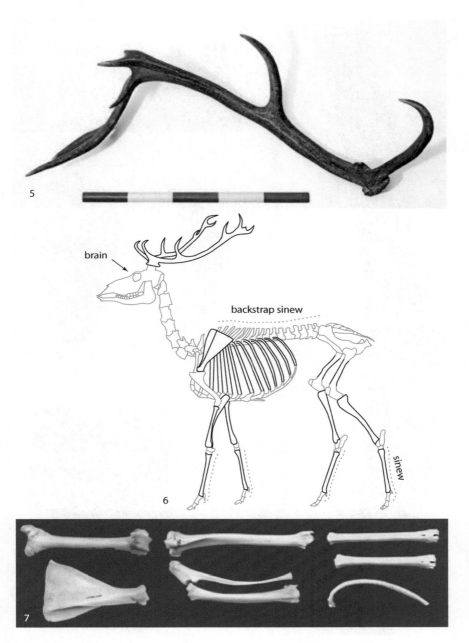

brain

backstrap sinew

sinew

5

6

7

PLATE 35 The raw materials available from one European red deer (*Cervus elaphus*) (cont.). Source: Hurcombe.

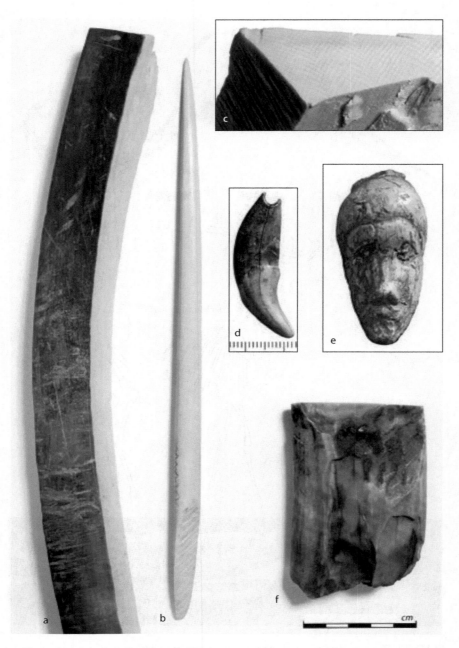

PLATE 36 Ivory and teeth: (a) curved piece of mammoth ivory; (b) spearhead; (c) polished surface showing distinctive patterns, and sawn and flaked surfaces; (d) tooth pendant, Iron Age; (e) Palaeolithic Dolní Věstonice; (f) fragments of flaked herbivore tooth.
Source: Hurcombe except e, Moravské Museum Brno.

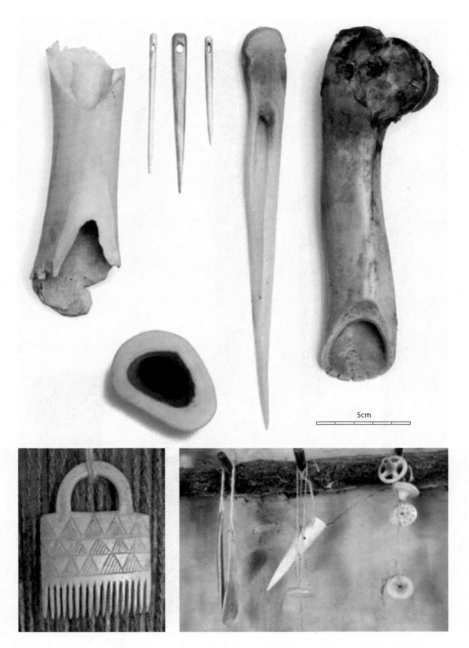

PLATE 37 Bone raw materials and artefacts: Shafts of bone with fractured ends and cross section to show thickness, needles, awl and defleshing tool, bone weaving comb, bone pin heads and point.

Source: Hurcombe.

PLATE 38 Bone awls from Wallace ruins showing a variety of lengths and point types, some
with wear traces.
Source: Bruce Bradley.

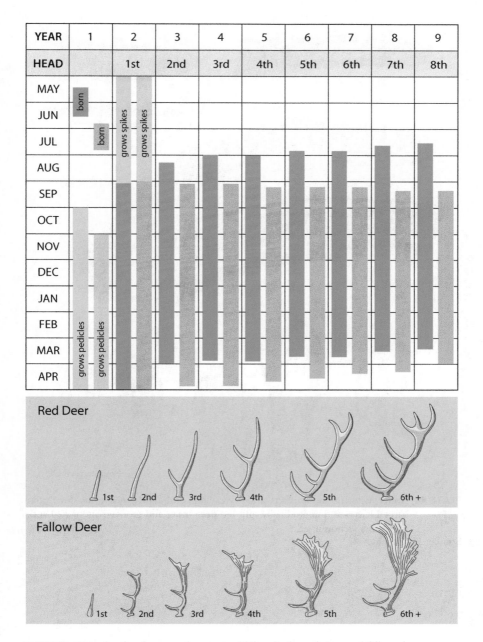

PLATE 39 Growth of antler over the year and lifecycle for red deer and fallow deer. Source: Hurcombe.

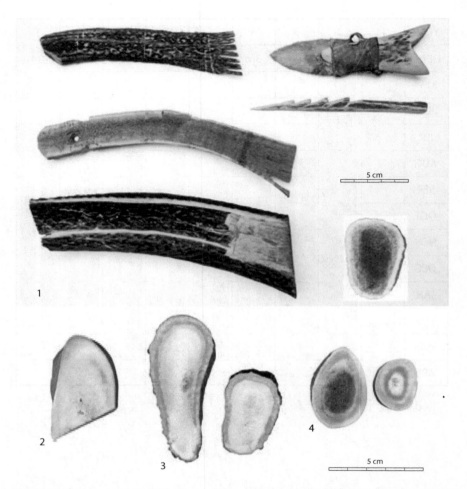

PLATE 40 Antler materials and artefacts: antler weaving comb, antler sleeve for stone point, barbed harpoon, longitudinally split red deer antler and grooved and flaked antler with cross section inset.

Source: Hurcombe.

PLATE 41 Horn materials and artefacts: horn comb, spoon and flexible needles, with curved horn vessel, and longitudinally split and solid cows horn (paler), longitudinally split and cross section of buffalo horn (darker) showing layered internal structure.
Source: Hurcombe.

PLATE 42 Feathers: top, detail of a Hawaiian headdress showing feathers worked into cordage base; middle, splitting turkey feathers prior to inserting them into cords for garments and ceremonial items; bottom, fletched arrow bound with sinew.
Source: Hurcombe.

PLATE 43 Shells as artefacts and materials: mask decorated with cowrie shells, detail, shells as decorative and colourful materials.
Source: Hurcombe.

PLATE 44 Hide processing: 1. detail of Eurasian elk (*Alces alces*) hide showing the different layers of epidermis, grain and corium; 2. frame to dry and work young *Alces alces* hide; 3. reindeer skins tacked to a barn to dry; 4. cleaning the flesh side of a cow hide using a stone scraper, scraping off the grain of an ostrich skin with a bone tool, stretching brain-tanned large hide as part of the softening process, smoking large hides sewn together to make a smoke tent.

Source: Hurcombe.

PLATE 45A Hides and furs: rolled hides and furs showing variations in thickness and drape.
Source: Hurcombe.

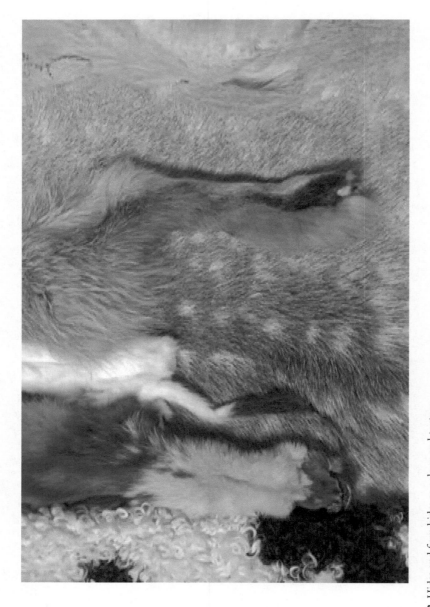

PLATE 45B Hides and furs: hides as colour and texture.
Source: Hurcombe.

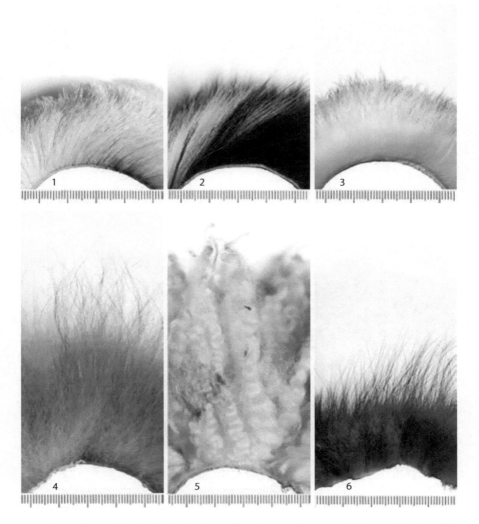

PLATE 46 Hair and fur: 1. deer hair; 2. goat hair showing longer and shorter hairs; 3. rabbit fur; 4. fox fur, showing longer guard hairs and fine underfur; 5. sheep wool modern breed, showing crimp (waviness) and long fine wool fibres; 6. pine marten showing underfur and guard hairs.

Source: Hurcombe.

PLATE 47A Hide tanning and processing effects: thickness of (a) bison tan bark tan grain on, compared to (b) bison wet scrape to take grain off, brain tan and smoke tan; (c) *Alces alces* grain on bark tan compared to (d) wet scrape grain off and brain tan, smoke tan. Left, grain side, right, flesh side. Source: Hurcombe.

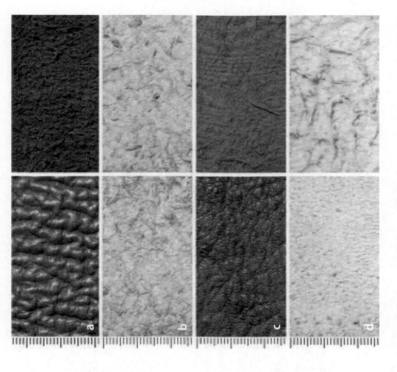

PLATE 47B Hide tanning and processing effects: thickness of (a) bison hide bark tan grain on, compared to (b) bison wet scrape to take grain off, brain tan and smoke tan; (c) *Alces alces* grain on bark tan compared to (d) wet scrape grain off and brain tan, smoke tan. Left, grain side, right, flesh side.

Source: Hurcombe.

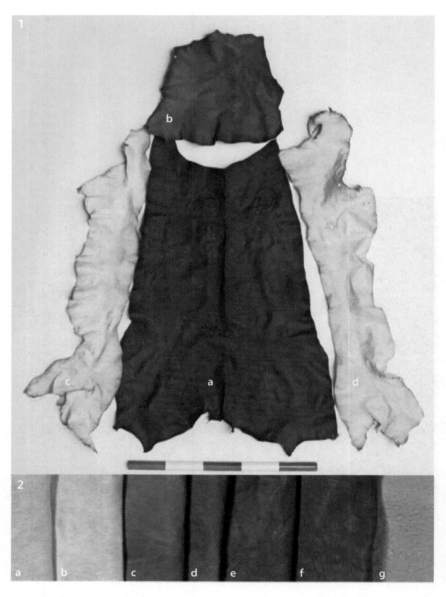

PLATE 48 Hide tanning treatments as colour: 1. a single reindeer hide, hair off, grain on divided into four, (a) willow bark tan and added fat, (b) willow bark tan with no fat, (c) brain tan, (d) urine tan; 2. (a) urine tan, (b) brain tan, (c) willow tan no fat, (d) willow and rowan tan, fat added, (e) willow tan, fat added, (f) spruce tan, fat added, (g) brain tan then smoked.

Source: Hurcombe.

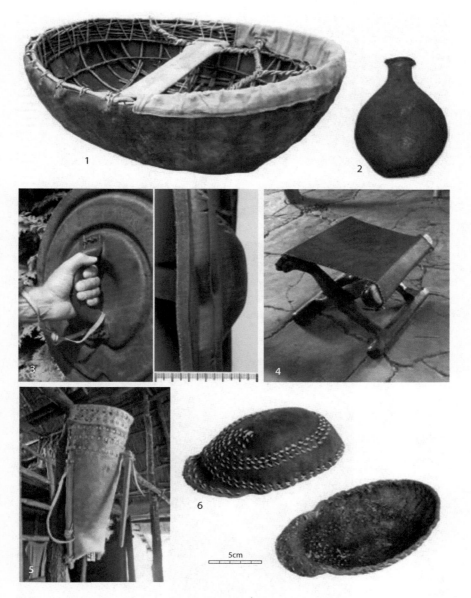

PLATE 49 Hide artefacts: coracle made by Clive Ó Gibne, goat bladder bottle, shield of cow hide, detail of edge, replica folding stool, Hallstatt style backpack, hide scoop.
Source: Hurcombe.

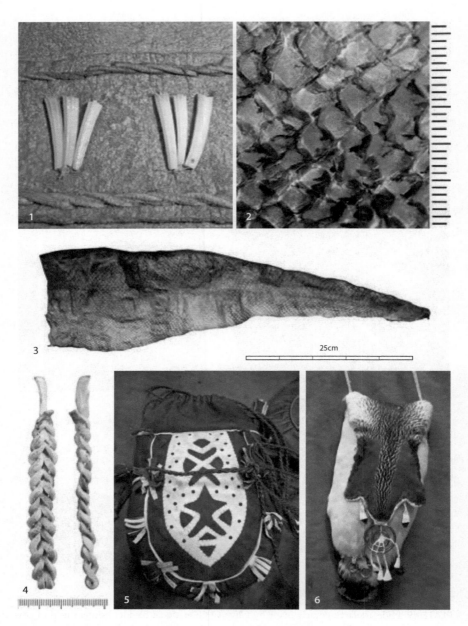

PLATE 50 Decorative effects in hide work: 1. *Dentalium* shell decoration; 2. salmon skin texture detail and 3. whole skin; 4. interwoven rawhide plait; 5. Sámi appliquéd fat hide-work over bark-tan; 6. loon skin bag used for shaman's items.
Source: Hurcombe.

25cm

PLATE 51 Felt work: 1. yurt with wood frame with felt wall; 2. Turkish Kepenek, traditional shepherd's cloak with no sleeve opening, detail shows fine couchwork; 3. felt made from multicoloured texcel alpine sheep showing the disordered fibres densely matted by the felting process.

Source: Hurcombe.

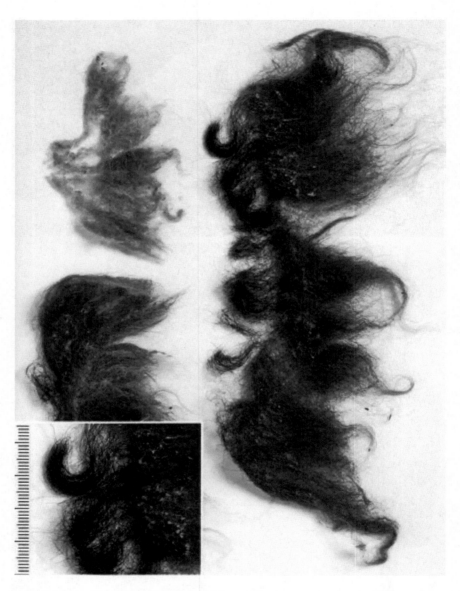

PLATE 52 Soay sheep's wool: naturally shed wool showing range of colours and wool fibre
lengths in the locks with a distinct short dark layer in places. Detail shows a layer
of skin cells and the short coarse fibres below the better locks of the rooed layer.
Source: Hurcombe.

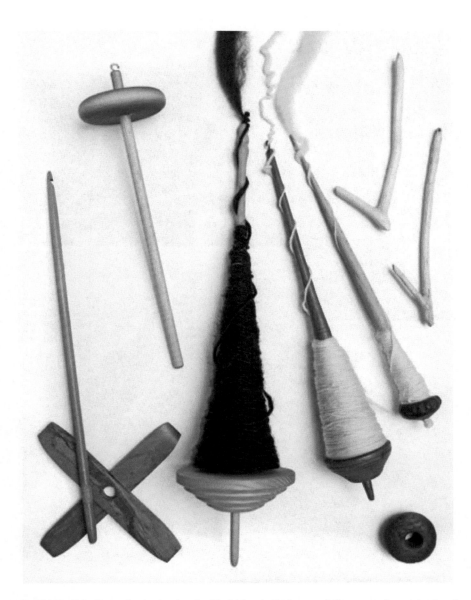

PLATE 53 Spindles and spinning hooks: Turkish spindle bottom left, range of top whorl and bottom whorl spindles with wooden and ceramic whorls and two spinning hooks. Source: Hurcombe.

PLATE 54 Uzbek ground loom: the long loom, heavy weaving sword and heddle suspension system of bent wood frame supporting heddle stick; all loom elements are minimally worked and shaped except weaving sword.
Source: Hurcombe.

PLATE 55 Looms: warp weighted loom showing the shed stick in the notch pulling out one set of threads, inset shows the shed stick against the frame allowing the other set of threads to reverse places, bentwood frame for sprang, back strap loom with belt around waist and tensioned by the body, tablet weaving.
Source: Hurcombe.

PLATE 56 Woollen textiles: 1. Iranian baby's blanket, 2. tablet woven warp faced braid; 3. ply split braiding, camel hair from Pakistan; 4. Wool tabby with two spin directions making a close weave; 5. twill weave with thicker threads making a textured pattern; 6. detail of check two tone weave pattern; 7. nalbinden (needle looping).

Source: Hurcombe.

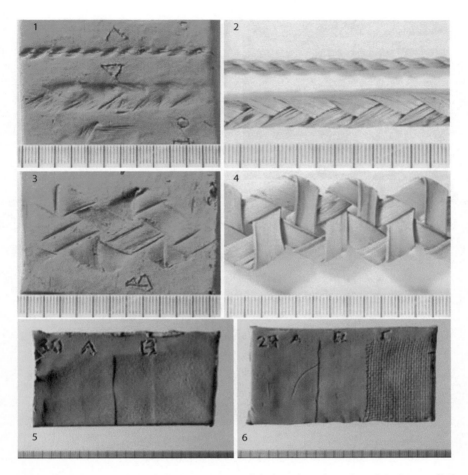

PLATE 57 Experimental fired clay impressions of cloth and cordage: 1. and 2. *Scirpus* plied cord and plait; 3. and 4. New Zealand Flax hexagonal plait; 5. felt and hide impressions; 6. linen cloth impressions.

Source: Hurcombe.

PLATE 58 Archaeological impressions of basketry and cordage: 1. Barnhouse Orkney, Neolithic; 2. Knackyboy, Scilly Isles, Bronze Age; 3. Upton Pyne, Devon. Source: Hurcombe.

PLATE 59 Archaeological finds from Etton, Neolithic causewayed enclosure: 1. and 2. Ebsfleet
bowl with bird bone impressions, shell and flint temper; 3. large shell tempered
rim sherd; 4. antler comb; 5. detail of twisted flax fibres; 6. Mildenhall bowl with
shell temper.
Source: Hurcombe.

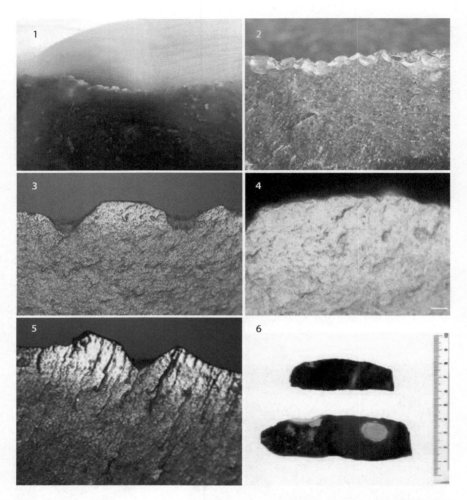

PLATE 60 Usewear on serrated edge flint tools: 1. macroscopic gloss on serration; 2. fine serrations; 3. usewear traces at 50x, and 4. 200x; 5. gloss on the tips; 6. serrated tools.

Source: Hurcombe.

remove loose stones and to keep the soil uniform. Thus the cultivated beds of sedge were able to give much better raw materials for basketry. The slight picking over of the soil and the management were advantageous to the plant as practices enabled individual plants to be thin enough on the ground not to become a tangled mat with poor resources for any one plant. Once a bed had been harvested it was left for several years before a repeat harvest. Thus there was not only a husbandry harvest period, there was also a management strategy over a cycle of several years. The advantages of using managed sedge beds can be understood because of the numbers needed for one item: a burden basket could take more than 1,000 rhizomes (Anderson 2005: 196). This phenomenal amount of plant material needed for cultural items also exists in other basketry materials. For example, a special basket took three thousand flower stalks from deergrass (*Muhlenbergia rigens*). Both harvesting and burning management practices for deergrass are reported to allow more light to the ground and to allow the plant to be more vigorous, with more young growth. Tules (also known as *Scirpus* or *Schoenoplectus*, various species) were also important basketry plants, where the stems were used, and in some species also the brown roots, which could be used for coloured pattern details. Clearing out dead material and cutting was beneficial to the plant and there were also stands that were managed by fire.

The management practices described did not stop with these sorts of smaller plants: they also included tree management. Here too the numbers are very important. For example, a winnowing basket, using shrub material, would take ten shrubs if they were unmanaged, but one shrub from a managed bush. For particular species and basketry types, such as the coiled cooking basket, the numbers were even greater: 150 shrubs if unmanaged plants were used, or six shrubs if managed plants were used (Anderson 2005: 216). The numbers of stalks and plants needed for cordage can likewise be phenomenal. Indian hemp and milkweed were both important for this, and for example, a large net would require 2,135m of string, which in turn took 35,000 plant stalks (Anderson 2005: 231). Plants with tall straight stems and no lateral branches would be more likely to occur after burns in the area. Throughout Anderson's groundbreaking account of Californian Native American management practices there is a detailed knowledge of the resources available and an imperative to manage those resources – and tend the wild – in order to obtain the best craft materials as well as find suitable food materials.

The methods of caring for the land included burning, practiced annually or in longer cycles, aiding irrigation by artificial channels, pruning and coppicing practices, sowing and casting seeds in recently burned areas, disturbing the ground to collect some species and promote new growth, and even transplanting, and weeding, as well as clearing out dead growth by hand and, if necessary, grubbing out young trees that were growing in too close competition to desired trees (Anderson 2005: 134–47). Clearing away dead material and renewing growth would also greatly reduce the pathogens and fungi that would otherwise attack both food and craft material crops. The knowledge of conditions of the plants for particular craft purposes in the annual cycle, and also according to local growing traditions, is well documented in many cultures. The detail provided by Anderson for the

Californian examples is indicative of the kind of local knowledge hunter-gatherers would have had.

Specific growing conditions were noticed (Anderson 2005: 53). The same kind of plant was differentiated and given different names according to where it was growing. White root (*Carex barbarae*) was valued for fine work if it was growing in boggy ground, but was better harvested when growing beside streams and banks if it were to be used for large coarse baskets and, where great strength was needed, it was collected from stands growing in gravels, where the roots and rhizomes were much stronger. The Karuk gathered pine roots after the tree had bloomed because the roots were tougher at this time. Hupa weavers preferred to gather a fern for making black colours (*Adiantum aleuticum*) at high altitudes because it gave better colour. The same people considered that the best yew (*Taxus brevifolia*) was gathered from stands growing alongside creek beds, because it grew straighter there. The Hupa gathered *Iris macrosiophon* for cordage, but did so preferentially from plants growing under oaks, not pines. This knowledge of the subtle differences in the use of plants according to their growing conditions is by no means surprising where the raw materials are produced locally and for important needs. Furthermore these were fitted into the annual cycle alongside the collection of other resources. The same principles also applied to animals. Rabbits were hunted when their fur was thickest, in the autumn, which was also when deer were in their best condition both foodwise and as a hide. Other annual round activities included harvesting materials for basketry in spring or autumn, when the sap was down, so the harvesting would not unduly affect the plant. There were important cues in the environment that would tell when certain resources were coming into season, by using other plants blooming, flowering or producing seed at about the same time.

The examples indicated here and elsewhere in this book, show how richly the knowledge of plants may have affected the way in which prehistoric peoples were attuned to their environment and its craft potential, as much as its food potential. Just as Mesolithic fire practices are considered as beneficial for hunting and for food production, so too we should think of such practices benefitting some of the plant and animal craft material needs for prehistoric peoples. There is likely to be far more tending and husbanding of wild material for crafts than we at present allow for. Furthermore this close intimacy between plants, animals and humans clearly affects the character of local stands of plants and associated animals. Where such practices are widespread and longstanding, they are also affecting the character of local and regional environments. At this level people are not just situating craft practices within a natural setting but affecting the landscape by creating taskscapes as well. Plants, animals and human actions are jointly making the ecosystem and giving places personalities and characteristics.

Animacy and agency

The concept of agency introduced in Chapter 1 has been applied to objects but it also applies to living things. Animals as totems have important meanings: they have agency as symbols because humans attribute agency to them. Animals can serve as metaphors, symbols and mythological beings, with many examples available from the ethnographic literature. In South America in particular, there are many ways of looking at the jaguar and other animals as totems. These have been explained as intensely ritual and as forming symbolic relationships with particular species. South American examples also benefit from iconography and texts relating to the belief systems: the role of the Puma skins and some other beasts to stand in for good or evil mythological beings connecting with other worlds, and totem spirits as both guides and powerful entities are well-known in ethnographic literature (Urton 1985; Viveiros de Castro 1992).[4]

These sorts of relationships with animals are also present in the way that Russell (2012) has dealt with the social aspects of animal behaviour as 'social zooarchaeology'. This is a welcome development but there is a greater depth of materiality to be teased from this theme of investigation. Sometimes these metaphors are dealt with in ways that involve the use of teeth, feathers or skins, or other ways in which the animal's materiality is used to invoke the whole animal. North American examples include the importance placed on eagle feathers and the role of big horn sheep in Crow culture. Humans relate to behavioural and physical characteristics, and the materiality of the animal can signify the social agency. For example, in early Neolithic sites such as Çatal Höyük in Turkey there are symbolic representations of horns. These can also be found in Central Asian sites as rams' horns. Thus the other significant product to come from a close relationship with animals may well be the ability to use this translucent, usefully shaped material that is easily malleable with hot water – the closest modern material equivalent would be a mouldable plastic. To people who were intimately connected with animals as they lived in the landscape, and as some of them were hunted for food and materials, the connection between the material from the animal and the animal itself would have been far more intense. There would be an strong knowledge of the animal species, how it moved about the landscape across the seasons and its habits for feeding, mating and rearing its young as well as the social grouping of the species and the relationship it had with other species of plants and animals. In some cases the relationship would be to a particular animal and place perhaps as observed or as a hunting event. The materiality of animals would have been part of this detailed knowledge and an aspect of the capture or death of the animal as a generic individual such as 'three-year-old male deer killed in full antler' or specifically 'the antlered stag stalked at dawn with visiting kin celebrating the birth of a child'. Animals would be individuals with agency and an association with particular or generic events. The material remains of animals have potency and there are archaeological examples of special social relationships. The most famous example in the Mesolithic is the modified red deer antlers from Star Carr. However, when looking for the origins of this kind of behaviour, there is one period where the relationship between animals and humans stands out as a fully developed rich aspect of their material culture – the Palaeolithic art of Europe, known from caves and objects.

Nowhere is there a more obvious connection between animals and humans at a symbolic and ideological level than in the set of evidence known colloquially as Ice

Age art. A recent exhibition at the British Museum brought together a stunning collection of material that showed the capacity of the human mind to deal with conceptual issues and to link those issues very firmly to people and animals. There is skilled execution, but also a conceptual mind at work in the cave paintings and the engraved drawings of the area that covers Northern Italy, Southern France and Southwest Germany. Further east there are also small sculptures of animals: 'the animals depicted are not a true reflection of the natural world or even human hunting patterns, but rather a selection based on the psychological and ideological needs of the people surviving in increasingly harsh environments' (Cook 2013: 146). Cook is commendable in noting the material culture items that could have been made from these animals ranging from skins as the walls of tents to skin bottles or perhaps bladders as storage containers with cordage, clothing and blankets all provided from animal materials. Some of the species found as prey on sites do not feature so heavily in the art. These are reindeer, Arctic fox and Arctic hare and this disjunction between the animals depicted and the key prey species is best explained by the art serving a conceptual purpose. In different areas the art is of a different size and the raw materials vary so there are also regional styles.

There are figures that appear to be part animal and part human; for example the 'lion man' from Stadel (30cm tall) and a second figure much smaller and less finely executed at 2.5cm tall similarly is a composite of lion and human characteristics; these may have referred to a legend or some form of belief system that was rendered into reality by art on more than one occasion (Cook 2013: 28–36). Such items suggest iconic or shamanistic behaviour and a rich imaginative spiritual life as well as animistic beliefs. Reindeer and other animals are drawn with fine details affecting the colouring and details of the heads, with shaggy coats (Cook 2013: 200–1, 268–69). The details use a variety of textures to create these visual effects. The details of the coat and the animal mean that 10,000 years later the animal is recognizable with regards to species, sex and age (Cook 2013: 195). Some engravings seem to have multiple images to indicate how the animal runs (Cook 2013: 202–3), and roundels of bone have also been used to create objects that seem designed to be twisted, or spun to different positions to animate animals, with the perforated roundel from Mas D'azil cave showing both an aurochs cow and a calf on the two sides of the disc (Cook 2013: 204–6). The centre of both animals is cleverly placed and when spun the images give the effect that the calf is growing into the adult.

Animated animals, finely rendered coat details, human-animal transitional forms and the location of the art all point to close observation and complex concepts of animals and a belief that gave them agency. There are other examples of conceptual relationships between animals and people but once animals are domesticated there is an unspoken assumption that they serve people's pragmatic interests rather than conceptual links, with the exception being animal remains in ritual contexts. However, agriculture need not reduce the herded animals to an inanimate economic product.

The domesticated animals of today are the product of many millennia of human breeding and the human–animal relationships are now on an industrial scale. In order to explore a closer small-scale set of relationships, one study stood out.

Mongolian herders

Natasha Fijn (2011) is a multidisciplinary film-maker and it is this perspective that she brings to her studies of a Mongolian herding community and the exploration of their relationship with their animals. This approach has ways of looking at that relationship that are of use to archaeologists thinking of human–animal relationships in the past. In her opening explanations, she lists the dairy products and key animal terms and behavioural terms for the community. There are no fewer than 15 dairy products, 26 different terms for the species, age and sex or other distinctions of animals and 29 separate behavioural terms for the same animals. Several authors have commented on the relationship between people and their animals (Fijn 2011; Ingold 1980; Haraway 2003). There is a close symbiotic relationship but a lack of sentimentality despite the care and recognition of individual animal personalities. The people and animals share the landscape and the domestic spaces in a complementary way.

The Mongolian herders that Fijn studied keep cattle (including yaks), goats and sheep (which are herded together) and horses, which are important for their milk as well as for transport. The horse herd has a stallion who protects a set of mares but there is also a lead mare. The Mongolian horses (*Equus caballus*) are short and stocky with thick coats. Yaks, used in the high areas, are slightly larger than the cattle with a skirt of longer hair. Both the yak and cattle breeds are hardy and produce milk and calves well, and make good draught animals. Mongolian sheep shed their slow-growing wool naturally in summer. The families' relationship with the wild animals recognizes the role that they believe they played in being relatives of their own domesticated animals. Mongolia also has *Equus przewalskii*, Bactrian camel (*Camelus ferus*), ibex (*Capra sibirica*) and Argali sheep (*Ovis ammon*). This mixed range of equid, bovid, ovi-caprid and caprid relationships taken together with Fijn's approach and attention to detail provided a coherent case study to explore thinking about the materiality of domestic animals.

The animals provide a range of skin, innards, horns, hair and felt products; dairy products include boiled butter and oils. Some dairy products such as fermented mare's milk are stored and cured inside cowskin bags. In spring the goats' under-coat is combed out, the sheep are clipped and horses have their manes clipped. Wool is made into felt for dwellings, known as *gers*. Horns can be used to feed orphan animals. Fijn (2011: 87) states that the herders believe the horns lose body heat in the winter. She notes that the cattle did sometimes have horns but that many of these were stumps because they fell off in the extreme cold. Felt was used as a binding along with cloth for an ox whose horn had broken off (Fijn 2011: 255). When an animal is killed, the men skin it and ladle the blood out, then the women deal with the stomach and intestines. The innards are washed so that they can be used as storage containers and the meat is stripped and dried inside a storage hut. The only items not eaten are the bones and the semi-digested contents from the stomach and intestines. There is no sentimentality as once the animal is dead it is seen as becoming something that is food and there to be used. Bones are seen as the places where the soul resides. The loss of a calf is overcome by removing the hide and placing it over an orphan calf, so that the smell of the original calf induces the original mother to adopt the new calf. They do not eat animals that are under one year of age. If a lamb does die, the herder will take the hide but not the meat. The practice of dealing with the hide is to immerse it in curd and then after an interval it is worked to make it pliable and suitable for sewing into winter clothing. These uses are recorded as cow hide stretched into strips to make horses' bridles or lassos, and plaited horse hair used to tie together the wooden lattice inside the *ger*. Sheep wool is beaten and made into felt for the linings of the *ger* or as linings for boots, ox horn is used as a bottle for feeding orphaned young animals (Fijn 2011: 226–28). The Mongolians have a musical instrument called a horse-head fiddle, which is made from a base of horse hide and the handle of the bow from a horse rib: the strings and bow were made from horse hair and the rhythm of the horse can be played upon it (Fijn 2011: 158–59). The horse facilitates the herding of the other animals and a favourite horse will not be eaten.

The milk-based form of pastoralism as opposed to meat-orientated pastoralism is predicated upon a very close relationship between herder and animal. This is evident throughout Fijn's account of Mongolian herders (2011) and is supported by Ingold (1980), who believed that milked reindeer herds were more tame. Habituating animals that are essentially otherwise wild to humans needs to be done early and consistently so that they become manageable. The continuity in handling is also important. For horses, individual animals are recognized and linked with their mothers immediately after birth by tying a cloth or some other system so that they can be brought to each other for suckling. In June, the mares start to give birth; this adds considerably to the workload because they need to be milked every two to three hours. The foal is kept beside the mare and is allowed to suck before and after milking. Thus, the mother and the foals become used to human interaction. The herders pick out animals who will be trained to become leaders. These are chosen because they interact well with humans and will allow strong relationships. While wild male animals would become quite dangerous and not want to approach humans, the herd's structure means that foals or male young animals are used to close interactions and handling by humans and, by the time they reach adulthood, most of them are castrated.

Cattle have a different relationship because once they have given birth then the individual animals have to be milked twice daily for much of the year. The herders communicate with their animals using songs, words and calls (Fijn 2011: 117). Because of the twice-daily milking relationship and the proportion of the year for which this happens, they have very close relationships with humans; cows that are regularly milked seem to know their own names and have some understanding of other commands, such as the names of their calves. The practice of using the young as a way of conditioning the mother to let down her milk is known from other cattle-using communities. In this society it is usually the woman who will be doing the milking and she will let an assistant to know when to bring the calf and when to remove it.

Domestic animals are not a disembodied group but individuals with close relationships with humans. What Fijn's intimate account suggests is that early and smaller-scale domesticated animals had specific individual relationships with individual humans and that there might well have been a gendered aspect to this bond. The hides and fibres of animals should be thought of in this intimately connected way. In particular, the intimate relationships formed by milking could have enabled animal fibres to be combed or rooed (plucked) out when the coat was shedding. The close relationships of milk-based pastoralism offers different opportunities to obtain secondary products. Furthermore, human–animal relationships may differ between males and females of the same species (Fijn 2011: 181). The women deal mostly with the female animals because of the milking practices; young children deal with younger animals because that suits their physical status; the stronger and larger animals are dealt with by the male herders. These differences are slightly staggered with respect to the male and female tasks as people go through the life cycle. Women will carry on milking whereas the role of men changes with age and it will be the younger generation who deal with the younger, stronger and more difficult animals. Tools go alongside the gender division of tasks so that men use the riding and traction-related tools whereas women use the objects related to activities such as milking and cooking. The gender relationships of the subsistence tasks thus colour the material culture and associations of objects with men and women.

The reason for this outline is because this ethnographic text epitomizes an intimacy between people and animals and offers several valuable insights into the way in which human–animal relationships may have tethered people (by gender and age) to places and to times on daily and seasonal cycles of activity. In turn this affects the availability of materials from animals and the associated material culture. The milking practices of Neolithic cattle can be thought through in different ways. Herd animals that are milked would also have presented opportunities for collecting their fibres either by combing or rooing. While the fibres could be naturally shed and collected from bushes, the suggestion that combing at a selected time offers the chance to influence the prevalence of finer fibres and the total amount gives a new way of thinking about human–animal relationships connected with fibre collection. The close relationship and new opportunities may both result in archaeological signatures.

Folk physics and bush chemistry

Many of the processing techniques described in the preceding chapters involve an understanding of physics and chemistry at some level, and it is useful to think through how some of the common physical and chemical principles of dealing with materials could be achieved and understood within prehistoric societies. It is not necessary to understand chemicals and physics in the way that modern scientists do, in order to understand how they work, and what cause and effects there might be. Instead, it is useful to think of them by borrowing the term 'folk physics' (Povellini 2000) and coining the term 'bush chemistry'. In any event, many of the chemical and physical principles in prehistory would have been varied because they were using natural resources, and not standardized materials or quantities of chemicals. Cracking open nuts using a hammer and anvil, or building a night nest are the kind of 'folk physics' that modern apes are known to employ. Building shelters and knapping stone tools also involve 'folk physics'. The flaking, splitting and smoothing of materials can be seen in the same way. The bush chemistry is more challenging, but bones in hot sun quickly denature and will start to exhibit sun cracks. Fresh sticks are more flexible than dry sticks, they also sound different. The skin on a freshly killed animal is soft and flexible but the dry skin is tough. These are both physical and chemical processes. Ripe fruit will ferment and change taste; a sudden shower will re-wet the dried skin and tendons remaining on a carcass making it flexible again. It is not hard to think of ways in which the pathway of human evolution included an appreciation of science. While the 'transformative' processes of firing clay and smelting metal occur in later prehistory, fire transforms wood and is a feature of much earlier prehistory. Fire also turns wood into smoke, which is a useful substance. Physical and chemical transformations of materials are part of the development of knowledge of materials. The processes described in the preceding chapters have some recurring themes of using chemicals to transform the physical properties of materials. There are important chemicals as part of simple bush chemistry; acids, alkalis, urine, fats and oils. Tannins and dyes are more complicated chemical processes.

Wood ash in solution forms an alkaline liquid known as lye. It is commonly used as a strong cleaning and degreasing agent. Wood ash feels different if you get it on your hands, which react if they are at all wet or if the ash reacts with sweat. Thus as soon as people started making fires, and cooking with those fires, there would have been ready amounts of wood ash, and a clear way of noticing the chemical reactions as they affected the body. Wood ash solutions are mentioned in fibre and cordage production processes. It can also be important as a dye assistant, or mordant, in dyeing. Although putting wood ash in water will produce a silty liquid, it is possible to pour this through a basket, sieve or plant materials, so that what drips through into a container is cleaner. Again, to use this material, containers may have been useful, although wood ash itself can be put onto surfaces and affect them, or ash can be placed in pits or rock hollows where rainwater collects.

The smoke produced from fire is also an important by-product of burning wood. It creates a powerful smell and can be used in cleansing processes, to keep insects away from drying meat and people, to cure hides and to preserve meats. Smoke is not one entity: different woods give different smells and flavours, some give off more smoke than others.

For acids, there are readily available plant materials such as willow bark, which will create acidic solutions. There are also many plants, such as sorrel (*Rumex acetocella*), which will give an acidic mash. The headache curing principles in willow bark tea are a well-known herbal remedy. Medicinal and herbal teas are thus one way in which people could have been forming liquids that were both acids and also tannin-rich. Again, tannins will help with dyeing and, where this is combined with iron rich substances, will darken as a dye bath and become more fixed. The technologies intersect plants link with animal processes and vice versa. In these ways wood ash, urine and tree bark teas may have been ways in which simple but effective ranges of acidic and alkaline solutions could have been produced for many different situations.

Urine, when fresh, can be used for tanning, and when stale it becomes ammonia and has bleaching properties. These sorts of changes over time in one solution are common, as many liquids go off, ferment or become mouldy as time progresses. If there are containers storing liquids, then these sorts of principles will be noticed. Thus in order to make some use of urine as an ammoniacal solution, a container would be needed, but there would have been a general awareness of colour changes associated with bodily wellbeing and dehydration that would affect the urine of individuals. In Ingalik society the ammonia seems to be important (Osgood 1940). Both men's and women's urine are collected in special baskets, and it is said that urine salts can help with tanning problem skins. It is also used as a dehairing solution prior to tanning. Urine is also used as an astringent wash and as a soap. Urine is collected, stored and used as a raw material, in liquid form and also as salt encrustations. Clearly, this community values this material for its chemical properties.

Fats and oils were also important to prehistoric societies. They can be extracted as lumps of fat, and also boiled and rendered. Since there are Upper Palaeolithic lamps, a general appreciation of fats and oils is known from at least that time. Oils can help with waterproofing or softening skins, and with the process of fat tanning, and could have been obtained from any fat-bearing animal or oil rich seed. However, in some areas, there are obvious animals to target. For example, near the coast fish or marine mammals are good sources of fats and oils. Ishi in native California (Heizer and Kroeber 1979) macerated salmon skins to produce oils.

In this cause-and-effect observation of relationships, folk physics would also have a role to play. In many of the bone, antler, ivory and horn technologies, it is easier to work these materials after they have been soaked, than it is to work them dry. Likewise, bark and basketry materials are easier to work once they have been soaked than if they are dry. In some cases this difference is crucial as to whether or not they will form the desired shapes. If people are using fires, then placing material to heat gently near the fire will also soften a wide range of branches and other plant materials. An earth oven for cooking works because it is a slow steam cooker, with a sealing layer keeping the heat in. This would also work for some kinds of artefact-processing activities. In the Palaeolithic the *baton de commandments* have possible roles as spear shaft straighteners. In later periods there are also arrow shafts to straighten. Thus for both straightening spears and arrow shafts gentle heat and steam could have helped the straightening process greatly. Herbal teas react differently if the water is boiled aggressively, or simmered, or steeped (where boiling water covers leaves and the liquid is left to cool). Coldwater soaking versus steeping, simmering or boiling can change the dye principle by altering the colour or permanence.

Some of the methods that are commonly used to help work the materials described in this book could have been available, and part of the knowledge of materials, from very early periods. The concepts of bush chemistry and folk physics would have been well embedded in the consciousness of people in prehistoric societies who relied on the ability to transform raw materials into material culture.

Colour

The sensory worldview of prehistoric communities could have emphasized colour in ways that are difficult for us to appreciate now. This is because colour is richly textured and deeply hued in our own world. As some of the collective images in this book show, the prehistoric colour pallet was full of earth tones and tonal contrasts. It was not until the use of Indigo became established, that most societies had a deep blue colour system. However, the ochre tones and greens are available from natural dyes and principals. There was also the use of shells and colourful furs and skins. The plumage of birds and the colours of skins could have been the first ways in which colourful hues were available to humans. Colour, shine and brilliance are important aspects of materiality and expression.[5] There is ochre from Blombos Cave 75,000–100,000 BP (Henshilwood et al 2011) inside two abalone (*Haliotis midae*) shells as containers, and there is associated grinding equipment, although Wadley (2010) believes the mix of ochre and charcoal could also be an adhesive of which there are other examples at 58,000 BC from Sibudu Cave. From this early period onwards, colour becomes part of the materiality of humans and needs to be considered by archaeologists as part of the worldview of prehistoric societies and thus as part of the likely desirable qualities in material culture. As demonstrated in Chapter 3 it is evident that the age of animals, and the kinds and colouring of coats, could be strong reasons for selectively seeking out particular species. That is particularly true of the furs. The use of bird skins with the feathers attached is another way in which colour could have been used in the past. However, a prime way to alter the colour is to select different aspects of the coat for processing and use in different parts of the system. At its simplest with sheep, this could involve using the lighter colour fibre and hair usually present on the underbelly, with a richer, deeper colour on the back. Careful sorting of the wool will allow the colours to be separated, and thus a two-tone colouring of a textile would be possible. More specific manipulation of colour is most likely a part of tanning technologies, as I have tried to show in Plates 47, 48 and 50. In particular the range of colours in Plate 48 are all achieved by varying the tanning method, and could be seen as coincidental by-products. However, they are also strong colours in their own right, and keep their colours relatively well, although the paler colours will quickly darken in smoky atmospheres and in contact with soil. This range of colours is achieved by simple methods, and almost all of them, and especially the tree bark tanning methods, could be darkened further by the addition of iron compounds to the tanning solution. This could be as simple as haematite or iron rich soils present or deliberately added. Light materials could also have designs painted on them. In these ways colour and pattern could have been part of very early skin clothing traditions. The tree tanning seen in the Neolithic Schnidejoch find from the Alps is an example of tree bark tanning that would probably have coloured the skins. Other ways of colouring materials can include burying them in iron rich soils, such as in mud cloth production, or producing a combination of tannins and soil contact, which – perhaps over days or weeks – gradually stains the material.

Berries that were commonly available would also have been able to stain, if not dye, the materials of the period. Conversely, bleaching, using stale urine solutions (ammonia) or sunlight, could have lightened material. Again the tonal contrasts might have been important in the design elements. Colour is well-known from traditional dyeing, and in general it is easier to dye wool textiles and fibres than it is to dye cellulose-based plant fibres. However, much depends on the kind of dye being discussed, and the use of mordants. Modern dyeing techniques use metallic salts as a way of enhancing the colours, brightening them and making them more colour-fast. Without these metallic salts, many of the colours are more fugitive, i.e. they wash out or fade in the sunlight, and the colours are more muted. In a society where colour was less evident this could still have been important.[6] Many of the plants that give dyes smell strongly, or have other uses. Some are also medicinal plants. Many are tannin-rich and part of the tanning traditions. In these ways it is not difficult to see societies developing the knowledge of the use of natural materials as part of the colouring of their material culture.

The role of colour in symbolism is strongly linked to ochre, and to red in particular as a colour, which has been used for burials and is also present in some of the very early examples of ochre use. Authors have commented on its blood-like colour, but it is also one of the strongest colours available to prehistoric people and could have been used to colour hide, where it would also have acted as a preservative. In addition there are ways of varying the kinds of colours available from one plant, by taking different elements of the plants, leaves versus bark, versus root, or taking that element at different times of the year, such as leaves in early spring, as opposed to full summer, and it is often possible to moderate the colour by the use of iron-rich elements. Colour is part of the symbolism and sensory worldviews discussed by authors in relation to stone (see, for example, Jones and MacGregor 2002; Cooney 2002). Stones seem to have been selected for their flecking and tonal contrasts, and these qualities may also be important in tempered pottery and colours in other items of material culture. Thus this short discussion of colour shows that it is part of the sensory arenas of the past and the sensory worldviews. It is also one where the elements of folk physics and bush chemistry combine into ones where people can show their crafts and artistry as individuals and as communities.

Sensory arenas

There is now a body of literature on sensory perceptions in anthropology and archaeology. Plant and animal materials and artefacts contribute strongly to the sensory worldviews of societies.[7] Throughout Fijn's (2011) account of living with Mongolian herders there is a sense of attunement between the animals being herded and the humans. This is also present in the way in which people engage with plants and their intimate knowledge of parts of landscape (Osgood 1940) and the ways in which the sensitivity of these people is attuned to their environment. It is difficult for a modern person to get a sense of this and in the past it was not often studied, but Fraser Darling (1937) has a closing chapter on the sensory perceptions of the deer that he studied in Scotland. In a prescient passage, Darling explains that the sight, although so crucial for humans, is a sense on which red deer do not rely. Darling uses observed patterns of behaviour and particular events where he was convinced that the deer needed the sense of smell to make better sense or to believe something that they could not otherwise accept through their eyesight. Humans in contrast tend to preference what they see above the other senses. Darling also makes an interesting observation on the sense of colour that animals have and the fact that light-coloured dogs do not work well with sheep as it seems as though the sheep do not see them in the same way. For sound, he notices that the red deer will sometimes lay up in 'a zone of silence' where it is easy to hear the approach of danger.

Darling's close observations of a herd of deer allowed zooarchaeological studies to investigate ways in which humans might have been following the deer or preying on them in particular ways according to seasons as the animals were observed to be a different part of the landscape in summer and winter. These classic kinds of studies fed into analyses of key sites such as Star Carr (Clark 1954) and areas such as Epirus in western Greece (Higgs et al 1967), and the way in which people exploited the landscape became a part of archaeological thinking. Thus animals started to become better characterized and the ways in which humans exploited them became better understood as a driving force for where their campsites might be found and where the interpretive archaeological information might be found. This is why these kinds of studies could now be rolled forward to look at what that exploitation pattern would provide for in the way of skins and antlers and the other resources to be had from these very important large animals. Certain animals are key to understanding particular periods or regions; for example, reindeer in the Upper Palaeolithic of Western Europe, and red deer in the Mesolithic of Northwest Europe. The sensory world of material culture is made from raw materials that have smells, textures, colours, sounds and tastes, and for organic materials these often relate back directly to the living organism and its sounds, smells, colours, textures and tastes. Thus there are two layers of sensory information from organic material culture; those emanating from the object itself and those connected with the living plant or animal, its place in the landscape and the places and people who obtained the living thing and worked it into the material culture item.

The sensory perception of tools incorporates a deep sense of how to use them. The change in materials from stone to metal requires changes elsewhere. Even if something is perceived as fundamentally a good tool, if it is novel it might be rejected in favour of the familiar. Different body actions are necessary when using metal tools as supposed to stone ones. In producing a Bronze Age sewn-plank boat with bronze axes, adzes and chisels, the sounds were very distinctive to any boat-builder walking past, but had a subtly different character because of the bronze tool edge. Furthermore, nobody in the modern world has really appreciated how a copper edge would seem to a person used to polished stone, or how polished stone would have seemed to a person accustomed to using flaked stone edges. In other words, nobody in modern societies has followed the journey that a past society made in the changing of the tool edge material and form and realigning their expectations of the amount of force, the angle of attack and the way in which that edge would have performed a given task. The nearest we can come to it is to work backwards ourselves and at least to experience them all. The modern volunteers on a recent project building a replica Bronze Age boat with replica Bronze Age tools in Falmouth, UK, perceived the bronze tools as 'soft' because their prior experience was with steel tools. Somebody who was used to polished stone axes would instead have perceived them as sharper and tougher and infinitely more forgiving of any mistaken blows. This aspect of the tool quality may have enabled the learning process to be rather easier since mistakes would not be so costly to the community's tool sets. If we see axes and adzes as important woodworking tools, these observations are relevant to perishable material culture as they may relate to the perception of the woodworker or the woodsperson.

Wells' (2012: 48–49) discussion of fire as a light source is well-handled but for this book it is worth drawing attention to the way in which we perceived the supply of wood for the fire. If a lamp is found inside a cave then we assumed that fat has been processed, a wick has been obtained or processed, and the two have been assembled together with a hollowed-out stone or similar object to act as the receptacle. It is an object of material culture to provide light. This is not so when we talk about firewood. Yet the fire consumes wood throughout its existence even if it is only allowed to flare up when cooking is being achieved. These statements bear further discussion. When people are cooking, the light may have been a soft red glow to the coals. When people are preparing to cook, the flames may have given off far more radiant light. If people wanted to engage in manufacturing projects, the flaring up of the fire immediately before it became useful for cooking could have been a key moment to capitalize on better qualities of light and greater intensity for more finely detailed work, before the fire was reduced and the soft glow of the embers signalled that food was being prepared. Should archaeologists therefore regard wood for fire in the same way that they do the preparation of materials for oils and lamps? It is certainly a key resource used within the home. The flavours and style of burning of different wood varies greatly and firewood for the house would have had to have been chosen for its suitability, and it would have been dried or stored somewhere. Thus a highly selected set of pieces of wood were brought back to the house and presumably consumed every day to provide heat and light. If this was happening from a pottery kiln, it would be seen as an important act of ceramic production sequence. Certainly, with metal-producing and using societies, the provision of charcoal for metalworking activities has to be part of the discussions about resourcing, but I would argue here that firewood is an important aspect of the demands made of wood as a resource in prehistory. The warmth, light and smell of the fire is the warmth, light and smell of home and all of them rely on the qualities of the wood gathered and placed in the fire.

The lamp and fires, and the smoke from them would permeate the clothing, the house and everything in it. Smoke is one of those processes that dries meat and imparts a distinctive texture and flavour, and therefore the smell of the smoke and the way in which it has been used to flavour that product will colour people's expectations. Oils all have a distinct smell, especially those from fish and animals. Just as much as a fibula preconditions people to know what else to expect that object to do and how to wear it (Gosden 2005), so too, smells and visions will trigger cognitive associations to which people will react. When polished, metal produces the ultimate shine but it also leaves a taste on the tongue and a smell on the fingers from handling it. These textures and smells would have been new when these materials were first introduced into a community, although they would gradually become part of the desired features of the social material culture repertoire.

Identities, personalities and places

Personalities indicate people as individuals with recognizable characteristics. This section draws out the numerous ways in which craft resources have personalities. In Chapter 1, I argued that both plants and animals have characters and react to human interventions but on different timescales. In Chapter 2 and in the 'Tending the wild' section of this chapter there are clear examples of particular growing conditions needed for the best plant resources for crafts with cues taken from the character of the soil, or the other plants growing alongside the resources. The biological term 'habitat' indicates a broad idea of the conditions where a plant will grow but the information from traditional harvest patterns show the best resources grow within more specific conditions and that the characteristics of the craft tree or plant and the other species growing alongside it constitute a more specific sense of place and personality of the resource. In some cases stands of plants can be known individually and repeated visits to collect the resource will need to be managed to ensure the resource is not compromised and, often alongside this, the resource itself will be improved. Given the intensity of this relationship it seems right to think of this as the harvested plants having personalities and places in the landscape.

A surprising number of activities and locations are about size and comfort. These can be the obvious ones, such as working heavy materials near where they are found, for example a tree in the forest can be worked down to a much smaller item to be brought back and worked up further. Throughout many of the specific references to taskscapes and stages of production as places there are references to things that archaeologists do not currently consider. These are practical, have a profound influence on where tasks are undertaken and the archaeological signatures that they would leave behind and yet are often not an evident line of interpretation to somebody who has not undertaken the task in the location and environment themselves. One such is the role of water, insects and other animals. Antlers can be cached under rocks or in water to prevent other animals finding and eating them. Bark can be stored for some days or even weeks underwater. Humans are irritated by mosquitoes. Working where there might be a breeze, lighting a fire at the entrance to a temporary house or bringing material back to the settlement so that one can work inside all help to avoid mosquitos.

Identity is not just material culture and site types, it is what people do to leave these archaeological signatures because identity is performed by actions as well as signalled by material culture. These aspects create the sensory worldviews of familiarity, choice, value and the exotic. In Chapters 2 and 3, the exploitation of plants and animals used to form material culture were important choices to create social identities. Processes and technologies as well as finished products are social markers. Tools, equipment and containers are used and created in social ways. Clothing is an important personal and communal identity. Changing the plants or animals or process used will result in different smells, drapes, flexibility, colours and textures. The aesthetics of these can be personal choices, but the characteristics of them can be deeply embedded aspects of the material culture repertoire. Harris' (2012) term 'cloth cultures' goes some way to outlining the common broad themes discerned despite the individuality in the clothing choices for the European Bronze Age. The reality is that all aspects of material culture have cultural elements. The prevalence and importance of some resources could constitute significant aspects of identity creation. The example below explores the significance of particular resources for Ingalik 'identity relationships'.

Osgood states:

> The outstanding fact about the materials used by the Ingalik is the predominance of the products of the spruce tree. In about 150 or approximately half of the items, some part of the spruce tree is a component. The only other comparable source of materials is the caribou, but in this case, out of somewhat fewer items, a large per cent of the representation is in babiche or sinew thread. In any event no other representatives of the flora or fauna even approach the role of the spruce tree or the caribou.
>
> (Osgood 1940: 432)

The use of spruce for 55 per cent of the material culture items listed is due to an interplay between availability, wood properties, and tools and technologies. Osgood goes on to make a pertinent comment as a list of the hardness of the different tree species wood is iterated with the clear note that, for the indigenous community, hardness equates to the difficulty of working the wood with the tools they had available. The properties of the material are tempered by the technologies and tools available. The hardness order is: 1. red grained wood of spruce or tamarack; 2. black birch; 3. white birch; 4. spruce or tamarack; 5. cottonwood; 6. alder; 7. willow; 8. spruce root; 9. spruce root near the trunk. Red grained wood is explained as a growth pattern to be found on the convex side of bent-over spruce trees. There are also comments about the relative hardness of different woods from different growing conditions for some of the other tree species. Hard wood is worth working and is chosen preferentially for artefacts such as wedges. For many other kinds of woodworking the pay-off between the tools and effort needed to work it, versus the toughness needed for the job in hand, gives a different preference. There are also comments about young wood generally being tougher than old wood, and that in the very coldest weather birch is better than other choices. Wood can be hardened if it becomes heated and mildly burned, but this will also make it more brittle. Wherever possible shortcuts are taken: where angled pieces of wood are needed, naturally formed pieces from root and trunk branch, or branch and trunk area are used. These are strong and can save a lot of shaping time.

In animal material culture, the dominance of caribou can be explained by its preferential use for clothes and babiche or sinew cordage. Both bone and antler from the animal are also used in a variety of worked tools for piercing, gouging and scraping. Bone is recognized as harder but more brittle, although this can be alleviated by regular oiling, whereas the antler is the toughest of the two, particularly if the antler is young, and referred to as 'taken in the velvet', i.e. when the soft outer covering is still protecting the growing antler (Osgood 1940: 435). The society that uses caribou products has detailed knowledge of their raw material qualities. These animals are material resources and not just food. Throughout Osgood's account there is a substance that stands out as an identity substance – urine. Urine baskets are kept inside the house to collect urine from different people in different ways, so that the liquids can be used as an astringent wash, as urine soap or as a tanning agent where both the liquid and the urine salts collected on the base of the bowls are used.

Reading through the whole volume on Ingalik material culture, one is struck by just how much they are dominated by particular kinds of smells and particular tree and prey species. In terms of their material culture, the dominant smells and textures are fire, spruce, fish oil and to a lesser extent caribou. Other species and processes are valued, of course, but nonetheless there is a significant set of connections with particular items and resources. Thus for the Ingalik it is the spruce and caribou that dominate the material culture items as raw materials, even though the birch bark canoes are the more widely known cultural item. The spruce root, bark and tree give shelters, structures, lashings and many other aspects of the society's material needs. These are balanced by a close relationship with one particular animal – the caribou, which meets a lot of the hide and cordage needs of that society.

Elsewhere, close relationships exist with other animals, most noticeably the domestic species. However, the switch from wild to domestic has to have come about from a gradual intensification in the areas where they were domesticated, but elsewhere there is a more sudden shift in areas where the farming package was introduced. These sorts of mental shifts in resources are going to be important, and should be considered alongside the more obvious food values and availability issues. These features will mean that changing key resources will create a cultural shift in smell, colour and textures of material culture as well as shifts in lifestyle and living conditions. These shifts could be powerful reason for resisting new possibilities and could also be explored as reasons why some cultural practices would be continued despite new lifestyles and subsistence strategies. This is no more than a marker for a phenomenon that deserves wider exploration, but it is useful to think through these sorts of intense relationships.

Conclusion

This outline explains how some of the choices relate to the environment, but how that environment and its complex interaction with kinds of tools affect the manner of working. The containers, clothing, hunting and fishing equipment, and tools to make other items of material culture all interweave and intersect in complex ways, drawing from both plants and animals, but they exist within the environment. The key question is, as an outsider looking into that community, the dominance of certain key species is very apparent. Were that particular resource to fail, there would have been considerable consequences on the material culture for that community. Quantity and size may also play a role, as materials such as sedges and grass, used as roofing, require large numbers of plants and have distinctive materials and smells, at least until the material has aged or taken up the smell of smoke inside a house. These materials are also used for insulation for shoes and mittens in the cold, and for making mats for sleeping on. Larger hides can be used as roofing and walls, so some larger scale structures, taken together with lightly processed but nonetheless useful material, can also be added into this complex interweaving of material culture usage. To quote Osgood:

> There is a balance between the individual creativity and what best serves a purpose for pragmatic reasons. On the one hand, the individual seems to have considerable latitude in what he makes and how he makes it, but on the other hand, utilitarian and environmental factors seem to have patterned things fairly definitely.
>
> (Osgood 1940: 437)

This is not a reductionist argument but a way of understanding the materiality behind the choices people make.

Thinking through the intensification of human–animal contact allows for a consideration of the use of the fibres well before any change in the animal's coat occurred. It is a strange oversight that archaeologists who are writing about animism, ritual and ideological animal concepts, as well as the intensification of economic relationships with them, routinely disregard any mention of fibre, fur, skins or horns. Indeed, this bias seems almost perverse. One of the aims of this book is to open people's eyes to thinking through the possibilities of fibres being collected as well as skins being an important by-product of whatever food value the animals provide. Again, to concentrate on the iconic significance of an animal but not the usefulness of its material by-products seems odd to me as this overlooks a potentially important source of evidence.

In this chapter, the discussions and ideas have led to one possibility: certain plants and animals have greater significance than others. This can come about because of the intense relationship, due to the prevalence of the animal or plant in the environment, and also the ability of people to exploit it. Perhaps that relationship intensifies over time, as familiarity explores more of the possibilities. In these complicated ways one should think potentially of plants and animals as having strong identities connected with groups of prehistoric peoples. These would be strong reasons for groups to keep current practices, or to quickly adopt new ones. Some of these plants and animals serve both food and material culture needs. A community that relied heavily on deer for meat, skins and antler would have clothing, containers and cordage made from the skins and tools made from the antlers. Switching to a different animal as a meat sources would have profound ripple effects on the material culture. Where animals are farmed the continuation of hunting practices could retain the connection for reasons of identity as well as utility. Willow is a medicinal material, a useful wood, and a very useful bast fibre source. It also tans skins, giving a very strong nut-brown colour. It can provide cordage, lashings, basketry, fencing, flexible brush-wood structures and more solid construction materials and frameworks. Much of a society's needs could be met with willow, and in Middle Neolithic Holland the family group depicted in the Science Museum in the Hague shows what a strong colour association would be given by the basketry and hide work produced using this material. Thus some elements of clothing, containers, tanning, house construction and col-ouration would interweave to give people a close association with this particular tree plant. An example of other key materials from the smaller plants would be bulrushes – the toughest, longest and most flexible of the rush plants – and also nettles, which are important as a source of greens and as medicinal plants as well as being part of fibre production and potentially fine material goods. There will be other candidates for identity plants in other areas and other regions. Hunted and managed animals can also have close links with the economy and identities of societies.

Thinking about the subsistence and craft possibilities from plants and animals in tandem offers different ways of considering lifestyles and landscape use and the intensity of relationships. Craft materials and products as well as food are important constituents of identity. This way of thinking offers new suggestions for interpretation and investigation, which can be summarized below.

- Wild plant resources can be tended and husbanded; environmental data needs to factor in potential human usage.
- Milking alters the social structure of both animals and humans, with females on both sides gaining in importance.
- Milking provides a platform for initiating and intensifying fibre collection (hair in cattle, wool in sheep).
- The concepts of bush chemistry and folk physics would have been well embedded in the consciousness of people in prehistoric societies who relied on the ability to transform raw materials into material culture.
- The sensory world of material culture is made from raw materials that have smells, textures, colours, sounds and tastes, and for organic materials these often relate back directly to the living organism and its sounds, smells, colours, textures and tastes.

Notes

1 The relationship of people with the plants and animals in their environment has filtered into a wide range of ideas about attitudes. The conceptual dimensions of these crafts are inherent in the positioning and placement of materials (Bernick and Deur 2002; Croes 2001; Curtis 1913; Descola 1996; Descola and Pálsson 1996; Hackenberger 2005; Hall 1981; Nicholas 1998; Lepofsky and Lyons 2003; Purdy 2001; Rozen 1978; Stewart

1984; Turner 1998; Turner and Bell 1971; Suttles 1990). Animal farming and management behaviour and people's relationship with animals has been covered in classic volumes and recent archaeological work (Anderson and Storm 2008; Ballard 2012; Boyce 1989; Boyle 2005; Cabanau 2001; Clutton-Brock and Pemberton 2004; O'Connor and Sykes 2010; Fothergill and Berlowitz 2011; Geist 1971; Goulding 2003; Grimstead 2010; Harrison 1985; Hodgetts 2005; Monks 2005; Pavao-Zuckerman 2011; Pryor 1996, 2006; Roe 1972).

2 Linda Lemieux, a professional basket-maker, worked with me as a consultant on my Leverhulme research project. She introduced me to her harvesting methods and management cycles for bulrush (*S. lacustris*) on a river in the Somerset Levels and for willow in her own field.

3 Latz (1995) has extensive coverage of aboriginal use of fire as a management tool in Australia with implications for the availability of plant resources Fire-stick farming and use of fire has been studied in Australia (Bliege Bird et al 2008; Jones 1969; Miller 2005; Mooney et al 2011).

4 Many ethnographic and historical accounts as well as some archaeological evidence, demonstrate the symbolic and ritual role animal and their products played (Cummings and Harris 2011; Gibson and Simpson 1998; Jones 2000; Legge 1992; Longworth and Varndell 1996; McNiven 2003; Pollard 2000; Robinson 2002; Sheridan et al 2003; Schulting 1996; Tola 2009; Turner 1985; Urton 1985; Vitebsky 2005; Viveiros de Castro 1992; Weedman 2002; Willerslev 2007).

5 See Boivin and Owoc (2004); Hartl and Hofmann-de Keijzer (2005); Henare (2005); Jones and MacGregor (2002); Saunders (1999).

6 The range of natural dye materials has already been covered in Chapter 2, note 28, but colour is important to the complexity of material culture and the use of lichens, mushrooms, plants and tree barks, as well as animal furs and skins, all impart smells and textures as well as colours.

7 For the contribution strongly related to the sensory worldviews of societies, see Classen (1997, 2005); Classen et al (1994); Cummings (2002); Howes (1991); Lazzari (2003); Scarre and Lawson (2006). For materiality, see Hurcombe (2007b); Parker Pearson and Ramilisonina (1998); Parker Pearson et al (2006); Renfrew (2004). However, few authors have specifically looked at venues and sensory perception, such as the role of light in a dwelling (Dawson et al 2007).

5

INTEGRATING CRAFT AND
SUBSISTENCE NEEDS

Introduction

Macro-scale changes in technologies are part of theoretical frameworks and broad comparative approaches. At one extreme, there are studies of how technology changes over large areas or periods, and then there are much smaller scale studies of that variation and its significance at a local scale.[1] Torrence (2001) points out the kinds of technologies and decisions available from studies of societies at different scales. She considers this question of scale and uses Oswalt's (1976) food-getting technology system to explore how hunter-gatherers deal with the risks and potential consequences involved in problems in the food supply. A large part of this is a matter of achieving a balance between the input of energy to obtain food, and the resulting output of energy or available calories. The approach addresses how hunter-gatherers have minimized risk by the application of material culture solutions to catching prey. Sometimes these material solutions are used directly by people and at other times they need only untended facilities such as traps and snares. My contention here is that the same approach might be applicable to ways of thinking about the obtaining and storing of craft materials from plants and animals throughout the yearly cycle. Nearer the equator, there may be rainy seasons, which affect resource availability. If resources are obtainable throughout the year, there is little point in storing them, unless they are part of the *chaîne opératoire* of, for example, the drying of materials prior to working them. In contrast, in northern latitudes, the seasonality of some of the resources makes distinct phases of seasonal activity. The winters may be prime times for making things ready for intense food-getting activities in the summer. Both Oswalt and Torrence focus on food and explain the complexity and diversity of material culture related to obtaining food as instruments, weapons, and tended and untended facilities as ways of minimizing risk and optimizing food. What they do not consider is the parallel nature of the technology used to make the food-getting material culture. Thus, the emphasis here is on shifting this perspective into thinking about the short productive seasons as an important craft way of exploiting the landscape throughout the entire year/yearly seasons.

To summarize, Oswalt (1976: 64) defines *instruments* as those tools that can be obtained in large numbers and with relatively little cost and risk to people. Examples might be digging sticks and some kinds of clubs. In contrast, *weapons* are implements such as spears, harpoons, bows and arrows and also on this definition items such as fish hooks, since they too directly catch a mobile prey by the delayed use of human energy. *Facilities* are described as tended versus untended. Tended facilities include hunting blinds and surrounds. Traps and snares are examples of untended facilities, where the presence of the person does not determine the success of the facility (and indeed, could well be detrimental). Oswalt's definitions for items for obtaining food can be shifted into a parallel set for obtaining raw materials for manufacture, i.e. the procurement of craft materials from plants and animals. In this way, implements such as a digging stick for digging up roots that are potentially usable for cordage and for basketry purposes could be seen as instruments, whereas a well-made harvesting tool used for obtaining plant materials for mats, cordage and thatch could be seen as a weapon because it involves the direct application of energy to 'capture' the material from its natural environment. It has also involved energy in shaping the handle, obtaining the resin or pitch and using these as settings for interchangeable blades of stone to form an ergonomic and efficient harvesting tool. Just as cereal crops need to be harvested efficiently in an optimum period, so many craft resources have similar time constraints. The hunting equipment used to obtain animals could be seen as weapons both for food and also for the capture of craft materials from their carcasses. Facilities could include the storage, collection and processing of plant and animal materials. For example, in craft terms, pits for storing or for soaking materials prior to using them would be facilities, as would be rock caches covering antlers to make sure that other predators did not gnaw them. Retting pits may not need to be tended all the time but they are systems that need to be maintained and also watched perhaps one or two times a day if the weather is warm. These are not without risk: in some cases, material left retting in a slow-moving river maybe at risk if there are flash floods. Thus, the energy systems that Oswalt is keen to see lying behind some of these technological systems for food-getting can be thought through in relation to procuring craft materials. Given this, we might expect that, as with the analysis of food-getting technologies and the associated stone tool systems that ameliorate risk, so too the material culture items and the raw materials for crafts would involve more inherent risks in higher latitudes where resources are not uniformly available throughout the year. In the same way, Torrence's (2001) discussion of storage as a way of ameliorating risk for food resources also applies to the raw materials for crafts and the production of material culture. Thus drying racks for preserving meat can also be used to dry the raw materials for basketry production or for hide-working prior to storage and use at some later date. Both plants and animal skins usually require drying in order to make sure that mould and other organisms will not compromise the quality of the material to be stored. These sorts of issues are broad scale comparative problems that are, at the moment, very rarely considered within material culture studies. In most cases, study of the material culture is dominated by stone, pottery or metal objects, but these form merely an impoverished subsection of what was once available. Where evidence of organic material culture does survive, its study often pales alongside the studies of stone and metal artefacts.

The role of variation, form, design, and the social codes of material culture are composite issues for all material culture, but are largely considered (if at all) through only stone tools and pottery. Torrence's overview of how archaeologists have used stone tools to explore relationships between genders and social roles in the production of tools and technologies does consider the social aspects. As she explains, some aspects of the technological systems for food-getting are not straightforward choices on pragmatic criteria alone, but can reflect symbolism and social meaning (Torrence 2001: 91–93). Different food-getting activities of male and female groups within a community could also translate into different aspects of material culture production. In the Ingalik example discussed later in this chapter there are indeed relationships that strongly associate gender issues of user and maker, but also ones that crosscut these. However, these are generally attributable to differing physical abilities or to the location of activities in the landscape that are associated with the gender that is extracting and exploiting them in that place. In these ways, the male and female food-getting technologies may also relate to the male and female craft ways and taskscapes. To put this at its simplest, if men are doing larger-scale hunting and women are doing more of the collecting of plant resources, it is highly likely that women will also be collecting plant materials for crafts while men may be working bone and antler. If fish trap and weirs are important tended and untended facilities, the withies and wood to make them need to be cut and split or worked further in the right season. The craft that makes the facility also needs its own procurement and manufacturing strategies. Where large-scale tended facilities such as hunting blinds are used and if large numbers of a large species are killed at one time, there is a considerable amount of food processing to undertake and these groups are likely to be larger and of mixed gender. To give an obvious example, if a herd animal such as buffalo is subjected to a large-scale kill, it is not just the meat that needs to be cut up and dried or dealt with so that it can be safely stored and transported. If the hides are to be used, they too will have to be processed in an initial phase by perhaps cleaning them at the kill site, or drying them before taking them to another site for cleaning. Associations with animals where men are doing most of the risky or long-range hunting tasks is a strongly gendered activity that may carry through into the associated craft activities from those remains. These are not concrete assertions, but they are considerations that would enrich archaeological debates arising from the evidence that survives from prehistory.

The seasonal round of subsistence and craftwork

Societies harvesting seasonal food resources also have to contend with seasonal craft resources. The information provided in Chapters 2 and 3 can be used as a starting point for assessing the seasonality of some key resources. Not all the resources collected would need to be used immediately because the *chaîne opératoires* could be broken up by periods of storage. This also suggests that storage for craft materials as well as for food was an important aspect of the annual cycle. The seasonal constraints for a selection of useful plant and animal resources are outlined below along with a short account of how a larger building project would be mapped over the seasons. The seasonality is affected also by the technologies available to work materials.

Two construction projects in Northern climates are outlined to show the seasonal mapping of the tasks. The first is building a birch bark canoe that, once built, would need annual maintenance but could last four or seven seasons depending upon its use for hunting or travelling, and the second is a larger barn construction in Norway that might last many decades.

Constructing a birch bark canoe (Osgood 1940: 359–71) starts with selecting and marking trees that might be suitable as much as a year in advance of construction. Spruce roots for the stitching, spruce gum for waterproofing and rough shaping of the spruce wood elements for the frame can all be undertaken in advance. In spring the place for the construction, usually a riverbank, is prepared and the bark on the selected trees is tested by removing small pieces to check that it has the right evenness and flexibility (only three or four out of ten marked trees prove suitable). Suitable bark is carefully removed shortly before an intensive assembly period in a dry weather slot. The fine shaping of the frame elements is undertaken by a few people. Mats or fish skin covers can keep the project materials dry and several processes need heat to shrink the bark for a tight fit around the frame and for the application of the gum around the stitches. Friends and family help with the final assembly, stitching and waterproofing so that this final phase takes around five days.

The construction of Norwegian barns in the recent past involved large-scale buildings (up to 18m × 60m) with complex carpentry. Høgseth (2012) outlines the construction tasks for barns and houses as they are built under the direction of a specialist craftsman and fitted alongside the farming year. The builder and farmer meet and discuss the farmer's needs around December. Winter activities include selecting and marking the trees, felling, some preliminary cutting and trimming at the felling site (depending upon location in relation to the building site and saw mills), moving timber out of the forest and from March to July the major green timber would be worked into the large structural elements alongside birch bark collecting in May/June with sowing and spring farming tasks in the earlier part of this phase. From May to August the timber would be trimmed further and the joints and structural elements assembled on the ground and adjusted where necessary with the whole building structure being raised towards the end of this period and fitted around mowing and harvesting tasks. In August/September the main elements of the house are completed, as well as the roofing, along with herring fishing. From October to January the fitting of smaller elements for windows and stairs from dried wood was undertaken, completing the building.

These two examples of larger projects give a sense of how the food and craft tasks had to dovetail one another as resources came into season and as people were available. Building houses, boats and major facilities such as fish weirs or storage structures would have had similar phases of activity as evident from the larger house structures and the sewn plank boat (Plates 5 and 6). Many individual plant and animal resources also have seasonal constraints, as outlined below:

- *Bark as sheets, cordage or tanning materials.* It is relatively straightforward to strip bark from the tree in spring/early summer but inordinately difficult at other times using simple technologies and the bark itself becomes less flexible. Thus if a new house is to be built and bark is used for roof or walls there is a specific time in the year when this activity would be planned to occur. The bark could be allowed to dry in the desired shape and kept for later use. Bark will soften with soaking and gentle heat but it is at its most flexible when newly removed from the tree. Bark for cordage can come from smaller trees and these may be able to be stripped for a slightly longer period depending on the growing conditions. There are more tannins in the bark as the sap is rising so it both easier and better to remove bark for tanning during May/June, the traditional 'barking' season in the UK. It is best dried in the shade. Bark can be chipped off at other times and leaving bark outside will allow rainwater to leach the tannins out.
- *Tree roots.* These are best dug up in Spring or Summer and the epidermis is easiest to remove after a few hours of light drying.
- *Rushes (Scheonoplectus or Scirpus spp.).* In the UK these are harvested in late June/ early July in a period of good weather after a period of low rainfall so that the river level is low and they can be dried before being stored. With care the bundle visible in Plate 12 would make several small bowls.
- *Reeds (Phragmites spp.).* If the dry stems are used such as in traditional thatch they are harvested in winter, and in this condition can make mat screens but they are more flexible in summer and stems with the leaves on can be used as matting and roofing materials.
- *Willow withies (Salix sp.).* Late winter while the sap is down is the best harvest season to preserve the rootstock.
- *Brambles (Rubus sp.).* Young runners from last year's growth are easily seen and harvested in winter.
- *Nettles (Urtica dioica).* The harvest period varies with the end product and the processing method. These plants make good cordage once they have grown. For stronger materials they need to be harvested before they are affected by frosts which can weaken them, for finer items processing immediately after first frosts can give good results. For textile fibres the retting process is quicker in warmer weather so harvesting in August or early September can work well allowing the retted stems to be dried and processed further at a later point. For manual processing harvesting in the summer to process over the winter can be flexibly scheduled.
- *Straw.* Stems can be harvested at the same time as the seed heads or in a second cut.
- *Sedges and grasses.* These can be harvested in summer so that the material can be dried before the bad weather. The material can be gathered in bundles for shoe hay, mats or basketry but use as thatch would require much larger quantities.

- *Antler.* Depending on the species the season when antlers are shed varies, but antlers can be gnawed or eaten entirely by dogs and foxes and will lose elasticity if left exposed on the ground for long periods. Thus targeting this resource in the season of shedding may make sense; for red deer this would be late March/ early April. Otherwise the material is available from animals killed in the right months of the year (for red deer, autumn and winter).
- *Furs.* These are usually at their best in winter.
- *Hides.* The best hides are from animals in good condition so after good feeding in the summer but before damage from the mating season. In spring/early summer the skins can be riddled with fly larvae holes. Skins will need to be cleaned and dried or stabilized in some other way before being stored until processed further.
- *Intestines.* The materials need to be cleaned thoroughly straightaway and either inflated or stuffed with grass so that they keep their tubular shape.
- *Hair and wool.* Naturally shed hair and woolly underfur could be collected from tree stumps and bushes where the moulting animals routinely graze in early summer.

This short review of the timing of resources shows that many plants and animals have seasons when they are at their best and often need at least a first stage in processing in order to enable them to be stored. Seasonal gluts are inevitable where there are herd animal movements or fish runs. These will need to have both the food and material resource needs factored into the set of tasks. Storage in roof spaces, under the eaves or in pits or caches will offer different possibilities. Drying racks will not be just for food. Separate storage buildings could work well for items needing shady cool storage but many house structures quickly become damp if a fire is not lit regularly as many of the roofing materials let in some water over time. Storing perishable craft resources could be expected to be part of lifestyle shifts with increased sedentism and a move to more farmed resources. Changes in technologies, tools and equipment would offer new ways of exploiting and processing perishable materials. The shift from flaked axe edge to polished stone axe edge to metal axe would make a difference to the performance characteristics of edge tools and woodworking in particular. The period boundaries of the Mesolithic, Neolithic and Bronze Age offer broad changes in the nature of perishable material culture which are worth exploring further.[2]

Mesolithic lifestyles

Rowley-Conwy (2001) convincingly argues that the 'original affluent society' is neither on its inevitable way to becoming an agricultural society, nor is it in any sense an original society. Rather, it is a highly complicated and developed set of exploitative strategies that has been successful but is not a second tier form of agriculture, nor a state that is attainable by all kinds of hunter-gatherers societies in all kinds of environment. Rowley-Conwy (2001) explores the different ways in which a four-fold typology of hunter-gatherers can be seen from an interdisciplinary perspective. The first has little or no mobility or food storage. The second has logistical groups for specialized activities but no defence of their territories. The third does defend their territories, and the fourth has more sedentary groups who defend their territories and also store resources. His four-fold typology is clearly in many respects a continuum. He makes a convincing case for considering the basis for some of the European Late Palaeolithic societies that were heavily dependent upon on salmon and reindeer as 'classic targets of logistic strategies ethnographically' (Rowley-Conwy 2001: 50). He points out that the decisions of hunter-gatherers about which animals to kill, in particular the selection of juvenile individuals, will not just maintain the size of the available animals but also result in the adults keeping their productivity even when year-on-year some of their offspring are killed. As long as others survive to adulthood, there will tend to be more animals available to be killed each year. These selective sets of behaviour, which deliberately or inadvertently result in maintaining or improving the type and abundance of resources in the future, has some counterpart in the plant-based interventions explained in the previous chapter. Clearly, some kinds of prey species may have been directly affected by humans to the point of local extinction, especially when stressed by environmental change.

In recent years, many European Mesolithic sites have seen interpretations shift from being envisaged as transient camps to ones where some form of sedentism was practised. Although not all members of the society need have been present throughout the entire year, nonetheless these sites show substantial ranges across seasons with a great diversity of tool types and prey species. Indeed, they could be seen as key camps or base camps depending on the terms selected. Such sites include Mount Sandel in Ireland (Woodman 1985) and Smakkerup Huse in Denmark (Price and Gebauer 2005). The evidence for these interpretations is based on the presence of seasonal birds and the eruption and wear patterns of teeth in pig jaws, the growth patterns of deer antler, and the seasonality of the birth of the young. In the case of Smakkerup Huse, there is also evidence from wood and plant remains such as hazelnut and hawthorn fruits indicating autumn activities as well as the cutting season from analyses of the patterns of growth in hazel poles. It is of course possible that the occupants of these kinds of settlements split up, and work parties went to different areas to obtain the maximum amount of food and materials prior to the winter. Thus, both fishing on the coast and inland activities could have been important summer activities. Price and Gebauer (2005: 30) conclude that sedentary residence of some form was normal in the late Ertebølle period. Part of this argument also rests on increasing complexity and diversity within the social systems of these communities.

Price and Gebauer (2005: 24, Fig. 1.5) outline the cultural sequences in Denmark and their associated fauna, which is augmented here by considering how these shifts would have changed the availability of perishable craft resources. This can be seen in the early periods to offer very different choices to potential hunting communities. In the Hamburgian period, there were large animals such as woolly mammoth and also reindeer but as the climate warmed Irish elk dominated along with reindeer, and this is followed in turn by an Ahrensburgian fauna in which reindeer gave way to horse, bison, and aurochs in the early and middle phases of the Mesolithic Maglemose and Kongemose periods (Price and Gebauer 2005: 24). The choice of prey species included aurochs, elk, red deer, roe deer and wild boar. I would argue that these offered different sizes and qualities of hides as well as meat. There are also different shapes and qualities of antler associated with elk, red deer and roe deer. It is clear that there is a significant component in the Mesolithic from the marine environment (Price and Gebauer 2005: 22, Fig. 1.4). To these resources must therefore be added the potential of using fish skins and oils. In the final Ertebølle phase or the very earliest Neolithic phase domesticated cattle can also be added to the list of potential items for material culture. Rowley-Conwy (1993) has characterized some of these Ertebølle sites and the seasonal materials available to them, in keeping with Binford's (1980, 1981) idea of a key base camp and then collecting strategies for hunter-gatherers in which part of the group move to other areas and collect food to be brought back and consumed along with other resources. Rowley-Conwy identifies the use of the base camp where red and roe deer would be available all year, supplemented in winter by wild boar along with fur-bearers over the winter period, with access on the coast to cod, flat fish, porpoises, oysters and birds such as ducks and swans. In the spring, this switched to a combination of oysters on the coast and furbearers inland. Spring is one of the periods where it is hardest to find seasonal indicators. Thus, this picture of a lean period may be real, but it may also be an artefact of our lack of indicators for this time of year within archaeological data sets. There are many plant resources in the summer and for the autumn, seals on the coast, and hazelnuts and acorns inland. The rich diversity of these late Mesolithic Ertebølle sites is shown by the faunal materials of such sites including 32 different animal species, of which aurochs, wild boar, red deer and roe deer were hunted for food. Animals such as pine marten, polecat, wolf, fox, lynx, wild cat, beaver and otter were hunted for their furs and skins and dog bones show skinning marks at Smakkerup Huse (Hede 2005: 96). Alongside an amber pendant there are two others that are made from pierced red deer teeth, demonstrating the significance of this animal.

The other aspect of the site of Smakkerup Huse is that the small fur animals and indeed fish are very thin skinned and after the initial skinning process, require very little in a way of scraping because not a great deal of force need be applied to clean them, the skin tends to come off fairly cleanly. Furthermore, the manner of spreading them out to dry is little more than a matter of pushing sticks or perhaps grass inside the skin to keep the sides from sticking together before working it with the hands so few tools are used for processing the smaller animal to make furs. Fish would need to be skinned, but the filleting might well be being done at the coast or wherever the fish are caught and then the fish skins, by analogy with the Ingalik example, could well be being pulled off after the fish is dried. This again, would mean that there was little in the way of tool-based scraping to be done and their processing could all be done by using mostly hands. Processing larger skins such as the deer hides is easier to do using some form of tool but beyond the initial pulling off of excess fat, which could be quite limited if the skinning has been done skilfully, then other phases of the processing could be undertaken with bone, antler and wood tools. Thus, thinking through the kinds of clothing likely to be worn by this people, analogies with material from graves from the region, suggests that skins perhaps with the addition of some forms of decoration might be useful. Even a small number of skins could have made substantial contribution to the repertoire of clothing. The use of plant material as some elements of plant-based clothing cannot be ruled out. Likewise, the variation in house sizes and shapes described for the region (Price and Gebauer 2005: 31) could mean that some of the skins might be used without further processing as elements for structures. Cemetery evidence shows the position of foot bones and in some cases ochre spreads signifying the use of skins as clothing at sites such as Vedbæk (Albrethsen and Brinch Petersen 1976).

From this assessment there would have been hides from red and roe deer brought in throughout the year; a variety of furs available from animals caught during the winter and spring which could have been caught at specialist fur trapping sites as well as closer to base (Andersen 1995a; Rowley-Conwy 1995a). In winter bird feathers and bird skins (swans, ducks) would be available as well as fish skins (cod were up to 50cm in length). In the autumn sealskins can be added to the list. Fish in winter and seals in the autumn could also have provided oils and fats for lamps, lubrication and waterproofing. Antlers, both shed and unshed, would have been available according to roe and red deer antler cycles and horns from the domestic cattle and aurochs. The animal bones were available for what is interpreted as marrow extraction (although this will also release the oils) with the metapodials not being smashed apart for marrow but seemingly reserved for use as tools such as awls and points. The spurdog (*Squalus acanthias* a kind of shark) has a sharp spine, which was used as a fine piercing tool at Smakkerup Huse (Price and Gebauer 2005: 118).

Research has also taken advantage of the excellent conditions for organic preservation to allow some consideration of the range of plant resources exploited. Although researchers have concentrated on those plants that are edible, some might have been significant resources for the material culture. These include acorns and even apple and sloe. Rowan berries along with hazelnuts, for example, make good food but the plants also offer materials for basketry and bast fibre for cordage. Hazel was used for stakes and general construction; yew and elm for bows and paddles, oak for shafts and handles, lime for dugout canoes, willow for baskets and traps. Evidence for the use of thatch (*Cladium mariscus*) has been reported from the inland Swedish settlement of Bökeberg (Regnell et al 1995). Other fibres were used for rope, string, and many other items (Kubiak-Martens 1999, 2002; Zvelebil 1995). Mason (in Price and Gebauer 2005: 80–83) points out that the remains of young acorns could be because they fell naturally from nearby oak twigs, or they could have entered the archaeological record in some anthropogenic way. They are found on several Mesolithic sites so they seem to be part of a more general issue. Mature ones may have been a food source but the immature acorns are more problematic to explain. However, acorns can be used as a tanning agent and the season for stripping bark is during bud burst and an early summer period thereafter so one alternative explanation for this phenomenon offered here is that they may potentially be collected as tannin-rich elements.

Sites such as Smakkerup Huse with good preservation conditions show fish traps and weirs, and bows of elm wood (Price and Gebauer 2005: Ch. 4). Other finds from the site include possible fragments of *Phragmites* as well as charred seeds including ones from *Juncus*, *Galium* and a Gramineae, and also charred fragments of *Tilia* (lime) bark. *Phragmites* is useful as a source of starch and as matting material and *Tilia* can be used for its bast fibres, as for example at Tybrind Vig, where it was worked into a looping around the core item of material culture. Other species such as *Rubus* (blackberry) can also be used to make binding material in loop work or used whole as bindings. The nettle *Urtica* is also present in small amounts but its presence could be very significant. Mason correctly concludes that the species is potentially useful, but the interpretation is problematic as they can also be a ruderal species. Fragments of the tree fungus (*Fomes* or *Polyporus fomentarius*) were found on the site and this material is known as a tinder fungus and can be harvested from trees such as birch and beech. Fragments of wooden artefacts, bark sheets and dugout canoes were also found, but most of the other artefacts are the bases of stakes. The bark is not identified, but noted as probably of lime or birch. These are certainly artefacts and are part of a pattern of such finds from other Scandinavian Mesolithic sites. They are assumed to have been used by people for construction material or as matting although they can also be soaked and prepared and used in more complex ways, see Chapter 2. The site also contains some woodchips, which suggest that material such as canoes might have been made at this site and while only a fragment was found on site, this was at the rear of the canoe as it had the characteristic section of clay-covered base with traces of fire. All of this material is in keeping with other log boats found from similar periods in the region. Perhaps the most famous is the one from Tybrind Vig, which was almost 10m long (Andersen 1987a, 1987b; Christensen 1990, 1997). They are commonly made from lime wood as is the one from Smakkerup Huse. There is a vast array of material culture elements represented here, from very large scale structures for housing, to large scale structures for transport in the form of dugout canoes to much smaller scale items such as general cordage. The lime bast bag from Tybrind Vig (see Chapter 2) is one such piece that could have been both bag or textile fabric. There were large quantities of hazelnuts, which are known to be a significant food resource in the Mesolithic. Although experimental evidence has shown that hazel bast fibres make excellent, strong cordage material, it seems likely that here the food resource took priority. A small fragment of either double plaited material or twining work was also found.

Stakes from Smakkerup Huse have been found in some quantity and their position in the ground suggests their use in making fishways and fish traps. The stakes were mostly made of coppiced hazel about 3cm in diameter. The tree ring analysis clearly shows that many were harvested after seven years. The dendrochronological work showed most of the material being cut in the summer at the end of the growing season. The suggestion that this might have been to allow the wood to dry before it was used is an interesting aspect of the hints of wood working practices arising from this material. In this respect at least, the harvest of coppiced hazel for wood was deliberate and took place before the tree would have been productive for hazelnuts, which typically were at their best after about 15 years of age (Price and Gebauer 2005: 89). The parenchyma and small numbers of *Juncus* and other softer plants are again likely to be underrepresented and underidentified in the archaeological record, but it is highly likely that the sorts of materials found at Tybrind Vig would also have been being made and used in this settlement as well.

Thus, the plant-based material culture show log boats that were likely to be created by selecting trees in the winter and then felling, trimming and moving them to the waterside for finishing. The fragments of bark and general use of bast fibres suggest there was a bark harvest season in late spring. The management of hazel for stakes could have carried into the management of other kinds of trees and shrubs. If they were using nettles, then these could have been collected in the summer or early autumn depending upon what characteristics were most required. There is no indication of what material was being used to attach the fishing hooks and make the line, nor the material used for net-working. In other areas such as the Northwest Coast of America, these kinds of artefacts are made from nettle. It is possible also to use willow and other species available in this environment.

The site itself has occupation from at least the last two phases of the Ertebølle and runs into the early Neolithic, since there are small numbers of domestic cattle. It is thus broadly dated from c. 4800 BC to c. 3950 BC. The brief review here has conflated some of this material. Nonetheless, the approach taken here to use a wide range of ethnographic data to try and understand a holistic approach across the seasons for both food and also material culture needs has made additions even to this well-excavated, well-preserved and well-analysed site. The skins from large animals such as the deer are assumed to be part of the raw materials for crafts. However, it is another step again to think through what kinds of tanning might have been taking place for these materials. The intriguing possibility of using small twigs of oak as a source of tannin has been raised but cannot be identified further. The sea mammals would have been able along with the fish to provide oil for lamps but also for working skins if fat tanning was being undertaken. The use of plant material as insulation for footwear is likely. Taking all of these elements together means that there may be some explanations offered of the kinds of perishable material culture crafts likely to have been carried out by this community. In general, the material from this region of the Ertebølle in South Scandinavian has a variety of sizes and shapes but most are found in the archaeological record as postholes. The evidence in at least one case of thatch from *Cladium* sp. shows that plants species could have been used as thatch, but it would also have been useful as insulating material.

The situation at Smakkerup Huse can also be seen in other iconic Mesolithic sites in Britain and Ireland. The classic excavations conducted by Clark (1954) at Star Carr showed unequivocally the role of perishable material cultures. These include rolled up birch bark that could have been soaking in water prior to being worked or stored in water for use as birch bark floats, and the famous red deer frontlets, which are undoubtedly significant objects showing a role for red deer in the conceptual life and beliefs of the community. The original excavations identified fragments of worked wood and a paddle and the recent excavations have added to this by identifying large scale split woodwork that shows the ability to produce planks in this phase of prehistory. If we imagine Star Carr as part of this larger more sedentary system, then here at least there is the possibility of plank-built structures. Although in general, the Mesolithic in Britain is characterized by post built structures where any such exist.

The recent excavations and publication of a broad range of material from Smakkerup Huse have enabled it to be given as a case study here, but these other sites could equally well be reconsidered for the missing component. The missing majority of the perishable material culture are likely to have gone alongside this seasonal round of food exploitation and the craft products obtained from the same environment, flora and fauna. It is in these ways that this works thus to address and place more prominence on the consideration of perishable crafts as part of the totality of resource exploitation and seasonal activities undertaken by a community and forming an important part of the material culture repertoire.

Neolithic lifestyles

Hunter-gatherer lifestyles persisted alongside and in close proximity to farming subsistence practices. The take-up of these elements of an agriculture system of farming was undoubtedly something that varied region to region. Linear Pottery Culture (in German *Linienbandkeramik* Culture, known as LBK) is a very distinctive central European farming community from which eventually many variations and stylistic changes led to the proliferation of more regional distinctive farming communities. The initial LBK phase which began in c. 5,500 BC was nonetheless a very rapid spread and despite a wide geographical distribution contained certain core elements. The most distinctive elements are the long, rectangular houses seen archaeologically as rows of large post-holes with internal divisions subdividing them. These large houses were clustered into small hamlets, but some show fortifications – or at least palisades – around them. However, these are best seen as islands within a largely forested landscape with the houses, forming a cluster and the fields surrounding them. There are ornaments on the body in the form of shells of *Spondylus*. These are marine shells and indicate extensive trading networks. There are also cemeteries where people were buried in distinctive ways with small amounts of individual material culture. Subsequently, there was a regionalization of the styles and varieties from the LBK to the societies that succeeded it and expanded its territory. Even these developed societies are far more egalitarian than their successors when copper metallurgy becomes more widely known and available.

The significant differences between Mesolithic and Neolithic lifestyles are summarized best by tying more people to sowing and tending crops in spring and early summer to make sure that weeds are not in competition with the crops and by the commitment to daily milking practices. Late spring and early summer are also periods for gathering raw materials such as bast fibres from trees. However, the way in which the society dealt with this could have been by splitting tasks up for different groups. Bast fibre cordage and clothing are important in the Bronze Age in the

Alpine region so it seems likely that tree basts and other plant-based clothing systems would have been important earlier. The plots of ground cultivated in the early Neolithic were probably not extensive. Therefore the scheduling conflict could have been resolved by segments of society undertaking different aspects of these crop tasks.

The key issue otherwise, is the animals. Once the Neolithic round of animals included not just cattle but also sheep, goats and pigs then there is a profound change in the way that hides might have become available. In the same way that the cow offers different possibilities for a large substantial hide with very tough properties, so too in the past, hunting would have fulfilled some of these needs for hides. However, hunting continues in the Neolithic. Therefore cattle could be seen as an additional resource kept mostly for milk and meat but with their hides available once they were slaughtered or died. It is essentially an add-on extra that probably did not compromise traditional ways of using hides. With the advent of sheep and goats, sets of much smaller hides come into the raw material chain when those animals are slaughtered. Because in the Neolithic the sheep were being kept for meat and only to a certain extent for wool, then these patterns are likely to have meant that young animals would not have been kept over winter if by doing so, they would have needed further feed and could have compromised the lifestyle of the community. There is a period of autumn slaughter in the bone evidence that could suggest a glut of small carcasses with small-scale skins ready for processing in the autumn. Drying them after slaughter to work on them at a later point in time would have been crucial. If the weather was fine then they could be dried in the wind outdoors but it would be necessary to ensure that flies did not lay eggs on them. Once dried, the hides could have been rolled up and brought inside, and brought out again during the winter to be worked on as and when the weather and other tasks permitted. These hides are small and would have presented no large problems for space or storage. They may also have been stored in roof spaces where the presence of smoke deterred pests and started the process of curing the hides. More, but smaller hides, arising from their meat sources would have led to different clothing patterns and eventually perhaps to different clothing traditions. This is all predicated on people relying largely on animal skins for key items of clothing. Into this mix for the Mesolithic to Neolithic transition should also be placed the other important crop of flax.

Although flax is only found in a handful of places, it is part of the Neolithic LBK cultural repertoire and seems to have been available for farmers. Its rarity in the archaeological record is more likely to be a factor of archaeological preservation and accumulation of evidence on site than a real issue. Flax as a double crop gives both the fibres from the stem and also the seeds which are rich in nutrients and also in oil. Oil as a component of the diet or for use in material culture production or for lamps could all be an important aspect of this crop. The other consequences of growing crops are that straw would have been available. Straw was almost certainly shorter than in modern crops and it is stronger and has more silica than some of the sedges and grasses that might have been being employed as matting and as duffel for insulation in the same periods. However, for societies that used much of these materials and would otherwise have to gather them, the idea that people would harvest the top of the cereal but ignored the straw needs to be justified if that is the argument being made. It seems more likely that they would have used the straw in some way perhaps as part of roofing, matting, bedding for humans or animals or as insulation within and around the settlement. Archaeologists who study usewear patterns on sickles have shown that in some cases it is harvested alone. If the same communities then wanted the straw it could be left to dry and then harvested in a second harvest round at a later point. Of course, all of this supposes that people wanted flax for cordage and fine net and line work and also for textiles. From the Mesolithic and Neolithic periods in much of the world, there are simply very few finds of fabric materials. In general, those present concur with Rast-Eicher's (2005) sequence of bast first, then hair and wool. Thus in the Neolithic and Mesolithic, the bast fibres might have been far more significant than we have at present allowed. This would give the interesting scenario that the crop of flax allowed the production of very fine bast fibres in larger quantities grown specifically for this purpose as well as for their food value as part of the Neolithic package. Prior to this, fine fibres were certainly available from nettles but also by soaking and splitting lime bast or rendering willow or hazel bast, very fine bast fibre work could still be achieved using Mesolithic as well as Neolithic style technologies. The Mesolithic Tybrind Vig material is made from lime bast using a looping around the core technology that it makes a wonderful flexible, resilient, and aromatic material for clothing or bags. Lime bast can be used in fairly large sections as twining material but if the finest quality is desired, the laminations will allow it to be split and worked much more finely.

The Neolithic is often seen as a period of deforestation. Polished stone tools offer new possibilities for exploiting trees in general and opening up areas for growing crops rather than a modern concept of deforestation as swathes of felling. Anybody who has used either a flint or a polished stone axe or a copper one on a tree trunk wider than a person's body would know all too well the amount of effort this takes. Much more likely is the gradual extension of the area of fields and plots around settlements. Trees can always be ring-barked, thus causing them to die slowly, so that the light gets through to the soil and the soil underneath standing trees could be used. This gradual and incremental idea of the slow loss of forest and equally gradual increase in farming land is a rather more likely scenario given this kind of technology. It might be much wiser to see the axes of prehistory, whether they are chipped stone, polished stone or copper or bronze as being essentially about wood and woodworking and woodland management exploitation. Many timber trees are much easier to work when they are green and newly felled. Once it is fully seasoned, oak hardens to a degree that even modern metal tools can find hard going. Thus, taking down trees for use in construction projects would be a major issue if axes are more effective tools for those trees that need to be felled for this purpose. It is still the case that the larger trees would present many more challenges than the smaller whole saplings or body-sized trunks. Felling forests as deliberate forest clearance would have been a massive investment of time and energy and would have consumed so many axes from these earlier periods. Instead, the light tillable soils were selected throughout Europe by early farming communities. The same soils have lighter, more patchy forest on them and there are areas with natural clearings perhaps caused by flood or by lightning that could be utilized as openings in the forest and expanded. From these small beginnings, people and their communities began to make appreciable difference to the amount of tree cover but not by anyone person – or even collectively – deliberately setting out to clear all the forest around them. Instead, the forest was cleared at the level of individual trees perhaps dealt with piecemeal, and in different ways. Some were felled for construction and building projects or for making log boats, or because trees were directly in the way of others to fell in a space to opening the forest floor to light for small patches of farm plot, and others rooted up by animals.

The advent of farming would have seen new forms of artefacts. Milking vessels robust enough to survive being kicked would be needed so perhaps would have been a wooden or hide vessel rather than a ceramic one. Hobbles and ties would have been important management tools for animals and some fencing or hedging may have been useful even if most grazing was free range. Wooden artefacts and cordage would also have been useful. All these items are of perishable material culture.

Metal-using lifestyles

Metal as the material for edge tools is significantly different from stone. It is the first time that a basic edge tool raw material is so geographically restricted. At first sight, this need have nothing to do with the perishable material culture. However, in the holistic view of the material culture these issues will be interconnected. Existing material technologies did not stop with the advent of metal, but would have changed and developed. Prior to metal, everybody would have been able to make some form of pottery, some form of stone work and some form of perishable hidework and cordage and basketry style work. Inequalities would have rested on precise ways of collecting and processing locally available materials, individual skill, the effort and hours put into finer processing and also to some extent on the manipulation of the material into its finished composite form. In these ways, even in the Neolithic, there was great equality, balanced and adjusted by individual skills and application. Some processes could have been regarded as having more closed, secretive knowledge: for example, the precise ways of achieving the colour on a hide or on textiles – but these are embellishments rather than fundamentals. However, the person that does not have access to metal is somebody who cannot obtain a significantly better tool for working wood and chopping wood or, in the case of a copper knife, a more maintainable tool, but in both cases one that flashes and shines. The other way in which metal fixes itself into the social framework is as pure decorative ornament as beads, bracelets, or as small pieces attached to clothing or covering other items such as buttons. Metal is an embellishment but it is one that only a few can access. Furthermore, there is the separation between maker and user in metalwork that is not present in societies that get most of their resources from close at hand. Access to metal is not like that.

Social change and early metallurgy

Two recent volumes have highlighted a much broader scale approach to understanding cultural change. They emphasize the later periods of prehistory and in particular pick out the warrior period as a significant aspect of change and with it the use of metal as the material culture of the swords and weaponry that go with notions of warriorhood. However, both have something extra to say about how archaeologists view longer term change. Vandkilde (2007: 31) in particular is clear that her overview considers both the *longue durée* of the French Annales School (Braudel 1949) and also the more detailed conjunctures. She makes the point that detailed analysis is possible to pick up the cyclical variations forming the dynamic stasis of the period. Much like Rowley-Conwy (2001) she too resists the idea that to change is part of an inevitable progress through an evolutionary sequence of social complexity. Instead, she points out that there are periods where the reverse seems to happen. There are also areas where the pace of change is not in step in a region. We inevitably reflect backwards in time and the sequence of changes may appear from this perspective far more inevitable than they are in practice and certainly than they are within one individual's lifetime or even across several generations.

The early Copper Age cultures saw the real flourishing of early metallurgy (Vandkilde 2007: 48). The metal is the shine and sparkle around which people otherwise construct their normal textiles and socially rich diverse lifestyles. Vandkilde shows some of these objects, selecting spiral loops and small things and labelling them copper trinkets of the late Neolithic after 5000 BC (Vandkilde 2007: 49, Fig. 10). These decorative items and the early axes did not belong to unclothed bodies. The axes were hafted onto well-made wooden – and thus perishable – shafts and could be seen as a personal tool that would also add to social status. While the clothing evidence on anthropomorphic stelae from the same period shows all too well the richness in textile design and the proliferation of detail and textures. By such means, the extra metal can be seen as embellishment of what was already happening to the textiles. Through much of Europe, cattle could be seen as a primary domesticated species for a household providing milk and on death, hides and horns. The sheep and goats would not be kept just for their meat but also for their coats, which could be collected during life. This image of the secondary productions revolution has one key problem. Cattle have over time, lost their better coat qualities and become more hairy. The reverse is true of sheep. These differences may not have existed in the earlier phases of the Neolithic as cattle might well have also provided useful hair and wool into the household. Eventually, oxen as well as cattle could have been used to provide transport and draught for ploughing.

Sherratt's so-called secondary products revolution has been a useful concept since he first put it forward in the early 1980s. However, analysis of the residues of ceramic pots shows that milk was an important element of the diet from the beginnings of the Neolithic (Evershed et al 2008), and that some of these elements may have to be thought of differently. Nonetheless, the opportunities that close proximity in control of animal and plant breeding cycles and selection gave to people undoubtedly allowed them to select for key advantages. In this sense, there was a secondary products revolution. However, the real revolution was in the change in sites and structures that went with the beginnings of that Neolithization process. Once the Corded Ware culture emerged in the third millennium BC (Vandkilde 2007: 65–77), the concept of warfare seems to be inherent in the society from the beginning and the Bell-Beaker cultures that came in to being later perpetuated this set of warriorhood accoutrements. Whether for every sword there is a hilt and sheath, for every spear a shaft, and a shaft and quiver for every bow and arrow, there has to have been a reaction. In this respect, the provision of shields and protective clothing that might have deflected weapons or at least improved the survival from wounds inflicted by them would have been imperative. The obvious materials for shields are wood or stiff hide, or some form of robust protective clothing could feature heavy leather at least over key body parts, or the provision of densely woven basketry body-wear that would have helped the person wearing it survive slashing and thrusting blades. In later periods, there are survivals of protective Mycenaean armour and helmets. However, for these early periods, most perishable material items are known only from images. There is currently little or no attention paid to 'defence' material culture as counterparts to the weapons of the day. Coles (1962) undertook experiments with thin bronze shields, showing that the shields were ineffective unless they were backed by more robust and shock-absorbing (and perishable) materials. He experimented with wooden backing and also with thick hide shields, both of which were more effective than metal alone at ensuring that the person survived a blow. Thus, if Vandkilde is right and warriors were an important part of the social changes of the *longue durée* in Europe, then alongside that there have to have been consequent changes in the perishable material culture that could also have set a premium on certain kinds of materials as part of the material culture of that era. Thick skins of oxen and larger cows would certainly have been expected to be at a premium. If this model is correct, the role of warriorhood as opposed to warfare was an important hier-archical structure within a society, and the production of the necessary pieces of equipment for this group would have been a substantial undertaking for those individuals In the meanwhile, the role of these objects has been supported by similar aggrandizement in their trading of other material culture items reinforcing social status. Thus, it seems likely that intensification and elaboration might have gone hand-in-hand with these developments in metal-using warriorhood. Textiles, dyes and more elaborate woodworking and hide-working could all be seen as part of this generalized phenomenon, which sees more specialized forms of craftwork.[3] Also in this period, there was the deposition of goods in wet places. While this is known primarily as the deposition of metal objects, in particular of accoutrements of war, there is no reason to suppose that perishable items were not also deposited there. There would simply be no trace left of any such practice.

Perishables are important to the use of metal in other ways. Smelting requires the use of effective mining equipment and material for hoisting and carrying the ore out of the mine as well as bags or containers of some sort. The smelting process would most likely also have had to use bellows made of hide and wooden pipes, hollowed out, rebound and used to feed the air from the bellows to the *tuyère* (the ceramic nozzle going into the fire). Also necessary were items to protect the hand, perhaps in the form of leather gloves, and also bindings for the two-piece moulds and arrangements for picking up the hot crucibles. All these would have been fashioned from perishable material culture. There is also the important addition of charcoal. In order to smelt effectively, and then to work metal effectively, raw wood and charcoal production would have been key components of the use of trees in regions where smelting and metalwork was undertaken.

Conclusions

In the preceding discussions on different periods, I have tried to tease out the way in which perishable material culture could have been interwoven with the subsistent patterns and seasonal round of activities.

Where there are good preservation conditions, as in areas of the circum-Alpine region in Europe, there is evidence that even in the Neolithic and Copper Ages, there are items of clothing which are made from grasses, straw and tree-bast fibres. In general, archaeologists have thought far more about animal skins and their role as clothing and fabric materials than they have considered bast fibres and plants such as reeds and grasses as the basis for clothing items. If nothing else, this chapter has highlighted this lack of perception of possibilities for plant fibre and whole plant clothing items. In the metal-using periods, the key changes in perishable crops are when sheep are kept more for their wool, and clothing shifts to wool based textiles. This may have enhanced the significance of those animals. The keeping of animals for longer also means that at any one point in time there will be fewer hides from those animals. In addition, the way in which metals have been used has traditionally been seen as woodworking and tree-felling activities. Of these, the former is likely to be a far more significant component than the later. The splitting of large trees is already known from the Neolithic and indeed from the Mesolithic in places such as Star Carr. The technologies that allow for more access to metal present new opportunities for finer woodworking and it is these periods that see the development of larger scale structures made from the larger trees. Until this time, the largest items of wood are the log boats. These are robust, could be expected to last for perhaps five years or so, if care was taken with them, and perhaps for longer. Once the log boat was compromised as a boat, it could still have been used as a trough for large scale extraction of oils for soaking large materials, and could thus have still had a significant use. The labour and energy invested in this kind of technology is considerable at the outset, but here is a long-term artefact initially fulfilling a unique role in water transport and then fulfilling other secondary activities for perhaps many years afterwards. Boats can also be built of skins and bark. The log boats offer longevity. The type of birch bark used in canoes grows only in northern regions, and therefore the log boat is a good alternative where there are large trees and where a robust craft is useful. Skin boats have the benefit of light portability, but they have to be hauled out of the water and dried off every so often. Thus the skin boats could have fulfilled a very important aspect of travel and food-getting across water, but they would have been limited to short journeys and of course the larger boats required a great number of large robust skins to cover them. The slender pointed craft of modern-day Inuit watercraft show what can be achieved with these boats and that they can operate in extreme conditions. In most prehistoric situations, offshore fishing does not form a major component of the diet and a major way of getting around the landscape in quite the same way. The Northern climate with its intense cold and its abundant large sea mammals exploitation strategy does present a special case. However, in the past, this kind of extreme reliance on boats may only have paid off where there were large numbers of good quality robust skins to make the boat in the first place, and also a keen and pressing need to invest in the materials and construction of larger boats either to obtain more resources and food either directly or through contact with distant societies as part of hierarchical exchange systems.

For animal resources, the shift to farming gave larger numbers of small skins from the slaughter of young animals and the occasional adult sheep and goat hides and much larger cattle hides, but as hunting continued there would still have been access to deer. Antler continues to be used as raw material for tools as well as bone from domestic and wild animals. Access to fibres becomes easier through proximity during moulting seasons. Crops can provide straw as well as seed heads, and flax adds to the farmed plant materials. Managed coppice stools contribute to basketry and stakes but other wild resources may be being managed more closely as people live nearer together and spend more time in one place in the landscape. There is more large-scale woodworking such as palisades.

Metal-using societies consume perishable material culture in several ways. First, as direct products for mining and smelting ores and casting, all of which require baskets, large carrying equipment, ladders, lamps, ropes, bellows, tongs and the management and collection of wood for charcoal production. Second, as an increase in the scale and quantity of wood used in constructions, some of which are palisades, gatehouses and monumental buildings. More personal protective equipment is made such as shields. Third, people are living together in larger groups and the perishable resources are more managed, and at the same time there is more specialization. The refinements in textile production go alongside increased centralization and hierarchical social structures.

Taken all together, in each of the key periods in transitions, perishable crafts react and interweave with other changes in lifestyle, changes in food-getting technologies and changes in how the main edge tools of that society work. The contention of this chapter is thus that the perishable crafts, which are so rarely seen in the archaeological records, are nonetheless important factors in how people live their lives and how they adopted and integrated older practices with new ways of life and new sets of raw materials and food. The perishable missing majority is not a silent partner in these macro-scale shifts: it is an integral part of them.

Notes

1 Culture is seen as a human trait, which in consequence has led to a focus on how materials can be used to understand the evolving mind (de Beaune et al 2009; Falk 2011; Hoffecker 2011; Ingold 2011; Russell 2012; Wells 2012).
2 Where there is good evidence and new well-dated finds, the interpretations are exploring broadscale changes and social issues reinterpreting old sites alongside the new evidence (Bailey et al 2005; Bamforth 2011; Beattie et al 2000; Crowell et al 2010; Cummings and Harris 2011; Downes and Ritchie 2003; Evans 2005a, 2005b; Ford and Pine 2003; Gibson and Simpson 1998; Gronnow 2009; Hoffecker 2002; Hungry Wolf 1982; Longworth and Varndell 1996; Louwe Koojimans 2000; Louwe Koojimans et al 2001a, 2001b; Magnusson 2010; Needham and Spence 1996; Owoc 2005a, 2005b; Panter-Brick et al 2001; Parker Pearson 2000; Pettit 2011; Pétrequin et al 2001; Pollard 2000; Price and Gebauer 2005; Pryor 2010; Robinson 2002; von den Driesch and Peters 1995).
3 The role of learning and skill in executing crafts has drawn authors from the social sciences as well as archaeology (Adamson 2007; Alfody 2005; Apel and Knuttson 2006; Ciszuk 2007; Crawford 2009; Dormer 1997a, 1997b, 1997c; Easton McLeod 2000; Greenhalgh 1997; Hosfield 2009; Meuli 1997; Risatti 2007; Sennett 2008; Spahan and Wherry 2010; Tabor 2008; Wherry 2006; Yair et al 2001). Additional sources deal with the practical aspects of craft transmission and skill acquisition (Andersson Strand 2008; Bamforth and Finlay 2008; Basketmaker's Association 1989; Bleed 2008; Ferguson 2008; Hammarlund 2005; Hurcombe and Lemieux 2005; Kania 2010; Malafouris 2010; Nørgaard 2008; Pelegrin 1990; Stout 2011; Stout and Chaminade 2009; Stout et al 2008; Tehrani and Riede 2008).

6

INTEGRATING ORGANIC AND INORGANIC MATERIAL CULTURE

Introduction

The holistic approach advocated in Chapter 1 explained that, although a large part of material culture is missing, it nonetheless existed and affected many of the other categories of material culture that survive more frequently. In particular the stone and ceramic evidence from sites can be used as ways of further exploring the organic material culture. In addition, many tools are used to work organic material, so if functional analysis by usewear traces or by analogy can be deployed, then tools and devices are important sources of evidence for the kinds of perishable technologies that may have been taking place. There are other less straightforward ways of exploring these relationships between organic and inorganic material culture. One of these is the phenomenon of skeuomorphism. Skeuomorphs are objects that allude to, by their features, an item made in a different material. These issues are explored below, and a foundation laid for thinking through the material culture from a site in a more holistic way. The final part of the chapter uses this approach to investigate the whole sense of material culture from the British Neolithic site of Etton, a causewayed enclosure in East Anglia, England. The basic premise is that, although artefacts are studied by archaeologists in categories that are defined by materials (for example, flint, pottery and metalwork), that is not how they existed in life. In life they were an integrated complex web of relationships between edge tools for working other materials, containers of many different materials for different purposes, and clothes and structures to keep people warm and safe. This whole material culture was bound up with people's ideas, identities and beliefs, and for most of prehistory people used materials that were around them in the environment, or for which they could exchange goods. This holistic approach to the 'missing majority' is underpinned by ethnographic and experimental data. It is also a way of thinking through from the known facts of a site, to interpretive possibilities. Those possibilities can be opened up to include the missing majority in ways that show new evidence trails and lend themselves to further investigations. The holistic approach advocated here, therefore, crosscuts different specialisms as they exist within archaeology, and also the boundary between evidence and interpretation. In much the same way that periods and regions have common themes in styles of pottery and stone tools, so these broader themes will exist in perishable material culture traditions. Therefore it is possible to use some particular sites to stand as examples of what might be happening on sites with a lesser range of material culture preserved. A key feature of the holistic approach is to put back some idea of the missing majority, and make it part of people's thinking, and to show that when this approach is applied, the whole is more than the sum of the parts.

Skeuomorphs

The study of skeuomorphs is both a practical and conceptual act. Skeuomorphs are lookalike objects, showing features resembling the characteristics found in other materials. An outline of the 'organics from inorganics' projects approach to skeuomorphs has already been provided (Hurcombe 2008b) and a short overview will be given here. Skeuomorphs can exist in many materials, referencing many others. The one that most archaeologists know is ceramic vessels imitating other materials. This is because pottery is a plastic medium that lends itself well to this kind of imitation. It is also one where a classic paper (Manby 1995) has set down the skeuomorphs for a set of small British prehistoric vessels known as accessory cups. These had decoration on the sides of the vessels, indicating basketry style features, and imitation spiral coiling on the base. The paper also drew attention to a ceramic scoop which appeared to imitate leather, and a vessel known as the Corbridge food vessel (Manby 1995: 86). Thus his classic article drew on ceramics that referenced coil baskets, a more complicated footed vessel of basketry style weave, and stitched leather. As part of the investigations of skeuomorphs, Plate 49.7 shows a leather scoop that has been recreated using a combination of tanning and heating technologies. The reconstruction of the leather version shows that the scoop functions well, and the stitching is a very distinctive feature. Likewise, the pottery vessels thought to be skeuomorphs have been explored by reconstruction projects undertaken in partnership with a professional basket-maker, and are illustrated and have been described (Hurcombe 2008b: 102–5). The physical recreation of objects possibly referenced by the prehistoric skeuomorphs was an interesting exploratory act, not a straightjacket. In each case, several different reconstructions of the versions were made, to allow for understandings to develop and to explore different materials in the reconstruction role. What the experiments collectively showed was that the visual references were indeed pragmatic and could be turned into workable objects. Some materials used in the process were not successful, while others were. The series of trials explored cause-and-effect of materials and processes, and ruled out some possibilities for these while addressing very broad themes of the styles of organic material culture referenced by skeuomorphs. They also showed, unsurprisingly, that the skeuomorphs did not necessarily recreate one particular object, but were a generalized category of object. Earwood (1993: 222) reaches similar conclusions for wooden vessels.

In our own society, this kind of visual referencing can occur when an original material is substituted by one that is more durable or more easily available. A concrete garden container will not fracture in the frost in the way a ceramic one might, a wooden sword will be safer as a toy than a metal one, and plastic allows for cheaper, lighter and infinitely varied copies of a whole range of materials. There are also skeuomorphs that refer to iconic items that are referenced as symbols. These higher level skeuomorphs can be facsimiles relating to rituals or art objects.

Sometimes in the modern world sizing changes, for example, shrinking of the material if is it to be a toy, or if it is signifying the larger object as a reference in art. Thus skeuomorphs in our own society are not one unique set of criteria and one phenomenon, they are a broad group and serve a variety of purposes. In the pre-historic example outlined by Manby, the accessory vessels were all buried items, deliberately placed in the ground. Thus these are likely to be part of significant ritual actions, even if they are versions of objects that were common in life. There are also broader references, such as the suggestion that Neolithic bowls reference round-based wooden vessels, or the other way around. Sometimes these similarities in form are difficult to unravel, because the relationship could be in both directions, or in tandem. Skeuomorphs are thus one of the conceptual ways in which the organic material culture of the past can be explored, but in ways that are open to debate. In prehistory the key ways in which features can be copied, are also concentrated in particular kinds of materials, which lend themselves more to a variety of forms. The obvious example is pottery, because of the plasticity of clay, and also wood, which can be carved into a range of shapes. Objects such as bone and stone items can be skeuomorphs but are not so often to be seen in this light. Clay is the ultimate plastic material for skeuomorphs.

Impressions in ceramics

Impressions in ceramics have long been a source of information about the missing perishable material culture. If nothing else, the direction of twist and size of cordage can be obtained from these sorts of features. In British prehistory it was thought that cord-wrapped sticks were producing many of the impressions on pottery, but closer analysis has shown that there is no one simple phenomenon in the materials used to place impressions on pots (Hurcombe 2008b). The research showed that three kinds of impressions could be categorized: chance impressions, impressions occurring as part of the production process but that were allowed to remain on the surface, and impressions that had been added deliberately for decorative effect. The significance of the production process is that the decorative ceramic impressions are deliberate. Impressions by chance should be a more random subset of the materials available in a society, whereas impressions as part of the production process are drawn from a subset of material remains used in ceramic production. The most obvious is a mat, basket or cloth used as a base to more easily turn the clay as the pot is being formed, and for this, mats and open basket forms might be preferred. For enabling clay to be taken out of moulds more successfully, more rounded baskets, or cloth-lined wooden or basketry moulds might have been useful. In practice, such impressions are not neutral acts. As a plastic material, clay can be reshaped for a considerable period of time as it dries. Thus a pot produced on a mat could be left for the top part to dry. When the pot was removed from the mat, the resulting impression could be obscured or removed before the firing process if it was not desired. In these ways ceramic impressions start as particular sets of finite evidence, but lead into intentionality, chance and more social aspects of the *chaîne opératoire*. However, the first step is to understand how such impressions effect themselves on clay.

The research which investigated this phenomenon[1] collected a wide range of materials and technologies to form different types of impressions, and used these to impress clay samples, which were then fired to serve as points of comparison and establish a reference collection. As examples, Plates 57.1 and 57.2 show a plied string and a plait made from bulrush (*Scirpus lacustris*) and the impressions in clay made by these items.

The twisted cord of the impression is clearly visible both as a direction of twist in the individual elements, and also as a direction in the finished plyed cord. It is possible to measure the length and angle of the ply and the twist direction. The way in which the clay impression is interrupted even though the impression is quite deep also indicates the firm rounded nature of the plied cord. This cord has never been used, so it is not worn, and although flexible, it is not flaccid. In these ways the hardness of the material, and its depth, affect the impression in the clay. Clearly some impressions will have been pushed into the clay with more force and this can result in slightly different images, but it is always possible to measure the relative depth and gaps to give some indication of the depth of the original. Thus measurements from ceramic impressions can be appropriate proxies for the real item. The same two images also show that the way in which *Scirpus* puffs up slightly and has small creases that are features which can be seen in the impressions. In contrast the New Zealand flax (*Phormium* tenax) worked into a hexagonal plait, is split material, which has curled slightly at the harder edges which also have a darker tone. Thus Plates 57.3 and 57.4 show the fine detail of the ribbing of the *Phormium* in some places, and the thicker edge curling upwards in others. Nonetheless, the technology and detail of the structure are characterized by the impression. Finer textures can also be perceived provided that the clay is not too heavily tempered with large materials. Plates 57.5 and 57.6 show a variety of impressions from felt, hide (flesh side after softening), and a set of three different plain weave linen textiles. For the woven samples it is possible to describe the weave structures and measure the clay impressions as proxies for the original material. There are also different textures created by the more amorphous materials of hide and felt. Furthermore, by impressing a range of different cord and textile materials it was obvious that even hard spun wool and hair have a lot of extraneous material with fibres escaping from the twisted yarn. These characteristics marked them out distinctly from plant-based materials. Sinew was intermediate. In these ways it is possible to rule out some kinds of fibres and to suggest a range of other fibre types from analogies with these impressions. However, as Chapter 2 has shown, there are many more plant materials than cotton or linen. The ceramic impressions on the Bronze Age accessory vessel illustrated in Plate 58.3 are distinctive and fine. They were assessed as being made from plant rather than animal material, but a range of different plants was explored to reproduce the cord marks. This vessel was replicated because it is an accessory cup similar to those described by Manby (1995) as it too has decoration on the base, imitating a spiral coil technique. The vessel was successfully reproduced using a very fine lime-bast plied cord, although other plant fibres would have worked as well. Thus for this small accessory cup the testing of possible materials could give plant material as the cordage, but not specify which one.

The bases of vessels have been assessed for their production impressions. Plates 58.1 and 58.2 show the bases of two vessels, the first from the Neolithic site of Barnhouse, Orkney, UK (Richards 2005), and the second from Knackyboy, a Bronze Age cairn from the Isles of Scilly off Southwest Britain (O'Neil 1952). Both show spiral coil technique baskets, with the Orkney example showing damage to the basketry item, exposure of a solid core in places, and firm thin stitching materials. The base from the Isles of Scilly has a bound bundle start and a well-worn regular spiral. Thus both basketry impressions demonstrate the coil technique, possible materials used, and the condition of the basket.

However, that is just the start of the interpretation. If these baskets were old when they were being used as part of the ceramic production process, then old could imply well-worn and now used for this process, or well-worn and deliberately used as part of a personal item associated with this ceramic and baked onto its surface in a more permanent way. While the Neolithic base, in Plate 58.1 could be described as quite tattered, the Bronze Age base in Plate 58.2 is worn but still intact. The Bronze Age impression was on the base of a funerary urn that was placed upside-down on the ground. Thus, this impression at least, would have been visible as part of the funeral rite for a person. Although this impression could have been obliterated before firing, it was not. Whether this was a chance production impression allowed to remain on the surface, or a production impression with significance, which was then a highly visible part of the ceremony, is open to interpretation.

In these ways the starting points of ceramic impressions lead into more conceptual issues and the role of mats and baskets within a society. It should be noted that both my own, and Mary Ann Owoc's (2005b) research of the Scillonian impressions suggests that there are a range of matting and basketry and cordage techniques. In many cases the existing basketry finds suggest rich diversity.

The success of the analyses of ceramic impressions can be assessed by the work of Soffer et al (2000), who have established the Palaeolithic presence of cordage technologies and weaves. Because of the richness of some impression traditions it has been possible to produce whole books on the missing majority of perishable textiles, based on the ceramic impressions. Drooker (1992) has assessed the textiles from a Mississippian village at Wickliffe. Impressions on ceramics do not just reflect cordage technologies, they are also made by combs, sticks and in some cases small bones, such as bird bones as shown in Plates 59.1 and 59.2 (see below).[2] Much depends upon the quality and quantity of impressions: the quantities of impressions at Wickliffe are not matched in number by a site in Europe.

Tools and devices as evidence for perishable technologies

Many of the images used in this book feature tools used to process materials into items of perishable material culture. These are broad-ranging and exist in many different kinds of materials. The most obvious are the stone tools that can be used to harvest and process the materials described in this book, but many perishable items can be produced by picking and processing the materials by hand. Nonetheless tools and devices form important evidence for perishable technologies. These include metal tools, such as the implement used to comb shoe hay, shown in Plate 14.2; the antler used as wedges for working wood, shown in Plate 4 along with shells used to scrape out charred wood; a wooden mallet used for beating bark fibre to extend and soften it in Plate 7, and the shell tool in Plate 13, used to process the New Zealand flax fibres. Natural materials, such as beaver teeth, can be used as tools, seen in Plate 31 and bones can be finely worked into combs, needles, awls and defleshers; see Plates 37 and 38. Several of these show specific items used for basketry production, such as bone awls, and weaving tools. A weaving comb of antler is shown in Plate 40 (top left) and a bone comb in Plate 37.2. Both the bone defleshing tool in Plate 37.1 (right) and the large shell in Plate 43, bottom right, have been used for working hides as defleshing tools and softening tools. The needles shown in Plate 37 could be for sewing in a traditional sense, but could also be associated with cordage technologies and the production of looping-around-the-core style material and netting. The defleshing tool is shown in action in Plate 44.5 removing the grain on an ostrich skin. Beside it is the image of a stone scraper, hafted in a stick, and below it Plate 44.6 shows the stretching of a skin; on the right hand side the toothed wooden implement seen on the post is another softening aid from traditional Sámi culture in northern Scandinavia.

The tools and technologies for weaving are amongst the best known examples of evidence for organic materials from inorganic materials (Andersson Strand 2003, 2007; Andersson Strand et al 2010, 2013). The evidence from spindle whorls, weights and loom elements have been covered in the previous chapter but it is important to remember that many pieces of equipment are made entirely from organic materials, and that some elements have very little modification. Weaving combs or picks (here, a pin-like instrument), and weaving-swords are the next most recognizable elements of the tools commonly associated with spinning and weaving. Spindle whorls and loom weights are ceramic evidence for spinning and weaving activities. However, as in the image in Plate 53 shows, there are many ways of spinning including using a hooked stick, and using spindle whorls of organic material that would not survive well. It has already been pointed out that the weaving structures shown in Plates 54 and 55 have many elements that are not going to be attributable directly to looms. Some of the more shaped items, such as the forked sticks visible in the warp-weighted loom images, and an arrangement of loom weights in the ground, might be the best evidence for the frameworks that could have been associated with weaving. Even the rigid wooden heddle rod in Plate 55.3, can be replaced by hide strips and need leave no trace. The string heddle system, shown in the other images of a warp-weighted loom, would also leave no trace. The tablets shown in Plate 55 are sometimes found if they are made of bone – and examples are known ethnographically of horn and wood – but the latter are not likely to survive often in the archaeological record. The most developed tool is the large weaving sword shown in Plate 54, but the close-up view of the ground loom shows that the rest of the material is composed of sticks and relatively amorphous shaped pieces of wood. Where weights and whorls are found these can be interpreted with the aid of experimental evidence as outlined in Chapter 3.

The wear system of some of the unusual shapes of weights is also an important feature of understanding their use and as shown in Figure 5, there are many ways in which frameworks could be used to aid the production of quite sophisticated and fine fabrics, using methods that do not involve ceramic weights. This brief review can be supplemented by looking at a recently published volume on textiles and textile production in Europe (Gleba and Mannering 2012), where many of the contributors outline the evidence for weights, tools and devices to augment and amplify the understanding available from the perishable material culture remains themselves.

Wear analysis of tools

Wear analysis is increasingly able to show the production of perishable technologies, using evidence from stone, bone and antler tools. This is supplemented by a great deal of experimental evidence which is drawing inspiration from the ethnographic data.[3] Some discussion on the usewear traces of awls has already been outlined (van Gijn 2005, 2006; and see Plate 38). Here it is proposed to concentrate on one neglected aspect of wear analysis as an example of the ways in which these sorts of studies can open up new ideas in the production of perishable technologies. It has long been recognized by European wear specialists that there are special stone tools with distinctive wear traces that, because of their bright distinctive characteristics, could be due to working plants. These tools are known from Neolithic contexts in Britain, and also in Denmark from Ertobølle Mesolithic deposits. They have a micro-denticulated, or serrated, edge, characterized by a macroscopically visible strong polish over a small section of the surface of the tool, extending not more than 1.5cm along it. These tools have fine transverse use actions. Furthermore, the wear traces are concentrated at the very tips of the serrations, and not in the hollows of the serrations. These characteristics are shown in Plate 60. The tools themselves come in a variety of shapes and sizes. Some have backing on the edge so that they are easy to hold, others have natural cortex on one side or made from very irregular flakes. They are found on longbarrows, causewayed enclosures, Neolithic settlement sites, and in association with the Sweet Track, a Neolithic trackway on the Somerset Levels, UK. They are thus a wide ranging tool type, and amongst the most numerous of all the formal tool types identified on Neolithic sites. On most British causewayed enclosure sites, these kinds of tools are as numerous, or nearly so, as scrapers (Hurcombe 2007c: 46, Fig. 5). The category of tool known as 'edge-trimmed flakes' or 'utilized flakes', when examined closely, have also included these distinctive traces so it is likely that the function they served is even more prevalent. The material looked at from the Somerset Levels and sites such as the causewayed enclosure at Ramsgate have demonstrated that many more flakes with this characteristic set of wear exist in these other tool categories,[4] which are themselves an interesting prospect of study. I have explored flax, hemp and nettle *chaîne opératoires* in traditional water retting methods (Hurcombe 2007c, 2010), and also because of the wear traces, processes that do not involve water, but manual processing, as described in Chapter 2. Using this varied approach to materials and technologies and *chaîne opératoires*, the best interpretation of these serrated tools to date is that they served a key role in plant processing traditions. Uses such as those described for the preparation of nettles and other raw materials can vary the *chaîne opératoire* considerably, but fit well within the broad framework of the archaeological wear traces. This experimental dataset strongly suggests that these serrated tools are part of plant-working traces associated with fibre and cordage technologies. It is obvious from the ethnographic data that even more possibilities deserve further experimental exploration. Harvesting of green materials, such as *Phragmites*, and processing these for different kinds of usage will create variations in the *chaîne opératoire* and the ensuing wear traces. Nonetheless, what this kind of data shows is the potential of wear analysis to open up possibilities and understandings on broad spectrums across the perishable material culture traditions.

Holistic site based studies: an example from Etton

In Neolithic Britain a causewayed enclosure, a typical Neolithic site type in Britain, was selected as an example of the kinds of interactions between organic and inorganic elements on site. Broadly speaking, these have been grouped into stone and pots, and then some of the organic evidence has been discussed. The site has been fully published by English Heritage (Pryor 1998). Along with many other causewayed enclosure sites, Etton has serrated flakes. These have very small flake scars creating a microserration, which can be as fine as 10 serrations to 1cm, although they can also be quite coarse, with layers of retouch. These pieces are characterized as well by a lustrous ventral surface in a narrow band. As explained in Chapter 2, these serrated flakes have been shown to be useful in the preparation of fibres for cordage technologies and fabric production. There were likewise many scrapers found on site, but these could have been used on a broad range of materials, including wood, bone, antler and horn, as well as hide. The polished stone axes and axe fragments could have been used to fell trees, but were also likely to have been woodworking tools, and one haft for a polished stone axe was also found. For the bone tools there were a variety of items, including a cattle rib with scored marks, whose size and appearance indicates that it could have been used as a polisher, beater or scutching knife, along with many other purposes. A scapula with cutmarks on the surface could have formed a work surface. Scapula shovels were also noted. The animal evidence includes gracile sheep, domestic and wild cattle, including an aurochs skull with horns, and also a fox mandible and a horse skull. Some of these deposits are ritual depositions and serve to show that the role of some animals was more than their food value. Certainly fox has useful and beautiful fur, and large thick hides could be obtained from cattle and horse. The sheep would have provided much smaller skins, but the presence of some red deer and roe deer indicates that these animals were also available. In at least one case a red deer fragment shows marks from skinning, indicating that the hide was removed and presumably exploited for material culture. The antler tools include red deer picks and a red deer crown, which could have been a rake, as well as a broken antler baton, and antler combs that could have been used for a variety of purposes. At Etton the material is too degraded to see wear traces, but at other causewayed enclosure sites these are present. Combs have been suggested to be hide processing and dressing tools, but they could also be used for many other purposes, from stripping seed heads, to aligning fibres prior to spinning. The pots present on site include some fine examples, and many are shell tempered, indicating the use of shells.[5] Plate 59 shows potsherds with shell temper. As can be seen from the top two images the shell was very evident on the surface, with large pieces of shell still visible on Plate 59.2. Shell temper was also seen in large vessels, such as in Plate 59.3, and in the small bowl in Plate 59.6. In each case the shell temper adds another layer of inference and involvement with organic material culture.[6]

Plate 59.4 shows the remains of the antler comb, with clear examples of the groove, which has been deepened to help form one of the tines, others of which have now broken. No wear traces were visible on this find. Plate 59.5 shows a detail of the so-called 'string' from Etton. This was found near a piece of birch bark, which may have aided its preservation, which is remarkable. The detail shows the slight thickening around a hole where a side branch has occurred, and the slight twist to the fibres as Z in the individual elements can clearly be seen, although elsewhere the piece is loosely plied, as S. The presence of the pots also indicates that wood has been used for fuel, and the piece in Plate 59.3 has been chosen because parts of the details and the thickening of the rim and the impressions can be seen as visual reminiscences of stitching. It is possible that this object has skeuomorphic characteristics. Other baked clay finds include a series of weights, which could be loom weights or net sinkers, and one piece that could be kiln furniture or serve another purpose. Plant finds include two pieces of birch bark, one of which was a small square, placed as a mat underneath a finely made small bowl, and the other of which was larger and slightly folded over. The larger piece was found near the flax 'string', which on close inspection does not appear to be retted but instead looks to be comprised of several stems, loosely processed, twisted and bundled up. Wooden finds on site include heeled points, which can be seen as awls. These would be suitable for basketry in the coil style, or looped basketry work. There are also quantities of chips of wood and a wooden axe haft made from a half split log, probably of alder. A wooden plank and tangentially split pieces were found at the site, with squared timber from one area. There are a number of Y-shaped sticks, one of which is short, but several of which are long and very similar to that illustrated in Plate 1. There are also a number of wooden bowls and trays from the site that appear to have a variety of shapes.

Taken altogether, some of this evidence suggests that coil basketry or looping work could have been undertaken on site, and that woodland was managed; coppice stools have been found. The Y-shaped sticks, potential weights and some of the bone and antler tools can be seen as potentially useful for weaving. The wooden bowls and pottery appear broadly similar to the extent that Taylor (1998) suggests that the bowls of wood are copying those of pot. In this respect much depends upon familiarity with the pieces, and the relationship could well be the other way around. There are flax remains from the site, which is highly unusual, although flax is known from other sites in Neolithic Britain. In addition to flax, other plant remains include much nettle and some other potentially useful species. For example, there are sedges, and plants such as *Typha* and *Scirpus*, which could all be useful for basketry and thatching materials. The nettles could indeed be weed species from disturbed or damp ground, but could also be part of the cordage and fabric production. Other plants found on the site can be used as dyes, for example *Galium* sp., can give a red dye but there is no other direct evidence of dyeing process other than the oak bark, which could be used as a mordant dye assistant. The presence of the arrowheads suggests that there were bows, and feathers used in the fletching, and that there was a bow string. Taken altogether, the evidence from the stone tools, with substantial numbers of serrated implements, can also be added to the material culture repertoire. Thus the site has interesting evidence for the use of hides, feathers and shell, and for the activities of woodworking, and potentially also fabric and basketry production. The bark that is present is from mature trees in some cases, which must have come from outside the immediate vicinity of the enclosure. In this respect, the bark has been imported, and can be seen as an important resource in its own right. The bark could have been used as a tanning agent for hides, or as a mordant for dye for plant and animal based fibres. The presence of birch bark likewise suggests that there were birch bark containers and mats available. The *chaîne opératoire* for the bark must have included its removal in the spring, and for the coppiced wood included cutting of the material towards the end of summer while the leaves were still present on the evidence of the final growth ring. There are other scheduling indications from the animals and the deer antler.

From this short review of one site, it can be seen that a more holistic approach to understanding what different materials and environmental evidence might indicate can offer more than the individual analysis. Integrating the organic and inorganic components of a site, and deploying an augmented idea of the kind of material culture being produced allows for broader interpretive possibilities. This short overview draws in data from possible skeuomorphs, organic temper in pottery, possible loom weights and tools and devices that could be used in the production of perishable material culture and some wear traces known from similar kinds of tools, as well as drawing on ethnographic knowledge and experimental data. The 'background' environmental data is both questioned as to assumptions about 'weed' and incidental materials, and also amplified as to the possible reasons why material was on site or draws attention to potential uses of the plants available in and around the site. It provides an idea of how the holistic approach to material culture might be undertaken. A key feature of the holistic approach is to put back some idea of the missing majority, and make it part of people's thinking, and to show that when this approach is applied, the whole is more than the sum of the parts.

Notes

1 This was part of a project funded by Leverhulme that looked at alternative methods of investigating cordage and basketry technologies. It involved assessing how materials would show their identity and features of technologies using impressions. There are a lot of pottery styles where the decoration is either direct impressions of shells, cordage, bone or other organic materials or a visual reference to organic materials (Gelbert 2001; Gosselain 2001; Kinnes and Varndell 1995; Salanova 1992, 1998; Wallaert 2008; Wentink 2006).

2 The techniques of using impressions and drawing evidence from tools used in textiles production and experimental evidence is well established (Drooker 2001; Ferrero 2013; Gerend 1904; King 1978; Knudsen 2007; Ryder 2005), from both the American scholarly traditions and also those in Europe (Adovasio et al 1996; Hurley 1979; Liddell 1929; Manske et al 2004).

3 See Anderson (1980); Beugnier (2007); Beugnier and Crombé (2007); Hurcombe (2000b, 2008b); Juel Jensen (1994); Owen (1999, 2000); van Gijn (1989, 1998a).

4 The discussion is informed by the full publication and also a visit to the British Museum stores, to view all of the potsherds and those organic materials available for study. All of the flakes from the Somerset Levels Project were examined in Taunton Museum, Somerset, UK, and a selection of serrated flakes and utilized flakes were examined for a report in press for the Ramsgate Harbour causewayed enclosure currently being published by Canterbury Archaeological Trust.

5 Shell has been studied as a temper material for its performance qualities and also for its significance (Blitz 1993; Feathers 1989; Stimmell et al 1982).

6 The sherd shown in Plates 59.1 and 59.2 is from an Ebbsfleet bowl, and is described by Pryor (1998: 197, Fig. 201) as a medium fabric with shell and flint temper and rows of fine bird bone impressions. These bird bone impressions were slightly different on the two sherd faces, with the articular surface of the distal humerus impressed on the interior and rim, and the proximal end on the exterior. The sherd comes from causeway G, section 177, layer 2, phase 2. Plate 59.3 shows sherd M39 (Pryor 1998: 162, 166, Fig. 178). This has a rolled over rim, with a fabric that includes medium–coarse shell, and inside diagonal decoration on the rim. The neck has panels divided by vertical applied cordons, and is decorated with stabs and impressions. The small bowl in Plate 59.6 is from layer 3, phase 1C, and is a simple Mildenhall bowl (Pryor 1998: 167, Fig. 180, 169).

7

CONCLUSIONS

In this short overview and summary, the aims of the work form the framework. The main problem identified in writing this book was the missing majority – the perishable aspects of material culture that rarely survive but that, more significantly, are missing from our thinking. The research presented here shows how an holistic approach can be used to put the missing majority back into archaeological thinking. It shows how plants and animals contribute to not just foods, but material culture, and do so in ways that integrate with subsistence practices and with the inorganic evidence from stone, pottery and metal, which survives far more often. The organic material culture component is a significant factor in broadscale shifts in lifestyles, and the material culture made from plants and animals deserves to be a feature of discussions and interpretations even when it is missing.

The first aim was to raise awareness of the missing majority, the perishable material culture of past societies and make the case for a more holistic approach to material culture. In Chapters 2 and 3, the missing majority has been explored in breadth, detail and full colour. Unusual plant materials in the modern world, such as tree bark, bast fibres and roots, have been discussed, and an augmented appreciation of how common plants such as nettles and bulrushes can be used has been presented. The range of usage of materials from animals, including sinews and feathers, fish skins and intestines as well as animals skins, and many different kinds of tanning technologies have all been outlined. Cordage and cordage technologies as sophisticated ways of meeting everyday needs for not just string but clothing, containers and shelters have been covered. This vast wealth of information has drawn on a wide range of examples and case studies from different parts of the world. Inevitably, this has been something of a whistlestop tour, but it has deliberately paused longer where the materials and technologies are less familiar. In this way I have hoped to increase knowledge and appreciation of the lesser known elements of the perishable material culture world. It is possible to write whole books on textiles, and many have already done so; therefore I have dwelt less on the better known techniques, because more is known about them.

Archaeologists have increasingly sophisticated techniques at their disposal, especially at the level of biological and chemical markers. These issues will become more refined in the coming decade and contribute to a micro-awareness of some of the identifications of species and technologies. However, right now, a better appreciation of these sorts of issues on the ground in the field units, and the ideas of the excavators as directors and as diggers, will lead to a better appreciation of these finds, as more are discovered and appropriately handled from the ground and into the field base or lab environment where they can be further excavated in controlled conditions. The research here will raise awareness of the possibilities; a morass of dark plant remains may be a form of textile, a clump of rush material could be a twined rain cloak, an oblong clump of moss all that remains of a shoe stuffed with moss, a gelatinous ooze the precious remnant of a fat-tanned bag, an irregular soil stain a hide wrapping and a thin soil layer the remains of a reed thatch now preserved as a layer rich in phytoliths.

I have also emphasized the beginnings of the *chaîne opératoire* and the object biographies because material culture does not spontaneously form any more than food does. Archaeologists think of subsistence practices as direct connections to landscapes and places. For food, archaeologists consider seasonal exploitation, equipment, processing and storage as well as cooking practices and for each there is a sense of location and strategy. For animal and plant craft resources the same rich strategic issues exist: they need to be considered in the same way. Any animals obtained for food will also need to have their material culture usage factored in to plans and strategies. Just because a plant or tree is in one place does not mean it is always available as a good resource. Even plants that are green all year will have cycles of activity that may make them 'at their best' for the intended purpose only for a short period. Or the resource is available over a more extended period but the dry weather slot to stabilize them prior to storage means that the strategic exploitation has to be within a smaller window of time. People's choices interweave with subsistence practices and other cultural aspects but they are strategies which are part of their cultural behaviour and on which their wellbeing relies. The opening phases of the *chaînes opératoires* have been given more attention here because they have more importance than commonly appreciated. By emphasizing places in the landscape, management cycles and exploitation strategies that form the start of material culture production the constraints and links with a resource taken from the landscape at a particular moment in time in a particular place can be given more prominence. Ideas about the intensity of that relationship and the management possibilities that could exist, from very early periods, have been explored and explained. There are new ways of seeing the landscape–people relationships, and interactions and these offer new interpretive possibilities.

The second aim was to adopt an intensely practical understanding of the possible roles of plants and animals in the formation of material culture repertoire, while emphasizing the social constructs of materiality and technological choices, and providing tacit and explicit knowledge in new approaches. My own intensely practical relationship with many of the specific *chaîne opératoires* in this book and the processing of plants and animals, has informed every image and every word. It is my belief that the concept of materiality is enriched by this practical understanding, which interweaves pragmatic and social issues and opens up new vistas. Traditional craft practices are a rich source of information, but there is much more to be learned from engaging in these activities one's self as well. Not all practices known in the world today were known and pursued by past societies. Conversely, not all possibilities known and pursued in the past are available and known today. This mismatch is inevitable, but this book has gone some way to redressing this balance, and bringing to the attention of a broad range of archaeologists and others a wealth of materials and technologies to serve many different purposes. There is no inevitable pathway of perishable material culture. The arguments here have not been reductionist or essentialist, but instead about interpretive possibilities and the broadening of the ideas about materiality and material culture production and use.

The third aim was to demonstrate by examples and case studies how to extract information about the missing majority from the inorganic artefacts and environmental data. The case studies presented throughout the volume and rounded off in the concluding chapters have demonstrated this holistic approach to material culture, interweaving the perishable and inorganic elements together, as a viable way forward. Wear analysis and impressions analysis are important tools to understanding perishable material culture. Overall, this book has set out an agenda, and it has shown that the prehistoric perishable material culture, absent from so much of the archaeological record, as the missing majority, was most probably rich, diverse and colourful. It gave people the means to express individuality and communal identities and relationships, and it took up large parts of their time and planning in the extraction and manipulation of resources from the environment. As people did these things they were also affected by them, and their relationships with the plants and animals in the environment were strengthened as part of that act of making. In some instances a case can be made for an intense relationship with particular species of plants and animals. What you do is a large part of who you are. And the making of material culture is an act of performing social identity at the level of person and community, in a very individual way.

Finally, I would like to consider what different audiences might find useful from the ideas expressed in this book. For academic archaeologists, I hope they find a way of envisaging the missing majority that allows them to engage with this, and to factor it into their excavation and survey strategies, and the overall interpretation of the evidence from a site or landscape. For environmental archaeologists and zooarchaeologists, I hope that they will more often consider, investigate and report the material culture possibilities of some of the wild resources and the dual nature of the food/raw material resources. For practical excavators, from students on training excavations upwards, I hope that they think again about trowelling through a slight anomaly that they can feel, or a slight shadow that is at the edge of what they can recognize visually. If this book has made just a couple more excavators think about what might be the consequences of that next trowelling action, then more organic material culture will be found, and added to the existing dataset. This will be a good outcome. If craft practitioners are reading this book, I hope the sense of the richness of your own craft traditions comes off the page and into your hands. There is great depth to the history of human engagement with the plants and animals that make up our material culture world.

The missing majority is significant, irrespective of how well or how often it survives. This research has shown that missing from the archaeological record is not a reason for perishable material culture to be missing from our thinking. The idea of plants and animals as material culture needs to ripple outwards through all the layers of archaeological data gathering, interpretation and presentation. Thinking about and discussing organic material culture only on the rare occasions when it is found misses out important facets of the cultural repertoire, and the relationships between the individuals of a society and between people and their environment. Plants and animals are about more than food. They sustain the soul, by also providing the material for making important practical and symbolic items, and forming a large part of who we are. Perishable materials along with stone, pots, and metals created smells, textures, tastes, colours and sounds that caught people's attention and led their sensory worldview. People across the world today and in the past did not just eat, they made, and they used the plants and animals around them to interact with their world and with one another in complicated ways. The human interventions in the environment also shaped it, sometimes consciously but always interactively. Perishable material culture played a major role and it is well worth investigating the missing majority. You are indeed what you eat, and also what you make, wear, use and inhabit.

BIBLIOGRAPHY

Abbott, M. (1989) *Green Woodwork: Working with Wood the Natural Way*, Lewes: Craftsman Publications.

——(2004) *Living Wood: From Buying a Woodland to Making a Chair*, Bishop's Frome: Living Wood Books.

——(2011) *Going with the Grain: Making Chairs in the 21st Century*, Bishop's Frome: Living Wood Books.

Adams, M.J. (1977) 'Style in Southeast Asian materials processing: some implications for ritual and art', in H. Lechtman and R.S. Merrill (eds) *Material Culture: Styles, Organization, and the Dynamics of Technology*, New York: West Publishing Co., pp. 21–52.

Adamson, G. (2007) *Thinking Through Craft*, Oxford: Berg.

Adovasio, J.M. (1970) 'The origin, development and distribution of western archaic textiles', *Tebiwa*, 13: 1–40.

——(1977) *Basketry Technology: A Guide to Identification and Analysis*, Chicago: Aldine.

Adovasio, J.M. and Gunn, J. (1977) 'Style, basketry, and basketmakers', in J.N. Hill and J. Gunn (eds) *The Individual in Prehistory: Studies of Variability in Style and Prehistoric Technologies*, New York: Academic Press, pp. 137–52.

Adovasio, J.M., Soffer, O. and Klìma, B. (1996) 'Upper Palaeolithic fibre technology: interlaced woven finds from Pavlov I, Czech Republic, c. 26,000 years ago', *Antiquity*, 70: 526–34.

Adovasio, J.M., Andrews, R.L., Hyland, D.C. and Illingworth, J.S. (1999) 'Perishable industries from the Windover Bog: an unexpected window into the Florida Archaic', paper prepared for the Conference on the Significance of Organic Materials from Archaeological Contexts 1–5 December 1999, Gainsville, Florida.

Adrosko, R. (1971) *Natural Dyes and Home Dyeing*, New York: Dover.

Aiano, L. (2006) 'Pots and drums: an acoustic study of Neolithic pottery drums', *Euro Rea: Journal of (Re) construction and Experiment in Archaeology*, 3: 31–42.

Albrethsen, S.E. and Brinch Petersen, E. (1976) 'Excavation of a Mesolithic cemetery at Vedbaek, Denmark', *Acta Archaeologica*, 47: 1–28.

Alfaro Giner, C. (1980) 'Estudio de los materiales de cesterìa procedentes de la cueva de los Murciélagos (Albuñol, Granada)', *Trabajos de Prehistoria*, 37: 109–46.

——(1992) 'Two Copper Age tunics from Lorca, Murcia (Spain)', in L. Bender-Jørgensen and E. Munksgaard (eds) *Archaeological Textiles in Northern Europe: Report from the 4th NESAT symposium, 1–5 May 1990 in Copenhagen, Tidens Tand Nr. 5*, Copenhagen: Konservatorskolen det Kongelige Danske Kunstakademi, pp. 20–30.

Alfody, S. (2005) *The Development of Professional Fine Craft in Canada*, Montreal: McGill-Queens University Press.

Alperson, N, Richter, D, Goren-Inbar, N. (2007) 'Phantom hearths and the use of fire at gerehser Benot Ya'aqov, Israel', *PaleoAnthropology* 2007: 1–15.

Ambrose, S.H. (2001) 'Palaeolithic technology and human evolution', *Science*, 291: 1748–53.

Andersen, P. (1967) *Brikvævning*, Kopenhagen: Borgen.

Andersen, S. (1987a) 'Tybrind Vig: a submerged Ertebølle settlement in Denmark', in J. Coles and A. Lawson (eds) *European Wetlands in Prehistory*, Oxford: Clarendon, pp. 253–80.

——(1987b) 'Mesolithic dugouts and pebbles from Tybrind Vig, Denmark', *Acta Archaeologica*, 57: 87–106.

——(1995a) 'Ringkloster: Ertebølle trappers and wild boar hunters in Eastern Jutland, a survey', *Journal of Danish Archaeology*, 12: 13–59.

——(1995b) 'Coastal adaptation and marine exploitation in Late Mesolithic Denmark with special emphasis on the Limfjord region', in A. Fischer (ed.) *Man and Sea*, Oxford: Oxbow Books, pp. 41–66.

Anderson, C. and Storm, A. (2008) *Seal: Handling After the Shot*, Nyköping: Svenska Jägareförbundet.

Anderson, M.K. (2005) *Tending the Wild: Native American Knowledge and the Management of California's Natural Resources*, Berkeley: University of California Press.

Anderson, P.C. (1980) 'A testimony of prehistoric tasks: diagnostic residues on stone tool working edges', *World Archaeology*, 12(2): 181–94.

Anderson, P.C., Georges, J.-M., Vargiolu, R. and Zahouani, H. (2006) 'Insights from a tribological analysis of the tribulum', *Journal of Archaeological Science*, 33(11): 1559–68.

Andersson Strand, E. (2003) 'Tools for textile production from Birka and Hedeby', *Birka Studies*, vol. 8, Stockholm: Riksantikvarieainbetet.

——(2007) 'Textile tools and production during the Viking age', in C. Gillis and M.B. Nosch (eds) *Ancient Textiles: Production Craft and Society*, Oxford: Oxbow Books, pp. 17–25.

——(2008) 'Tools, textile production and society in Viking Age Birka', in M. Gleba, C. Munkholt and M.-L. Nosch (eds) *Dressing the Past*, Oxford: Oxbow Books, pp. 68–85.

Andersson Strand, E. and Nosch, M.L. (eds) (2013) *Tools, Textiles and Contexts*, Oxford: Oxbow Books.

Andersson Strand, E., Mårtensson, L., Nosch, M.-L. and Rahmstorf, L. (2008) 'New research on Bronze Age textile production', *Institute of Classical Studies of the University of London Bulletin*, 51: 171–74.

Andersson Strand, E., Gleba, M., Mannering, U., Munkholt, C. and Ringgard, M. (eds) (2010) *North European Symposium for Archaeological Textiles X*, Oxford: Oxbow Books.

Andrews, P. (1995) 'Experiments in taphonomy', *Journal of Archaeological Science*, 22: 147–53.

Andrews, P. (ed.) (1997) *Nomad Tent Types in the Middle East*, 2 vol, Wiesbaden: Ludwig Reichert.

Andrews, R.L. and Adovasio, J.M. (1996) 'The origins of fiber perishables production east of the Rockies', in J.B. Patterson (ed.) *A Most Indispensable Art: Native Fiber Industries from Eastern North America*, Knoxville: University of Tennessee Press, pp. 30–49.

Antipina, Y. (2001) 'Bone tools and wares from the site of Gorny (1690–1410 BC) in the Kargaly mining complex in the south Ural part of the east European steppe', in A.M. Choyke and L. Bartosiewicz (eds) *Crafting Bone: Skeletal Technologies through Time and Space, Proceedings of the 2nd Meeting of the (ICAZ) Worked Bone Research Group Budapest, 31 August–5 September 1999*, Oxford: British Archaeological Reports International Series 937, pp. 171–78.

Apel, J. and Knutsson, K. (eds) (2006) *Skilled Production and Social Reproduction*, Uppsala: Societas Archaeologica Upsaliensis.

Atzei, A.D. (2009) *Le piante nella tradizione popolare della Sardegna*, Sassari: Carlo Delfino.

Aveling, E.M. and Heron, C. (1998) 'Identification of birch bark tar at the Mesolithic site of Star Carr', *Ancient Biomolecules*, 2: 69–80.

——(1999) 'Chewing tar in the early Holocene: an archaeological and ethnographic evaluation', *Antiquity*, 73: 579–84.

Backwell, L.R. and d'Errico, F. (2001) 'Evidence of termite foraging by Swartkrans early hominids', *PNAS*, 98: 1358–63.

Bahn, P.G. and Vertut, J. (1988) *Images of the Ice Age*, Leicester: Windward.

Bahnson, A. (2005) 'Women's skin coats from West Greenland – with special focus on formal clothing of caribou skin from the early nineteenth century', in J.C.H. King, B. Pauksztat and R. Storrie (eds) *Arctic Clothing of North America – Alaska, Canada, Greenland*, London: British Museum Press, pp. 84–90.

Bailey, D., Whittle, A. and Cummings, V. (eds) (2005) *(Un)settling the Neolithic*, Oxford: Oxbow Books.

Baillargeon, M. (2005) 'Hide tanning: the act of reviving', in L. Frink and K. Weedman (eds) *Gender and Hide Production*, Lanham: Altamira Press, pp. 143–52.

Balfour-Paul, J. (1997) *Indigo in the Arab World*, Richmond: Curzon.

Ballard, J. (2012) *Elk*, Guilford, CT: Globe Pequot Press.

Bamforth, D. (2011) 'Origin stories, archaeological evidence, and post-Clovis Paleoindian bison hunting on the Great Plains', *American Antiquity*, 76(1): 24–40.

Bamforth, D. and Finlay, N. (2008) 'Introduction: archaeological approaches to lithic production skill and craft learning', *Journal of Archaeological Method and Theory*, 15: 1–27.

Barber, E.J.W. (1991) *Prehistoric Textiles: The Development of Cloth in the Neolithic and Bronze Ages, With Special Reference to the Aegean*, Princeton: Princeton University Press.

Basketmaker's Association (1989) *The National List of Basic Wage Rates in the Basketry Industry 1956: List of Basket Specifications*, Ware: Basketmaker's Association.

Bayman, J.M. (2002) 'Hohokam craft economies and the materialization of power', *Journal of Archaeological Method and Theory*, 9: 69–95.

Bazzanella, M. and Mayr, A. (2009) *I reperti tessili, le fusaiole e i pesi da telaio: dalla palafitta di Molina di Ledro*, Trento: Provincia Autonoma di Trento Soprintendenza Per i Beni Librari, Archivistici e Archaeologici.

Bazzanella, M., Mayr, A., Moser, L. and Rast-Eicher, A. (2003) *Textiles – Intrecci e tessuti dalla preistoria europea*, Catalogo della mostra tenutasi a Riva del Garda dal 24 maggio al 19 ottobre 2003, Trento: Esperia.

Beach, H. (2001) *A Year in Lapland: Guest of the Reindeer Herders*, Washington: University of Washington Press.

Beattie, O., Apland, B., Blake, E.W., Cosgrove, J.A., Gaunt, S., Greer, S., Mackie, A.P., Mackie, K.E., Straathof, D., Thorp, V. and Troffe, P.M. (2000) 'The Kwäday Dän Tsìinch discovery from a glacier in British Columbia', *Journal Canadien d'Archeologie*, 24: 129–47.

Beaudry, M.C. (2006) *The Material Culture of Needlework and Sewing*, Newhaven: Yale University Press.

Beck, C.W. and Borromeo, C. (1990) 'Ancient pine pitch: technological perspectives from a Hellenistic shipwreck', in A.R. Biers and P.E. McGovern (eds) *Organic Contents of Ancient Vessels: Materials Analysis and Archaeological Investigation*, Philadelphia: University of Pennsylvania Museum, pp. 51–58.

Belgrave, A. (1995) *How to Make Felt: Create Hats, Bags, Rugs, Masks, and Much More*, Tunbridge Wells: Search Press Ltd.

Belitzky, S., Goren-Inbar, N. and Werker, E. (1991) 'A Middle Pleistocene wooden plank with man-made polish', *Journal of Human Evolution*, 20: 349–53.

Bender-Jørgensen, L. (1986) *Forhistoriske Textiler I Skandinavien (Prehistoric Scandinavian Textiles)*, Copenhagen: Det Kongelige Nordiske Oldskriftselskab.

——(1992) *North European Textiles until AD 1000*, Aarhus: Aarhus University Press.

——(1994) 'Ancient costumes reconstructed: a new field of research', in G. Jaacks and K. Tidow (eds) *Archäologische Textilfunde – Archaeological Textiles, Textilsymposium Neumünster, 4–7 May 1993 (NESAT V)*, Neumünster: Textilmuseum Neumünster, pp. 109–13.

——(2007) 'The world according to textiles', in C. Gillis and M.-L.B. Nosch (eds) *Ancient Textiles: Production, Craft and Society*, Oxford: Oxbow Books, pp. 7–12.

Bender-Jørgensen, L. and Munksgaard, E. (eds) (1992) *Archaeological Textiles in Northern Europe*, Copenhagen: Kons Skol.

Bender-Jørgensen, L. and Walton, P. (1986) 'Dyes and fleece types in prehistoric textiles from Scandinavia and Germany', *Journal of Danish Archaeology*, 5: 177–88.

Bennett, N. and Bighorse, T. (1971) *Working With The Wool: How to Weave a Navajo Rug*, Arizona: Northland Press.

——(1997) *Navajo Weaving Way: The Path from Fleece to Rug*, Colorado: Interweave Press.

Bennike, P., Ebbeson, K. and Bender-Jørgensen, L. (1986) 'Early Neolithic skeletons from Bolkilde bog, Denmark', *Antiquity*, 60: 199–209.

Benson, L.V., Hattori, E.M., Taylor, H.E., Poulson, S.R. and Jolies, E.A. (2006) 'Isotope sourcing of prehistoric willow and tule textiles recovered from western Great Basin rock shelters and caves: proof of concept', *Journal of Archaeological Science*, 33: 1588–99.

Bergerbrant, S. (2010) 'Differences in the elaboration of dress in Northern Europe during the Middle Bronze Age', in E. Andersson Strand, M. Gleba, U. Mannering, C. Munkholt and M. Ringgaard (eds) *NESAT X The North European Symposium for Archaeological Textiles*, Oxford; Oxbow Books, pp. 21–25.

Bergfjord, C., Mannering, U., Frei, K.M., Gleba, M., Scharff, A.B., Skals, I., Heinemeier, J. and Nosch, M.-L.B., Holst, B. (2012) 'Nettle as a distinct Bronze Age textile plant', *Scientific Reports*, 2: 664.

Bernick, K. (1998a) *Basketry and Cordage from Hesquiat Harbour*, Victoria, BC: Royal British Columbia Museum.

——(1998b) *Hidden Dimensions: The Cultural Significance of Wetland Archaeology*, Vancouver: University of British Columbia Press.

——(1998c) 'Stylistic characteristics of basketry from Coast Salish area wet sites', in K. Bernick (ed.) *Hidden Dimensions: the Cultural Significance of Wetland Archaeology*, Vancouver: University of British Columbia Press, pp. 139–56.

Bernick, K. and Deur, D. (2002) 'Rethinking Pre-Colonial plant cultivation on the Northwest Coast of North America', *The Professional Geographer*, 54: 140–57.

Betancourt, P.B. (2007) 'Textile production at Pseira: the knotted net', in C. Gillis and M.-L.B. Nosch (eds) *Ancient Textiles: Production, Craft and Society*, Oxford: Oxbow Books, pp. 185–89.

Beugnier, V. (2007) 'Préhistoire du travail des plantes dans le nord de la Belgique. Le cas du Mésolithique ancien et du Néolithique final en Flandre', in V. Beugnier and P. Crombé (eds) *Plant Processing from a Prehistoric and Ethnographic Perspective*, Oxford: BAR International Series 1718, pp. 23–40.

Beugnier, V. and Crombé, P. (eds) (2007) *Plant Processing from a Prehistoric and Ethnographic Perspective*, Oxford: BAR International Series 1718.

Bevan-Jones, R. (2004) *The Ancient Yew: A History of Taxus Baccata*, Cheshire: Windgather Press.

Beyries, S. and Audouin-Rouzeau, F. (eds) (2002) *Le Travail du Cuir de la Préhistoire à Nos Jours*, Antibes: APDCA.

Beyries, S., Vasil'Ev, S.A., David, F., D'Iachenko, V.I., Karlin, C. and Chesnokov, Y.V. (2001) 'Uil, a Palaeolithic site in Siberia: an ethno-archaeological approach', in S. Beyries and P. Pétrequin (eds) *Ethno-Archaeology and its Transfers*, Oxford: British Archaeological Reports International Series 983, pp. 9–21.

Binford, L.R. (1980) 'Willow smoke and dog's tails: hunter-gatherer settlement systems and archaeological site formation', *American Antiquity*, 45: 4–20.

——(1981) *Bones – Ancient Men and Modern Myths*, New York: Academic Press.

——(2009) 'Nunamiut subsistence provinces – the mountain area: hunting with bow versus gun', in B. Grønnow (ed.) *On the Track of the Thule Culture from Bering Strait to East Greenland*, Copenhagen: National Museum, pp. 211–22.

Blaine, M.R. (1979) *The Ioway Indians*, Norman: University of Oklahoma Press.

Bleed, P. (2008) 'Skill matters', *Journal of Archaeological Method and Theory*, 15: 154–66.

Bliege Bird, R., et al (2008) 'The "fire stick farming" hypothesis: Australian Aboriginal foraging strategies, biodiversity and anthropogenic fire mosaics', *Proceedings of the National Academy of Sciences*, 105: 14796–801.

Blitz, J.H. (1993) 'Big pots for big shots: feasting and storage in a Mississippian community', *American Antiquity*, 58(1): 80–96.

Blumenschine, R.J., Marean, C.W. and Capaldo, S.D. (1996) 'Blind tests of inter-analyst correspondence and accuracy in the identification of cut marks, percussion marks, and carnivore tooth marks on bone surfaces', *Journal of Archaeological Science*, 23: 493–507.

Bocquet, A. (1994) 'Charavines il y a 5000 ans', *Dossiers d'Archeologie*, 199: 1–104.

Bodman, M. (2008) *Devon Leather: An Outline History of a Lost Industry: Nineteenth-Century Tanners and Tanneries*, Tiverton, Exeter: Leat Press.

Boeger, L. (2008) *Intertwined: The Art of Handspun Yarn, Modern Patterns, and Creative Spinning*, Beverly, MA: Quarry Books.

Boetzkes, M. and Lüth, J.B. (eds) (1991) *Woven Messages – Indonesian Textile Tradition in Course of Time*, Hildesheim: Roemer-Museum.

Boivin, N. (2008) *Material Cultures, Material Minds: The Impact of Things on Human Thought, Society and Evolution*, Cambridge: Cambridge University Press.

Boivin, N. and Owoc, M.A. (eds) (2004) *Soils, Stones and Symbols: Cultural Perception of the Mineral World*, London: UCL Press.

Bolton, E.M. (1960) *Lichens for Vegetable Dyeing*, London: Longacre.

Bonnichsen, R., Hodges, L., Ream, W., Field, K.G., Kirner D.L., Selsor, K. and Taylor, R. E. (2001) 'Methods for the study of ancient hair: radiocarbon dates and gene sequences from individual hairs', *Journal of Archaeological Science*, 28: 775–85.

Bourdieu, P. (1977) *Outline of a Theory of Practice*, Cambridge: Cambridge University Press.

Bowes, B.G. (2010) *Trees and Forests: a colour guide*, London: Manson.

Boyce, M.S (1989) *The Jackson Elk Herd: Intensive wildlife management in North America*, New York: Cambridge University Press.

Boyle, K.V. (2005) 'Late Neolithic seal hunting in Southern Brittany: a zooarchaeological study of the site of Er Yoh (Morbihan)', in G.G. Monks (ed.) *The Exploitation and Cultural Importance of Sea Mammals*, Oxford: Oxbow Books, pp. 77–94.

Brandt, L.Ø., Tranekjer, L.D., Mannering, U., Ringgaard, M., Frei, K.M., Willerslev, E., Gleba, M. and Gilbert, M.T.P. (2011) 'Characterising the potential of sheep wool for ancient DNA analyses', *Archaeological and Anthropological Sciences* 3: 209–21.

Brandt, S.A. and Weedman, K.J. (1997) 'The ethnoarchaeology of hide working and flaked stone tool use in southern Ethiopia', in K. Fukui, E. Kurimoto and M. Shigeta (eds) *Ethiopia in Broader Perspective: Papers of the 13th International Conference of Ethiopian Studies, Vol. 1*, Kyoto: Shokado Book Sellers, pp. 351–61.

Braudel, F. (1949) *La Mediterraneé et al Monde mediterranéen a l'à époch de Philippe II*, Paris.

Brauner, D.R. (2000) *Approaches to Material Culture Research for Historical Archaeologists*, Pennsylvania: Society for Historical Archaeology.

Breniquet, C. (2010) 'Weaving in Mesopotamia during the Bronze Age: archaeology, techniques, iconography', in C. Michel and M.-L. Nosch (eds) *Textile Terminologies in the Ancient Near East and Mediterranean from the Third to the First Millennia BC*, Oxford: Oxbow Books, pp. 52–67.

Briard, J. (1976) *L'Age de Bronze en Europe barbare*, trans. M. Turton (1979) *The Bronze Age in Barbarian Europe: From the Megaliths to the Celts*, London: Book Club Associates with Routledge and Kegan Paul Ltd.

Brisbane, M. and Hather, J. (2007) *Wood Use in Medieval Novgorod*, Oxford: Oxbow Books.

British Leather Manufacturers' Research Association (1957) *Hides, Skins and Leather under the Microscope*, Egham, Surrey: Milton Park Press.

Broholm, H.C. and Hald, M. (1940) *Costumes of the Bronze Age in Denmark*, Copenhagen: Arnold Busck.

——(1948) *Bronze Age Fashion*, Copenhagen: Gyldendalske Boghandel Nordisk Forlag.

Bronitsky, G. and Hamer, R. (1986) 'Experiments in ceramic technology: the effects of various tempering materials on impact and thermal-shock resistance', *American Antiquity*, 51(1): 89–101.

Brown, R. (1995) *Beeswax*, Burrowbridge: Bee Books.
Bryan, N.G. and Young, S. (1940) *Navajo Native Dyes: Their Preparation and Use*, New York: Dover.
Brzeziński, W. and Piotrowski, W. (eds) (1997) *Proceedings of the First International Symposium on Wood Tar and Pitch: Held by the Biskupin Museum (Department of the State Archaeological Museum in Warsaw) and the Museumsdorf Düppel (Berlin) at Biskupin Museum, Poland, July 1st–4th 1993*, Warsaw: Domu Wydawniczym Pawła Dąbrowskiego.
Buchanan, R. (1995) *A Dyer's Garden: From Plants to Pot, Growing Dyes for Natural Fibres*, Loveland, CO: Interweave Press.
Buijs, C. (2005) 'Clothing as a visual representation of identities in East Greenland', in J.C.H. King, B. Pauksztat and R. Storrie (eds) *Arctic Clothing of North America – Alaska, Canada, Greenland*, London: British Museum Press, pp. 108–14.
Bunn, S. (2010) *Nomadic Felts*, London: British Museum Press.
Burenhult, G. (1997) *Ajvide Och Den Moderna Arkeologian, Falköping*: Gotland: Anders Raham,
Burke, B. (2007) 'The kingdom of Midas and royal cloth production', in C. Gillis and M.-L.B. Nosch (eds) *Ancient Textiles: Production, Craft and Society*, Oxford: Oxbow Books, pp. 64–70.
Burkett, M.E. (1979) *The Art of the Feltmaker*, Kendal, Cumbria: Abbot Hall Art Gallery.
Burnham, H.B. (1965) 'Catal Huyuk: the textiles and twined fabrics', *Anatolian Studies*, 15: 169–74.
Burningham, V. (1998) *Weaving Without a Loom*, Tunbridge Wells: Search Press Ltd.
Burov, G.M. (1998) 'The use of vegetable materials in the Mesolithic of northeast Europe', in M. Zvelebil, L. Domańska and R. Dennell (eds) *Harvesting the Sea, Farming the Forest: The Emergence of Neolithic Societies in the Baltic Region*, Sheffield: Sheffield Academic Press Ltd., pp. 53–63.
Butcher, M. and Hogan, J. (2008) *European Baskets*, Kilkenny: Crafts Council of Ireland.
Cabanau, L. (2001) *Wild Boar in Europe*, Cologne: Könemann, The Hunter's Library.
Callanaupa Alvarez, N. (2007) *Weaving in the Peruvian Highlands: Dreaming Patterns, Weaving Memories*, Loveland, CO: Interweave Press.
Candilo, M.D., Ranalli, P., Bozzi, C., Focher, B. and Mastromei, G. (2000) 'Preliminary results of tests facing with the controlled retting of hemp', *Industrial Crops and Products*, 11: 197–203.
Cannon, J. and Cannon, M. (1994) *Dye Plants and Dyeing*, London: Herbert Press in association with the Royal Botanic Gardens, Kew.
Cardon, D. (2007) *Natural Dyes: Sources, Tradition, Technology and Science*, London: Archetype Press.
Carey, J. (2002) *Round the Twist: Creative Cordmaking*, Ottery St Mary, Devon: Carey Company.
——(2003) *Braids and Beyond: A Broad Look at Narrow Wares*, Ottery St Mary, Devon: Carey Company/Braid Society.
Carrie, M.S. and Woodroffe, F.W. (1960) *Fellmongers Handbook*, New Zealand: New Zealand Department of Scientific and Industrial Research.
Carter, B.F. (1933) 'The weaving technic of Winnebago bags', *The Wisconsin Archeologist*, 12: 33–48.
Cartwright, C. (2003) 'The bark vessels and associated wood fragments', in S Preston (ed) *Prehistoric, Roman and Saxon Sites in Eastern Berkshire*, Reading: Thames Valley Archaeolgical Services, pp. 52–60.
——(2005) 'Bronze Age wooden tomb furniture from Jericho: the micrscopical reconstruction of a distinctive carpentry tradition', *Plaestine Exploration Quarterly*, 137: 99–138.
Casselman, K.L. (1993) *Craft of the Dyer: Colour from Plants and Lichens*, 2nd edition, New York: Dover.
Chadwick, E. (1980) *The Craft of Hand Spinning*, London: Batsford.

Chahine, C. (2000) *Changes in the Hydrothermal Stability of Leather and Parchment with Deterioration: A DSC study, Thermchimica Acta,* 365(1–2): 101–10.

Charters, S., Evershed, R.P., Goad, L.J., Heron, C. and Blinkhorn, P. (1993a) 'Identification of an adhesive used to repair a Roman jar', *Archaeometry,* 35: 91–101.

Charters, S., Evershed, R.P., Goad, L.J., Leyden, A., Blinkhorn, P.W. and Denham, V. (1993b) 'Quantification and distribution of lipids in archaeological ceramics: implications for sampling potsherds for organic residue analysis', *Archaeometry,* 35: 211–23.

Choyke, A.M. (2007) 'Objects for a lifetime – tools for a season: the bone tools from Ecsegfalva 23' in A. Whittle (ed.) *The Early Neolithic on the Great Hungarian Plain; investigations of the Körös culture site of Ecsegfalva 23, County Békés,* Budapest: Publicationes Instituti Archaeologici Academiae Scientiarum Hungaricae Budapestini, pp. 641–66.

Choyke, A.M. and Bartosiewicz, L. (eds) (2001) *Crafting Bone: Skeletal Technologies through Time and Space, Proceedings of the 2nd Meeting of the (ICAZ) Worked Bone Research Group Budapest, 31 August–5 September 1999,* British Archaeological Reports International Series 937, Oxford: Archaeopress.

Choyke, A.M. and Schibler, J. (2007) 'Prehistoric stone tools and the archaeozoological perspective: research in Central Europe', in C. Gates St-Pierre and R.B. Walker (eds) *Bones as Tools: Current Methods and Interpretations in Worked Bone Studies,* Oxford: BAR International Series 1622, pp. 51–65.

Christensen, C. (1990) 'Stone Age dug-out boats in Denmark: occurrence, age, form and reconstruction', in D. Robinson (ed.) *Experimentation and Reconstruction in Environmental Archaeology,* Copenhagen: National Museum, pp. 119–42.

——(1997) 'Wood from fishways – forestry', in L. Pedersen, A. Fischer, B. Aaby (eds) *Storebælt i 10.000 år: Mennesket, Havet Og Skoven,* Copenhagen: Storebæltsforbindelsen, pp. 147–56.

Christiansen, C.A. (2004) 'A reanalysis of fleece evolution studies', in J. Maik (ed.) *Priceless Invention of Humanity: NESAT VIII, Akta Archeologica Lodziensia 50(1),* Lodz: Institute of Archaeology and Ethnology, pp. 11–17.

Ciszuk, M. (2007) 'The academic craftsman – a discussion of knowledge of craft in textile research', in C. Gillis and M.L. Bert-Nosch (eds) *Ancient Textiles: Production, Craft and Society,* Oxford: Oxbow, pp. 13–15.

Claassen, C. (1998) *Shells,* Cambridge: Cambridge University Press.

Clark, J.G.D. (1954) *Star Carr,* Cambridge: Cambridge University Press.

Clark, J.G.D. and Thompson, M.W. (1953) 'The groove and splinter technique of working antler in Upper Palaeolithic and Mesolithic Europe', *Proceedings of the Prehistoric Society,* 6: 148–60.

Clark, P. (ed.) (2004) *The Dover Bronze Age Boat in Context: Society and Water Transport in Prehistoric Europe,* Oxford: Oxbow Books.

Clarke, D.V., Cowie, T.G. and Foxon, A. (1985) *Symbols of Power at the Time of Stonehenge,* London: Her Majesty's Stationery Office.

Classen, C. (1997) 'Foundations for an anthropology of the senses', *International Social Sciences Journal,* 153: 401–12.

——(ed.) (2005) *The Book of Touch,* Oxford: Berg.

Classen, C. and Howes, D. (2006) 'The museum as sensescape: Western sensibilities and indigenous artefacts', in E. Edwards, C. Gosden and R. B. Phillips (eds) *Sensible Objects: Colonialism, Museums and Material Culture,* Oxford: Berg, pp. 199–222.

Classen, C., Howes, D. and Synnott, A. (1994) *Aroma: The Cultural History of Smell,* London: Routledge.

Clutton-Brock, T.H. and Pemberton, J. (2004) *Soay Sheep: Dynamics and Selection in an Island Population,* Cambridge: Cambridge University Press.

Coccolini, G.B.L. (2006) 'The wooden artefacts of the Bronze Age lakeshore dwellings of Ledro belonging to Italian museum collections', *Journal of Wetland Archaeology,* 6: 127–35.

Cogswell, J.W, Neff, H. and Glascock, M.D. (1998) 'Analysis of shell-tempered pottery replicates: implications for provenance studies', *American Antiquity,* 63(1): 63–72.

Cohen, N.S., Odlyha, M. and Foster, G.M. (2000) 'Measurement of shrinkage behavior in leather and parchment by dynamic mechanical thermal analysis', *Thermchimica acta*, 361(1): 111–17.

Coles, B. (ed) (1992) *The Wetland Revolution in Prehistory*, Southampton: Prehistoric Society and WARP.

Coles, B., Jorgensen, M.S. and Croes, D. (eds) (1999) 'The Hoko River wet site, a joint tribe/university research project', in *Bog Bodies, Sacred Sites and Wetland Archaeology*, Wetland Archaeology Research Project (WARP) Paper No. 12., Exeter: Department of History and Archaeology, University of Exeter.

Coles, J.M. (1962) 'European Bronze Age shields', *Proceedings of the Prehistoric Society*, 28: 156–90.

——(1973) *Archaeology by Experiment*, London: Hutchinson.

——(1979) *Experimental Archaeology*, London: Academic Press.

——(1982) 'The Bronze Age in northwestern Europe: problems and advances', in F. Wendorf and A.E. Close (eds) *Advances in World Archaeology*, vol. 1, London: Academic Press, pp. 265–321.

——(2006) 'Ancient wood, woodworking and wooden houses', *Euro Rea: Journal of (Re)construction and Experiment in Archaeology*, 3: 50–57.

Collingwood, P. (1974) *The Techniques of Sprang: Plaiting on Stretched Threads*, London: Faber and Faber.

——(1982) *The Techniques of Tablet Weaving*, London: Batsford.

——(1998) *The Techniques of Ply-Split Braiding*, Bellew.

Conard, N.J. (2003) 'Palaeolithic ivory sculptures from southwestern Germany and the origins of figurative art', *Nature*, 426: 830–32.

Connan, J. (1999) 'Use and trade of bitumen in antiquity and prehistory: molecular archaeology reveals secrets of past civilizations', *Philosophical Transactions of the Royal Society of London*, 354: 33–50.

Connan, J. and Nissenbaum, A. (2003) 'Conifer tar on the keel and hull planking of the Ma'agan Mikhael Ship (Israel, 5th century BC): identification and comparison with natural products and artefacts employed in boat construction', *Journal of Archaeological Science*, 30: 709–19.

Conneller, C. (2011) *An Archaeology of Materials: Substantial Transformations in Early Prehistoric Europe*, New York: Routledge.

Conneller, C., Milner, N., Tayler, B. and Taylor, M. (2012) 'Substantial settlement in the European Early Mesolithic: new research at Star Carr', *Antiquity* 86: 1004–20.

Connolly, T., Erlandson, J.M. and Norris, S.E. (1995) 'Early Holocence basketry and cordage from Daisy Cave, San Miguel Island, California', *American Antiquity*, 60: 309–18.

Conte, I.C. and Solana, D.C. (2011) 'Instrumentos de Trabajo de Concha', in *El poblat lacustre del Neolitic antic de La Draga, Excavacions 2000–2005*, Girona: Museu d'Arqueologia de Catalunya.

Cook, J. (2013) *Ice Age Art: The Arrival of the Modern Mind*, London: British Museum Press.

Cooney, G. (2002) 'So many shades of rock: colour symbolism and Irish stone axeheads', in A. Jones and G. MacGregor (eds) *Colouring the Past*, Oxford: Berg, pp. 93–107.

Cooper, F. (2006) *The Black Poplar: Ecology, History and Conservation*, Cheshire: Windgather Press.

Copley, M.S., Berstan, R., Mukherjee, A.J., Dudd, S.N., Straker, V., Payne, S. and Evershed, R.P. (2005a) 'Dairying in antiquity, III: evidence from absorbed lipid residues dating to the British Neolithic', *Journal of Archaeological Science* 32: 523–46.

Copley, M.S., Berstan, R., Dudd, S.N., Aillaud, S., Mukherjee, A.J., Straker, V., Payne, S. and Evershed, R.P. (2005b) 'Processing of milk products in pottery vessels through British prehistory', *Antiquity*, 79: 895–908.

Costin, C.L. (1993) 'Textiles, women, and political economy in prehispanic Peru', *Research in Economic Anthropology*, 14: 3–28.

Covington, A.D. (2009) *Tanning Chemistry: The Science of Leather*, Cambridge: Royal Society of Chemistry.

Crane, E. (1983) *The Archaeology of Beekeeping*, London: Duckworth.

Crawford, M. (2009) *The Case for Working With Your Hands*, London: Penguin.

Cribb, J. (ed.) (1986) *Money: From Cowrie Shells to Credit Cards*, London: British Museum Publications.

Cribb, R.L.D. (1987) 'The logic of the herd: a computer simulation of archaeological herd structure', *Journal of Anthropological Archaeology*, 6: 376–415.

——(1991) *Nomads in Archaeology*, Cambridge: Cambridge University Press.

Croes, D.R. (1997) 'The north-central cultural dichotomy: its evolution as suggested by wet-site basketry and wooden fish hooks', *Antiquity*, 71: 594–615.

——(2001) 'Birth to death: Northwest Coast wet site basketry and cordage artifacts reflecting a person's life-cycle', in B.A. Purdy (ed.) *Enduring Records: The Environmental and Cultural Heritage of Wetlands*, Oxford: Oxbow Books.

Crook, J. (2007) *Natural Dyeing*, London: Gaia.

Crowell, A., Worl, R., Ongtooguk, P.C. and Biddison, D. (eds) (2010) *Living our Cultures, Sharing our Heritage, The First Peoples of Alaska*, Washington: Smithsonian Books.

Čufar, K., Kromer, B., Tolar, T. and Velušček, A. (2010) 'Dating of 4th millennium BC pile-dwellings on Ljubljansko barje, Slovenia', *Journal of Archaeological Science*, 37: 2031–39.

Cummings, V. (2002) 'Experiencing texture and transformation in the British Neolithic', *Oxford Journal of Archaeology*, 21(3): 249–61.

Cummings, V. and Harris, O. (2011) 'Animals, people and places: the continuity of hunting and gathering practices across the Mesolithic–Neolithic transition in Britain', *European Journal of Archaeology*, 14(3): 361–82.

Curtis, E.S. (1913) *The North American Indian: Being a Series of Volumes Picturing and Describing the Indians of the United States, the Dominion of Canada, and Alaska*, vol. 9 Norwadd, MA: Plimpton.

Dalland, M. (ed.) (1999) 'Sand Fiold: the excavation of an exceptional cist in Orkney', *Proceedings of the Prehistoric Society*, 65: 373–413.

Darling, F. (1937) *A Herd of Red Deer*, Oxford: Oxford University Press.

Dart, R. (1957) 'The Osteodontokeratic culture of Australopithecus Promethus', *Transvaal Museum Memoir*, No. 10.

Daugherty, R.T. (1986) *Splintwoven Basketry*, Loveland, CO: Interweave Press.

David, E. (2007) 'Technology on bone and antler industries: a relevant methodology for characterizing early post-glacial societies (9th–8th millenium BC)', in C. Gates St-Pierre and R.B. Walker (eds) *Bones as Tools: Current Methods and Interpretations in Worked Bone Studies*, Oxford: BAR International Series 1622, pp. 35–50.

David, N. and Kramer, C. (2001) *Ethnoarchaeology in Action*, Cambridge: Cambridge University Press.

Dawson, P., Levy, R., Gardner, D. and Walls, M. (2007) 'Simulating the behaviour of light inside Arctic dwellings: implications for assessing the role of vision in task performance', *World Archaeology*, 39(1): 17–35.

Dean, J. (2010) *Wild Colour: How to Grow, Prepare and Use Natural Paint Dyes*, London: Mitchell Beazley.

de Beaune, S.A., Coolidge, F.L. and Wynn, T. (2009) *Cognitive Archaeology and Human Evolution*, Cambridge: Cambridge University Press.

Deguilloux, M.F., Bertel, L., Celant, A., Pemonge, M.H., Sadori, L., Magri, D. and Pett, R. J. (2006) 'Genetic analysis of archaeological wood remains: first results and prospects', *Journal of Archaeological Science*, 33: 1216–27.

Dehn, T. and Hansen, S.I. (2006) 'Birch bark in Danish passage graves', *Journal of Danish Archaeology*, 14: 23–44.

Delamare, F. and Guineau, B. (2000) *Colour: Making and Using Dyes and Pigments*, London: Thames & Hudson.

Delaporte, Y. (2004) *Le Vêtement Lapon: Formes, Fonctions, Évolution*, Paris/Oslo: Peeters/ Institute for Comparative Research in Human Culture.

Del Mar, F. (1924) *A Year Among the Maoris: A Study of their Arts and Customs*, London: Ernest.

Densmore, F. (1929) *Chippewa Customs*, Washington: Smithsonian.

——(1974) *How Indians Use Wild Plants for Food, Medicine and Crafts*, New York: Dover Publications.

d'Errico, F. and Vanhaeren, M. (2002) 'Criteria for identifying Red Deer (*Cervus elaphus*) age and sex from their canines: application to the study of Upper Palaeolithic and Mesolithic ornaments', *Journal of Archaeological Science*, 29: 211–32.

d'Errico, F., Henshilwood, C. and Nilssen, P. (2001) 'Enraved bone fragment from c. 70,000-year-old Middle Stone Age levels at Blombos Cave, South Africa: implications for the origin of symbolism and language', *Antiquity*, 75(288): 309–18.

d'Errico, F., Henshilwood, C.S., Lawson, G., Vanhaeren, M.,Tillier, A.-M., Soressi, M., Bresson, F., Maureille, B., Nowell, A., Lakarra, J., Backwell, L. and Julien, M. (2003) 'Archaeological evidence for the emergence of language, symbolism and music: an alternative multidisciplinary perspective', *Journal of World Prehistory*, 17(1): 1–70.

Descola, P. (1996) *In the Society of Nature: a Native Ecology in Amazonia*, Cambridge: Cambridge University Press.

Descola, P. and Pálsson, G. (1996) *Nature and Society: Anthropological Perspectives*, London: Routledge.

Desrosiers, S. (2010) 'Textile terminologies and classifications: some methodological and chronological aspects', in C. Michel and M.-L. Nosch (eds) *Textile Terminologies in the Ancient Near East and Mediterranean from the Third to the First Millennia BC*, Oxford: Oxbow, pp. 23–51.

Deutscher, G. (2010) *Through the Language Glass: How Words Colour Your World*, London: Heinemann.

De Waal, F. (1982) *Chimpanzee Politics*, London: Jonathan Cape Ltd.

Dobres, M.-A. (2000) *Technology and Social Agency: Outlining a Practice Framework for Archaeology*, Oxford: Blackwell.

Dobres, M.-A. and Hoffman, C.R. (eds) (1999) *The Social Dynamics of Technology: Practice, Politics and World Views*, Washington, DC: Smithsonian Institution Press.

Dobres, M.-A. and Robb, J.E. (eds) (2000) *Agency in Archaeology*, London: Routledge.

Docherty, M., and Emerson, J. (2004) *Simply Felt*, Loveland, CO: Interweave Press.

Dockstader, F.J. (1993) *Weaving Arts of the North American Indian*, New York: Harper Collins.

Donald, M. and Hurcombe, L. (eds) (2000a) *Gender and Material Culture in Archaeological Perspective*, London: Macmillan.

——(2000b) *Gender and Material Culture in Historical Perspective*, London: Macmillan.

——(2000c) *Gender and Material Culture: Representations of Gender from Prehistory to the Present*, London: Macmillan.

Dormer, P. (ed.) (1997a) *The Culture of Craft*, Manchester: Manchester University Press.

——(1997b) 'Textiles and technology', in P. Dormer (ed.) *The Culture of Craft*, Manchester: Manchester University Press, pp. 168–75.

——(1997c) 'Craft and the Turing test for practical thinking', in P. Dormer (ed.) *The Culture of Craft*, Manchester: Manchester University Press, pp. 137–57.

Douglass, J.M. (1946) 'Textile imprints on Wisconsin Indian pottery', *The Wisconsin Archeologist*, 27: 71–80.

Downes, J. and Ritchie, A. (eds) (2003) *Sea Change: Orkney and Northern Europe in the Later Iron Age AD 300–800*, Angus: The Pinkfoot Press.

Drooker, P.B. and Webster, L.D. (eds) (2000) *Beyond Cloth and Cordage: Archaeological Textile Research in the Americas*, Salt Lake City: University of Utah Press.

Drooker, P. (1981) *Hammock Making Techniques*, New Hampshire: Penelope B. Drooker.

——(1992) *Mississippian Village Textiles at Wickliffe*, Tuscaloosa: University of Alabama Press.

——(ed.) (2001) *Fleeting Identities: Perishable Material Culturein Archaeological Research*, Carbondale: Centre for Archaeological Research, Southern Illinois University.

Dufault, R. J. (2013) *Stalking the Wild Sweetgrass: Domestication and Horticulture of the Grass used in African-American Coiled Basketry*, New York: Springer.

Dunsmore, S. (1985) *The Nettle in Nepal: A Cottage Industry*, Surbiton: Land Resources Development Centre.

——(1993) *Nepalese Textiles*, London: British Museum Press.
Earwood, C. (1993) *Domestic Wooden Artefacts*, Exeter: Exeter University Press.
——(1998) 'Primitive ropemaking: the archaeological and ethnographic evidence', *Folk Life*, 36: 45–51.
Easton McLeod, E. (2000) *In Good Hands: The Women of the Canadian Handicrafts Guild*, Montreal: McGill-Queens University Press.
Edwards, E., Gosden, C. and Phillips, R.B. (eds) (2006) *Sensible Objects: Colonialism, Museums and Material Culture*, Oxford: Berg.
Edwards, R. (1984) *Homemade Leatherworking Tools*, Kuranda, Australia:Rams Skull Press.
Egg, M. and Spindler, K. (2009) *Kleidung und Ausrüstung der Kupferzeitlichen Gletschermumie aus den Ötztaler Alpen*, Mainz: Römisch-Germanischen Zentralmuseums.
Egg, M., Goedecker-Ciolek, R., Groenman-van Waateringe, W. and Spindler, K. (1993) *Die Geltschermumie vom Ende der Steinzeit aus den Ötztaler Alpen*, Mainz: Römisch-Germanischen Zentralmuseums.
Ellis, Richard S. (1976) 'Mesopotamian crafts in modern and ancient times: ancient Near Eastern weaving', *American Journal of Anthropology* 80(1): 76–77.
Emery, I. (1966) *The Primary Structures of Fabrics: An Illustrated Classification*, Washington, DC: Textile Museum.
English, N.B., et al (2001) 'Strontium isotopes reveal distance sources of architectural timber in Chaco Canyon, New Mexico', *PNAS* 1998: 11891–96.
Evans, C. (1989) 'Perishables and worldly goods – artifact decoration and classification in the light of wetlands research', *Oxford Journal of Archaeology*, 8: 179–202.
——(2005a) *A Woodland Archaeology: Neolithic Sites at Haddenham*, Cambridge: McDonald Institute for Archaeological Research.
——(2005b) *Marshland Communities and Cultural Landscapes: From the Bronze Age to Present Day*, Cambridge: McDonald Institute for Archaeological Research.
Evans, E. (1957) *Irish Folk Ways*, London: Routledge.
Evershed, R.P. (2008) 'Experimental approaches to the interpretation of absorbed organic residues in archaeological ceramics', *Experimental Archaeology*, 40(1): 26–47,
Evershed R.P., Payne, S., Sherratt, A.G., Copley, M.S., Coolidge, J., Urem-Kotsu, D., Kotsakis, K., Özdoğan, M., Özdoğan, A.E., Nieuwenhuys, O., Akkermans, P.M.M.G., Bailey, D., Andeescu, R.R., Campbell, S., Farid, S., Hodder, I., Yalman, N., Özbasaran, M., Bıçakc, E., Garfinkel, Y., Levy, T. and Burton, M.M. (2008) 'Earliest date for milk use in the Near East and southeastern Europe linked to cattle herding', *Nature* 455: 528–31.
Falk, D. (2011) *The Fossil Chronicles: How Two Controversial Discoveries Changed our View of Human Evolution*, Berkley: University of California Press.
Fariello, M. Anna (2009) *Cherokee Basketry: From the Hands of our Elders*, Charleston: History Press.
Feathers, J.K. (1989) 'Effects of temper on strength of ceramics: response to Bronitsky and Hamer', *American Antiquity*, 54(3): 579–88.
Ferguson, J. (2008) 'The when, where, and how of novices in craft production', *Journal of Archaeological Method and Theory*, 15: 51–67.
Ferrero, L.J. (2013) *An Experimental Comparison of Impressions Made from Replicated Neolithic Linen and Bronze Age Woollen Textiles on Pottery*, unpublished BA dissertation, University of Exeter.
Field, A. (2010) *Spinning Wool: Beyond the Basics*, Aukland: David Bateman Ltd.
Fienup-Riordan, A. (2005) '*Tupigat* (twined things): Yup'ik grass clothing, past and present', in J.C.H. King, B. Pauksztat and R. Storrie (eds) *Arctic Clothing of North America – Alaska, Canada, Greenland*, London: British Museum Press, pp. 53–61.
Fijn, N. (2011) *Living with Herds: Human–animal Coexistence in Mongolia*, Cambridge: Cambridge University Press.
Firth, R. (2007) 'Reconsidering Alum on the Linear B Tablets' in C. Gillis and M.-L.B. Nosch (eds) *Ancient Textiles: Production, Craft and Society*, Oxford: Oxbow Books, pp. 130–38.
Flint, I. (2008) *Eco Colour: Botanical Dyes for Beautiful Textiles*, Miller's Point, NSW: Murdoch Books.

Florance, N. (1962) *Rush-work*, London: G. Bell & Sons.
Follensbee, B.J. (2008) 'Fiber technology and weaving in formative-period Gulf Coast cultures', *Ancient Mesoamerica*, 19: 87–110.
Fontales Ortiz, C.M. (2006) *Cestería de los Pueblos de Galicia*, Vigo: Ir Indo Edicions.
Ford, S. and Pine, J. (2003) 'Neolithic ring ditches and Roman landscape features at Horton (1989–96)', in S. Preston (ed.) *Prehistoric, Roman and Saxon Sites in Eastern Berkshire: Excavations 1989–1997*, Reading: Thames Valley Archaeological Services, pp. 13–86.
Fothergill, A. and Berlowitz, V. (2011) *Frozen Planet: A World Beyond Imagination*, London: BBC Books.
Fournier, N., and Fournier, J. (1995) *In Sheep's Clothing: A Handspinner's Guide to Wool*, Colorado: Interweave Press.
Franck, R.R. (2005) *Bast and Other Plant Fibres*, Cambridge: Woodhead Publishing Limited.
Frank, B.E. (1998) *Mande Potters and Leather-workers: Art and Heritage in West Africa*, Washington, DC: Smithsonian Institution Press.
Franquemont, A. (2009) *Respect the Spindle*, Loveland: Interweave Press.
Fraser, J. (1996) *Traditional Scottish Dyes and How to Make Them*, Edinburgh: Cannongate.
Frei, K.M. (2010) *Provenance of Pre-Roman Textiles – Methods, Development and Applications*, Copenhagen: Humanities Faculty PhD.
Frei, K.M., Skals, I., Gleba, M. and Lyngstrøm, H. (2009b) 'The Huldremose Iron Age textiles, Denmark: an attempt to define their provenance applying the Strontium isotope system', *Journal of Archaeological Science*, 36: 1965–71.
Frei, K.M., Vanden Berghe, I., Frei, R., Mannering, U. and Lyngstrøm, H. (2010) 'Removal of natural organic dyes from wool-implications for ancient textile provenance studies', *Journal of Archaeological Science*, 37: 2136–45.
Frei, K.M., Frei, R., Mannering, U., Gleba, M., Nosch, M.-L. and Lyngstrøm, H. (2009a) 'Provenance of ancient textiles-a pilot study evaluating the strontium isotope system in wool', *Archaeometry*, 51: 252–76
Friedl, E. (1989) *Women of Deh Koh: Lives in an Iranian Village*, London: Smithsonian Institution Press.
Frink, L. (2005) 'Gender and the hide production process in Colonial Western Alaska', in L. Frink and K. Weedman (eds) *Gender and Hide Production*, Lanham: Altamira Press, pp. 89–104.
Frink L. and Weedman, K. (eds) (2009) *Gender and Hide Production*, Lanham: Altamira Press.
Gabra-Sanders, T. (1994) 'Textiles and fibres from the late Bronze Age hoard from St Andrew's, Fife, Scotland: a preliminary report', in G. Jaacks and K. Tidow (eds) *Textilsymposium Neumünster: Archäologische Textilfunde – Archaeological Textiles*, Neumunster: Textilmuseum Neumünster, pp. 34–42.
Gabriel, S. and Goymer, S. (1991) *The Complete Book of Basketry Techniques*, Newton Abbot: David & Charles.
Gaddum, P.W. (1968) *Silk: How and Where it is Produced*, Macclesfield: H.T. Gaddum and Company Limited.
Gage, J. (1993) *Colour and Culture: Practice and Meaning from Antiquity to Abstraction*, London: Thames & Hudson.
Gale, R. and Cutler, D. (2000) *Plants in Archaeology*, West Yorkshire: Westbury Publishing.
Garrick, D. (1998) *Shaped Cedars and Cedar Shaping: A Guidebook to Identifying, Documenting, Appreciating and Learning from Culturally Modified Trees*, Canada: Western Canada Wilderness Committee.
Gates St-Pierre, C. (2007) 'Bone awls of the St Lawrence Iroquoians: a microwear analysis', in C. Gates St-Pierre and R.B. Walker (eds) *Bones as Tools: Current Methods and Interpretations in Worked Bone Studies*, Oxford: BAR International Series 1622, pp. 107–18.
Gates St-Pierre, C. and Walker, R.B. (eds) (2007) *Bones as Tools: Current Methods and Interpretations in Worked Bone Studies*, Oxford: British Archaeological Reports 1622.
Gaudzinski, S. (1999) 'Middle Palaeolithic bone tools from the open air site Salzgitterlebenstedt', *Journal of Archaeological Science*, 26: 125–41.

Gaudzinski, S., et al (2005) 'The use of large Proboscidean reminas in everyday Paleolithic life', *Quaternary International*, 126–28: 179–94.

Geib, P.R. and Jolie, E.A. (2008) 'The role of basketry in Early Holocene small seed exploitation: implications of a ca. 9,000 year-old basket from Cowboy Cave, Utah', *American Antiquity*, 73(1): 83–102.

Geist, V. (1971) *Mountain Sheep: A Study in Behaviour and Evolution*, London: University of Chicago Press.

Gelbert, A. (2001) 'Ethnoarchaeological study of ceramic borrowings: a new methodological approach applied in the middle and upper valleys of the Senegal River', in S. Beyries and P. Pétrequin (eds) *Ethno-Archaeology and its Transfers*, Oxford: British Archaeological Reports International Series 983, pp. 81–94.

Gell, A. (1998) *Art and Agency: An Anthropological Theory*, Oxford: Clarendon.

Gelvin-Reymiller, C., Reuther, J.D., Potter, B.A. and Bowers, P.M. (2006) 'Technical aspects of a worked proboscidean tusk from Inmachuk River, Seward Peninsular, Alaska', *Journal of Archaeological Science*, 33: 1088–94.

Gerdes, P. (2010) *Tinhalèló: Interweaving Art and Mathematics*, Morriville: Lulu Enterprises.

Gerend, A. (1904) 'Potsherds from Lake Michigan shore sites in Wisconsin', *The Wisconsin Archeologist*, 4: 3–19.

Gianno, R. (1990) *Semelai Culture and Resin Technology*, New Haven: Connecticut Academy of Arts and Sciences.

Gibson, A. and Simpson, D. (eds) (1998) *Prehistoric Ritual and Religion: Essays in Honour of Aubrey Burl*, Stroud: Sutton Publishing.

Gibson, J.J. (1979) *The Ecological Approach to Visual Perception*, Hillsdale: Lawrence Erlbaum.

Gilligan, I. (2010) 'The prehistoric development of clothing: the archaeological implications of a thermal model', *Journal of Archaeological Method and Theory*, 17: 15–80.

Gillis, C. and Bert-Nosch, M.-L. (eds) (2007a) *Ancient Textiles: Production, Craft and Society*, Oxford: Oxbow Books.

——(2007b) *First Aid for the Excavation of Archaeological Textiles*, Oxford: Oxbow Books.

Gillooly, M. (ed.) (1992) *Natural Baskets*, Vermont: Storey Publishing.

Gillow, J. (2003) *African Textiles: Colour and Creativity Across a Continent*, London: Thames & Hudson.

Gilmore, K.P. (2005) 'These boots were made for walking: moccasin production, gender and the Late Prehistoric hideworking sequence on the High Plains of Colorado', in L. Frink and K. Weedman (eds) *Gender and Hide Production*, Lanham: Altamira Press, pp. 13–36.

Gilmour, G.H. (1997) 'The nature and function of astralagus bones from archaeological contexts in the Levant and Eastern Mediterranean', *Oxford Journal of Archaeology*, 16: 167–75.

Gleba, M. and Mannering, U. (2012) 'Introduction: textile preservation, analysis and technology', in M. Gleba and U. Mannering (eds) *Textiles and Textile Production in Europe From Prehistory to AD 400*, Exeter: Short Run Press, pp. 1–24.

Gleba, M., C Munkholt and M.-L. Nosch (eds) (2008) *Dressing the Past*, Oxford: Oxbow Books.

Goldstein, L. and Freeman, J. (1997) 'Aztalan – a middle Mississippian village', *The Wisconsin Archeologist*, 78: 223–48.

Good, I. (2001) 'Archaeological textiles: a review of current research', *Annual Review of Anthropology*, 30: 209–26.

Goodwin, J. (2003) *A Dyer's Manual*, Hessle: Ashman.

Gosden, C. (2005) 'What do objects want?' *Journal of Archaeological Method and Theory*, 12: 193–211.

——(2006) 'Material culture and long-term change', in C. Tilley (ed.) *Handbook of Material Culture*, London: Sage.

Gosden, C. and Marshall, Y. (1999) 'The cultural biography of objects', *World Archaeology*, 31(2): 169–78.

Goss, R.J. (1983) *Deer Antlers: Regeneration, Function and Evolution*, New York: Academic Press .

Gosselain, O.P. (2001) 'Globalizing local pottery studies', in S. Beyries and P. Pétrequin (eds) *Ethno-Archaeology and its Transfers*, Oxford: British Archaeological Reports International Series 983, pp. 95–111.

Goulding, M. (2003) *Wild Boar in Britain*, Wiltshire: Whittet Books Ltd.

Grabner, R. (2009) 'Prehistoric forest and wood utilization', in Kern, A., K. Kowarik, A. Rausch and H. Reschreiter (eds) *Kingdom of Salt*, Vienna: Natural History Museum, pp. 224–25.

Gramsch, B. (1992) 'Friesack Mesolithic wetlands', in B. Coles (ed.) *The Wetland Revolution in Prehistory*, Exeter: WARP Occasional Paper 6, pp. 65–72.

Grant, B. (1972) *Encyclopedia of Rawhide and Leather Braiding*, Atglen, PA: Cornell Maritime Press.

——(1978) *Leather Braiding*, Atglen, PA: Cornell Maritime Press.

Green, W. (1997) 'Middle Mississippian peoples', *The Wisconsin Archeologist*, 78: 202–22.

Greenhalgh, P. (1997) 'The history of craft', in P. Dormer (ed.) *The Culture of Craft*, Manchester: Manchester University Press.

Grierson, S. (1986) *The Colour Cauldron: The History and Use of Natural Dyes in Scotland*, Perth: Mill Books.

Grieve, M. (1931) *A Modern Herbal: The Medicinal, Culinary, Cosmetic and Economic Properties, Cultivation and Folklore of Herbs, Grasses, Fungi, Shrubs and Trees with all their Modern Scientific Uses*, London: Jonathan Cape Ltd.

Griffiths, M. (1997) *The Marram Weavers of Newborough: An Ancient Anglesey Craft*, Anglesey: Magma Books.

Grimstead, D.N. (2010) 'Ethnographic and modeled costs of long-distance, big-game hunting', *American Antiquity*, 75(1): 61–80.

Groenman-van Waateringe, W. (1967) *Romeins lederwerk uit Valkenburg Z.H.*, Groningen: J.B. Wolters.

——(1993) 'Analyses of the hides and skins from the Hauslabjoch', in M. Egg, R. Goedecker-Ciolek, W. Groenman-van Waateringe and K. Spindler (eds) *Die Geltschermumie vom Ende der Steinzeit aus den Ötztaler Alpen*, Mainz: Römisch-Germanischen Zentralmuseums, pp. 114–28.

Gronnow, B. (ed.) (2009) *On the Track of the Thule Culture from Bering Strait to East Greenland*, Denmark: National Museum.

Gustafson, P. (1980) *Salish Weaving*, Vancouver: Douglas & McIntyre.

Habicht-Mauche, J.A. (2005) 'The shifting role of women's labour on the Protohistoric Southern High Plains', in L. Frink and K. Weedman (eds) *Gender and Hide Production*, Lanham: Altamira Press, pp. 37–56.

Hackenberger, M. (2005) *The Ecology of Power: Culture, Place and Personhood in Southern Amazon AD 1000–2000*, London: Routledge.

Hageneder, F. (2001) *The Heritage of Trees: History, Culture, Symbolism*, Edinburgh: Floris.

——(2005) *The Living Wisdom of Trees*, London: Duncan Baird.

Hald, M. (1980) *Ancient Danish Textiles from Bogs and Burials*, Copenhagen: National Museum of Denmark.

Hall, A.R., Tomlinson, P.R., Hall, R.A., Taylor, G.W. and Walton, P. (1984) 'Dyeplants from Viking York', *Antiquity*, 58: 58–60.

Hall, E.R. (1981) *The Mammals of North America*, vol. 2, New York: Wiley.

Hamann, B. (1997) 'Weaving and the iconography of prestige: the royal gender symbolism of Lord 5 Flower's/Lady 4 Rabbit's family', in C. Claassen and R.A. Joyce (eds) *Women in Prehistory. North America and Mesoamerica*, Philadelphia: University of Pennsylvania, pp. 153–72.

Hamilton, S. and Whitehouse, R. (2006) 'Phenomenology in practice: towards a methodology for a "subjective" approach', *European Journal of Archaeology*, 9(1): 31–71.

Hammarlund, L. (2005) 'Handicraft knowledge applied to archaeological textiles', *The Nordic Textile Journal*: 86–119.

Hannus, L.A. (1985) *The Lange-Ferguson Site: An Event of Clovis Mammoth Butchery with the Associated Bone Tool Technology: The Mammoth and Its Track*, PhD Dissertation, Salt Lake City: University of Utah.

——(1989) 'Flaked mammoth bone from the Lange-Ferguson site, White River Badlands area South Dakota', in R. Bonnichsen and M. Sorg (eds) *Bone Modification Orono,* The Centre for the Study of the First Americans, pp. 395–412.

——(1997) 'Mammoth bone flake tools from the Lange/Ferguson site, South Dakota', in L.A. Hannus, L. Rossum and R.P. Winham (eds) *Proceedings of the 1993 Bone Modification Conference, Hot Springs, South Dakota,* Sioux Falls, SD: Archaeology Laboratory, Augustana College, pp. 220–35.

Haraway, D. (2003) *The Companion Species Manifesto: Dogs, People and Significant Others,* Chicago: University of Chicago Press.

Harding, A. (2000) *European Societies in the Bronze Age,* Cambridge: Cambridge University Press.

Harding, A. and Kavruk, V. (2010) *A Prehistoric Salt Production Site at Băile Figa, Romania,* www.academia.edu.

——(2013) *Explorations in Salt Archaeology in the Carpathian Zone,* Budapest: Archaeolingua.

Hardman, J. and Pinhey, S. (2009) *Natural Dyes,* Marlborough: Crowood.

Hardy, K. (2007) 'Where would we be without string? Ethnographic evidence for the use, manufacture and role of string in the Upper Palaeolithic and Mesolithic of Northern Europe', in V. Beugnier and P. Crombé (eds), *Plant Processing from a Prehistoric and Ethnographic Perspective,* Oxford: BAR International Series 1718, pp. 9–22.

Harris, J. (ed.) (1999) *5000 Years of Textiles,* London: British Museum Press.

Harris, S. (2007) 'Investigating social aspects of technical processes: cloth production from plant fibres in a Neolithic lake dwelling on Lake Constance, Germany', in V. Beugnier and P. Crombé (eds) *Plant Processing from a Prehistoric and Ethnographic Perspective,* Oxford: BAR International Series 1718, pp. 83–100.

——(2010) 'Smooth and cool, or warm and soft: investigating the properties of cloth in prehistory', in E. Andersson Strand, M. Gleba, U. Mannering, C. Munkholt and M. Ringgard (eds) *North European Symposium for Archaeological Textiles X,* Oxford: Oxbow Books, pp. 104–12.

——(2012) 'From the parochial to the universal: comparing cloth cultures in the Bronze Age', *European Journal of Archaeology,* 15: 61–97.

Harrison, R.J. (1985) 'The "Policultivo Ganadero", or the secondary products revolution in Spanish agriculture, 5000–1000 BC', *Proceedings of the Prehistoric Society,* 51: 75–102.

Hartl, A. and Hofmann-de Keijzer, R. (2005) 'Imitating ancient dyeing methods from the Hallstatt period – dyeing experiments with weld, indigo and oak bark', in P. Bichler, K. Grömer, R. Hofmann-de Keijzer, A. Kern and H. Reschreiter (eds) *Hallstatt Textiles: Technical Analysis, Scientific Investigation and Experiment on Iron Age Textiles,* Oxford: BAR International Series 1351, pp. 91–96.

Harvey, J. (1996) *Traditional Textiles of Central Asia,* London: Thames & Hudson.

Harvey, V.I. (1976) *Split-Ply Twining,* Santa Ana, CA: HTH Publishers.

Hather, J. (1993) *An Archaeological Guide to Root and Tuber Identification, Volume 1, Europe and South West Asia,* Oxford: Oxbow Books.

Hayden, B. (1990) 'The right rub: hide working in high ranking households', in B. Gräslund, H. Knutsson, K. Knutsson and J. Taffinder (eds) *The Interpretive Possibilities of Microwear Studies,* Uppsala: Societas Archaeologia Upsaliensis, pp. 89–102.

Hays-Gilpin, K. (2000) 'Gender constructs in the material culture of seventh-century Anasazi farmers in north-eastern Arizona', in M. Donald and L.Hurcombe (eds) *Representations of Gender from Prehistory to the Present,* Basingstoke: Macmillan, pp. 31–44.

Heckman, A.M. (2005) 'Cultural communication of ethnicity through clothing: the Qocha-Lake symbol in contemporary textiles from Ausangate, Peru', in R.M. Reycraft (ed.) *Us and Them: Archaeology and Ethnicity in the Andes,* Los Angeles: Cotsen Institute of Archaeology, University of California, pp. 104–14.

Hede, S.U. (2005) 'The finds: mammal, bird and amphibian bones', in T. D. Price and A. B. Gebauer (eds) *Smakkerup Huse,* Aarhus: Aarhus University Press, pp. 91–101.

Hedges, J. (2006) *Ply-Split Braiding: An Introduction to Designs in Single Course Twining,* Trowbridge: Cromwell Press.

Heizer, R. and Kroeber, T. (1979) *Ishi the Last Yahi,* Berekley: University of California Press.

Helbaek, H. (1963) 'Textiles from Catal Huyuk', *Archaeology* 16: 39–46.

Henare, A. (2005) '*Nga Aho Tipuna* (ancestral threads): Maori cloaks from New Zealand', in S. Küchler and D. Miller (eds) *Clothing as Material Culture*, Oxford: Berg, pp. 121–38.

Henshall, A. (1950) 'Textiles and weaving appliances from prehistoric Britain', *Proceedings of the Prehistoric Society*, 16: 130–62.

Henshilwood, C.S., d'Errico, F., Marean, C.W., Milo, R.G. and Yates, R. (2001) 'An early bone tool industry from the Middle Stone Age at Blombos Cave, South Africa: implications for the origins of modern human behaviour, symbolism and language', *Journal of Human Evolution*, 41(6): 631–78.

Henshilwood, C.S., d'Errico, F., van Niekerk, K.L., Coquinot, Y., Jacobs, Z., Lauritzen, S.-E., Menu, M. and Garcìa-Moren, R. (2011) 'A 100,000 year old ochre-processing pwrkshop at Blombos Cave, South Africa', *Science*, 334: 219–22.

Herbert, M. (1976) *The Reindeer People: Travels in Lapland*, London: Hodder and Stoughton.

Heron, C., Nilsen, G., Stern, B., Craig, O. and Nordby, C. (2010) 'Application of lipid biomarker analysis to evaluate the function of "slab-lined" pits in Arctic Norway', *Journal of Archaeological Science*, 37: 2188–97.

Hetherington, K. (2003) 'Spatial textures: place, touch and praesentia', *Environment and Planning A*, 35: 1933–44.

Higgs, E.S., Vita-Finzi, C., Harris, D.R. and Fagg, A.E. (1967) 'The climate, environment and industries of Stone Age Greece: Part III', *Proceedings of the Prehistoric Society*, 33: 1–29.

Hilu, S. and Hersey, I. (2004) *Bogolanfini Mud Cloth*, Atglen PA: Schiffer.

Hodgetts, L. (2005) 'Dorset palaeoeskimo harp seal exploitation at Phillip's Garden (Eebi-1), Northwestern Newfoundland', in G.G. Monks (ed.) *The Exploitation and Cultural Importance of Sea Mammals*, Oxford: Oxbow Books, pp. 62–76.

Hofenck de Graaff, J.H. (2004) *The Colourful Past: Origins, Chemistry and Identification of Natural Dyestuffs*, London: Archetype.

Hoffecker, J.F. (2002) *Desolate Landscapes: Ice Age Settlement in Eastern Europe*, New Jersey and London: Rutgers University Press.

——(2011) *Landscape of the Mind: Human Evolution and the Archaeology of Thought*, New York: Columbia University Press.

Hoffmann, M. (1991) *Fra Fiber til Tøy – Tekstilredskaber og bruken av dem i Norsk*, Tradisjon: Landsbrugforlaget.

Hogan, J. (2001) *Basketmaking in Ireland*, Co. Wicklow: Wordwell Ltd.

Høgseth, H.B. (2012) 'Knowledge transfer, the craftsmen's abstraction', in W. Wendrich (ed) *Archaeology and Apprencticeship*, Tucson: University of Arizona Press, pp. 61–78.

Holmes, W.H. (1896) *Prehistoric Textile Art of Eastern United States*, Washington, DC: United States Bureau of Ethnology.

——(1901) 'Prehistoric textile fabrics of the United States, derived from impressions on pottery', in J.W. Powell (ed.) *Third Annual Report of the Bureau of Ethnology*, Washington: Smithsonian, pp. 393–425.

Hopkins, H. (ed.) (2013) *Ancient Textiles Modern Science*, Oxford: Oxbow Books.

Hosfield, R. (2009) 'Modes of transmission and material culture patterns in craft skills', in S. Shennan (ed.) *Pattern and Process in Cultural Evolution*, London: University of California Press, pp. 45–60.

Hoskins, J. (2006) 'Agency, biography and objects', in C. Tilley, W. Keane, S. Küchler, M. Rowlands and P. Spyer (eds) *Handbook of Material Culture*, London: Sage, pp. 74–84.

Howes, D. (ed.) (1991) *The Varieties of Sensory Experience: A Source Book in the Anthropology of the Senses*, Toronto: University of Toronto Press.

——(2006) 'Scent, sound and synaesthesia: intersensoriality and material culture theory', in C. Tilley, W. Keane, S. Küchler, M. Rowlands and P. Spyer (eds) *Handbook of Material Culture*, London: Sage, pp. 161–72.

Hungry Wolf, B. (1982) *The Ways of my Grandmothers*, New York: Quill.

Hurcombe, L. (1992) *Use Wear Analysis and Obsidian: Theory, Experiments and Results*, Sheffield: Sheffield Academic Press.

——(1993) 'Experimentell arkeologi och stenredskap', *Forntida Teknik*, 2(93): 4–16.

——(1998) 'Plant-working and craft activities as a potential source of microwear variation', *Helinium*, 34(2): 201–9.

——(2000a) 'Plants as the raw materials for crafts', in A. Fairbairn (ed.) *Plants in Neolithic Britain and Beyond*, Oxford: Oxbow/Neolithic Studies Group.

——(2000b) 'Time, skill and craft specialisation as gender relations', in M. Donald and L. Hurcombe (eds) *Gender and Material Culture in Archaeological Perspective*, London: Macmillan, pp. 88–109.

——(2004a) 'Experimental Archaeology', in C. Renfrew and P. Bahn (eds) *Archaeology: The Key Concepts*, London: Routledge, pp. 110–15.

——(2004b) 'The lithic evidence from the Pabbi Hills', in R.W. Dennell (ed.) *Early Hominin Landscapes in Northern Pakistan: Investigations in the Pabbi Hills*, Oxford: British Archaeological Reports International Series 1265, pp. 222–91.

——(2007a) *Archaeological Artefacts as Material Culture*, London: Routledge.

——(2007b) 'A sense of materials and sensory perception in concepts of materiality', *World Archaeology*, 39: 532–45.

——(2007c) 'Plant processing for cordage and textiles using serrated flint edges: new chaînes opératoires suggested by combining ethnographic, archaeological and experimental evidence for bast fibre processing', in V. Beugnier and P. Crombé (eds) *Plant Processing from a Prehistoric and Ethnographic Perspective*, Oxford: BAR International Series 1718, pp. 41–66.

——(2008a) 'Looking for prehistoric basketry and cordage using inorganic remains: the evidence from stone tools', in L. Longo and N. Skakun (eds) *'Prehistoric Technology' 40 Years Later: Functional Studies and the Russian Legacy*, Oxford: British Archaeological Reports International Series 1783, pp. 205–16.

——(2008b) 'Organics from inorganics: using experimental archaeology as a research tool for studying perishable material culture', *World Archaeology*, 40: 83–115.

——(2010) 'Nettle and bast fibre textiles from stone tool wear traces? The implications of wear traces on archaeological late Mesolithic and Neolithic micro-denticulate tools', in E. Andersson Strand, M. Gleba, U. Mannering, C. Munkholt and M. Ringgaard (eds) *NESAT X The North European Symposium for Archaeological Textiles*, Oxford: Oxbow Books, pp. 129–39.

Hurcombe, L.M. and Lemieux, L. (2005) 'Basketry', in J. Gardiner (ed.) *Before the Mast: Life and Death Aboard the Mary Rose*, London: English Heritage, pp. 400–8.

Hurcombe, L. and Österman, J. (2010) 'Seminar on traditional skin tanning', in H. Tunón (ed.) *Seminarietrapport Traditionell Skinngarvning*, NAPTEK, Centrum för Biologisk mångfald, Uppsala, CBM skriftserie 35 and bäckedals Folkhögskola, Sveg, pp. 74–78.

Hurcombe, L. and Williams, L. (2002) 'Fish skin as a prehistoric material', *Bulletin of Primitive Technology*, 23: 39–41.

Hurley, W.M. (1979) *Prehistoric Cordage: Identification of Impressions on Pottery*, Washington, DC: Taraxacum, Chicago.

Hwang, M.S. (2010) 'Morphological differences between ramie and hemp: how these characteristics developed different procedures in bast fiber producing industry', *Textile Society of America Symposiuim Proceedings*, paper 23, digital commons at University of Nebraska, Lincoln.

Ibanez Estévez, J.J., González Urquijo, J.E., Peña-Chocarro, L., Zapata, L. and Beugnier, V. (2001) 'Harvesting without sickles. Neolithic Examples from humid mountain areas', in S. Beyries and P. Pétrequin (eds) *Ethno-Archaeology and its Transfers*, Oxford: BAR International Series 983, pp. 23–36.

Ingold, T. (1980) *Hunters, Pastoralists and Ranchers: Reindeer Economies and their Transformation*, Cambridge: Cambridge University Press.

——(1993) 'The temporality of landscape', *World Archaeology*, 25: 152–74.

——(2000a) *The Perception of the Environment: Essays in Livelihood, Dwelling and Skill*, London: Routledge.

——(2000b) 'Making culture and weaving the world', in P. Graves-Brown (ed.) *Matter, Materiality and Modern Culture*, London: Routledge, pp. 50–71.

——(2007) *Lines: A Brief History*, London: Routledge.
——(2011) *Being Alive: Essays on Movement, Knowledge and Description*, London: Routledge.
Innes, R.A. (1977) *Non-European Looms in the collections at Bankfield Museum, Halifax*, Calderdale: Calderdale Museums.
Issenman, B.K. (1997) *The Living Legacy of Inuit Clothing*, Vancouver: UBC Press.
Jakes, K.A. and Ericksen A.G. (1997) 'Socioeconomic Implications of Prehistoric Textile Production in the Eastern Woodlands, Materials Issues.' *Materials Issues in Art and Archaeology V; a Symposium Held Dec. 3–5, 1996*, edited by P. Vandiver, J. Druzik, J.F. Merkel, and J. Stewart, 462: 281–86.
Jakes, K.A., Sibley, L.R. and Yerkes, R. (1994) 'A comparative collection for the study of fibres used in prehistoric textiles from eastern North America', *Journal of Archaeological Science*, 21: 641–50.
Jensen, G. (2001) 'Macro wear patterns on Danish Late Mesolithic antler axes', in A.M. Choyke and L. Bartosiewicz (eds) *Crafting Bone: Skeletal Technologies through Time and Space, Proceedings of the 2nd Meeting of the (ICAZ) Worked Bone Research Group Budapest, 31 August–5 September 1999*, Oxford: BAR International Series 937, pp. 165–70.
Johnson, M.H. (1989) 'Conceptions of agency in archaeological interpretation', *Journal of Anthropological Archaeology*, 8(2): 189–211.
Jones, A. (2000) 'Life after death: monuments, material culture and social change in Neolithic Orkney', in A. Ritchie (ed.) *Neolithic Orkney in its European Context*, Cambridge: McDonald Institute for Archaeological Research, pp. 127–38.
Jones, A. and MacGregor, G. (eds) (2002) *Colouring the Past*, Oxford: Berg.
Jones, A.M. (1978) *The Rural Industries of England and Wales, Vol. IV: Wales*, Wakefield: E.P. Publishing.
Jones, D. and Cloke, P. (2002) *Tree Culture: The Place of Trees and Trees in their Place*, Oxford: Berg.
Jones, R. (1969) 'Fire-stick farming', *Australian Natural History*, 16: 224.
Juel Jensen, H. (1994) *Flint Tools and Plant Working: Hidden Traces of Stone Age Technology*, Copenhagen: Aarhus University Press.
Kania, K. (2010) 'Experiment and knowledge base: bringing historical textile workers together', in *Euro Rea: Journal of (Re)construction and Experiment in Archaeology*, 7: 15–18.
Karali, L. (1999) *Shells in Aegean Prehistory*, Oxford: BAR International Series 761.
Karsten, P. and Knarrström, B. (2003) *The Tågerup Excavations*, Trelleborg: National Heritage Board.
Keates, S. (2002) 'The flashing blade: copper. Colour and luminosity in northern Italian Copper Age society', in A. Jones and G. Macgregor (eds) *Colouring the Past: The Significance of Colour in Archaeological Research*, Oxford: Berg, pp. 109–25.
Keeley, L.H. and Toth, N. (1981) 'Microwear polishes on early stone tools from Koobi Fora, Kenya', *Nature*, 293: 464–65.
Keith, K. (1998) 'Spindle whorls, gender, and ethnicity at Late Chalcolithic Hacinebi Tepe', *Journal of Field Archaeology*, 25: 497–515.
Kemp, B.J. and Vogelsang-Eastwood, G. (2001) *The Ancient Textile Industry at Amarna*, London: Egypt Exploration Society.
Kent, K.P. (1957) *The Cultivation and Weaving of Cotton in the Prehistoric Southwestern United States*, Philadelphia: American Philosophical Society.
——(1983) *Pueblo Indian Textiles: A Living Tradition*, Santa Fe, NM: School of American Research Press.
Kihlberg, K. (2003) *Masters of Sámi Handicraft: Duodji – Slöjdens Mästare*, Sweden: Förlagshuset Nordkalotten.
Killen, G. (1994) *Ancient Egyptian Furniture: Boxes, Chests and Footstools*, Warminster: Aris and Phillips.
Killen, J.T. (2007) 'Cloth production in Late Bronze Age Greece: the documentary evidence', in C. Gillis and M.-L.B. Nosch (eds) *Ancient Textiles: Production, Craft and Society*, Oxford: Oxbow Books, pp. 50–58.

King, J.H.C., Pauksztat, B. and Storrie, R. (2005) *Arctic Clothing of North America – Alaska, Canada, Greenland*, London: British Museum Press.

King, M.E. (1978) 'Analytical methods and prehistoric textiles', *American Antiquity*, 43: 89–96.

Kinnes, I. and Varndell, G. (eds) (1995) *Unbaked Urns of Rudely Shape: Essays on British and Irish Pottery, for Ian Longworth*, Oxford: Oxbow Books.

Kitchell, J.A. (2010) 'Basketmaker and archaic rock art of the Colorado Plateau: a reinterpretation of palaeoimagery', *American Antiquity*, 75(4): 819–40.

Kiviat, E. and Hamilton, E. (2001) 'Phragmites use by Native North Americans', *Aquatic Botany*, 69(2): 341–57.

Knappett, C. (2005a) *Thinking through Material Culture: An Interdisciplinary Perspective*, Philadelphia: University of Pennsylvania Press.

——(2005b) 'The affordances of things: a post-Gibsonian perspective on the relationality of mind and matter', in E. DeMarrais, C. Gosden and C. Renfrew (eds) *Rethinking Materiality: the Engagement of Mind with the Material World*, Cambridge: McDonald Institute Monographs, pp. 43–51.

Knudsen, L.R. (2007) 'Translating archaeological textiles', in C. Gillis and M.B. Nosch (eds) *Ancient Textiles, Production, Craft and Society*, Oxford: Oxbow, pp. 103–11.

Koller, J., Baumer, U. and Mania, D. (2001) 'High-tech in the middle Palaeolithic: Neandertal-manufactured pitch identified', *European Journal of Archaeology*, 4: 385–97.

Kooistra, L. (2008) 'Artefacten van hout en bast', in H. Koot, L. Bruning, L. and R.A. Houkes (eds) *Ypenburg-Locatie 4: Een Nederzetting met Grafveld uit het Midden-Neolithicum in het West-Nederlandse Kustgebied*, pp. 269–75.

Körbe-Grohne, U. (1988) 'Microscopic methods for identification of plant fibres and animal hairs from the Princes' Tomb of Hochdorf, SW Germany', *Journal of Archaeological Science*, 15: 73–83.

Kovačič, V., Moravec, V. and Svoboda, J. (2000) 'Fotografická dokumentace textilnich Otisků Z Lokality Pavlov I', in *Archeologické rozhledy LII*, pp. 303–15.

Krzyszkowska, O. (1990) *Ivory and Related Materials: An Illustrated Guide*, London: Institute of Classical Studies.

Krzyszkowska, O. and Morkot, R. (2000) 'Ivory and related materials', in P.T. Nicholson and I. Shaw (eds) *Ancient Egyptian Materials and Technology*, Cambridge: Cambridge University Press, pp. 320–31.

Kubiak-Martens, L. (1999) 'The plant food component of the diet at the late Mesolithic settlement at Tybrind Vig, Denmark, vegetation', *History and Archaeobotany*, 8: 117–27.

——(2002) 'New evidence for the use of root foods in pre-agrarian subsistence recovered from the late Mesolithic site of Halsskov, Denmark', *Vegetation History and Archaeobotany*, 11: 23–31.

Küchler, S. (2002a) 'Binding in the Pacific: between loops and knots', in V. Buchli (ed.) *The Material Culture Reader*, Oxford: Berg, pp. 63–80.

——(2002b) 'The anthropology of art', in V. Buchli (ed.) *The Material Culture Reader*, Oxford: Berg, pp. 57–62.

Kuoni, B. (1981) *Cestería Tradicional Ibérica*, Barcelona: Ediciones del Serbal.

Kuttruff, J.T. and Kuttruff, C. (1996) 'Mississippian textile evidence on fabric-impressed ceramics from Mound Bottom, Tennessee', in J.B. Patterson (ed.) *A Most Indispensible Art: Native Fiber Industries from Eastern North America*, Knoxville: University of Tennessee Press, pp. 160–73.

Lammers-Keijsers, Y.M.J. (2008) *Tracing Traces from Present to Past: A Functional Analysis of Pre-Columbian Shell and Stone Artefacts from Anse à la Gourde and Morel, Guadeloupe, FWI*, Leiden: Leiden University Press.

Langenheim, J.H. (2003) *Plant Resins: Chemistry, Evolution, Ecology and Ethnobotany*, Cambridge: Timber Press.

Langsner, D. (1995) *Green Woodworking: A Hands-on Approach*, Asheville, NC: Lark Books.

Larsen, R. (2000) 'Experiments and observations in the study of environmental impact on historical vegetable tanned leathers', *Thermchimica Acta*, 365: 85–99.

Lasiter, M.E. (1946) 'The textile world of the Ozark Bluff dwellers', *The Arkansas Historical Quarterly*, 5: 274–77.

Latz, P. (1995) *Bushfires and Bushtucker: Aboriginal Plant Use in Central Australia*, Alice Springs: Iad Press.

Lazzari, M. (2003) 'Archaeological visions: gender, landscape and optic knowledge', *Journal of Social Archaeology*, 3(2): 194–222.

Leach, B. and Tait, J. (2000) 'Papyrus', in P.T. Nicholson and I. Shaw (eds) *Ancient Egyptian Materials and Technology*, Cambridge: Cambridge University Press, pp. 227–53.

Lee, M. (2005) 'Hairnets and fishnets: the Yup'ik Eskimo *Kaapaaq* in historical context', in J.C.H. King, B. Pauksztat and R. Storrie (eds) *Arctic Clothing of North America – Alaska, Canada, Greenland*, London: British Museum Press, pp. 127–30.

Legge, A.J. (1992) *Excavations at Grimes Graves, Norfolk 1972–1976: Animals, Environment and the Bronze Age Economy*, London: British Museum Press.

Legrand, A. and Sidéra, I. (2007) 'Methods, means and results when studying European bone industries', in C. Gates St-Pierre and R.B. Walker (eds) *Bones as Tools: Current Methods and Interpretations in Worked Bone Studies*, Oxford: BAR International Series 1622, pp. 67–79.

LeMoine, G.M. (2007) 'Bone tools and bone technology: a brief history', in C. Gates St-Pierre and R.B. Walker (eds) *Bones as Tools: Current Methods and Interpretations in Worked Bone Studies*, Oxford: BAR International Series 1622, pp. 9–22.

LeMoine, G.M. and Darwent, C.M. (1998) 'The walrus and the carpenter: late Dorset ivory working in the High Arctic', *Journal of Archaeological Science*, 25: 73–83.

Lemonnier, P. (1986) 'The study of material culture today: toward an anthropology of technical systems', *Journal of Anthropological Archaeology*, 5: 147–86.

——(ed.) (1993) *Technological Choices: Transformations in Material Cultures since the Neolithic*, London: Routledge.

Lepofsky, D. and Lyons, N. (2003) 'Modeling ancient plant use on the Northwest Coast: towards an understanding of mobility and sedentism', *Journal of Archaeological Science*, 30(11): 1357–71.

Leroi-Gourhan, A. (1964) *Le Geste et la Parole, Vol. I: Technique et Langage; Vol. II: La Mémoire et les Rythmes*, Paris: Albin Michel.

Leuzinger, U. (2004) 'Experimental and applied archaeology in lake-dwelling research', in F. Menotti (ed.) *Living on the Lake in Prehistoric Europe: 150 Years of Lake-Dwelling Research*, London: Routledge, pp. 237–50.

Lev-Yadun, S.(2007) 'Wood remains from archaeological excavations: a review with a near Eastern perspective', *Israel Journal of Earth Sciences*, 56: 139–62.

Lewis, J. and Terry, J. (2004) 'The excavation of an early Bronze Age cemetery at Holly Road, Leven, Fife', *Tayside and Fife Archaeological Journal*, 10: 23–53.

Liddell, D.M. (1929) 'New light on an old problem', *Antiquity*, 3(11): 283–91.

Ling Roth, H. (1918) *Studies in Primitive Looms*, Halifax: Bamkfield Museum Notes.

Lockhart-Smith, C.J. and Elliott, R.H.G. (1974) *Tanning of Hides and Skins*, London: Tropical Products Institute.

Longworth, I. and Varndell, G. (1996) *Excavations at Grimes Graves, Norfolk 1972–1976: Mining in the Deeper Mines*, London: British Museum Press.

Louwe Koojimans, L.P. (2000) 'Living in the Neolithic: habitation and landscape', in A. Ritchie (ed.) *Neolithic Orkney in its European Context*, Cambridge: McDonald Institute for Archaeological Research, pp. 323–31.

Louwe Koojimans, L.P., Oversteegen J.F.S. and van Gijn, A.L. (2001b) 'Artefacten van been, gewei en tand', in *Hardinxveld-Giessendeam Polderweg: Een Mesolithisch jachtkamp in het rivierengebied (5500–5000 v. Chr.)*, Rapportage Archeologische Monumentenzorg 83, pp. 285–324.

Louwe Koojimans, L.P., van Gijn, A.L., Oversteegen J.F.S. and Bruineberg, M. (2001a) 'Artefacten van been, gewei en tand', in *Hardinxveld-Giessendeam De Bruin: Een kampplaats uit het Laat-Mesolithicum en het begin van de Swifterbant-cultuur (5500–4450 v. Chr.)*, Rapportage Archeologische Monumentenzorg 88, pp. 327–67.

Lucas, A.T. (1958) 'Furze, a survey and history of its uses in Ireland', *Béaloideas* 26: 1–203.

Luik, H., Choyke, A.M., Batey, C.E. and Lougas, L. (eds) (2005) *From Hooves to Horns, from Mollusc to Mammoth: Manufacture and Use of Bone Artefacts from Prehistoric Times to the Present*, Tartu: Ajaloo Instituut.

Lupo, K.D. and Schmitt, D.N. (2002) 'Upper Palaeolithic net-hunting, small prey exploitation, and women's work effort: a view from the ethnographic and ethnoarchaeological record of the Congo basin', *Journal of Archaeological Method and Theory*, 9: 147–79.

Lyford, C.A. (1943) *Ojibwa Crafts*, Lawrence, KS: Bureau of Indian Affairs.

——(1945) *Iroqois Crafts*, Lawrence, KS: Bureau of Indian Affairs.

Lyman, R.L. (1994) *Vertebrate Taphonomy*, Cambridge: Cambridge University Press.

Lyman, R.L., O'Brien, M.J. and Hayes, V. (1998) 'Mechanical and functional study of bone rods from the Richey-Roberts Clovis Cache, Washington, USA', *Journal of Archaeological Science*, 25: 887–906.

Mabey, R. (2001) *Food for Free*, London: HarperCollins.

MacGregor, A. (1976) 'Bone skates: a review of the evidence', *Archaeological Journal*, 133: 57–74.

——(1985) *Bone, Antler, Ivory and Horn*, Beckenham: Croom Helm.

——(1998) 'Hides, horns and bone: animals and interdependent industries in the early urban context', in E. Cameron (ed.) *Leather and Fur: Aspects of Early Medieval Trade and Technology*, London: Archetype Publications Ltd., pp. 11–26.

MacGregor, A. and Currey, J. (1983) 'Mechanical properties as conditioning factors in the bone and antler industry of the 3rd to the 19th century', *Journal of Archaeological Science*, 10: 71–77.

MacGregor, A. and Mainman, A. (2001) 'The bone and antler industry in Anglo-Scandinavian York: the evidence from Coppergate', in A.M. Choyke and L. Bartosiewicz (eds) *Crafting Bone: Skeletal Technologies through Time and Space, Proceedings of the 2nd Meeting of the (ICAZ) Worked Bone Research Group Budapest, 31 August–5 September 1999*, Oxford: BAR International Series 937, pp. 343–54.

MacKenzie, M. (1991) *Androgynous Objects: String Bags and Gender in Central New Guinea*, Chur: Harwood Academic.

MacKenzie McCuin, J. (2009) *The Intentional Spinner: A Holistic Approach to Making Yarn*, Colorado: Interweave Press.

MacPhilib, S. (2000) 'Rush rafts in Ireland', *Ulster Folklife*, 46: 1–8.

——(2007) 'Relics of Water World: boat and fishery collections in the National Museum of Ireland – Country Life' in E. Flegg (ed.) *The Future of Maritime and Inland Waterways Collections*, Kilkenny: Heritage Council, pp. 25–28.

Madden, R. (2010) *Being Ethnographic: A Guide to the Theory and Practice of Ethnography*, London: Sage.

Magnusson, S. (2010) *Life of Pee: The Story of How Urine Got Everywhere*, London: Aurum.

Maier, U. (1999) 'Agricultural activities and land use in a Neolithic village around 3900 BC, Hornstaad-Hörnle IA, Lake Constance, Germany', *Vegetation History and Archaeobotany*, 8: 87–94.

Maier, U. and Schlichtherle, H. (2011) 'Flax cultivation and textile production in Neolithic wetland settlements on Lake Constance and Uper Swabia (south-west Germany)', *Vegetation History and Archaeobotany*, 20: 567–78.

Maier, U. and Vogt, R. (2001) *Siedlungsarchäologie im Alpenvorland VI: Botanische und Pedologische Untersuchungen zur Ufersiedlung Hornstaad-Hörnle IA*, Stuttgart: Theiss.

Maik, J. (ed.) (2004) *Priceless Invention of Humanity – Textiles: NESAT VIII, 8–10 May, 2002. Acta Archaeologica Lodziensia Nr. 50/1*, Łódź: Łódzkie Towarzystwo Naukowe, Instytut Archeologii i Etnologii PAN.

Mairet, E. (1964) *Vegetable Dyes: Being a Book of Recipes and Other Information Useful to the Dyer*, London: Faber and Faber.

Malafouris, L. (2010) 'The brain-artefact interface (BAI): a challenge for archaeology and cultural neurosciences', *Social, Cognitive and Affective Neuroscience*, 5: 264–73.

Mallow, J.M. (2001) *Pine Needle Basketry: From Forest Floor to Finish Project*, New York: Black Crafts.

Manby, T.G. (1995) 'Skeuomorphism: some reflections of leather, wood and basketry in Early Bronze Age pottery', in I. Kinnes and G. Varndell (eds) *'Unbaked Urns of Rudely Shape': Essays on British and Irish Pottery for Ian Longworth*, Oxford: Oxbow, pp. 81–88.

Mannering, U. (1996) 'Oldtidens brændenældeklæde: førsog med fremsstilling af brænder-nældegarn', in. M. Meldgaard and M. Rasmussen (eds) *Arkæologiske Eksperimenter i Lejre*, Lejre: Arkæologisk Forsøgscenter, pp. 73–80.

——(2008) 'Iconography and costume from the Late Iron Age in Scandinavia', in M. Gleba, C. Munkholt and M.-L.B. Nosch (eds) *Dressing the Past*, Oxford: Oxbow Books, pp. 59–67.

Mannering, U., Gleba, M. and Bloch Hansen, M. (2012) 'Denmark', in M. Gleba and U. Mannering (eds) *Textiles and Textile Production in Europe From Prehistory to AD 400*, Exeter: Short Run Press, pp. 91–118.

Manske, K., Owoc, M.A., Greek, M., Illingworth, J. and Adovasio, J. (2004) *Island Threads: Bronze Age Textile Production and Identity on the Isles of Scilly, UK*, poster presented at the 69th annual meeting of the SAA, Milwaukee, WI.

Mansur-Franchomme, M.E. (1983) 'Scanning electron microscopy of dry hide working tools: the role of abrasives and humidity in microwear polish formation', *Journal of Archaeological Science*, 10: 223–30.

Martial, E. and Médard, F. (2007) 'Acquisition et traitement des matières textiles d'origine végétale en Préhistoire: l'exemple du lin', in V. Beugnier and P. Crombé (eds) *Plant Processing from a Prehistoric and Ethnographic Perspective*, Oxford: BAR International Series 1718, pp. 67–82.

Mason, Carol I. (1997) 'The Historic Period in Wisconsin Archaeology, Native Peoples.' *The Wisconsin Archeologist* 78: 298–319.

Mason, O.T (1889) *Aboriginal Skin-Dressing: A Study Based on Material in the US National Museum*, Report of the US National Museum under the direction of the Smithsonian Institute.

——(1890) *Basket-Work of the North American Aborigines*, Washington: Smithsonian Institution.

——(2010) *Indian Basketry*, Memphis: General Books.

Maynard, B. (1977) *Cane Seating*, Leicester: Dryad Press.

——(1989) *Modern Basketry Techniques*, London: Batsford.

Mazza, P.P.A., Martini, F., Sala, B., Magi, M., Colombini, M.P., Giachi, G., Landucci, F., Lemorini, C., Modugno, F. and Ribechini, E. (2006) 'A New Palaeolithic discovery: tar-hafted stone tools in a European Mid-Pleistocene bone-bearing bed', *Journal of Archaeological Science*, 33: 1310–18.

McCarthy, F.D. (1976) *Australian Aboriginal Stone Implements: Including Bone, Shell and Tooth Implements*, 2nd edn, Sydney: Australian Museum Trust.

McCorriston, J. (1997) 'The fiber revolution: textile extensification, alienation, and social stratification in ancient Mesopotamia', *Current Anthropology*, 38: 517–49

McGrail, S. (1982) *Woodworking Techniques Before AD 1500: Papers Presented to a Symposium at Greenwich in September, 1980, Together with Edited Discussion*, Oxford: BAR International Series S129.

——(1987) *Ancient Boats in North-Western Europe: The Archaeology of Water Transport to AD 1500*, London: Longmans.

——(2002) *Boats of the World: From the Stone Age to Medieval Times*, Oxford: Oxford University Press.

McGregor, R. (1992) *Prehistoric Basketry of the Lower Pecos, Texas*, Madison, WI: Prehistory Press.

McGuire, J. (1990) *Basketry: The Nantucket Tradition*, New York: Lark Books.

McNiven, I.J. (2003) 'Saltwater people: spiritscapes, maritime rituals and the archaeology of Australian indigenous seascapes', *Seascapes: World Archaeology*, 35(3): 329–49.

Médard, F. (2000) *L'Artisanat Textile au Néolithique*, Montagnac: Monique Mergoil.

——(2005) 'Les textiles préhistoriques: anatomie des écorces et analyse des traitements mis en œuvre pour en extraire la matiére textile', in P. della Casa and M. Trachsel (eds) *WES'04: Wetland Economies and Societies*, Zürich: Schweizerisches Landesmuseum, pp. 99–104.

Médard, F. and Moser, F. (2006) 'Observations sur la fabrication expérimentale des étoffes cordées', *Euro Rea: Journal of (Re)construction and Experiment in Archaeology*, 3: 19–22.

Meeks, N.D. and Cartwright, C.R. (2005) 'Caribou and seal hair: examination by scanning electron microscope', in J.C.H. King, B. Pauksztat and R. Storrie (eds) *Arctic Clothing of North America – Alaska, Canada, Greenland*, London: British Museum Press, pp. 42–44.

Meiggs, R. (1982) *Trees and Timber in the Ancient Mediterranean World*, Oxford: Clarendon Press.

Menz, D. (2004) *Color Works: The Crafter's Guide to Colour*, Loveland, CO: Interweave Press.

Merleau-Ponty, M. (1962) *The Phenomenology of Perception*, London: Routledge.

Meskell, L. (2005) 'Introduction: object orientations', in L. Meskell (ed.) *Archaeologies of Materiality*, Oxford: Blackwell, pp. 1–17.

Meuli, J. (1997) 'Writing about objects we don't understand', in P. Dormer (ed.) *The Culture of Craft*, Manchester: Manchester University Press, pp. 202–18.

Michel, C. and Nosch, M.-L. (eds) (2010) *Textile Terminologies in the Ancient Near East and Mediterranean from the Third to the First Millennium BC*, Oxford: Oxbow Books.

Militello, P. (2007) 'Textile industry and Minoan palaces', in C. Gillis and M.-L.B. Nosch (eds) *Ancient Textiles: Production, Craft and Society*, Oxford: Oxbow Books, pp. 36–45.

Miller, G.H. (2005) 'Ecosystem collapse in Pleistocene Australia and a human role in megafaunal extinction', *Science*, 309: 287–90

Miller, H.M.L. (2007) *Archaeological Approaches to Technology*, Amsterdam: Elsevier.

Milliken, W. and Bridgewater, S. (2004) *Flora Celtica: Plants and People in Scotland*, Birlinn: Edinburgh.

Moir, B.G. (1990) 'Comparative studies of "fresh" and "aged" *Tridacna gigas* shell: preliminary investigations of a reported technique for pre-treatment of tool material', *Journal of Archaeological Science*, 17: 329–46.

Möller-Wiering, S. (2005) 'Textiles for transport', in F. Pritchard and J.P. Wild (eds) *Northern Archaeological Textiles, NESAT VII Textile Symposium in Edinburgh, 5–7 May 1999*, Oxford: Oxbow Books, pp. 75–79.

——(2007) 'Under canvas', in C. Gillis and M.-L.B. Nosch (eds) *Ancient Textiles: Production, Craft and Society*, Oxford: Oxbow Books, pp. 122–26.

Monks, G.G. (2005) 'An oil utility index for whale bones', in G.G. Monks (ed.) *The Exploitation and Cultural Importance of Sea Mammals*, Oxford: Oxbow Books, pp. 138–53.

Mooney, S.D., et al (2011) 'Late Quaternary fire regimes of Australasia', *Quaternary Science Reviews*, 30: 28–46

Morrell, P.L. and Clegg, M.T. (2007) 'Genetic evidence for a second domestication of barley (*Hordeum vulgare*), east of the fertile crescent', *Proceedings of the National Academy of Sciences*, 104: 3289–94.

Morsbach, H. (2002), *Common Sense Forestry*, Vermont: Chelsea Green Publishing Company.

Mould, R. and Mould, Q. (eds) (2011) *Leather Tanneries: The Archaeological Evidence*, London: Archetype Publications Ltd. in association with the Archaeological Leather Group.

Mowat, L., Morphy, H. and Dransart, P. (1992) *Basketmakers: Meaning and Form in Native American Baskets*, Oxford: Pitt Rivers Museum.

Mrozowski, S.A., Franklin, M. and Hunt, L. (2008) 'Archaeobotanical analysis and interpretations of enslaved Virginian plant use at Rich Neck Plantation (44WB52)', *American Antiquity*, 73(4): 699–728.

Musée de Préhistoire d'Ile-de-France (2004) *La Vannerie dans l'Antiquité*, Nemours: Musée de Préhistoire d'Ile-de-France.

Myking, T., Hetzberg, A. and Skrøppa, T. (2005) *History, Manufacture and Properties of Lime Bast Cordage in Northern Europe*, Oxford: Oxford University Press.

Nabokov, P. and Easton, R. (1989) *Native American Architecture*, Oxford: Oxford University Press.

Nagar, M. and Misra, V.N. (1994) 'Survival of the hunter-gathering tradition in the Ganga Plains and Central India', in B. Allchin (ed.) *Living Traditions: Studies in the Ethnoarchaeology of South Asia*, Columbia, MO: South Asia Publications, pp. 169–92.

Needham, S.P. (2000) *The Passage of the Thames: Holocene Environment and Settlement at Runnymede*, London: British Museum Press, Runnymede Bridge Research Excavations, Vol. 1.

Needham, S. and Spence, T. (1996) *Refuse and Disposal at Area 16 East, Runnymede*, London: British Museum Press.

Newman, R. and Serpico, M. (2000) 'Adhesives and binders', in P.T. Nicholson and I. Shaw (eds) *Ancient Egyptian Materials and Technology*, Cambridge: Cambridge University Press, pp. 475–94.

Nicholas, G.P. (1998) 'Wetlands and hunter-gatherers: a global perspective', *Current Anthropology*, 39: 720–31.

Nishida, I. (ed.) (2008) *The Higashimyo Wetland Site: The Basket Makers of the Jomon Period around 7000 BP*, Nara: Meishinsha.

Nordfors, J. (1974) *Needle Lace and Needleweaving: A New Look at Traditional Stitches*, New York: Nostrand Reinhold.

Nørgaard, A. (2008) 'A weaver's voice: making reconstructions of Danish Iron Age textiles', in M. Gleba, C. Munkholt and M.-L.B. Nosch (eds) *Dressing the Past*, Oxford: Oxbow Books, pp. 43–58.

North House Folk School (2007) *Celebrating Birch: The Lore, Art, and Craft of an Ancient Tree*, East Petersburg: Fox Chapel Publishing Company Inc.

Nosch, M.-L.B. (2008) 'Haute couture in the Bronze Age: a history of Minoan female costumes from Thera' in M. Gleba, C. Munkholt and M.-L.B. Nosch (eds) *Dressing the Past*, Oxford: Oxbow Books, pp. 1–12.

Novellino, D. (2009) 'From museum collection to field research', *Indonesia and the Malay World*, 37: 203–24.

Oakley, K.P. (1965a) 'Folklore of fossils part I', *Antiquity*, 39: 9–16.

——(1965b) 'Folklore of fossils part II', *Antiquity*, 39: 117–25.

——(1985) *Decorative and Symbolic Uses of Fossils: Selected Groups, Mainly Invertebrate*, Oxford: Pitt Rivers Museum, University of Oxford.

Oaks, R. and Mills, E. (2010) *Coppicing & Coppice Crafts: A Comprehensive Guide*, Wiltshire: The Crowood Press Ltd.

O'Brien, R. (2010) 'Spindle-whorls and hand-spinning in Ireland', in M. Stanley, E. Danaher and J. Eogan (eds) *Creative Minds: Production, Manufacturing and Invention in Ancient Ireland*, Dublin: National Roads Authority, pp. 15–26.

O'Connor, S. and Veth, P. (2005) 'Early Holocene shell fish hooks from Lene Hara Cave, East Timor establish complex fishing technology was in use in Island South East Asia five thousand years before Austronesian settlement', *Antiquity*, 79: 249–56.

O'Connor, T. and Sykes, N. (eds) (2010) *Extinctions and Invasions: A Social History of British Fauna*, Oxford: Windgather Press.

Okey. T. (1912) *An Introduction to the Art of Basket-making*, London: Pitman.

Olsen, S.L. (1989) 'On distinguishing natural from cultural damage on archaeological antler', *Journal of Archaeological Science*, 16: 125–36.

O'Neil, B. (1952) 'The excavation of Knackyboy cairn, St. Martin's, Isles of Scilly, 1948', *Antiquaries Journal*, 32: 21–34.

Orchard, W.C. (1971) *The Technique of Porcupine Quill Decoration among the Indians of North America*, 2nd edn, New York: Museum of the American Indian Heye Foundation.

——(1975) *Beads and Beadwork of the American Indians*, New York: Museum of the American Indian Heye Foundation.

Osgood, C. (1940) *Ingalik Material Culture*, Newhaven: Yale University press.

Osipowicz, G. (2007) 'Bone and antler: softening techniques in prehistory of the north eastern part of the Polish Lowlands in the light of experimental archaeology and micro trace analysis', *Euro Rea: Journal of (Re)construction and Experiment in Archaeology*, 4: 11–21.

Oswalt, W.H. (1976) *An Anthropological Analysis of Food-getting Technology*, New York: Wyley.

Outram, A. (ed.) (2008) 'Introduction to experimental archaeology', *World Archaeology*, 40: 1–6.

Outram, A.K., Knüsel, C.J., Knight, S. and Harding, A.F. (2005) 'Understanding complex fragmented assemblages of human and animal remains: a fully integrated approach', *Journal of Archaeological Science*, 32: 1699–1710.

Overstreet, D.F. (1997) 'Oneota prehistory and history', *The Wisconsin Archeologist*, 78: 250–96.

Owen, L.R. (1998) 'Gender, crafts and the reconstruction of tool use', *Helinium*, 34: 186–200.

——(1999) 'Questioning stereotypical notions of prehistoric tool functions: ethno-analogy, experimentation and functional analysis', in L.R. Owen and M. Porr (eds) *Ethno-analogy and the Reconstruction of Prehistoric Artefact Use and Production*, Tübingen: Mo Vince Verlag, pp. 17–30.

——(2000) 'Lithic functional analysis as a means of studying gender and material culture in prehistory', in M. Donald and L. Hurcombe (eds) *Gender and Material Culture in Archaeological Perspective*, Basingstoke: Macmillan, pp. 185–205.

Owoc, M.A. (2005a) 'From the ground up: agency, practice, and community in the Southwestern British Bronze Age', *Journal of Archaeological Method and Theory*, 12: 257–81.

——(2005b) 'Just an impression: cordage and textiles as invisible materiality', paper presented at the Theoretical Archaeology Group Conference, December 2005, Sheffield, UK.

Paama-Pengelly, J. (2010) *Maori Art and Design; Weaving, Painting, Carving and Architecture*, Auckland: New Holland.

Paine, S. (1990) *Embroidered Textiles: Traditional Patterns from Five Continents, with a Worldwide Guide to Identification*, London: Thames & Hudson.

——(1994) *The Afghan Amulet: Travels from the Hindu Kush to Razgrad*, London: Penguin Books.

Pante, M.C. and Blumenschine, R.J. (2010) 'Fluvial transport of bovid long bones fragmented by the feeding activities of hominins and carnivores', *Journal of Archaeological Science*, 37: 846–54.

Panter-Brick, C., Layton, R.H. and Rowley-Conwy, P. (eds) (2001) *Hunter-Gatherers: An Interdisciplinary Perspective*, Cambridge: Cambridge University Press.

Park, J.A. (2004) *Simmans, Sookans and Straw Backed Chairs*, Orkney: Orkney Heritage.

Parker Pearson, M. (2000) 'Ancestors, bones and stones in Neolithic and Early Bronze Age Britain and Ireland', in A. Ritchie (ed.) *Neolithic Orkney in its European Context*, Cambridge: McDonald Institute for Archaeological Research, pp. 203–14.

Parker Pearson, M. and Ramilisonina (1998) 'Stonehenge for the ancestors: the stones pass on the message', *Antiquity*, 72: 308–26.

Parker Pearson, M., Pollard, J., Tilley, C., Welham, K. and Albarella, U. (2006) 'Materialising Stonehenge: the Stonehenge Riverside Project and new discoveries', *Journal of Material Culture*, 11: 227–61.

Patterson, M. (2007) *The Senses of Touch: Haptics, Affects and Technologies*, Oxford: Berg.

Pavao-Zuckerman, B. (2011) 'Rendering economies: Native American labor and secondary animal products in the eighteenth-century Pimería Alta', *American Antiquity*, 76(1): 3–23.

Payne, S. (1973) 'Kill-off patterns in shepp and goats: the mandibles from Askale', *Anatolian Studies*, 23: 281–303.

Peabody Turnbaugh, S. and Turnbaugh, W.A. (1986) *Indian Baskets*, Atglen, PA: Schiffer Publishing.

Pedersen, K. (2005) 'Eskimo sewing techniques in relation to contemporary sewing techniques – seen through a copy of a Qilakitsoq costume', in J.C.H. King, B. Pauksztat and R. Storrie (eds) *Arctic Clothing of North America – Alaska, Canada, Greenland*, London: British Museum Press, pp. 70–73.

Pelegrin, J. (1990) 'Prehistoric lithic technology, some aspects of research', *Archaeological Review from Cambridge*, 9: 116–25.

Penniman, T.K. (1984) *Pictures of Ivory and Other Animal Teeth, Bone and Antler, with a Brief Commentary on their Use and Identification*, 2nd edn, Oxford: Pitt Rivers Museum.

Peter, K. (1980) *Nats'ats'a' ch'adhah ahkhii, How I Tan Hides*, Athabaskan: Alaska Native Language Centre, University of Alaska.

Peterson, J.B. (ed.) (1996) *A Most Indispensible Art: Native Fiber Industries from Eastern North America*, Knoxville: University of Tennessee.

Pétrequin, A.-M. and Pétrequin, P. (1988) *Le Neolithique du Lacs*, Montligeon: Errance.

Pétrequin, P., Weller, O., Gauthier, É., Dufraisse, A. and Piningre, J.-F. (2001) 'Salt springs exploitation without pottery during prehistory. From New Guinea to the French Jura' in S. Beyries and P. Pétrequin (eds) *Ethno-Archaeology and its Transfers*, Oxford: BAR International Series 983, pp. 37–65.

Pettit, P. (2011) *The Palaeolithic Origins of Human Burial*, London and New York: Routledge.

Phillips, J. (2000) 'Ostrich eggshells', in P.T. Nicholson and I. Shaw (eds) *Ancient Egyptian Materials and Technology*, Cambridge: Cambridge University Press, pp. 332–33.

Pitts, M. and Roberts, M. (1997) *Fairweather Eden: Life in Britain Half a Million Years Ago as Revealed by the Excavations at Boxgrove*, London: Century.

Platt, S.G. and Brantley, C.G. (1997) 'Canebrakes: an ecological and historical perspective', *Castanea*, 62: 8–21.

Plisson, H. (1993) 'Le travail des matières premières animales tendres: de l'outil vers le processus', in M. Otte (ed) *Traces et Fonction: Les Gestes Retrouvés*, Liège: Etudes et recherches archéologiques de l'Université de Liège, pp. 50–51.

Polakoff, C. (1982) *African Textiles and Dyeing Techniques*, London: Routledge and Kegan Paul.

Pole, L., Doyal, S. and Burkinshaw, J. (2004) *Second Skin: Everyday and Sacred uses of Bark*, Exeter: Royal Albert Memorial Museum and Art Gallery.

Pollard, J. (2000) 'Neolithic occupation practices and social ecologies from Rinyo to Clacton', in A. Ritchie (ed.) *Neolithic Orkney in its European Context*, Cambridge: McDonald Institute for Archaeological Research, pp. 363–69.

Povinelli, D. (2000) *Folk Physics for Apes: Chimpanzees, Tool-use, and Causal Understanding*, Oxford: Oxford University Press.

Price, T.D. and Gebauer, A.B. (eds) (2005) *Smakkerup Huse: A Late Mesolithic Coastal Site in Northwest Zealand*, Denmark: Aarhus University Press.

Pringle, H. (1997) 'Ice Age communities may be earliest known net hunters', *Science*, 277: 1203–4.

Procter, H.R. (1922) *The Principles of Leather Manufacture*, London: E. & F.N. Spon.

Pryor, F. (1996) 'Sheep, stockyards and field systems: Bronze Age livestock populations in the Fenlands of eastern England', *Antiquity*, 70: 313–24.

——(1998) *Etton: Excavations at a Neolithic Causewayed Enclosure Near Maxey, Cambridgeshire 1982–7*, London: English Heritage.

——(2006) *Farmers in Prehistoric Britain*, Stroud, Gloucestershire: Tempus Publishing Ltd.

——(2010) *The Making of the British Landscape: How We Have Transformed the Land from Prehistory to Today*, London: Allen Lane.

Purdy, B.A. (ed.) (2001) *Enduring Records: The Environmental and Cultural Heritage of Wetlands*, Oxford: Oxbow.

Quimby, G.I. (1961) 'Cord marking versus fabric impressing of woodland pottery', *American Antiquity*, 26: 426–28.

Rackham, O. (1996) *Trees and Woodland in the British Landscape: The Complete History of Britain's Trees, Woods and Hedgerows*, London: Phoenix.

Rahme, L. (2003) *Skinn Garvning och Beredning med Traditionella Metoder*, Sigtuna: Lottas Garfveri.

——(2006) *Fiskskinn Garvning och Sömnad*, Sigtuna: Lottas Garfveri.

Ramseyer, D. (ed.) (2001) *Objets Méconnus*, Paris: Société Préhistorique Française.

Rasmussen, M. (ed.) (2007) 'Iron Age houses in flames: testing house reconstruction at Lejre', *Studies in Technology and Culture*, vol. 3, Lejre: Lejre Historical-Archaeological Experimental Centre.

Rast-Eicher, A. (1992) 'Neolitische Textilien im Raum Zürich' in L. Bender-Jørgensen and E. Munksgaar (eds) *Archaeological Textiles in Northern Europe*, Copenhagen: Konservatorskolen det Kongelige Danske Kunstakademi, pp. 9–19.

——(2005) 'Bast before wool: the first textiles', in P. Bichler, K. Grömer, R. Hofmann-De Keijzer, A. Kern and H. Reschreiter (eds) *Hallstatt Textiles: Technical Analysis, Scientific Investigation and Experiment on Iron Age Textiles*, Oxford: BAR International Series 1351, pp. 117–31.

Rast-Eicher, A. and Bender-Jørgensen, L. (2013) 'Sheep wool in Bronze Age and Iron Age Europe', *Journal of Archaeological Science*, 40: 1224–41.

Rast-Eicher, A. and Schweiz, E. (1994) 'Gewebe im Neolithikum', in G. Jaacks and K. Tidow (eds) *Textilsymposium Neumunster: Archologische Textilfunde – Archaeological Textiles*, NESAT V, Neumunster: Textilmuseum, pp. 18–26.

Rast-Eicher, A. and Windler, R. (eds) (2007) *NESAT IX, Archäologische Textilfunde – Archaeological Textiels, Braunwald, 18–21 mai 2005* Näfels: Lotteriefonds des Kanton Glarus.

Reed, F. (2005) 'The poor man's raincoat: Alaskan fish-skin garments', in J.C.H. King, B. Pauksztat and R. Storrie (eds) *Arctic Clothing of North America – Alaska, Canada, Greenland*, London: British Museum Press, pp. 48–52.

Reed, R. (1972) *Leathers, Skins and Parchments*, London: Academic Press.

Regnell, M., Gaillard, M.-J., Bartholin, T. S. and Karsten, P. (1995) 'Reconstruction of environment and history of plant use during the late Mesolithic at the inlands settlement of *Bökeberg* tree, Southern Sweden', *Vegetation History and Archaeobotany*, 4: 67–91.

Renfrew, C. (2004) 'Towards a theory of material engagement', in E. DeMarrais, C. Gosden and C. Renfrew (eds) *Rethinking Materiality: The Engagement of Mind with the Material World*, Cambridge: McDonald Institute for Archaeological Research, pp. 23–31.

Renouf, M.A. (2009) 'Dorset paleoeskimo whalebone use', in H.C. Gullov (ed.) *On the Track of the Thule Culture from Bering Strait to East Greenland*, Copenhagen: National Museum, pp. 91–104.

Reschreiter and Kowarik, K. (2009) 'The Carrysacks – strict division of labour and high efficiency in Kermn', in A.K. Kowarik, A. Rausch and H. Reschreiter (eds) *Kingdoom of Salt*, Vienna: Natural History Museum, pp. 60–62.

Rhoads, J.W. (1992) 'Significant sites and non-site archaeology: a case-study from south-east Australia', *World Archaeology*, 24: 198–217.

Rice, M. (1980) *Mushrooms for Color*, California: Mad River Press Inc.

Richards, C. (ed.) (2005) *Dwelling Among the Monuments: The Neolithic Village of Barnhouse, Maeshowe Passage Grave and Environs*, Cambridge: McDonald Institute Monographs.

Richards, M. (2004) *Deerskins into Buckskins: How to Tan with Brains, Soap or Eggs*, 2nd edn, Cave Junction, OR: Backcountry Publishing.

Rimantiene, R. (1992) 'Neolithic hunter-gatherers at Sventoji in Lithuania', *Antiquity*, 66: 367–76.

Rimkuté, V. (2010) 'The Neolithic mats of the Eastern Baltic Littoral' in E. Andersson Strand, M. Gleba, U. Mannering, C. Munkholt and M. Ringgaard (eds) *NESAT X The North European Symposium for Archaeological Textiles*, Oxford: Oxbow Books, pp. 217–20.

Risatti, H.A (2007) *Theory of Craft: Function and Aesthetic Expression*, Chapel Hill: University of North Carolina Press.

Rizopoulou-Egoumenidou, E. (2009) *Tanning in Cyprus from the 16th to the 20th Century: From Traditional Tanneries to Modern Industries*, Nikosia: Cyprus Research Centre.

Robinson, D.B. (2002) *The Sámi of Northern Europe*, Minneapolis: Lerner Publications Company.

Robson, D. and Ekarius, C. (2011) *The Fleece and Fiber Sourcebook*, Massachusettes: Storey Publishing.

Rodman, A.O. and Lopez, G.A.F. (2005) 'North Coast style after Moche: clothing and identity at El Brujo, Chicama Valley, Perud', in R.M. Reycraft (ed.) *Us and Them: Archaeology and Ethnicity in the Andes*, Los Angeles: Cotsen Institute of Archaeology, University of California, pp. 115–33.

Roe, F.G. (1972) *The North Americal Buffalo: A Critical Study of the Species in its Wild State*, Newton Abbot: David and Charles.

Rœder Knudsen, L (2007) 'Translating "archaeological textiles"', in C. Gillis and M.-L.B. Nosch (eds) *Ancient Textiles: Production, Craft and Society*, Oxford: Oxbow Books, pp. 103–11.

Ronald Smith, J. (1975) *Taaniko: Maori Hand-Weaving*, New York: Charles Scribner's Sons.

Rothe, L. (1934) *Studies in Primitive Looms*, Halifax: F. King & Sons Ltd.

Rots, V. 2010 *Prehension and HaftingTraces on Flint Tools: A Methodology*, Leuven: Leuven University Press.

Roux, V. (1989) *The Potter's Wheel: Craft Specialization and Technical Competence*, New Delhi: Oxford & IBH Publishing Co. Pvt Ltd.

Rowley-Conwy, P. (1993) 'Season and reason: the case for a regional interpretation of Mesolithic settlement patterns', in G.L. Peterkin, H.M. Bricker and P. Mellars (eds) *Hunting and Animal Exploitation in the Later Paleolithic and Mesolithic of Eurasia*, Washington, DC: American Anthropological Association, pp. 179–88.

——(1995a) 'Wild or domestic, on the evidence for the earliest domestic cattle and pigs in Southern Scandinavia and Iberia', *International General Osteoarchaeology*, 5: 115–26.

——(1995b) 'Making first farmers younger: the West European evidence', *Current Anthropology*, 36: 346–53.

——(2001) 'Lines of enquiry', in C. Panter-Brick, R.H. Layton and P. Rowley-Conwy (eds) *Hunter-Gatherers: An Interdisciplinary Perspective*, Cambridge: Cambridge University Press, pp. 1–11.

——(2006) 'The concept of prehistory and the invention of the terms "prehistoric" and "prehistorian": the Scandinavian origin, 1833–1850', *European Journal of Archaeology*, 9(1): 105–30.

Rozen, D.L. (1978) *The Ethnozoology of the Cowichan Indian People: Fish, Beach Foods and Marine Mammals*, Vancouver: Ethno-Arch Consultants.

Rudkin, L. (2007) *Natural Dyes*, London: A. & C. Black Publishers Ltd.

Russell, M. (1982) *Trees and Timber in the Ancient Mediterranean World*, Oxford: Clarendon Press.

Russell, N. (2012) *Social Zooarchaeology: Humans and Animals in Prehistory*, Cambridge University Press.

Ryder, M.L. (1964) 'Fleece evolution in domestic sheep', *Nature*, 204(4958): 555–59.

——(1965) 'Report of textiles from Catal Huyuk', *Anatolian Studies*, 15: 175–76.

——(1969) 'Changes in the fleece of sheep following domestication', in P.J. Ucko and G.W. Dimbleby (eds) *The Domestication of Plants and Animals*, London: Duckworth, pp. 495–521.

——(1970) 'Remains derived from skin', in D. Brothwell and E.S. Higgs (eds) *Science and Archaeology*, London: Thames & Hudson, pp. 539–54.

——(1980) 'Hair remains throw light on early British cattle', *Journal of Archaeological Science*, 7: 389–92.

——(1984) 'The first hair remains from an aurochs (*Bos primigenius*) and some medieval domestic cattle hair', *Journal of Archaeological Science*, 11: 99–101.

——(1987) 'The evolution of the fleece', *Scientific American*, 255: 112–19.

——(1991) 'The last word on the golden fleece legend', *Oxford Journal of Archaeology*, 10: 57–60.

——(1992) 'Iron Age haired animal skins from Hallstatt, Austria', *Oxford Journal of Archaeology*, 11: 55–68.

——(1999) 'Probable fibres from hemp in Bronze Age Scotland', in G. Jones (ed.) *Environmental Archaeology 4*, Oxford: Oxbow Books, pp. 93–95.

——(2000) 'The fibres in textile remains from the Iron Age salt-mines at Hallstatt, Austria', *Annalen des Naturhistorischen Museums Wien*, 102A: 223–44.

——(2001) 'Fibres in Iron Age textiles from the Dürrnberg (Austria)', *Archaeological Textiles Newsletter*, 33: 2–5.

——(2005) 'The human development of different fleece-types in sheep and its association with the development of textile crafts', in F. Pritchard and J.P. Wild (eds) *Northern Archaeological Textiles, NESAT VII textile symposium in Edinburgh, 5–7 May 1999*, Oxford: Oxbow Books, pp. 122–28.

Ryder, M.L. and Gabra-Sanders, T. (1987) 'A microscopic study of remains of textiles made from plant fibres', *Oxford Journal of Archaeology*, 6: 91–108.

Salanova, L. (1992) 'Le Décor a la Coquille dans le Campaniforme du Sud-Finistere', *Rev. archeol. Ouest*, 9: 79–81.

——(1998) 'Technological, ideological or economic European union? The variability of Bell Beaker decoration', *Bell Beakers Today*, pp. 91–102.

Saunders, N.J. (1999) 'Biographies of brilliance: pearls, transformations of matter and being, c. AD 1492', *World Archaeology*, 31(2): 243–57.

Sayer, C. (1985) *Mexican Textiles*, London: British Museum Publications.

Scarre, C. and Lawson, G. (eds) (2006) *Archaeoacoustics*, Cambridge: McDonald Institute for Archaeological Research.

Scheinsohn, V. and Ferretti, J.L. (1995) 'The mechanical properties of bone materials in relation to the design and function of prehistoric tools from Tierra del Fuego, Argentina', *Journal of Archaeological Science*, 22: 711–18.

——(1997) 'Design and function of prehistoric tools of Tierra Del Fuego (Argentina) as related to the mechanical properties of bone materials utilized in their manufacture', in L.A. Hannus,

L. Rossum and R.P. Winham (eds) *Proceedings of the 1993 Bone Modification Conference, Hot Springs, South Dakota*, Sioux Falls, SD: Archaeology Laboratory, Augustana College, pp. 65–75.

Schiffer, M.B. (1987) *Formation Processes of the Archaeological Record*, Alburquerque: University of New Mexico Press.

Schlanger, N. (2004) '"Suivre les gestes, éclat par éclat": la chaîne opératoire de Leroi-Gourhan', in F. Adouze and N. Schlanger (eds) *Autour de l'Homme: Contexte et Actualité de Leroi-Gourhan*, Paris: Editions APDCA.

——(2005) 'The chaîne opératoire', in C. Renfrew and P. Bahn (eds) *Archaeology: The Key Concepts*, London: Routledge, pp. 25–31.

Schlick, M.D. (1994) *Columbia River Basketry: Gift of the Ancestors, Gift of the Earth*, Seattle and London: University of Washington Press.

Schlumbaum, A., Campos, P.S., Volken, S., Volken, M., Hafner, A. and Schibler, J. (2010) 'Ancient DNA, a Neolithic legging from the Swiss Alps and the early history of goat', *Journal of Archaeological Science*, 37: 1247–51.

Schmidt, A.L. and Pederson, K.B. (2009) *Skin Clothing from the North: Abstracts from the Seminar at the National Museum of Denmark, November 26–27, 2009*, Denmark: National Museum of Denmark.

Scholtz, S.C. (1975) *Prehistoric Plies: A Structural and Comparative Analysis of Cordage, Netting, Basketry, and Fabric from Ozark Bluff Shelters*, Fayetteville: University of Arkansas Museum.

Schulting, R.J. (1996) 'Antlers, bone pins and flint blades: the Mesolithic cemeteries of Téviec and Hoëdic, Brittany', *Antiquity* 70: 335–50.

Schutten, T. (1975) *Spinnen met Plezier: de techniek van een oud ambacht*, Wageningen: Zomer & Keuningen.

Schwebke, P.W. and Krohn, M.B. (1970) *How to Sew Leather, Suede and Fur*, New York: Simon and Schuster.

Semaw, S. (2000) 'The world's oldest stone artefacts from Gona, Ethiopia: their implications for understanding stone technology and patterns of human evolution between 2.6–1.5 million years ago', *Journal of Archaeological Science*, 27: 1197–1214.

Sennett, R. (2008) *The Craftsman*, London: Penguin Books.

Serpico, M. and White, R. (2000a) 'Oil, fat and wax', in P.T. Nicholson and I. Shaw (eds) *Ancient Egyptian Materials and Technology*, Cambridge: Cambridge University Press, pp. 390–429.

——(2000b) 'Resins, amber and bitumen', in P.T. Nicholson and I. Shaw (eds) *Ancient Egyptian Materials and Technology*, Cambridge: Cambridge University Press, pp. 430–74.

Shaham, D., Grosman, L. and Goren-Inbar, N. (2010) 'The red-stained flint crescent from Gesher: new insights into PPNA hafting technology', *Journal of Archaeological Science*, 37: 2010–16

Sharples, N. (2000) 'Antlers and Orcadian rituals: an ambiguous role for red deer in the Neolithic', in A. Ritchie (ed.) *Neolithic Orkney in its European Context*, Cambridge: McDonald Institute for Archaeological Research, pp. 107–17.

Shaw-Smith, D. (2003) *Traditional Crafts of Ireland*, London: Thames & Hudson.

Sheridan, A., Kochman, W. and Aranauskas, R. (2003) 'The grave goods from the Knowes of Trotty, Orkney: reconsideration and replication', in J. Downes, and A. Ritchie (eds) *Sea Change: Orkney and Northern Europe in the Later Iron Age AD 300–800,* Angus: Pinkfoot Press, pp. 177–88.

Sherratt, A. (1983) 'Secondary exploitation of animals in the old world', *World Archaeology* 15: 90–104.

Shutova, N. (2006) 'Trees in Udmurt religion', *Antiquity*, 80: 318–27.

Sillar, B. (2000) *Shaping Cultures: Making Pots and Correcting Households*, Oxford: BAR International Series 883.

Sillitoe, P. and Hardy, K. (2003) 'Living Lithics: ethnoarchaeology in Highland Papua New Guinea', *Antiquity*, 77(297): 555–66.

Silvester, R. (1994) 'The ethnoarchaeology of Kalinga basketry: a preliminary investigation', in W.A. Longacre and J.M. Skibo (eds) *Kalinga Ethnoarchaeology: Expanding Archaeological Method and Theory*, Washington, DC: Smithsonian Institution Press, pp. 199–207.

Skeates, R. (1991) 'Triton's trumpet: a Neolithic symbol in Italy', *Oxford Journal of Archaeology*, 10: 17–32.

Skinner, A. (1923) 'Observations on the ethnology of the Sauk Indians', *Bulletin of the Public Museum of the City of Milwaukee*, 5(1): 1–57.

——(1926) 'Ethnology of the Ioway Indians', *Bulletin of the Public Museum of the City of Milwaukee*, 5(4): 181–354.

Soffer, O. (2004) 'Recovering perishable technologies through use wear on tools: preliminary evidence for Upper Palaeolithic weaving and net making', *Current Anthropology*, 45: 407–25.

Soffer, O., Adovasio, J.M., and Hyland, D.C. (2000) 'The "Venus" figurines: textiles, basketry, gender, and status in the Upper Paleolithic', *Current Anthropology*, 41: 511–37.

Soffer, O., Adovasio, J.M. and Hyland, D.C. (2001) 'Perishable technologies and invisible people: nets, baskets, and "Venus" wear ca. 26,000 BP', in B.A. Purdy (ed.) *Enduring Records: The Environmental and Cultural Heritage of Wetlands*, Oxford: Oxbow Books, pp. 233–45.

Soffer, O., Adovasio, J.M., Kornietz, N.L., Velichko, A.A., Gribchenko, Y.N., Lenz, B.R. and Suntsov, V.Y. (1997) 'Cultural stratigraphy at Mezhirich, an Upper Palaeolithic site in Ukraine with multiple occupations', *Antiquity*, 71: 48–62

Spahan, R. and Wherry, C.C. (2010) *SMASH International Indigenous Weaving: Salish, Mi'kmaq Alaskan Southwest, Hawaiian* (exhibition catalogue), Victoria, BC: Art Gallery of Greater Victoria.

Spangenberg, J.E.M.F., Tschudin, P., Volken, M. and Hafner, A. (2010) 'Microstructural, chemical and isotopic evidence for the origin of Late Neolithic leather recovered from an ice field in the Swiss Alps', *Journal of Archaeological Science*, 37: 1851–65.

Spencer-Wood, S. (2005) 'Feminist boundary crossings: challenging androcentric assumptions and stereo types about hideworking', in L. Frink and K. Weedman (eds) *Gender and Hide Production*, Lanham: Altamira Press, pp. 197–214.

Spindler, K. (1995) *The Man in the Ice*, London: Phoenix.

Stanford, D., Bonnichsen, B.R. and Morlan, R.E. (1981) 'The Ginsberg experiment: modern and prehistoric evidence of a bone-flaking technology', *Science*, 212(4493): 438–40.

Steinkeller, P. (1980) 'Mattresses and felt in Early Mesopotamia', *Oriens Antiquus*, 19: 79–100.

Stevenson, I.N. (1974) *Andean Village Technology: An Introduction to a Collection of Manufactured Articles from Santiago de Chocorvos, Peru*, Oxford: Pitt Rivers Museum.

Stewart, H. (1973) *Indian Artefacts of the Northwest Coast*, Seattle: University of Washington Press.

——(1977) *Indian Fishing: Early Methods on the Northwest Coast*, Vancouver: Douglas and McIntyre.

——(1984) *Cedar – Tree of Life to the Northwest Coast Indians*, Vancouver: Douglas and Macintyre.

Stig-Sørenson, M.L. (1997) 'Reading dress: the construction of social categories and identities in Bronze Age Europe', *Journal of European Archaeology*, 5: 93–114.

Stimmell, C., Heimann, R.B. and Hancock, R.G.V (1982) 'Indian pottery from the Mississippi Valley: coping with bad raw materials', in J.S. Olin and A.D. Franklin (eds) *Archaeological Ceramics*, Washington, DC: Smithsonian Institution Press, pp. 219–28.

Stocks, D. (1993) 'Making stone vessels in Ancient Mesopotamia and Egypt', *Antiquity*, 67: 596–603.

Stout, D. (2011) 'Stone toolmaking and the evolution of human culture and cognition', *Philosophical Transactions of the Royal Society Biological Sciences*, 366: 1050–59.

Stout, D. and Chaminade, T. (2009) 'Making tools and making sense: complex, intentional behaviour in human evolution', *Cambridge Archaeological Journal*, 19: 85–96.

Stout, D., Toth, N., Schick, K. and Chaminade, T. (2008) 'Neural correlates of early stone age toolmaking: technology, language and cognition in human evolution', *Philosophical Transactions of the Royal Society Biological Sciences*, 363(1499): 1939–49.

Suttles, W. (ed.) (1990) *Northwest Coast: Handbook of North American Indians, Vol. 7*, Washington, DC: Smithsonian.

Taber, B. and Anderson, M. (1975) *Backstrap Weaving*, London: Pitman.

Tabor, R. (2008) *The Encyclopedia of Green Woodworking*, Bath: Ecologic Books.

Tapio, M., Marzanov, N., Ozerov, M., Cinkulov, M., Gonzarenko, G., Kiselyova, T., Murawski, M., Viinalass, H. and Kantanen, J. (2006) 'Sheep mitochondrial DNA variation in European, Caucasian, and central Asian areas', *Molecular Biology and Evolution* 23(9): 1776–83.

Taylor, M. (1992) 'Flag Fen: the wood', *Antiquity*, 66: 476–98.

——(1998) 'Wood and bark from the enclosure ditch', in F. Pryor (ed.) *Etton: Excavations at a Neolithic Causewayed Enclosure Near Maxey, Cambridgeshire, 1982–7*, London: English Heritage, pp. 115–60.

Teal, P. (1976) *Hand Woolcombing and Spinning: A Guide to Worsteds from the Spinning-Wheel*, Petaluma, CA: Unicorn Books and Crafts Inc.

Tebbs, B. (ed.) (1984) *Trees of the British Isles*, London: Orbis.

Tehanetorens (1983) *Wampum Belts*, Onchiota, NY: Six Nations Indian Museum.

Tehrani, J.J. and Riede, F. (2008) 'Towards an archaeology of pedagogy: learning, teaching and the generation of material culture traditions', *World Archaeology*, 40: 316–31.

Thieme, H. (1997) 'Lower Paleolithic hunting spears from Germany', *Nature*, 385: 807–10.

Thomson, R. (1998) 'Leather working processes', in E. Cameron (ed.) *Leather and Fur: Aspects of Early Medieval Trade and Technology*, London: Archetype Publications Ltd., pp. 1–9.

Thompson, J. (1994) *From the Land: 200 Years of Dene Clothing*, Quebec: Canadian Museum of Civilisation.

Thompson, A.J. and Jakes, K.A. (2002) 'Replication of textile dyeing with sumac and bedstraw', *Southeastern Archaeology*, 21(2): 252–56.

Tilley, C. (2002a) 'Metaphor, Materiality and Interpretation', in V. Buchli (ed.) *The Material Culture Reader*, Oxford: Berg, pp. 23–26.

Tilley, C. (2002b) 'The Metaphorical Transformations of Wala Canoes', in V. Buchli (ed.) *The Material Culture Reader*, Oxford: Berg, pp. 27–55.

Tola, F.C. (2009) *Les Conceptions du Corps et de la Personne dans une contexte Amérindien: Indiens toba du Gran Chaco Sud-Américan*, Paris: L'Harmattan.

Torrence, R. (2001) 'To gather at technology: macro- and microscale approaches', in C. Painter-Brick, R.H. Layton and P. Rowley-Conwy (eds) *Hunter-gatherers: An Interdisciplinary Perspective*, Cambridge: Cambridge University Press, pp. 73–98.

Tunón, H. (ed.) (2010) 'Seminarierapport', *Seminarierapport: Traditionell skinngarvning*, CBM:s skriftserie 35. Bäckedals folkhögskola, Sveg & Naptek, Centrum för biologisk mångfald, Uppsala.

Turner, A.R. (1973) *Finger Weaving: Indian Braiding*, New York: Stirling.

Turner, N.J. (1998) *Plant Technology of First Peoples in British Columbia*, Vancouver: University of British Columbia Press.

——(2001) '"Keeping it living": applications and relevance of traditional plant management in British Columbia to sustainable harvesting of non-timber forest products', *NTFP Conference Proceedings*, pp. 66–77.

——(2004) *Plants of Haida Gwaii, Winlaw, British Colombia*, British Colombia: Sono Nis Press.

Turner, N.J. and Bell, M.A.M. (1971) 'The ethnobotany of the Coast Salish Indians of Vancouver Island', *Economic Botany*, 25: 63–104.

Turner, N.J., Boelscher Ignace, M. and Ignace, R. (2000) 'Traditional ecological knowledge and wisdom of aboriginal peoples in British Columbia', *Ecological Applications*, 10: 1275–87.

Turner, T. (1985) 'Animal symbolism, totemism and the structure of myth', in G. Urton (ed.) *Animal Myths and Metaphors in South America*, Salt Lake City: University of Utah Press, pp. 49–106.

Tzachili, I. (2007) 'Weaving at Akrotiri, Thera: defining cloth-making activities as social process in a Late Bronze Age Aegean town', in C. Gillis and M.-L.B. Nosch (eds) *Ancient Textiles: Production, Craft and Society*, Oxford: Oxbow Books, pp. 190–96.

Urton, G. (1985) 'Animal metaphors and the lifecycle in an Andean community', in G. Urton (ed.) *Animal Myths and Metaphors in South America*, Salt Lake City: University of Utah Press, pp. 251–84.

Van de Noort, R. (2003) 'An ancient seascape: the social context of seafaring in the early Bronze Age', *Seascapes, World Archaeology*, 35(3): 404–15.

van Driel-Murray, C. (2000) 'Leatherwork and skin products', in P.T. Nicholson and I. Shaw (eds) *Ancient Egyptian Materials and Technology*, Cambridge: Cambridge University Press, pp. 299–319.

——(2002) 'Practical evaluation of a field test for the identification of ancient vegetable tanned leathers', *Journal of Archaeological Science*, 29: 17–21.

Vanden Berghe, I., Devia, B., Gleba, M. and Mannering, U. (2010) 'Dyes: to be or not to be. An investigation of Early Iron Age dyes in Danish peat bog textiles', in E. Andersson Strand, M. Gleba, U. Mannering, C. Munkholt and M. Ringgaard (eds) *NESAT X The North European Symposium for Archaeological Textiles*, Oxford: Oxbow Books, pp. 247–51.

Vandkilde, H. (2007) *Culture and Change in Central European Prehistory 6th to 1st Millennium BC*, Aarhus: Aarhus University Press.

van Gijn, A. (1989) 'The wear and tear of flint: principles of functional analysis applied to Dutch Neolithic assemblages', *Analecta Praehistoria Liedensia*, Leiden: Faculty of Archaeology, Leiden University.

——(1998a) 'Traditions in tool-use behaviour: evidence from the Dutch Neolithic', *Helinium*, 34: 261–80.

——(1998b) 'Craft activities in the Dutch Neolithic: a lithic viewpoint', in M. Edmonds and C. Richards (eds) *Understanding the Neolithic of North-Western Europe*, Glasgow: Cruithne, pp. 328–50.

——(2005) 'A functional analysis of some Late Mesolithic bone and antler implements from the Dutch coastal zone', in H. Luik, A.M. Choyke, C.E. Batey and L. Lougas (eds) *From Hooves to Horns, from Mollusc to Mammoth: Manufacture and Use of Bone Artefacts from Prehistoric Times to the Present*, Tartu: Ajaloo Instituut, pp. 47–66.

——(2006) 'Implements of bone and amber: a Mesolithic tradition continued', in L.P. Louwe Kooijmans and P.F.B. Jongste (eds) *Analecta Praehistorica Leidensia*, Leiden: Faculty of Archaeology, Leiden University, pp. 207–24.

——(2007) 'The use of bone and antler tools: two examples from the Late Mesolithic in the Dutch Coastal Zone', in C. Gates St-Pierre and R.B. Walker (eds) *Bones as Tools: Current Methods and Interpretations in Worked Bone Studies*, Oxford: BAR International Series 1622, pp. 81–92.

van Gijn, A. and Boon, J. (2006) 'Birch bark tar', in L.P. Louwe Kooijmans and P.F.B. Jongste (eds) *Analecta Praehistorica Leidensia*, Leiden: Faculty of Archaeology, Leiden University, pp. 261–66.

van Gijn, A. and Raemaekers, C.M. (1999) 'Tool use and society in the Dutch Neolithic: the inevitability of ethnographic analogies', in L.R. Owen and M. Porr (eds) *Ethno-Analogy and the Reconstruction of Prehistoric Artefact Use and Production*, Tübingen: Mo Vince Verlag, pp. 43–52.

Vanhaeren, M. and d'Errico, F. (2006) 'Aurignacian ethno-linguistic geography of Europe revealed by personal ornaments', *Journal of Archaeological Science*, 33: 1105–28.

Vanhaeren, M., d'Errico, F., Stringer, C., James, S.L., Todd, J.A. and Mienis, H.K. (2006) 'Middle Palaeolithic shell beads in Israel and Algeria', *Science*, 312: 1785–88.

Vaughan, S. (1994) *Handmade Baskets from Nature's Colourful Materials*, Tunbridge Wells: Search Press.

Vellanoweth, R. L. (2001) 'AMS radiocarbon dating and shell bead chronologies: middle Holocene trade and interaction in Western north America', *Journal of Archaeological Science*, 28: 941–50.

Vickrey, A.E. (1987) *Felting by Hand*, Geneva, New York: Craft Works Publishing.

Vitebsky, P. (2005) *Reindeer People: Living with Animals and Spirits in Siberia*, London: HarperCollins.

Viveiros de Castro, E. (1992) *From the Enemy's Point of View: Humanity and Divinity in an Amazonian Society*, Chicago and London: University of Chicago Press.

Vogelsang-Eastwood, G. (2000) 'Textiles', in P.T. Nicholson and I. Shaw (eds) *Ancient Egyptian Materials and Technology*, Cambridge: Cambridge University Press, pp. 268–98.

Vogt, E. (1949) 'The birch as a source of raw material during the Stone Age', *Proceedings of the Prehistoric Society*, 5: 50–51.

von den Driesch, A. and Peters, J. (1995) 'Zur ausrüstung des Mannes im Eis: gegenstände und knochenreste tierischer herkunft', in K. Spindler, H. Rastbichler-Zissernig, H. Wilfing, D. zur Nedden and H. Nothdurfter (eds) *Der Mann im Eis: neue funde und ergebnisse*, Vienna: Springer-Verlag, pp. 59–66.

Wadley, L. (2005) 'Putting ochre to the test: replication studies of adhesives that may have been used for hafting tools in the Middle Stone Age', *Journal of Human Evolution*, 49: 587–601.

——(2010) 'Cemented ash as a receptacle or work surface for ochre powder production at Sibudu, South Africa, 58,000 years ago', *Journal of Archaeological Science*, 37: 2397–406.

Wadley, L., Hodgkiss, T. and Grant, M. (2009) 'Implications of complex cognition from the hafting of tools with compound adhesives in the middle Stone Age, South Africa', *PNAS*, 106: 9590–94.

Waetzoldt, H. (2007) 'The use of wool for the production of strings, ropes, braided mats, and similar fabrics', in C. Gillis and M.-L.B. Nosch (eds) *Ancient Textiles: Production, Craft and Society*, Oxford: Oxbow Books, pp. 112–21.

Waldner Mcgrath, J. (1977) *Dyes from Lichens and Plants*, Toronto: Reinhold.

Wallaert, H. (2008) 'The Way of the Potter's Mother: apprenticeship strategies among Dii potters from Cameroon, West Africa', in M.T. Stark, B.J. Bowser and L. Horne (eds) *Cultural Transmission and Material Culture: Breaking Down Boundaries*, Tucson: University of Arizona Press, pp. 178–98.

Walsh, P. (2009) *Spinning, Dyeing and Weaving*, London: New Holland.

Warburg, L. (1974) *Spindebog*, Høberg: Borgen.

Warnier, J.-P. (2006) 'Inside and outside: surfaces and containers', in C. Tilley, W. Keane, S. Küchler, M. Rowlands and P. Spyer (eds) *Handbook of Material Culture*, London: Sage, pp. 186–96.

Webley, L. (2005) 'Hideworking among descendants of Khoekhoem Pastorailists in the Northern Cape, South Africa', in L. Frink and K. Weedman (eds) *Gender and Hide Production*, Walnut Creek: Altamira Press, pp. 153–73.

Weedman, K.J. (2002) 'On the spur of the moment: effects of age and experience on hafted stone scraper morphology', *American Antiquity*, 67(4): 731–44.

——(2005) 'Gender and stone tools: an ethnographic study of the Konso and Gamo hideworkers of Southern Ethiopia', in L. Frink and K. Weedman (eds) *Gender and Hide Production*, Lanham: Altamira Press, pp. 175–96.

Wells, O. (1969) *Salish Weaving Primitive and Modern*, Sardis, BC: Oliver Wells.

Wells, P.S. (2012) *How Ancient Europeans Saw the World: Visions, Patterns and the Shaping of the Mind in Prehistoric Times*, New Jersey: Princeton University Press.

Wendrich, W. (1991) 'Basketry: a textile technique?', *Archaeological Textiles Newsletter*, 12: 18–20.

——(1994) *Who is Afraid of Basketry?*, Leiden: Leiden University.

——(1999) *The World According to Basketry: An Ethno-archaeological Interpretation of Basketry Production in Egypt*, Leiden: Leiden University Press.

——(2000) 'Basketry', in P.T. Nicholson and I. Shaw (eds) *Ancient Egyptian Materials and Technology*, Cambridge: Cambridge University Press, pp. 254–67.

Wentink, K. (2006) 'An interview with potters in the southernmost part of Malawi', *Leiden Journal of Pottery Studies*, 22.

West, A. (1989) *Aboriginal Australia: Culture and Society*, Woden: Aboriginal and Torres Strait Islander Commission.

West, G. (2005) *Leatherwork: A Manual of Techniques*, Marlborough, Wiltshire: Crowood Press.

Wherry, F. (2006) 'The nation-state identity management and indigenous crafts: constructing markets and opportunities in Northwest Costa Rica', *Ethnic and Racial Studies*, 29: 124–52.

White, R. (1989a) 'Production complexity and standardization in early Aurignacian bead and pendant manufacture: evolutionary implications', in P. Mellars and C. Stringer (eds) *The Human Revolution*, Edinburgh: Edinburgh University Press, pp. 366–90.

——(1989b) 'Toward a contextual understanding of the earliest body ornaments', in E. Trinkaus (ed.) *The Emergence of Modern Humans: Biocultural Adaptations in the Later Pleistocene*, Cambridge: Cambridge University Press, pp. 211–31.

——(1989c) 'Visual thinking in the Ice Age', *Scientific American*, 260: 92–99.

——(1992) 'Beyond art: toward an understanding of the origins of material representation in Europe', *Annual Review of Anthropology*, 21: 537–64.

Whittaker, J. and Kamp, K. (1992) 'Sinagua painted armbands', *Kiva*, 58: 177–87.

Wickens, H. (1983) *Natural Dyes for Spinners and Weavers*, London: Batsford.

Wild, J.P. (1970) *Textile Manufacture in the Northern Roman Provinces*, London: Cambridge University Press.

——(1988) *Textiles in Archaeology*, Aylesbury: Shire Publications.

Wilder, E. (1976) *Secrets of Eskimo Skin Sewing*, Fairbanks, Alaska: University of Alaska Press.

Willerslev, R. (2007) *Soul Hunters: Hunting, Animism, and Personhood among the Siberian Yukaghirs*, California and London: University of California Press.

Willink, R.S. and Zolbrod, P.G. (1996) *Weaving a World: Textiles and the Navajo Way of Seeing*, Santa Fe: Museum of New Mexico Press.

Wilson, A. S., Dodson, H.I., Janaway, R.C., Pollard, A.M. and Tobin, D.J. (2010) 'Evaluating histological methods for assessing hair fibre degradation', *Archaeometry*, 52: 467–81.

Wincott Heckett, E. (2007) 'Clothing patterns as constructs of the human mind: establishment and continuity', in C. Gillis and M.-L.B. Nosch (eds) *Ancient Textiles: Production, Craft and Society*, Oxford: Oxbow Books, pp. 208–14.

Wood, J. (2003) 'The Orkney Hood: an ancient re-cycled textile', in J. Downes and A. Ritchie (eds) *Sea Change: Orkney and Northern Europe in the Later Iron Age AD 300–800*, Angus: Pinkfoot Press, pp. 171–76.

Wood, R. (2005) *The Wooden Bowl*, Carmarthenshire: Stobart Davies Ltd.

Woodman, P.C. (1985) *Excavations at Mount Sandel 1973–77, County Londonderry*, Belfast: Her Majesty's Stationery Office.

Woodroffe, D. (ed.) (1949) *Standard Handbook of Industrial Leathers: Dealing with the Production, Testing, Application and Care and Maintenance of Industrial Leathers*, London: National Trade Press Ltd.

Woodward, A., Hunter, J., Ixer, R., Roe, F., Potts, P.J, Webb, P.C., Watson, J.S. and Jones, M.C. (2006) 'Beaker age bracers in England: sources, function and use', *Antiquity*, 80(309): 530–43.

Wright, D. (1972) *Baskets and Basketry*, Newton Abbot: David and Charles.

——(1983) *The Complete Book of Baskets and Basketry*, 2nd edn, Newton Abbott: David and Charles.

Yair, K., Press, M. and Tomes A. (2001) 'Crafting competitive advantage: crafts knowledge as a strategic resource', *Design Studies*, 22: 377–94

Yarish, V., Hoppe, F. and Widess, J. (2009) *Plaited Basketry with Birch Bark*, New York: Sterling.

Young, G.S. (1998) 'Thermodynamic characterisation of skin, hide and similar materials composed of fibrous collagen', *Studies in Conservation*, 43: 65–79.

Zola, N. and Gott, B. (1992) *Koorie Plants, Koorie People*, Melbourne: Koorie Heritage Trust.

Zvelebil, M. (1995) 'Plant use in the Mesolithic and its role in the transition to farming', *Proceedings to the Prehistoric Society*, 60: 35–74.

INDEX

T - #0019 - 070524 - C64 - 234/156/16 - PB - 9780415537933 - Gloss Lamination